The Free State of Jones

THE
FREE
STATE

THE UNIVERSITY OF
NORTH CAROLINA PRESS
CHAPEL HILL

OF
JONES

MISSISSIPPI'S
LONGEST
CIVIL WAR

VICTORIA E. BYNUM

with a new afterword by the author

Portions of this book have been reprinted in revised form with permission from the following works: Victoria E. Bynum, "Misshapen Identity: Memory, Folklore, and the Legend of Rachel Knight," in *Discovering the Women in Slavery: Emancipating Perspectives on the American Past*, edited by Patricia Morton (Athens: University of Georgia Press, 1996), © 1996 University of Georgia Press; "Misshapen Identity: Memory, Folklore, and the Legend of Rachel Knight," in *Sex, Love, Race: Crossing Boundaries in North American History*, edited by Martha Hodes (New York: New York University Press, 1999); " 'White Negroes' in Segregated Mississippi: Miscegenation, Racial Identity, and the Law," *Journal of Southern History* 64 (May 1998); and "Telling and Retelling the Legend of the Free State of Jones," in *Guerrillas, Unionists, and Violence on the Confederate Home Front*, edited by Daniel Sutherland (Fayetteville: University of Arkansas Press, 1999).

Designed by April Leidig-Higgins
Set in Joanna

The paper in this book meets the guidelines for permanence and durability of the Committee on Production Guidelines for Book Longevity of the Council on Library Resources.

ISBN 978-1-4696-2705-2 (pbk: alk. paper)
ISBN 978-1-4696-2706-9 (ebook)

The Library of Congress has cataloged the original edition of this book as follows:
Bynum, Victoria E. The free state of Jones: Mississippi's longest civil war / by Victoria E. Bynum.
p. cm.—(The Fred W. Morrison series in southern studies) Includes bibliographical references (p.) and index.
1. Jones County (Miss.)—History—19th century. 2. Jones County (Miss.)—Social conditions —19th century. 3. Military deserters—Mississippi—Jones County—History—19th century. 4. Unionists (United States Civil War)—Mississippi—Jones County. 5. Mississippi—History— Civil War, 1861–1865—Social aspects. 6. United States—History—Civil War, 1861–1865—Social aspects. 7. Knight family. 8. Racially mixed people —Mississippi—Jones County—History—19th century. 9. Jones County (Miss.)—Biography. I. Title. II. Series.
F347.J6 B95 2001   976.2'55—dc21
2001027040

stated with a grant
Figure Foundation
civil may we rest

To the memory of my father,
Oma Stanley Bynum
Now I understand

Contents

Part Two. Civil War, Reconstruction,
and the Struggle for Power

Illustrations, Maps, and Tables

Illustrations

Maps

Tables

Acknowledgments

Throughout my journey into Jones County's colorful past, Gregg Andrews, my husband and colleague, has been my constant companion, and
moreover, he proved indispensable to the research and writing of this
book. Together we have traversed the South summer after summer, researching his books as well as mine. Gregg's social and professional skills
have aided me time and again. For example, without his presence and
prodding as we searched for the old homesite of Newt Knight's parents, I
doubt that I would have stopped to ask a farmer working in his field for
directions. That chance encounter with local resident Julius Huff led to one
of my most memorable excursions into Mississippi's past. On hearing that
I was a historian, Julius dropped his work and drove us in his truck
through swampy dirt roads to the cemetery of John "Jackie" Knight,
Newt's grandfather. There he shared with us the stories he had heard all his
life as he directed us to the stone marking the mass grave of three members
of the Knight Company who were executed in 1864 by Confederate cavalry. After that experience, Gregg and I carried pad and pencil wherever we
went, including the momentous day when we drove with another local
resident, eighty-nine-year-old Earle Knight, to the Newton Knight cemetery. After landowner Jerry Jones kindly unlocked the gated fence, we were
on our way. Over dirt roads strewn with debris and thick with weeds up to
the hood of the car, and with thunderclouds gathering overhead, we
searched and searched—and finally found the graves of Newt and Rachel.

Early in the adventure, it was clear that I would learn far more about the past from informal visits and conversations with people like Julius and Earle than by conducting formal interviews. Many families in Jones and Covington Counties opened their homes to us upon learning of my research and treated us with wonderful hospitality. In 1993 Carliona Ingram Forsythe prepared us a sumptuous Southern meal and arranged for us to meet with Ethel Knight, author of *The Echo of the Black Horn*. That same summer DeBoyd Knight and his wife, Robbie, regaled us with stories, photos, newspaper clippings, and other memorabilia related to the Free State of Jones. In the summer of 1994 Earle Knight not only arranged for us to visit the Newt Knight cemetery but also shared several meals with us and escorted us to the historic Amos Deason home. I am deeply saddened that neither Earle nor Carliona lived to see this book in print. Sometime after Earle's death in 1998, I received a telephone call from his friend and cousin William Pitts, who shared that sadness with me and added his own thoughts about the legacy of Newt Knight.

It took a trip to Oakwood College (founded for African Americans in 1896 by the Seventh-Day Adventist Church) in Huntsville, Alabama, and the assistance of Minneola Dixon, Oakwood library's archivist, and, finally, a phone call to Winona Knight Hudson of Fresno, California, to connect me with descendants of Rachel Knight. In the summer of 1995, Florence Knight Blaylock, Rachel's great-granddaughter, and her husband, Eugene Blaylock, opened their home in Soso to me. For three wonderful days, Gregg and I visited with descendants of Rachel, including Dorothy Knight Marsh, Olga Watts Nelson, Annette Knight, Lois Knight Wilson, Flo Wyatt, Jeannette Smith, Saundra Shaw, and Audrey Knight Crosby, who shared stories, documents, and photographs. I am equally grateful to Florence for her tireless campaign throughout the past five years to gather additional information and photographs for the book. Through her, I gained contact with Ardella Knight Barrett of St. Louis, Missouri, Rachel's great-granddaughter, who donated numerous photographs and documents. Florence also put me in touch with Kenneth Welch, whose research on the Knights is unsurpassed. I am particularly honored that Florence invited Gregg and me to attend the 1999 Knight-Booth family reunion, at which I delivered the keynote address, and that the Seventh-Day Adventist Church of Soso welcomed us at its service during that reunion weekend. Needless to say, without the trust and generosity extended to me by members of this branch of the Knight family, I could never have pieced together the history of the mixed-race Knight community.

Although most of the research for this book was conducted in libraries, archives, courthouses, and people's homes, it has also been shaped by the incredible breadth of communication made possible by the Internet. Genealogical discussion forums, websites, and electronic mail have introduced me far and wide to descendants of Jones County families. In March 1996, for example, historian Rudy Leverett contacted me by e-mail and initiated a fruitful exchange of ideas and information about the Free State of Jones. Rudy also generously provided me with a copy of his unpublished biography of Confederate major Amos McLemore.

I was equally elated in late 1998 when Gerald W. Johnson, whose Welborn kinfolk comprised a sizable chunk of the Knight band, also contacted me by e-mail. As I hoped he would, Gerald provided a wealth of information and insights about the band's operations. Also helpful were several e-mail messages from Welborn descendant Johnny Pryor. In regard to the Welborn, Reddoch, and Duckworth families of eighteenth-century North and South Carolina, Ann Beason Gahan, Eleonore Crespo, Eddie Josey-Wilson, Barbara Thornton, Dorothy Cavendish, Jean Duckworth Paleschic, and John Duckworth all contributed valuable insights and information.

I have had equally good fortune in researching the Collins and Bynum families on the Internet. Beyond communicating with me by e-mail, Mary Bess Gamero-Adams and Judy Smith of Texas, Regina Roper of Florida, and Wayne and JoAnn Wingate of Louisiana all shared documents, photographs, letters, and genealogical research with me. I am also grateful to Frances Montgomery, T. J. Bynum, Robin Fisher, and Ron Griffin for sharing their genealogical information about these families.

My knowledge about the Knight family was likewise greatly expanded thanks to the Internet. On the Louisiana, Texas, and Arkansas branches of the Knights, Rhonda Benoit, Versie Frederick, Mabel Riddle, and Frances Jackson furnished me with charts, stories, and photographs. Also helpful were e-mail messages from Sondra Bivens, Paula Bolan, Paula Broussard, Kecia Carter, Audrey Dorgan, Frances Gandy-Walsh, Lonnie Knight, Frances Nosser, and Dolores Rutherford.

My kinfolk back in California, especially Jim and LouAnne Bynum, enabled me to leave the South every now and then to enjoy rare summer vacations devoid of archive and courthouse visits. At the same time, they exhibited ongoing curiosity about my work-in-progress. It was my mother, Margaret Bynum, who first suggested that I contact Earle Knight, an old acquaintance of hers and my father's, since he "might" be kin to Newt Knight. Bill Bynum and Tammie Loftin were interested enough in the Free State of Jones to drive through Ellisville one summer day and sit on the porch of the haunted house in which Newt Knight allegedly murdered Amos McLemore.

My colleagues at Southwest Texas State University have attended many talks and brown-bag luncheons on the Free State of Jones, and I thank them for their interest and support. I also thank the Advancement of Women in Higher Education, Phi Alpha Theta, the Center for Multicultural and Gender Studies, and the Campus Christian Community Center for sponsoring those forums. Widespread campus interest in Mississippi's Free State of Jones reinforced the popular notion that all nineteenth-century Southerners eventually moved to Texas, especially when Robert Cavendish, manager of grants administration at SWT and a graduate student in history, discovered that his direct ancestor, Jimmie Reddoch, had once owned the land that sheltered Deserters' Den on the Covington County side of the Leaf River. Likewise, Dr. Ramona Ford of SWT's sociology department deserves special thanks for arranging my meeting with Carliona Ingram Forsythe of Covington County, Mississippi, through Carliona's daughter, Nicole Smith Boozer, in 1993 a student at SWT.

Numerous colleagues from the wider profession critiqued earlier drafts of this work, led me to new materials, or simply cheered me on with supportive comments. They include Gregg Andrews, Peter Bardaglio, John Boles, Charles C. Bolton, Shearer Davis Bowman, Susan Branson, Stephanie Cole, Cita Cook, Edward Countryman, Jane Dailey, Thomas Dublin, Laura Edwards, Ann Elwood, Paul Escott, Lesley Gordon, Kenneth Hamilton, Stanley Harrold, Martha Hodes, John Inscoe, Dolores Janiewski, Marjoleine Kars, Neil McMillen, Wayne Mixon, Christopher Morris, Patricia Morton, Evelyn Thomas Nolen, Nell Painter, Philip Paludan, Michael Pierson, Jonathan Sarris, Margaret Storey, Daniel Sutherland, William Thomas III, Elizabeth Hayes Turner, Marjorie Spruill Wheeler, LeeAnn Whites, David Williams, Joel Williamson, and Karen Zipf.

Throughout this long journey, Kate Douglas Torrey of the University of North Carolina Press has been the soul of patience. She trusted my judgment when I expanded the scope of my study to include both the origins and the legacy of the Free State of Jones even though it meant more summers spent conducting research at the expense of writing. Altina Waller and Ted Ownby read the first draft of my manuscript for the press and helped me to clarify my ideas, eliminate unnecessary details, and sharpen my analysis in critical areas. Project editor Paula Wald, followed by copyeditor Stephanie Wenzel, made certain that the final product was accurate and stylistically well crafted. If any shortcomings remain in the book, I bear full responsibility for them.

None of my travels to libraries, archives, and courthouses in Washington, D.C., North Carolina, Georgia, Alabama, and Mississippi would have been possible without the support of Southwest Texas State University. In the fall of 1992 the university granted me a one-semester research and development leave; between 1992 and 1996 I was awarded three research enhancement grants. Completion of the book was greatly facilitated by a much-appreciated fellowship from the National Endowment for the Humanities in January 2000. Now that the book is written, I can hardly imagine what it will be like to no longer be searching for people and places associated with the Free State of Jones. Neither can Gregg.

Timeline: The Free State of Jones

The Era of the American Revolution, 1765–1812

1765–71: The Regulator Movement erupted in North Carolina as farmers and planters rose up against local elites. Issues of corrupt government and unfair taxes anticipated the colonial revolt against Great Britain that followed.

April 18, 1775: Fighting broke out between American colonists and British soldiers.

July 4, 1776: The Declaration of Independence, issued in Philadelphia, Pennsylvania, by the Continental Congress, declared U.S. sovereignty as war raged between the colonies and Great Britain.

September 3, 1783: The Treaty of Paris was signed between United States and Great Britain, ending the Revolutionary War.

September 17, 1787: A majority of delegates to the Constitutional Convention voted to ratify the U.S. Constitution

1812–15: The War of 1812, sometimes called the "second war of Independence," broke out over issues of U.S. sovereignty vis-à-vis Great Britain. The Creek Nation was defeated by U.S. forces during this war, opening up Alabama and Mississippi territories to white settlers.

The American Civil War and Reconstruction, 1860–1875

November 6, 1860: Republican Abraham Lincoln elected president of the
United States. Southern slaveholders rejected Lincoln and the
Republican Party platform, which opposed expansion of slavery
into the western territories.

December 20, 1860: South Carolina seceded from the Union in protest
to Lincoln's election.

January–February 1861: Alabama, Florida, Georgia, Louisiana,
Mississippi, and Texas seceded from the Union.

April 12–13, 1861: Confederates fired the first shots of the Civil War at
Ft. Sumter, South Carolina. Lincoln called on the remaining
Southern states to supply troops to put down the insurrection.

April–May 1861: Virginia, North Carolina, Tennessee, and Arkansas
responded to President Lincoln's call for troops by seceding
from the Union.

October 3–4, 1862: The battle of Corinth, Mississippi. Significant
numbers of Jones County soldiers from the 7th Battalion,
Mississippi Infantry, fought at Corinth and deserted in the
aftermath of a Confederate defeat.

January 1863: The Emancipation Proclamation freed slaves in the
Confederate states.

May 18–July 4, 1863: The siege of Vicksburg, Mississippi. This Union
victory gave federal forces control of the Mississippi River,
including ports at Memphis and New Orleans. Following the
siege, men of the 7th Battalion, Mississippi Infantry, from Jones
County deserted the Confederacy in large numbers.

June 27, 1864: The battle of Kennesaw Mountain, northwest of Atlanta,
Georgia. This battle resulted in several members of the Knight
band being sent to Yankee prison camps after being forced back
into the Confederate army by Colonel Robert Lowry.

April 9, 1865: Confederate general Robert E. Lee surrendered to Union
general Ulysses S. Grant at Appomattox Court House in Virginia.
Though more battles and skirmishes occurred after this date,
the Civil War was over.

August 1865: The Mississippi Constitutional Convention of 1865 established a "white man's government," passing "black codes" that denied freedpeople personal rights, mobility, and voting rights.

1868: The Ku Klux Klan emerged in Mississippi.

January–May 15, 1868: The Mississippi State Convention of 1868, made up of black and white delegates, attempted reforms in suffrage, property, and education that benefited freedpeople and poor whites. Voters refused to ratify the new constitution.

February 3, 1870: The state of Mississippi was restored to the Union. Several members of the Knight band, including its leader, Newt Knight, received political appointments or won elective office.

November 1875: Pro-Confederate Democrats regained control of the Mississippi legislature. The last federal troops were removed in 1877. Reconstruction in Mississippi was over.

From Racial Segregation to Civil Rights

1878–80: The Mississippi legislature declared biracial education and interracial marriages illegal.

November 1890: The Mississippi Constitutional Convention of 1890 codified the state's laws against interracial schools and marriages and disfranchised black men.

May 18, 1896: Plessy v. Ferguson. Under the doctrine of "separate but equal," the U.S. Supreme Court upheld state laws that mandated racial segregation of public facilities.

May 17, 1954: Brown v. Board of Education of Topeka, Kansas. The U.S. Supreme Court declared racial segregation of public schools unconstitutional, overturning the Plessy v. Ferguson decision.

June 12, 1967: Loving v. Virginia. Nineteen years after Davis Knight's 1948 miscegenation trial, the U.S. Supreme Court declared state laws against interracial marriage to be unconstitutional.

Preface

When I began researching the legend of the Free State of Jones ten years ago, I had little sense of the journey I was about to undertake. Fifteen years earlier my interest in the legend had been piqued by a Civil War history textbook which noted that Confederate disaffection ran so deep in Jones County, Mississippi, that during the Civil War the county had allegedly seceded from the state and created the Republic of Jones. I was attracted not only by the county's bold actions but also because Jones County was the birthplace of my father. My memories of childhood visits to Jones County—which were few and far between—were vivid ones, especially because its rural setting so contrasted with my own experience of growing up in suburban Florida and California. Indeed, my lifelong interest in the Old South sprang from those childhood visits with my father's kinfolk in Piney Woods Mississippi. Yet I had no idea before I began my research that my Bynum ancestors were deeply involved on both sides of the conflict over the Free State of Jones.

I was initially uncertain whether to write a full-length book since a courthouse fire had destroyed most of Jones County's court records in 1887. I was also aware that many articles and a few books had already been written on the topic. Still, I believed, the story of this Civil War uprising should be retold from the perspective of its anti-Confederate dissidents and understood within the larger context of economic and political divisions among white Southerners. I was eager as well to analyze the role that women played, since the uprising's geographic center was not the battlefields of the Civil War but, rather, the swamps, fields, and homes of a community engaged in an inner civil war.

My first research trip to Mississippi, combined with extensive reading on the folklore of Civil War Jones County, revealed a true story of the South that no novelist's fantasy could rival, one that begged to be told from a historical perspective, not to be treated as legend or gossip. It was easy to see why the legend had endured. Its characters were larger than life: men bound to one another by kinship, economic status, and membership in a paramilitary band armed against the Confederacy; women equally bound by kinship and unfettered by the chains of ladylike behavior; and even some slaves, although Piney Woods Mississippi was not a major slaveholding region. Towering above all other characters in popular memory were "Captain" Newt Knight, the grandson of a slaveholder, and Rachel Knight, the slave of Newt's grandfather. Their relationship added the specter of interracial intimacy to the story. Furthermore, the intermarriage in 1878 of several of their children began a mixed-race community that endures today. Small wonder, I soon realized, that over a century ago the legend of the Free State of Jones had generated a civil war of words and memory that seemingly would not die.

Retelling and analyzing a story so complex in its details and so controversial in its meanings proved to be a daunting task and a truly awesome responsibility. From the time I began writing, in 1992, my primary concern was to tell the story as fully and accurately as possible. Yet because so much of the literature pertaining to the Free State of Jones is based on legends and memories shaped by family loyalties and Lost Cause principles, I also felt compelled to analyze that literature throughout the book. Thus, although my analysis of Jones County's uprising and its various chroniclers is deeply rooted in historical scholarship, I struggled against the temptation to stray too far from the story; in service to that goal, I have confined most of my discussions of scholarly works of history to endnotes.

The Free State of Jones

No, [Rachel] wasn't no half-mixture, wasn't no
half-mixture to it.—Tom Knight, trial of Davis
Knight, 1948

[Rachel's] hair was curly, wasn't no kinky about
it.—Henry Knight, trial of Davis Knight, 1948

Introduction

Sacred Wars

Race and the Ongoing
Battle over the
Free State of Jones

In December 1948 the Jones County Circuit Court in Ellisville, Mississippi, debated the racial identity of Rachel Knight, a woman who had been dead for fifty-nine years. At stake was the fate of her twenty-three-year-old great-grandson, Davis Knight, who was on trial for the crime of miscegenation. Davis, a white man in physical appearance, had married Junie Lee Spradley, a white woman, on April 18, 1946. Whether Davis was white or black, and therefore innocent or guilty of marrying across the color line, hinged on the racial identity of a distant ancestor whom he had never met, but who still excited the memories and passions of older citizens of Jones, Jasper, and Covington Counties in southeastern Mississippi.[1]

For four days in the Ellisville courthouse, Davis Knight's neighbors and relatives argued over whether Rachel Knight was a Creole, an Indian, or "just a regular Negro woman." Of special interest to the court was Rachel's relationship to Newton Knight, the legendary leader of Mississippi's most notorious band of deserters during the Civil War. In 1948, however, the state of Mississippi expressed no interest in Newt's Civil War exploits but only in the intermarriages of his daughter Molly and son Mat with Rachel's son Jeff and daughter Fannie. These marriages, contracted around 1878, began the mixed-race community of so-called "white Negroes" into which Davis Knight was born; thus, both Newton and Rachel were his ancestors.[2]

How had Davis Knight managed to avoid legal entanglement and maybe even a lynching before 1948? After all, he had been married for two years before the court indicted him. Perhaps it was his light skin that allowed him to "pass," at least outside his immediate community, but probably equally important was who his white ancestors were. His legal problems in 1948 were precipitated not only by local and national developments but also by his connections to the infamous Newt Knight.[3]

In the years surrounding Davis Knight's marriage, his great-grandfather received an unusual amount of public attention. Journalist James Street, who grew up near Jones County, was inspired by tales he had heard as a boy to write the popular Civil War novel *Tap Roots* (1943), about "Captain" Newt Knight and his band of deserters. Determined to offer readers a radically different Civil War South from the one portrayed in Margaret Mitchell's *Gone with the Wind*, Street abandoned the world of mansions, cotton fields, and the noble cause. Instead, he highlighted pro-Union Southerners, centering his story around the fictional Dabney family of "Lebanon" County in southeastern Mississippi. Although Street denied having modeled the book's main character and hero, Hoab Dabney, after Newt Knight, he did acknowledge the influence of Newt, whom he called a "rather splendid nonconformist."[4]

On the heels of *Tap Roots*, Thomas Jefferson Knight expanded and re-published *The Life and Activities of Captain Newton Knight*, a biography of his father originally released in 1935. Tom portrayed "Captain Newt" as a principled Robin Hood who had defied the Confederacy and created the Free State of Jones in order to protect the community's women and children from its depredations. In Tom's biography, however, he omitted an open secret long whispered in Jones County: that his father had crossed the sexual color line during the war with a former slave woman named Rachel and that his own sister and brother had later married children of Rachel.

Except for occasional gossip and rumors, white branches of the Knight family had mostly ignored their interracial branch. In fact, nearly all published accounts of Newt's life ignored the mixed-race community in which he lived after the Civil War. Tom Knight's own erasure of Rachel from the narrative of his father's life enabled him to replace painful memories of miscegenation with a glorified interpretation of his father's Civil War behavior.[5]

Thanks to Tom Knight and James Street, Newt reemerged as a folk hero, but the notion that Confederate deserters might be heroes disturbed many Mississippians. By the 1940s many decades of "Lost Cause" education had created far more reverence for the Confederacy than existed in the 1860s. Members of the Knight family whose ancestors fought for the Confederacy seemed particularly galled by Newt's renewed fame, especially when *Tap Roots* was released in 1948 as a movie starring Van Heflin and Susan Hayward.[6]

It was in the midst of Newt Knight's renewed popularity that his great-grandson Davis was indicted, then convicted, for the crime of miscegenation. According to *Time* magazine, "a relative, irked by an old family feud, had dug up Davis Knight's genealogy." On November 14, 1949, however, the Mississippi Supreme Court reversed the lower court's decision, ruling that it had failed "to prove beyond all reasonable doubt that the defendant has one-eighth or more negro blood." In effect, the high court proclaimed that Davis Knight was legally white.[7]

Although Davis Knight's legal ordeal was over, the local debate over the "purity" of the Knight family's blood raged on. In 1951, two years after the state supreme court's decision and at a critical juncture in U.S. race relations, Newt Knight's grandniece, Ethel Knight, published *The Echo of the Black Horn*, a damning biography of Newt Knight. In an obvious reference to James Street, Ethel announced her intention to counter "fiction writers with itching palm, which has too often been greased."[8] Dedicated to the memory of the "Noble Confederates who lived and died for Jones County," the book was a thinly disguised effort to discredit the anti-Confederate uprising and to rid the white branches of the Knight family of the taint of miscegenation. It is widely read by Mississippians even today.[9]

An avid segregationist who insisted that the South was in the midst of a holy war, Ethel linked Newt Knight's heightened popularity to national assaults on "class distinction and racial segregation," blaming both on society's "communistic elements." She even claimed that Newt had forced his children to commit miscegenation. Davis Knight might *appear* to be white, yet she *knew* that African blood flowed through his veins. To a white supremacist such as Ethel, his marriage to a white woman injected African blood, like the insidious virus of communism, into the white race. In her view, miscegenation was as un-American as opposition to the Confederacy; Davis Knight was guilty of miscegenation, and Newt was guilty of both.[10]

Davis Knight's trial enabled Ethel to trump Tom Knight's version of his father's life by reshaping the public's understanding of the Free State of Jones. Both authors wrote within white supremacist frameworks but with a very important difference. Tom presented his father as the hero of plain white folk, whereas Ethel attacked him as a traitor and misguided hero of disloyal slaves like the "strumpet" Rachel.

On one hand, Ethel's effort to exploit the scandal of miscegenation breathed life into the long-buried story of Rachel, who had been all but erased by the numerous tales of the legendary Free State of Jones. Ethel not only restored Rachel's historical role, but she also unveiled a powerful, larger-than-life woman who had endured slavery, sexual exploitation, the Civil War, Reconstruction, and Mississippi's mounting campaign for white supremacy and racial segregation. Most strikingly, Rachel seemed to have had as much impact on the world around her as it had on her.

On the other hand, Ethel Knight buried the class and cultural origins of Jones County's internal civil war beneath a barrage of titillating, racist tales of interracial sex, violence, and debauchery. She presented Newt Knight as a bloodthirsty killer who manipulated nearly one hundred men and a few good women into dishonoring their community and nation. Missing were the stories of yeoman families like the Collinses, who opposed secession from the beginning, who only reluctantly enlisted in the Confederate Army, and who deserted the army rather than fight a "rich man's war and a poor man's fight." Except for a brief acknowledgment of the unionism of the outspoken Collins family, Ethel granted deserters little agency or political consciousness. According to her, they merely "obeyed [Newt Knight] in every respect, and carried out his instructions to a letter, fearing death at his hands if he were displeased."[11]

To separate fact from fiction in regard to the legend of the Free State of Jones is no easy task. Few, if any, memories of participants in Jones's inner civil war were published before the twentieth century. The Civil War generation passed its stories on to succeeding generations, where they entered the realm of folktales that vary in detail depending on who is doing the telling. What is certain, however, is that by early 1864, Jones County deserters were well organized and well known to the Confederacy. Their self-styled military unit, the Knight Company, had its main hideout on the Leaf River, one of many sites in the South where deadly civil wars were fought between Confederate and anti-Confederate forces. The Knight Company attracted men from Jones and the surrounding counties of Covington, Jasper, Perry, and Smith. Its major leaders included Capt. Newton Knight, First Lieut. Jasper Collins, and Second Lieut. William Wesley Sumrall. Its core members came primarily from the Knight, Collins, Valentine, and Welch families.

Before Ethel Knight injected the volatile issue of race, two important questions divided those who told the story of the Free State of Jones: first, why did so many people in this region defy the Confederacy, and second, what were the thoughts and motives that impelled Knight, Collins, Sumrall, and others to organize a band of deserters in October 1863? Were Captain Knight and his men union-loving Robin Hoods who protected helpless women and children from marauding Confederate cavalry, as some portrayals suggest, or were they mere desperadoes, content to murder, pillage, and lay out in the swamps rather than fight for their country? Or, as others insist, were they simply hardheaded, individualistic poor whites defending a "primitive" or "pastoral" existence?[12]

None of these descriptions adequately portrays the self-sufficient—even prosperous—nonslaveholding yeomen who joined the Knight Company or the men and women who supported the Republic of Jones. Instead of analyzing the social and economic forces that gave rise to Jones County's anti-Confederate rebellion, twentieth-century journalists, folklorists, and historians continually debated the long-standing legend that Jones County had formally seceded from the Confederacy during the war. Time and again they chased the same story, wrangling over whether Jones County deserters in fact had created an independent Republic of Jones. For New South writers who increasingly romanticized the Confederate cause and in an era of growing racial segregation exaggerated the image of a "Solid [white] South," the idea that Jones's deserters had attempted secession-within-secession was more entertaining and believable than the notion that they had supported the Union. Jones County deserters thus devolved into degraded poor whites who responded savagely in knee-jerk fashion to any and all authority. In contrast, stung by the story's connotations of poor white ignorance and violence, local residents frequently denied that any such secession took place, while deserters and their descendants continued to assert that they had supported the Union during the Civil War.[13]

Whether seeking to vindicate or to condemn the Knight band, or simply to tell a good story, professional and nonprofessional historians have told us little about the origins of this uprising in a county that boasted few members of the planter class and a comparatively small slave population. Yet Col. William N. Brown, who spent more than a month chasing deserters with Robert Lowry's Confederate cavalry in Jones County, provided an important clue at the time. In 1864 Brown expressed his frustration to Governor Charles Clark that "old and influential citizens, perhaps their fathers or relatives," had imbued deserters with "union ideas" based on the "principles" of the "agrarian class."[14]

Likewise, in a letter published in the *Mobile Evening News* a few weeks after the raid, an anonymous officer blamed "older citizens" for inciting young men to question the legitimacy of the Confederacy. After mentioning Col. Lowry's ambush near Newt Knight's home, the officer cited Lowry's capture of "Sim Collins and boys." Simeon Collins was one of seven sons of Stacy Collins, all of whom armed themselves against the Confederacy. His sister, Sarah "Sally" Parker, was notorious for providing food and shelter to the deserters. Four Collins brothers participated in the Free State of Jones, while three others—Warren, Stacy Jr., and Newton—formed their own band of jayhawkers in the Big Thicket of East Texas, where half the family had moved around 1853. Much more so than the Knights, the Collinses represented a Unionist yeoman viewpoint solidly grounded in the agrarian principles to which Colonel Brown alluded.[15]

Postwar authors nevertheless made Newt Knight the central figure of the Free State of Jones not only because he was captain of the renegade company but also because he crossed the color line in his personal affairs. Precisely because authors have focused almost exclusively on the enigmatic Newt Knight, determined to expose the "true" driving force behind "his" rebellion, they have ignored the Collinses and only superficially examined the larger question that Brown attempted to answer: why did so many people in this region of Mississippi oppose the Confederacy?

Anti-Confederate women in Jones County were also erased from the past when "redeemed" versions of the Lost Cause enshrined Confederate white womanhood. White women became passive victims of either Confederate cavalry or Knight's band of deserters rather than active participants on both sides. Among black women, one of the most dynamic participants, Rachel Knight, disappeared altogether in accounts written by authors seeking to redeem the image of Newt Knight or Jones County. Rachel reappeared only because Ethel Knight hoped to destroy Newt's heroic image by raising the specter of miscegenation. In lurid, racist prose, Ethel portrayed her as a manipulative Jezebel who provided sexual favors to the deserters while serving as Newt's most important female accomplice.

Tom Knight and Ethel Knight had opposite goals when they wrote their versions of the history of the Free State of Jones. Tom hoped to sanctify his father, whereas Ethel sought to vilify him. Although they wrote from different motivations, both provided rich evidence of civilian participation in the anti-Confederate uprising. Both authors appropriated and reshaped community stories, using them as parables to vindicate their own positions to "prove" which of their mutual ancestors stood on the "right" or "wrong" side of the war. Although neither author analyzed the gender- or race-based contours of the uprising, both provided overwhelming evidence that entire communities, not simply men, participated in it. Their accounts belie glib assumptions that Jones's inner war amounted to nothing more than a contest between civil order and lawlessness, or that it was simply an economic conflict between slaveholders and nonslaveholders that was unaffected by local family, religious, and cultural divisions.

We stand to lose a distinctive episode of Southern history if we simply dismiss the competing personal narratives of the Free State of Jones as hopelessly biased, unverifiable folktales, although many are just that. For a half-century, literary images of a noble, genteel, and "lost" Solid South left no place for a story so revealing of the South's internal contradictions as that of the Free State of Jones. At best, Newton Knight became a primeval Robin Hood, a kind of Anglo-Saxon Noble Savage. At worst, he was a demented, ignorant, backwoods murderer who cowed others into joining him.

Questions regarding the motives of the men and women who supported the Knight Company receded further and further into the background after Ethel Knight transformed the legend of the Free State of Jones into a saga of sex, greed, and murder. For fifty years *The Echo of the Black Horn* has filled readers with the lurid specter of cold-blooded murderers and interracial mixing, which in turn merged easily with stereotypical images of violent and degraded poor whites. In the dawn of the new millennium, from Ethel's modest white frame house located near the Leaf River woods and "deserters' den," she still stands guard over her version of the Free State of Jones. Indeed, she has become as much a part of the area's living past as the people and events that she chronicled. More than simply a version of the past, however, *The Echo of the Black Horn* sanctions domination of whites over blacks and conventional authority over dissent, imprisoning Rachel and Newt within a "New South" glorification of the Old South's Lost Cause of slavery and Confederate nationalism.

To understand the origins of Jones County's yeoman uprising against the Confederacy, we must first release Newt Knight, who flouted both the rules of war and the rules of race, from the Lost Cause mentality that holds him and the important story of the Free State of Jones its prisoner. More importantly, the uprising must be studied within the context of both local and national events, not merely from the perspective of Newt alone. Only then can we better understand the motives and behavior of the men who joined the Knight band, as well as the parents, wives, slaves, and children who supported them.[16]

Part One

The Origins of Mississippi's Piney Woods People

We can't boast of our ancestors because,
when we get started talking about our
families, out jumps the ghost of a pirate
or a cousin of color.—Sam Dabney, from
James Street's *Tap Roots*, 1943

[The Knights were of] the old aristocracy,
bringing in slaves and finery from an older
civilization.—Ethel Knight, *Echo of the Black
Horn*, 1951

Chapter One

Jones County's
Carolina Connection

Class and Race
in Revolutionary
America

Although South Carolina was the birthplace of most Jones County settlers, most of the parents of these settlers, especially those born before 1820, came from North Carolina. Swept by the forces of evangelical revivalism, the Regulator Movement, and the American Revolution, they participated in various "uncivil" wars, creating antiauthoritarian traditions among their descendants that later would support desertion of the Confederacy as well as secession from the Union. Thus the divisions that ripped apart families and neighborhoods in Civil War Jones County would be nothing new for the Welborns, Knights, Collinses, Sumralls, Bynums, Valentines, and Welches, who shared with one another a rich heritage of dissent and conflict.[1]

While it would be a mistake to attribute Southern dissenters' political views and behavior to their ancestors' experiences, that heritage did influence descendants' future economic, geographic, and marital choices, which in turn influenced their Civil War behavior. So important, in fact, is the historical background of participants in the Free State of Jones that it, too, became contested terrain between novelist James Street and local historian Ethel Knight.

Street's allusions to pirates and cousins of color in *Tap Roots* were part of his effort to link the origins of anti-Confederate sentiment in Piney Woods Mississippi to the ancestry of its participants. Interwoven within his tale of action and romance were the Revolution, the War of 1812, the settling of the frontier, and the historical evolution of relations of class and race from the perspective of his fictional characters. As an author of history as well as fiction, Street wanted readers to understand that the past weighed mightily on the Civil War generation.

To understand Street's effort to connect the Free State of Jones to the Revolutionary era, however, one must read his earlier novel, *Oh, Promised Land*, published in 1940. The popularity of *Tap Roots*, reflected in Universal Studio's release in 1948 of a movie by the same name, overshadowed his earlier novel in which he discussed not only race relations but also the class origins and political backgrounds of Piney Woods settlers. Using the Dabneys as a fictional composite of Jones County's early Anglo settlers, Street placed them in frontier Georgia as former Tories, Indian fighters, and plain folk who eventually came to hate the institution of slavery.[2]

If Street had gone back one more generation, he likely would have added Revolutionary era Regulators and radical Baptist exhorters from North and South Carolina to his cast of characters. Between 1750 and 1815 in the Carolinas, plain folk participated in religious schisms, civil disorders, and battles with Indians over possession of lands. Political and economic conflict rocked both colonies, driving people from one frontier to another until finally they headed to the Southwest. Baptist Separates, Regulators, Tories, and especially, land-hungry farmers fled from North Carolina into Tennessee and Georgia, but particularly over the border into South Carolina's districts of Camden, Orangeburgh, and Ninety Six. In 1766 tensions over taxes and lands culminated in North Carolina when farmers organized the Regulator Movement to overturn corrupt local governments dominated by elite planters, merchants, and lawyers. Regulators struggled to maintain their status as independent producers who enjoyed a "competency" based on both self-sufficiency and commercial exchange.[3]

Among these families were many ancestors of Jones County settlers who later shared a historical predisposition to view the Civil War as a "rich man's war and a poor man's fight." Still, traditions of civil disaffection among the Southern yeomanry did not in and of themselves cause later generations to oppose the Confederacy. Indeed, in Jones County as else-where, many white Southerners believed that rebellion against the Union was the ultimate act of principled civil disobedience against greedy tyrants. The local context in which a family encountered Confederate authority greatly influenced whether that family would be anti- or pro-Confederate, and branches of the same families frequently adopted opposite stances.[4]

Ethel Knight, raised to revere the American Revolution and slavery, as well as the supremacy of the white race, could not abide such a history for her ancestors. She assured her readers that although many early white migrants to Jones County were "without lands or money," or "simply adventurers and vagabonds," the founding families, including the Knights, were part of "the old aristocracy, bringing in slaves and finery from an older civilization." Historical records, however, do not bear out such aris-tocratic claims. As Street recognized, the ancestors of Jones County fami-lies were mostly plain folk who migrated to Mississippi Territory in search of elusive prosperity.[5]

In 1951, however, Street's images of racially mixed ancestors disturbed Ethel Knight more than his class-conscious characters and drove her to write *Echo of the Black Horn*. Street's creation of the *Tap Roots* character Kyd Fermat Dabney, a Cajun orphan adopted by Hoab and Shellie Dabney who secretly possessed "Moorish blood," seemed particularly to disturb Ethel. Although Kyd was not by birth a Dabney, Street's description of her as an orphan suggested that she might be modeled after Mason Rainey Knight, Newt Knight's mother and Ethel's direct ancestor.[6]

The mysterious tales about Mason Knight, who was reputed to have been the "ward" of Jackie Knight before she married his son Albert, were tailor-made for Street's novel of adventure and scandal, and he may indeed have built on legends about her to create Kyd. In 1935 Tom Knight described his grandmother as an orphan whose surname was actually Griffin, not Rainey. He further explained that she was raised by Jackie and Keziah Knight alongside their own children. Around the same time, Martha Wheeler, a former Knight family slave, told Works Projects Admin-istration (WPA) writer Addie West that "she had always been told" that Mason Rainey had "attached herself" to the Knights in Asheville, North Carolina, after her own people died of the flux. Strikingly similar to Wheeler's story was Street's description of how a yellow-fever epidemic killed the parents of Kyd Fermat, causing her to turn to the Dabneys for sustenance.[7]

Kyd Dabney's resemblance to Mason Rainey disturbed some Knights because of her mixed-blood ancestry. "Those black eyes of Kyd's," mused Kyd's adoptive father, Sam Dabney, "ay they glow like bits of polished ebony in a tiny spoon of milk. And those full lips. And her happy nature. She's too unrestrained to be all white." Ethel Knight thus widened the distance between Street's fictional Kyd and her great-great-grandmother by expanding on Tom Knight's and Martha Wheeler's tales. She insisted that Mason Rainey's true name was Rebecca Griffith and that she and her brother were orphaned by their wealthy parents' death from the "bloody flux" during their move west. Shortly thereafter, she claimed, a group of Masons rescued the orphaned children and found a new home for the girl among the Knights. Ethel claimed that the Masons showed up on the Knights' doorstep on a rainy night—hence, the Knights renamed her Mason Rainey.[8]

To further counter any suggestion that Mason, like Kyd Dabney, might have had "black blood," Ethel described her as a "strange and beautiful" "Spanish-type lady." Since it was important to Ethel in 1951 that Mason's body contain not a drop of African blood, she explained her apparent lack of ivory skin and aquiline features by endowing her with an exotic (but European) ancestry. Because of *Tap Roots* and Davis Knight's trial, the racial identity of all Jones County Knights was openly in question at that time, and Ethel placed the blame for that squarely on the shoulders of James Street and Newt Knight.[9]

Although Ethel Knight's racial attitudes conformed to those exhibited by many white Southerners of her generation, these sentiments had evolved over a period of three centuries. By the 1840s, claims of Indian, Iberian, or Mediterranean ancestry defended one's whiteness against race-based laws and social harassment. But before the nineteenth century—and especially before slavery became firmly entrenched in the Carolina and Georgia back-countries—racial identity was more fluid, even negotiable in some cases. Nothing better exemplified its uncertain meaning in the era of the American Revolution than the prominent role played by Gideon Gibson, a light-skinned slaveholder of partially African ancestry, in South Carolina's Regulator Movement. As enforcement of race laws hardened, mixed people, including many of Gideon Gibson's descendants, migrated west in search of whiteness as well as fresh lands.[10]

During North America's colonial period, the yeoman ancestors of Jones County settlers lived in a patriarchal world bounded by lines of gender, class, and increasingly, race. The decision by colonial planters—the overwhelming majority of whom were white men—to abandon bound labor in favor of chattel slavery hastened their disproportionate control over land and wealth. In this world of expanding agricultural commerce and slavery, ordinary men understood that attaining economic success and individual honor depended on their ability to gain and cultivate land through the violent dispossession of Indians and ownership of African slaves.[11]

The rise of white men in the expansive colonial economy in turn gave rise to a racialized class structure. Even though slaveowners comprised only a minority of North Carolina's white population, their replacement of white servants with black slaves nonetheless sent the message to ordinary white men and women that servitude was uncomfortably close to slavery. As whiteness became the essential basis for freedom, white women became the crucial vessels of racial purity; black men, its despoilers. The policing of white women's and black men's sexual behavior revealed most strikingly the need for discrete categories of race in a society undergirded by the labor of enslaved Africans. Black women were designated as bearers of racially "polluted" offspring—whether fathered by black or white men—while notions of racial and sexual purity converged in the "chaste" white woman. Legally and socially, white women who crossed the color line entered a racialized realm of whoredom. As whites increasingly associated unbridled carnality, lust, and "nasty" sexual impulses with Africans, the term "wench" became almost synonymous with a female slave. At the same time, blame for the mixing of the races was placed squarely on the shoulders of white women, the designated repositories of chastity and racial purity, for their lewd "polluting" of white bloodlines.[12]

Male honor also became wedded to whiteness in this structure. A white man's success as patriarch depended not only on his owning land and mastering a household but on conquering "savage" Indians or owning "barbarian" Africans. Nevertheless, the bifurcation of racial identity into discrete categories of black and white was a long and ultimately illusory process. People of mixed racial ancestry were legally restrained and socially ostracized, but they could not be erased. Whether labeled Mulattoes, Mustees, Melungeons, Creoles, Cajuns, or the like, the mixing of peoples in early America was a visible fact.[13]

Despite increasingly close connections between racial and class identity in Revolutionary America, lower and middling white men continued to resent powerful white men, and an interracial subculture continued to flourish underground. Even slaveholders clandestinely participated in activities that regularly occurred among slaves and free blacks, often in wooded areas outside mainstream society. Sexual relationships, illicit trade, feasts, and religious celebrations flourished in what Rhys Isaac has termed an "alternative territorial system." Although whites moved in and out of this world, they asserted the prerogatives of whiteness when it served their interests to do so.[14]

In a world that increasingly linked white male honor to the ownership of African Americans, white men who openly shared their hearths and homes with blacks beyond the use of their labor were considered dishonorable. So embedded became the construction of whiteness as a marker of both racial and class supremacy that, one hundred years later, few whites questioned that Newton Knight and his children's interracial relationships were the result of degraded, "unnatural" impulses.[15] Interracial mixing had not abated; it had merely moved underground. Had Newt and his children treated their proscribed relationships as shameful liaisons to be kept secret, they would have posed little threat to society. Instead, Newt welcomed Rachel Knight and her children into the fold of his own family, thereby severing masculine honor from the prerogatives (and responsibilities) of whiteness, an act more shocking to his neighbors than his rebellion against the Confederacy.[16]

To help drive home her contention that Newt was an aberrant, deviant member of an otherwise distinguished family, Ethel Knight emphasized that his grandfather Jackie Knight was the son of a Revolutionary soldier and one of Jones County's largest slaveholders. While it is true that Jackie Knight owned twenty-two slaves by 1850, he did not begin adult life as a large slaveholder, nor could Ethel prove that he, her great-great-grandfather, was the son of a Revolutionary patriot soldier. And like most of his Piney Woods cohorts, Jackie Knight was descended from North Carolinians who grew up amid profound political, economic, and religious struggles that included the Regulator Movement, evangelical revivals, Indian Wars, and the Revolution.[17]

The Revolutionary generation's own ancestors were plain folk driven south from Pennsylvania, Maryland, and Virginia during the seventeenth and eighteenth centuries by rising populations, land pressures, and the Chesapeake's glutted tobacco economy.[18] Many of them had moved directly to the Piedmont region of North Carolina, while those from Virginia's south side often entered the state's coastal region and settled in Albemarle County. The ingredients for class and racial strife reemerged in setting after setting. In North Carolina, as in Virginia and Maryland, the final decades of the seventeenth century were filled with violent strife, as small freeholders and "new men" struggled to achieve economic prosperity and political power. Culpeper's Rebellion, Bacon's Rebellion, and by the mid-eighteenth century, the Seven Years' War, were all symptomatic of societies in painful transition.[19]

This was the New World, where a free man was supposed to rise by his own efforts, but old worlds, it seemed, constantly encroached on new ones. The more fluid economic conditions of the early seventeenth century, produced by large immigrant populations, high death rates, and bound labor, were eroded by rising populations of planters, yeomen, and landless freedmen who competed for land that became increasingly dear. And so it went, generation after generation.[20]

Map 1.1. North Carolina at the Beginning of 1760

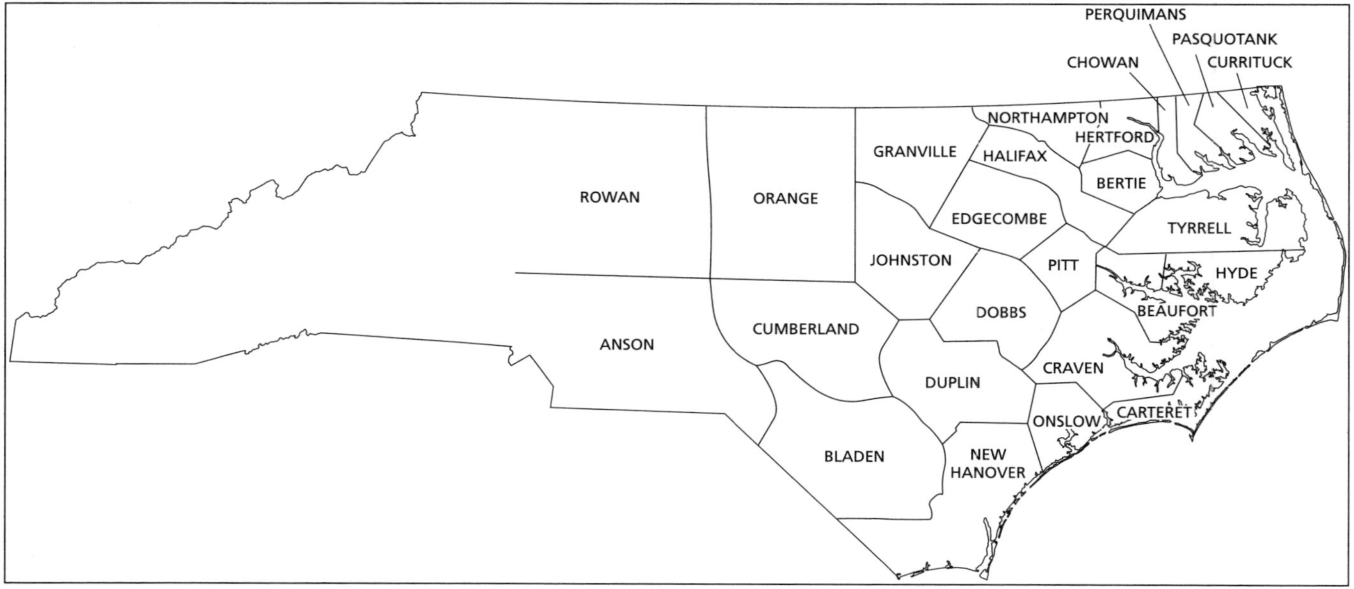

Source: D. L. Corbitt, Formation of North Carolina Counties, 1663–1943 (Raleigh: State Department of Archives and History, 1980).

Map 1.2. North Carolina at the Beginning of 1775

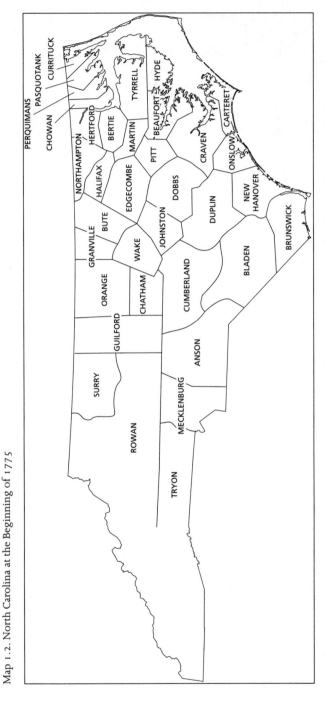

Source: D. L. Corbitt, Formation of North Carolina Counties, 1663–1943 (Raleigh: State Department of Archives and History, 1980).

During the eighteenth century, many yeoman families like the Knights struggled to rise beyond the status of mere landowners and began entering the ranks of slaveholders. Increasingly, the hallmark of the upper classes was more than mere prosperity and education; it was the practice of the polite rituals of "gracious living," including engagement in social events centered around formal dancing and ceremonious dinners. This genteel living necessitated ever more money for the acquisition of space and material goods. Separate rooms for separate functions and household goods—linens, tableware, and silverware—enabled members of the upper class to display their "refinement."[21]

By comparison, lower-class people appeared ever more "rude," too governed by their material poverty and unremitting labor—or so many of the upper class thought—to participate meaningfully in society. The daily hard work required of nonslaveholders and small slaveholders who farmed and raised livestock left little capital for the purchase of material possessions. Many yeomen occupied sparsely furnished, one-room log homes that might include additional sleeping space in overhead lofts or offer sheds that provided extra shelter or storage space. The badges of their class were painfully visible: leather pants derisively labeled "buckskins"; a diet of cornpone, pork, and milk; and the modest, sometimes disorderly structures they called home. Still, these were propertied free men who voted and sat on juries; gentlemen had to treat them with at least a modicum of respect.[22]

As in the Chesapeake, white North Carolinians built their society on the principles of a domestic patriarchy wherein men dominated public and private institutions. Women contributed to household economies by laboring both in fields and at hearths and were especially valued for their breeding capabilities. The good wife assured her husband's prosperity by obediently and cheerfully serving as his helpmeet in return for his protection. Unlike slaves, considered incapable of honor by whites, wives gained status to the extent that their husbands succeeded financially. Fortunately land was cheap and plentiful in eighteenth-century North Carolina. Propertied men became powerful patriarchs of status, however, to the extent that they were masters to slaves and servants as well as wives and children.[23]

The expanding network of Knights who lived in Edgecombe County understood this well and rose in stature during the second half of the eighteenth century. Although the exact birthplace of Jackie Knight and the name of his father are unknown, Jackie was likely descended from these Knights. Born in North Carolina on September 7, 1773, his mother, Mary, was from neighboring Hertford County. Jackie's grandfather may well have been William Knight of Bertie County, who raised both livestock and tobacco, apparently without slaves. William's 1752 will directed that his son John, who perhaps had already received land, inherit his "smith tools" and "wipsaw"; his second son, William, received land and a horse, and his third son, Nehemiah, received land.[24]

Slaveholding was more common among the next generation of Knights. In 1770 the estate of John Knight included two slaves and the household goods of a prosperous man: three featherbeds, a table, a desk, a chest, a brandy still, iron pots, pewter basins, dishes, and eating utensils. Nehemiah Knight, who appears in the tax and land records of late-eighteenth-century Georgia in the region to which Jackie Knight's family moved, was a slaveholder at the time of his death in 1819. Yet not all Knights were entirely comfortable with slavery. In 1789, in the midst of the nation's constitutional debates over the institution, Ephraim Knight of Halifax County (formed from Edgecombe in 1758) manumitted two mulatto slaves, Richard and Alexander.[25]

Several other ancestors of Jones County immigrants had made their way into the ranks of slaveholders before the close of the eighteenth century. In 1751 Younger Welborn's great-grandparents William and Isabel Teague arrived in North Carolina with their family, including several grown sons, from western Maryland. Their son Moses Teague moved to Rowan County in 1756, where his children intermarried with those of his neighbor, William Welborn, also from Maryland. The Rowan County Welborns remained nonslaveholders, but Moses Teague eventually acquired "one negro man, Abraham."[26]

Several Bynums of the North Carolina Piedmont also advanced into the ranks of slaveholders. When William Bynum Sr. died in 1746, he owned six slaves, forty head of cattle, and numerous household items that included featherbeds, books, and Bibles—items not commonly found in the homes of ordinary farmers. James Bynum (probably William's brother) was less prosperous; his 1763 will directed that three slaves, some supplies of corn and bacon, five cows, several featherbeds, and several unspecified items of furniture be distributed among his heirs.[27]

The acquisition of land, slaves, and material comforts brought a new anxiety to household patriarchs. Not all men could rise in this world; nor could those who did advance be certain that their rise would continue or that they could maintain the wealth they had gained. Those who became Regulators sought what they believed was a just reordering of power. Eighteenth-century farmers knew that their livelihood—indeed, their very survival—depended on participation in the developing commercial economy. Their fears of economic decline reflected a rational assessment of the changing world they faced.[28]

Slave-based commercial agriculture contributed vitally to the modern Atlantic trade system between 1730 and 1815, but most farmers participated only marginally in this golden age of plantation agriculture. Consequently, thousands of people in western North Carolina supported the Regulator Movement during the 1760s, and on May 15, 1771, two thousand men participated in the Battle of Alamance. Regulators condemned lawyers and merchants as parasites who made their wealth off the productive labor of farmers. In particular they resented the coteries of men who assigned exorbitant taxes, seized people's lands, and appropriated public monies through dominance of county politics.[29]

Among the ancestors of future members of the Knight Company, for example, the Welborns were most visible in the Regulator Movement. Aaron Welborn, the ancestor of numerous settlers of Piney Woods Mississippi, including three members of the Knight Company and Serena Knight, wife of Newton Knight, grew up in Rowan County, North Carolina. During the 1760s the Abbotts Creek neighborhood of Aaron's birth bristled with excitement from the activities of Regulators and New Light Baptists.[30] Likewise, from Anson County the early kinfolk of the Jones County Collinses—Jacob and Joshua—participated in the Regulator Movement.[31] The Collinses were two of ninety-nine men who protested the county's unfair taxation policies, arguing that "no people have a right to be taxed but by consent of themselves or their delegate."[32] And, among the North Carolina Bynums, James Bynum was indicted on March 11, 1771, for Regulator activities.[33]

The explosive effects of the Great Awakening lent force to North Carolina's Regulator Movement. Less than a decade before Regulators organized their activities, several Separatist New Light Baptist ministers had traveled to the North Carolina Piedmont from New England. The most successful New Light minister was Shubal Stearns, who led North Carolina Baptists in 1758 in forming the Sandy Creek Separate Association. Although New Light preachers offended most upper-class members of society, they touched the hearts of angry people when they condemned the greed of merchants and planters in their fiery jeremiads.[34]

Moreover, several New Light preachers were intimately connected to ancestors of Knight Company members. Philip Mulkey of Orange County, one of Shubal Stearns's chief disciples, was related by marriage to Regulator James Bynum. Stearns himself and his brother-in-law, Daniel Marshall, intermarried with the Regulator Welborn family. Two Welborns also married daughters of Regulator James Younger, a lesser known Baptist exhorter whose piety and "earnest exhortations" converted many of his neighbors to the Baptist faith.[35]

Evangelical radicals optimistically urged personal engagement in the world, promising that if people would only act in God's name, they could build morally pure republican communities. Although slaveholders and nonslaveholders alike responded to New Light preaching, those who became Regulators tended toward middling economic status. They were not simple rustics confused and frightened by a rapidly expanding market economy. Many, like the Teagues, Welborns, Youngers, Collinses, and Bynums, were prosperous farmers whose self-interest fueled their opposition to political and economic corruption. They voiced their complaints in the language of republican rights and Awakening morality, suggesting that white people could remain uncorrupted if they owned few, if any, slaves in a nonplantation region. Accepting the necessity of a commercial economy, many Regulators believed that land and slaves must be widely diffused among free white men in order to prevent greed and political corruption.[36]

The use of unordained "lay" ministers to spread the gospel had obvious appeal to women and to men of humble origins, such as James Younger, who infused his political activism as a Regulator with New Light morality. Around 1756 he visited Daniel Marshall in the Sandy Creek settlement and brought him back to Abbotts Creek, where Marshall founded the Abbotts Creek Baptist Church. Because Marshall was as yet unordained, Shubal Stearns accompanied the men to the new church, located not far from Welborn's (or Kimbrough's) Meeting House, where Regulators sometimes met. Stearns applied to Nicholas Bedgegood, minister of the Welsh Tract Baptists on the Peedee River in South Carolina, to assist in the ordination of Marshall. Bedgegood, a regular Baptist, refused, denouncing Separate Baptists as a "disorderly set, suffering women to pray in public, and permitting every ignorant man to preach that chose."[37]

Bedgegood's words suggest that not only men but also women in Civil War Jones County might draw on an antiauthoritarian heritage. Although most radical theologians did not question women's subordination to men, religious activism encouraged some women to enter the public world, seizing forbidden public spaces, as did some Jones County women during the Civil War. During the Great Awakening, exhorters Martha Stearns Marshall (sister of Shubal and wife of Daniel), Eunice Marshall (sister of Daniel), and Nancy Mulkey, whose exhortations "neither father nor brother could equal," crossed gendered boundaries in the name of delivering God's Word. As it has done historically, social crisis drew some women onto male fields of action.[38]

Persecution and criticism from political leaders and conservative clergy drove many itinerant New Lights to seek fresh fields of converts. Around 1762, on Fairforest Creek in the Ninety Six District, Philip Mulkey and his

North Carolina followers founded the first Baptist church of the South Carolina backcountry. Daniel and Martha Marshall left Abbotts Creek in 1760 for the South Carolina backcountry and, eventually, Georgia, with several Stearns and Welborn kinfolk. In 1771, at age sixty-five, Daniel and his family settled on Kiokee Creek, about twenty miles northwest of Augusta. Almost immediately Daniel was arrested under Georgia's legislative act of 1758 that forbade preaching outside the Church of England.[39]

Martha Stearns Marshall's spirited defense of her husband anticipated women's protection of husbands and sons in Civil War Jones County. Drawing on her skills as an exhorter, Martha allegedly quoted scripture to both the constable who arrested Daniel and the magistrate who tried him. Legend has it that she converted both. Whether true or not, the story's importance lies in its retelling to generation after generation of Baptist women. In times of moral crisis, New Light Baptists granted Christian women power to act outside their traditional sphere.[40]

The radical behavior of New Lights continually drew fire from the established ministries, who considered them rude and déclassé. Charles Woodmason, the famous Anglican backcountry minister, railed against the newly arrived and "infamous" Philip Mulkey. According to Woodmason, Mulkey came to South Carolina "in Rags, hungry, and bare foot" but could, "at his beck, or Nod, or Motion of his finger lead out four hundred Men into the Wilderness." Woodmason judged the Carolina backcountry's people through upper-class lenses and thought no better of them than he did Mulkey. The "Indians are better cloathed and lodged" than the plain people of Beaver Creek, he wrote, because of the latter's "Indolence and laziness." He described Beaver Creek folks as a "pack of wretches" who were "wild as the deer."[41]

Woodmason's class-based disgust had sexual overtones when directed toward backcountry women. Just as white colonial leaders questioned the chastity of white women who crossed the color line, so also did Woodmason suggest that those who followed itinerant preachers were sexually corrupt. He scolded pretty young women for attending church in "shifts" and "short petticoats, . . . barefooted and Barelegged," and he shamed them by inviting them to ponder what upper-class ladies would think of them. Sexual impurity thus merged with religious exuberance in his image of backcountry Baptist women.[42]

Woodmason's negative images of plain backcountry folk anticipated stereotypes that by the late nineteenth century would be staples of Northern and New South rhetoric (see Chapters 7 and 8). Small wonder, given the steady barrage of degrading images of plain people that spewed forth for the next century and a half, that status-conscious Ethel Knight would recast her Jones County ancestors as aristocratic slaveholding patriots rather than Regulators, itinerant preachers, and Tories.[43]

As New Light preachers moved into the South Carolina–Georgia back-country, many Regulator families followed their paths. Several sons and daughters of James Welborn Sr. and James Younger moved from North Carolina to the Pendleton district of South Carolina's old Ninety Six District. In 1788, under the leadership of the Reverend Moses Holland, they helped establish the Big Creek Church near the Saluda River. In 1801 James Welborn Jr., a nonslaveholder, served as a deacon. These families had successfully reestablished themselves as solid citizens of the South Carolina backcountry.[44]

The Welborns' kinsman, outlawed Regulator Joshua Teague, fled across the North Carolina border around 1770 and settled at Bush River, where he soon joined Philip Mulkey's New Light Bush River Baptist Church.[45] Migration to the South Carolina backcountry brought the Welborns and Teagues into a region with its own conflicted history, including the brutal Cherokee war of 1760–61, Great Awakening schisms, the Regulator Movement, and a vicious inner civil war between Whigs and Tories during the Revolution. Before displaced North Carolina Regulators arrived, however, South Carolina Regulators had generally quelled the violence, thievery, hand-to-mouth existence, and general lawlessness that flourished in the South Carolina backcountry after the Cherokee war.[46]

There were important differences between the Regulator Movements of North and South Carolina and, accordingly, in the forces that determined whether a family supported the Revolutionary movement or remained loyal to the Crown. The South Carolina backcountry's leading men of property and local stature launched their Regulator campaign against anarchy and disorder in 1767–68. By 1770, often by excessive means, they had successfully transformed chaos into order. Unlike North Carolina's Regulators, they directed their movement toward consolidation of their own economic and political power, gaining dominance by dispossessing Indians and disciplining or driving off outlaws, thieves, and hunters.[47]

The experiences of Jacob Summerall, great-great-grandfather of Newton Knight's second lieutenant, William Wesley Sumrall, demonstrated that South Carolina's Regulators sought more to expand and protect their own wealth than to promote economic democracy. Summerall was an anti-Regulator who later helped lead the Moderator Movement against Regulator excesses in South Carolina. In 1762 he was justice of the peace in the Edgefield district (formerly part of Ninety Six) and owned 550 acres of land in New Windsor Township, near the Savannah River. Summerall's friendship with British superintendent of Indian affairs John Stuart and the importance of New Windsor as an Indian trading post indicate that Sum-

Map 1.3. Georgia's Revolutionary War Counties

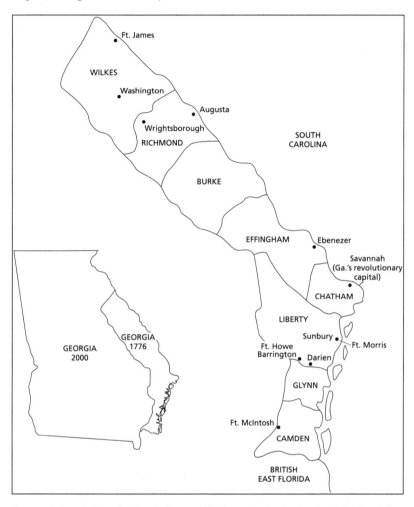

Source: Robert S. Davis Jr., *Georgia Citizens and Soldiers in the American Revolution* (Easley, S.C.: Southern Historical Press, 1979).

merall probably engaged in the Indian trade. That fact alone would have displeased Regulators, who blamed Indian traders and agents for many of their problems with the Cherokees. Also, Summerall's brother Henry had been convicted of horse theft, which raised questions about his own stance toward crime. Regulators frequently brutalized magistrates whom they considered too "easy" on criminals. Several of them dragged Summerall from his home in New Windsor Township, stripped him, tied him to a tree, and whipped him. When Summerall sued them, they retaliated by seizing him yet again.[48]

Col. John Stuart freed Summerall from the Regulators after Summerall's

Map 1.4. South Carolina, 1790

Source: Adapted from William Thorndale and William Dollarhide, *Map Guide to the U.S. Federal Censuses, 1790–1920* (Baltimore: Genealogical Pub. Co., 1992).

wife, Ann, appealed to him directly. Shortly thereafter, Summerall warned Stuart that Regulators were after him, too. On November 10, 1768, he wrote to Stuart that Regulator Laurence Rambo "thinks your Honor ought to be taken and whipped and your goods taken from you as you are giving to the damn'd Indians to kill the Back Woods people." Not surprisingly, Summerall's experience at the hands of Regulators led him into the Moderator Movement, organized in March 1769. As in the case of many back-country people, Regulator oppression encouraged Jacob to become a Tory, while his brother Jesse supported the Revolution.[49]

The Summeralls were typical of many families who found themselves politically divided during the American Revolution. Fierce local schisms generated by Indian wars, the Great Awakening, and the Regulator Movement often determined whether one became Whig or Tory. In the South Carolina backcountry, Regulators and Regular Baptists tended to be Whigs, while those whom they attempted to "order" tended toward loyalism.

Particularly in the Ninety Six and Camden Districts, Whigs and Tories chose sides according to neighborhood loyalties. Thus, relatives living in different neighborhoods might easily find themselves on opposite sides of the Revolution.[50]

Clearly, the memory of past conflicts blended with one's immediate political concerns to determine Revolutionary allegiances. There were both Whig and Tory ancestors among families that migrated from the Carolinas and Georgia to Piney Woods Mississippi, and many men may pragmatically have served both armies at different times. According to family tradition, the South Carolina Valentine family was so divided during the Revolution that the patriot branch of the family changed its name to Vollentine to separate itself from the Tory side. In Georgia, where New Lights were persecuted by those who had supported the Revolutionary cause, Daniel Marshall, Luke and James Bynum, and William and Thomas Welch all became Tories. So did most members of the Wrightsborough Quaker community, many of whom were former Regulators from North Carolina. It would be no different some ninety years later in Civil War Jones County, where many families linked by kinship and shared histories would split over whether to support the Confederacy.[51]

As exhilarating as it appeared in hindsight, the Revolution created social chaos and sowed bitter divisions among families. The trials of nation building put enormous social strains on Americans, temporarily flattening the heady ferment of religious zeal and doctrinal conflict. Churches were destroyed, and many congregations and ministers lost their spiritual moorings. Evangelical Whigs persevered, however, arguing that God had decreed America's victory over the British. Their efforts to revitalize religious piety through organization and missionary activity bore fruit with the Second Great Awakening.[52]

Such were the forces—evangelical revivalism, commercial growth, and the Revolution—that propelled people to move west. Fittingly, the main character of James Street's *Oh, Promised Land*, Sam Dabney, began his trek west in 1795 as a scout for frontier settlers. Like Jackie Knight, he hungered for wealth and status, which he eventually achieved by acquiring land and slaves. Sam, wrote Street, "was a Georgia redneck with a pocket full of yellow gold. He was the New South, the get-rich-quick South. He drank too much and talked too much, ready to fight, hyper-sensitive, trying to hide his red neck under a fine collar." Yet, in Sam Dabney, Street also introduced readers to a white Southern man who eventually turned against slavery and who believed by 1861 that secession was madness.[53]

In *Tap Roots* Street transformed the brash Sam Dabney from a cotton nabob into an older and wiser yeoman farmer, chastened by his long life on the

Southwestern frontier. Unlike Jackie, Sam died a nonslaveholder, convinced by his own "bad investments" that slavery was "economic stupidity." As Sam approached death in the summer of 1858, his granddaughter reminded him that a newspaper editor had once referred to him as the "aristocrat of the aristocrats." By now an old man disgusted by Mississippi's pretensions of gentility, Sam snorted, "God's jawbone! There are not enough aristocrats in Mississippi to serve as pallbearers of a-a-a gnat."[54]

After presenting the Revolution as an important force shaping the lives of Jones County ancestors, Street's novels revealed the frontier to be of equal importance. Whether they intended to become slaveholders or not, families such as the Dabneys rolled onto the frontier in pursuit of Thomas Jefferson's agrarian republic of prosperous white farmers. They would soon face again what many hoped to escape—a rapidly commercializing economy in which powerful planters bought the best lands, owned the most slaves, and all too often, determined political policy.[55]

It was a land of deep, dark water, with black
earth along the rivers. Pines stood at attention
on the ridges, scarcely swaying in the gentle
wind that blew up from the Gulf.—James Street,
Oh, Promised Land, 1940

He said he and his wife walked from South
Carolina [to] here, and that Betsy toated Mat,
the baby, and he carried his gun; so they made
their way down, you might say, by Indian paths.
—M. P. Bush, address before the DAR, 1912

Chapter Two

The Quest for Land

Yeoman Republicans
on the Southwestern
Frontier

By 1790 most of the ancestral families of Jones County settlers had left for
the South Carolina backcountry, and by early 1795 some had begun to
migrate toward Mississippi Territory. Throughout their long frontier trek,
many traveled in groups of allied families, intermarrying along the way.[1]
Together they fought Indians at practically every juncture of their migration across state and territorial borders. Often settling by choice in Hill
Country, Pine Barren, and Piney Woods regions, they strove to reproduce
economic, religious, and political styles of life that were rapidly disappear-
ing in the Southeast. Time and again individuals, families, and entire
neighborhoods moved to yet another sparsely settled frontier where they
repeated the process of building cabins, clearing land to farm, and releas-
ing their cattle and hogs to forage in the woods.[2]

In a rapidly changing world, however, yeoman farmers could not reproduce old ways of life merely by moving west, for they could escape neither

the pressures nor the temptations brought by a growing commercial economy. Just as a rising class of slaveholders in South Carolina had earlier appropriated the Regulator Movement to expand its power over the backcountry, so, too, did it consolidate that power after the Revolution through intense land speculation and by shifting the direction of evangelicalism in favor of slaveholders during the Second Great Awakening. Once again, small farmers were "free" to seek their fortunes elsewhere. Like Benjamin Franklin, Thomas Jefferson, and James Madison, for whom many frontier yeomen reverentially named their sons, most of them agreed that commercial farming facilitated a higher level of civilization than did mere subsistence farming. Most accordingly aspired to be commercially successful farmers and herders.[3]

The lure of cheap Western lands encouraged yeoman farmers to believe that they might strike a balance between primitive simplicity and corrupt wealth. For many, however, the desire for success was tempered by the popular republican belief that too much commercial success led to moral decay as greed overtook industriousness and as luxuries replaced the utilitarian products of a virtuous people. In effect, their migrations west represented attempts to divorce economic progress from the moral and political corruptions of "over-civilization."[4]

The simultaneous westward expansion of commercial agriculture and slavery put those who settled east of the Pearl River (where Covington County would be formed in 1819 and Jones County in 1826) on divergent economic paths. Some farmers would compromise economic self-sufficiency in favor of commercial profits, in the process buying slaves, while others would remain nonslaveholders, limiting their market production to surplus livestock and foodstuffs.[5]

Two settlers of this region, Norvell Robertson and Stacy Collins, illustrate the different responses of Piney Woods yeomen to Mississippi's rising cotton empire. The economic path chosen by Robertson would set his sons and grandsons on a course leading later to support for secession and the Confederacy, but Collins's path would lead his descendants not only to oppose secession but also to take up arms against the Confederacy.[6]

Frontier experiences played an important role in determining their choices. In Robertson's autobiography, completed in March 1846 when he was almost eighty-one years old, he explained why an ordinary man like himself chose the Piney Woods as his permanent home. He claimed that before he moved to Mississippi, he sold a tract of fertile land that he had won in the Georgia land lottery because "it had nothing to recommend it but the richness of the soil." The equally rich tracts of land that surrounded it further convinced him that the region "would in a short time be settled up by a dense population, a large proportion [of] which would probably be slaves. . . . In a short time there would be scarcely a spear of grass to be found in the country outside of the plantations." Robertson preferred owning land on Mississippi's Leaf River even though it was of "inferior quality." He liked the climate in Covington County, which he described as "dry, pleasant, and healthy." Like so many migrants to the Piney Woods, he found its ranges ideal for raising livestock.[7]

In deliberately settling outside the plantation belt, Robertson sought to minimize his competition with wealthier men, not to escape the world of commerce and slavery. Not only did he farm and raise livestock with the aid of several slaves, but he also operated a mill from which he "realized a moderate profit" and, later, a cotton gin. Moving west enabled him to prosper economically and socially despite the disadvantages of his birth. Like so many others, he sought escape from the "evil" effects of consolidated wealth while hoping that access to fresh, cheap land would bring him commercial success. And so it did. Though modest by plantation belt standards, Robertson's level of prosperity assured his family exalted status in Piney Woods society.[8]

To Stacy Collins, as to Norvell Robertson, the frontier represented propertied independence and selective access to markets, but there the similarity between the men ended. As Collins moved across the Southwestern frontier, he developed a strong sense of nationalism and, during crucial moments of conflict, joined others in petitioning the federal government for protection of settlers against corrupt local officials and Indians in remote frontier outposts. Most importantly, he never became a slaveholder.[9]

Born in 1786 in Spartanburg, South Carolina, Stacy Collins headed for the frontier while still a young man. Before 1808 he had settled in Georgia, where he apparently met and married Sarah Anderson Gibson, described by several descendants as a young widow of Native American ancestry.[10] After a brief stay in Twiggs County, Georgia, the couple settled around 1812 in Buckatunna, just west of the Chickasawhay River, in Wayne County, Mississippi Territory. Here Stacy owned eighty acres of land, as did Joshua Collins, who accompanied Stacy and Sarah in their move west, and Christopher Collins, who arrived ahead of them. Sometime between 1817 and 1820 Stacy and Sarah again moved, this time to nearby Covington County (later Jones County), where by 1829 his and Norvell Robertson's paths would cross.[11]

Robertson and Collins were part of the flood of yeoman farmers who moved west during the first decades of the nineteenth century in response to the growing boom in cotton production that accompanied the rise of backcountry planters. Their individual responses to the chaotic conditions of frontier life during the first two decades of the nineteenth century were repeated by other yeoman families who migrated to southeastern Mississippi. In Jones and Covington Counties the McLemores, Baylises, Shows, Duckworths, and Andersons would follow the economic path of Norvell Robertson, but the Valentines and Welches would follow that of the Collinses. For other Jones and Covington County families, the path was not so clear. The Knights, Bynums, Welborns, Reddochs, and Sumralls would all develop slaveholding as well as nonslaveholding branches.[12]

While cheap land in the West beckoned forebears of Jones County families, protracted struggles over economic changes hastened their exodus from the Southeast. The growing popularity of slave labor was evident to people leaving the Carolinas. In both states, any tendency among the yeomanry to criticize the institution of slavery during the Regulator Movement and the Revolution was blunted by 1790. Common white men mostly protested planters' abuse of class prerogatives rather than the system that underlay those privileges.[13]

In the Carolinas and Georgia, for example, citizens clashed over the appropriate use of waterways during the South's transition from a semi-subsistence to a market-based economy. Traditional methods of fishing and hunting, which remained important sources of livelihood and powerful symbols of manliness and independence among rural American men, were threatened by commercial development. Fishermen were especially frustrated by commercial millers who built dams that blocked the flow of their fishing streams.[14]

In framing their arguments, petitioners borrowed from the egalitarian rhetoric of the American Revolution. One South Carolina petition—which bore several signatures from the Welch family, whose descendants intermarried with the Collinses in Jones County, Mississippi—cited the "inalterable laws of nature" and the "common rights of mankind." Such republican rhetoric would appear again and again in the petitions from yeoman frontiersmen to the federal government.[15]

Southwestern frontiersmen such as Stacy Collins expressed fierce concern for their rights as free citizens of the United States, demanding that the national government protect those rights. The building of the Federal Road; the conquest of the Chickasaw, Cherokee, Creek, and Choctaw Indians; and the achievement of statehood for Mississippi (1817) and Alabama (1819) stimulated ever greater migration of farmers, hunters, fishermen, and herdsmen into the Southwest. Many of these men had served in the War of 1812. That experience, buttressed by stories and memories of past struggles of fathers and grandfathers, stimulated a fervent nationalism and republicanism among the generation that came of age in the first decade of the nineteenth century.[16]

Map 2.1. Principal Lines of Mississippi Territory prior to Statehood, 1798–1819

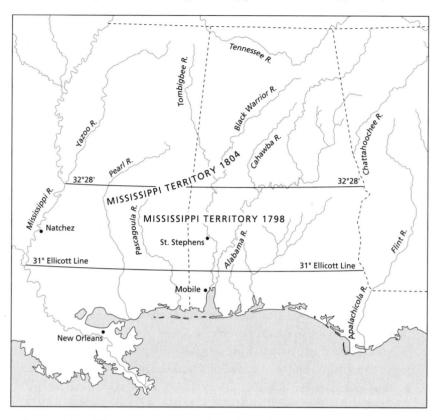

Source: Adapted from Henry DeLeon Sutherland Jr. and Jerry Elijah Brown, *The Federal Road through the Creek Nation and Alabama*, 1806–1836, maps by Charles Jefferson Hiers (Tuscaloosa: University of Alabama Press, 1989).

As men and women steadily streamed west toward Mobile and beyond to the Pearl River, their frontier experiences reinforced old suspicions about the corrupting force of wealth. Just as Regulators had complained to their colonial governments about the machinations of local elites, so frontier men griped to the federal government about Indians and inadequate territorial governments in the post-Revolution Southwest. Those who settled east of the Pearl River in Mississippi Territory, where Covington and Jones Counties would be founded, resented the preferential treatment given by the federal government to wealthy planters living in the Natchez District, west of the River.[17]

Although Presidents Thomas Jefferson and James Madison hoped that the availability of cheap lands would disperse landed and slave property widely and enable agricultural production to remain dominant over manufacturing, it was not always clear that government officials respected the "common man." For example, on May 1, 1804, Ephraim Kirby, U.S. commissioner for Washington County in the territory, described the "country" on the west side of the Mobile and Tombigbee Rivers to President Jefferson as a "Pine-baren of great extent," suitable only for raising cattle. With undisguised contempt, he characterized the region's settlers as "wild and savage" Tories, fugitives from the law, or at best, poor people who hoped "to gain a precarious subsistence in a wilderness."[18]

Despite Kirby's obvious chauvinism, there were important truths in his disdainful statements. Great Britain's designation of West Florida as an official asylum for Tory refugees in 1775 had drawn many Southeastern loyalists into the Lower Mississippi Valley. After the United States purchased Louisiana Territory in 1803, it claimed all of West Florida that lay west of the Perdido River, although Spain did not relinquish control until 1810. Tory planters, farmers, and adventurers reached the Natchez region by traveling from Nashville to the lower Mississippi River via the Natchez Trace. Poorer refugees from the Georgia and South Carolina backcountry sometimes traveled from the Savannah River across Creek lands, building settlements along the way as they pressed toward the Mississippi River.[19]

Kirby acknowledged that many English-speaking white settlers were poor people trying to escape poverty or prosecution. Indeed, many migrants to Mississippi Territory had spent their childhoods in transit, reaching adulthood in Georgia, Alabama, or Tennessee. In the Mississippi Valley, loyalists joined earlier Acadian, Canary Island, and Anglo-American settlers in a multiethnic, racial, and cultural setting enlivened by competition over land and trade and by conflicts over national customs and boundaries. Great Britain's colonization of West Florida helped transform the Mississippi Valley's subsistence economy into one of commercial plantations. Before commercial agriculture took hold, however, whites, free blacks, and slaves from the United States participated in a semisubsistence frontier economy that centered on exchanges of deerskins, horses, and alcohol with Indian, Spanish, and French traders.[20]

By 1804 about two hundred families, most of which were nonslaveholders, lived on the Mobile and Tombigbee Rivers in the eastern portion of Mississippi Territory (in present-day Alabama). Approximately sixty families lived in the Tensaw settlement, north of Mobile. Their numbers were quickly augmented after Congress approved in 1805 the building of a postal horse path extending through the Upper and Lower Creek lands from Middle Georgia to the Tombigbee and Alabama Rivers, just above Mobile, in Lower Alabama. Government officials hoped that this path would facilitate faster, safer transportation of U.S. mail to New Orleans. It quickly became an emigrants' route west, however, and in 1811 was the basis for the Federal (or Military) Road.[21]

Map 2.2. The Travelers' Road, 1815–1836

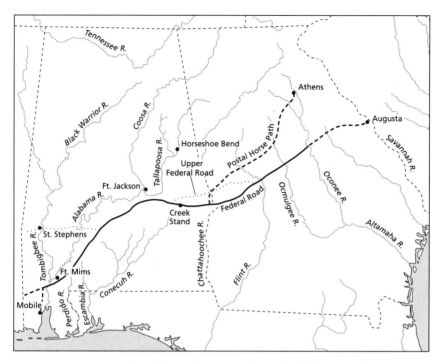

Source: Adapted from Henry DeLeon Sutherland Jr. and Jerry Elijah Brown, *The Federal Road through the Creek Nation and Alabama, 1806–1836*, maps by Charles Jefferson Hiers (Tuscaloosa: University of Alabama Press, 1989).

Most ancestors of Piney Woods Mississippians traveled west on the Federal Road. In 1808 several ancestors of Jones County deserters were among a small settlement of families on the Chickasawhay River in the future state of Mississippi. Daniel Whitehead, Tom Sumrall, Giles Sumrall, and Calvin Sumrall joined seventy-eight others to call on the U.S. General Assembly on December 16, 1808, to create a new county. Complaining that settlements were located forty to sixty miles from the courthouse, petitioners reminded Congress that they had "families depending alone on our labor" and that "high watters" made it "sometimes next to Impossible" to attend court sessions. They won their battle, and by 1810 there were 1,166 families living in the new county of Wayne, which included the future counties of Jones, Covington, and Perry.[22]

In 1809 Tom Sumrall and Daniel Whitehead joined William Coleman, John Landrum, John Mills, Robert Welch, several Loftins and Sullivans, and ninety-five others in petitioning the president and Congress to waive restrictions on their preemptive rights to Choctaw lands on which they had already settled. Using republican rhetoric, despite the fact that several signers bore Tory surnames, the men assured the government that they were "real American citizens well attached to the present government and administration of the U. States."[23]

In contrast to Commissioner Kirby's description ten years earlier, frontier people living on the Tombigbee and Alabama Rivers in 1815 saw themselves as the antithesis of wild and savage people, and they certainly were not "disunited." Their greatest fear was of landlessness and political powerlessness, which would render them dependent and seal their social degradation. Referring to the Creek War, they laid claim to the right to dispossess "savage" Indians from the soil. Two centuries of Indian dispossession had convinced most white men that this was their natural right.[24]

In the summer of 1813, settlers living in the Tensaw settlement suffered the horrors of the Fort Mims massacre. Hundreds of white settlers and their black slaves died in this episode of the Creek War, although some slaves managed to cross over into Indian society. Those whites who survived the massacre began the painful process of rebuilding or abandoning their settlements. Seventy-six claimants—survivors and heirs of individuals killed—filed claims with the government for losses that totaled over $121,000. In December 1815 settlers in this region offered a "repetition of their grievances" to the U.S. government. Explaining that their settlement had been the "theatre of Savage depredations," they complained not only about Creeks but also about the "more unnatural, but not less ferocious warfare by the ALLIES of SAVAGES," referring to U.S. troops who plundered settlers' livestock while fighting Indians.[25]

Between 1804 and 1815 complaints about inadequate or corrupt local government became a tradition among the plain people of the frontier South. In December 1815 several ancestors of future members of the Knight band—Stacy Collins, William Coleman, Samuel Colman (Coleman), Thomas Hollaman (Holliman), and Edward Arnel (Arnold)—and 323 other settlers living east of the Pearl River petitioned the federal government to suspend interest payments on public lands purchased by settlers before the outbreak of the War of 1812. Admonishing Congress to consider that war with Great Britain "had deprived them of a market" and "made their property the sport of the desolating savage," they implored its members to apply their past payments to a "fraction or quarter of a section" of the lands that they had originally purchased. In return the men promised to release their claims to the rest of their lands. Their economic goals matched their principles. As the petition explained, "to be on the safe side—they would rather have a little land, and be able to call it their own, than become the sport of future casualties—or the petitioners for future indulgences."[26]

In their quest for title to a "little land," frontier yeomen feared more than Indian "barriers" to progress. The engrossment of wealth by Eastern merchants, lawyers, and planters had driven many of them west in the first place. From beleaguered settlements in Mississippi Territory, settlers such as Stacy Collins complained not only that Indians had destroyed their houses, mills, cattle, grain, and furniture but also that the volunteer militia sent there to "protect" them "have been oblidged to consume the corn & stock of the Inhabitants of this frontier to a very considerable amount." Frontier yeomen had made the painful discovery that their escape from corrupt officials was more apparent than real.[27]

Harry Toulmin, the only federal judge appointed for the Washington District of Mississippi Territory, joined settlers in expressing to territorial delegate William Lattimore a sense of governmental abandonment. Washington District, Toulmin pointed out, was "five or six times as large as that west of Pearl River [the Natchez District], and to which three judges are allotted." He pleaded for the appointment of two additional judges to his district, explaining that "my own idea is that there ought to be a *proper federal court in this part* of the Mississippi territory."[28]

To gain an equal voice in shaping governmental policy, many settlers urged Congress to conduct an official census of Mississippi Territory and reapportion its representatives accordingly. In 1815 Stacy Collins, Joshua Collins, Samuel Coleman, and Thomas Holliman, along with 181 other men (including Tom Sumrall Sr., Tom Sumrall Jr., and Tom Jr.'s sons, Giles and Calvin), once again employed self-consciously republican prose, this time to remind Congress of their "EQUAL RIGHTS" to representation within a republican government. Denouncing the "political evils" that gave inhabitants living west of the Pearl River greater representation in Congress despite their district's smaller population, petitioners anxiously anticipated the moment "when in the course of human events" that Mississippi Territory would become a "Sister State" in the "American Union."[29]

Moving west plunged people into devastating wars and forbidding physical environments. For men these challenges stimulated political discourse and enhanced manly reputations for courage, fortitude, and physical strength. They struggled to attain economic independence and to protect their families, two core components of masculine honor. In such distinctly "masculine" and dangerous surroundings, the place of women was far less clearly defined than in the settled Eastern states.

In the novel *Tap Roots*, Street employed a common stereotype of the dangers that awaited women and children on the frontier when he described the early life of Hoab Dabney's wife, Shellie: "She was a child at Ft. Mims, a ragged dirty child orphaned while an infant and brought up by

Indians. She even had an Indian name then—the Princess of the Wind." Like many such fictional tales, Shellie's story began in disaster and ended in romance. Hinting once again at interracial mixing, Street also fed readers' insatiable appetite for damsels in distress and manly rescuers by having Hoab Dabney himself pluck Shellie from her Indian captors and deliver her to his mother in Mississippi until she was old enough for him to marry.[30]

In truth, of course, the frontier was hardly a romantic adventure for most women. Society dictated that women acquiesce to husbands, fathers, and masters' decisions to move west regardless of their own desires or interests. What lay before them was frightening: not only Anglo-Indian wars but diseases and deaths suffered in lonely, isolated outposts and, for enslaved women, distant slave markets. Maria Crump, a white woman living in Huntsville, Alabama, must have steeled herself during the war-torn year of 1814 to present so cheerful a picture of life in Mississippi Territory to her brother- and sister-in-law back in Virginia. In regard to Indians, she assured them that General Jackson had accomplished "Glorious Victories . . . over these inhuman creatures." Nonetheless, Maria's lonely existence as a frontier wife was evident. She implored Joseph and Judith Michaux to consider moving to Huntsville, complaining that her own relatives had not written her in six months. Meanwhile her husband had been absent for six weeks and would not return home for two or three more. Still, she stoically assured her in-laws that "altho I have ties of the dearest nature which binds me to Virginia, I would not return for no consideration."[31]

White women such as Maria Crump who shared the bonds and rewards of kinship, race, and class with husbands were far more amenable to obeying the will of white men than were Native Americans and blacks. Still, not all accepted their subordination so graciously as did Maria. Mary Elizabeth Lide, unmarried at the advanced age of twenty-eight, was forced in 1835 to accompany her father, older brother, and other family members from South Carolina to Alabama. In a letter to a married sister back home, she complained bitterly about her new frontier home, portraying herself as a prisoner of male prerogatives. "So you see," she wrote, "what brother [has] done with us; brought us out here and put us in the penitenciary."[32]

A few women refused altogether to move west. From the South Carolina backcountry in 1823, the husband of Margaret Castleberry placed the following notice in the *Pendleton District Messenger*: "Whereas I am about to remove from the state, and my wife Margaret positively refuses to accompany me, I hereby caution all persons not to credit her on my account, as I am determined not to pay any debts contracted by her, while she persists in her disobedience."[33]

Of course not all women opposed moving west. Although men measured frontier goals in distinctly masculine terms, white women might have their own reasons for wanting to leave home. Boredom with the narrowness of one's social life, exasperation over too many responsibilities to a wide network of kin, or simple weariness from an unending cycle of poverty could make a woman restless for escape. Some women of the Mississippi Territory sought to expand their horizons through divorce, taking advantage of the territory's relatively liberal laws on divorce at least as frequently as did men.[34]

White frontier women looked to male patriarchs for protection from "savages," but even when shielded by men, they toted guns, cleared fields, and helped build communities under conditions unknown to Eastern ladies. When Mary Mills of Georgia married Sam Coleman, she was already a widow with three children. With her new husband, a rising slaveholder who owned two slaves in 1820 and seventeen by 1840, she pioneered in the settling of Mississippi Territory. Until the Civil War ended slavery, Mary struggled to maintain the slaveholding lifestyle she had achieved by marrying Sam. She apparently taught her daughter Elizabeth, who married Jackie and Keziah Knight's son Daniel, to do the same. When Sam died, around 1842, Elizabeth Coleman Knight inherited several slaves from his estate, which she owned independently from her husband thanks to having filed a deed of separate estate. Sam and Mary Coleman's wealth also reportedly enabled their son Thomas Jefferson Coleman to affect the demeanor of an educated gentleman in rural Piney Woods Mississippi.[35]

Despite Mary Coleman's slaveholding status and relative wealth, the struggles of frontier life would contribute to the circumstances that led to the deaths of her two grandsons during the Civil War. During her marriage to Sam, she gave birth to eight children, several of whom, like Sam, died before she did. Then came the murder of her son Tom shortly before the Civil War (see Chap. 4). Tom's three orphaned children—Silman, Martha Cornelia, and Noble—were left in the charge of Mary, their aging grandmother. Although the children were only teenagers during the Civil War, all three became allies of their cousin Newton Knight, a decision that would result in the Confederacy's execution of the two boys (see Chap. 6).[36]

For Mary Harper, a white woman of Clarke County, Alabama, the frontier brought danger, adventure, and perhaps in the end a taste of power and independence. In the aftermath of the Ft. Mims massacre, she filed a claim for $275 in losses. She was probably "Polly" Harper, the lone woman to sign an 1815 petition from the Washington District that implored Congress to grant settlers relief from payments on public lands. Less than a year later, on October 10, 1816, she bought land from Martha Griffin. In 1823 she still lived on her own land in Marengo County (formerly Clarke), Alabama.[37]

Women who were born rather than transported to the frontier frequently displayed diverse ethnic roots. Peggy Summerlin, who lived not far from Mary Harper on the Alabama River, was of Native American and Euro-American ancestry. Her surname (a version of Summerall) suggests that she was kin to the South Carolina Summeralls who migrated to the Alabama River during the 1790s. Summerlin shared Mary Harper's harrowing experience of the Creek War, but her plight was complicated by her mixed ethnic roots. When she filed a claim for $597 in the aftermath of the war, she testified to being a "half-breed" of the Creek Nation. She described her flight from "hostile Indians" in 1813, during which she abandoned the "half-breed" settlement on the Alabama River for refuge at Pierce's Fort near Fort Mims. In the process she suffered the loss of 100 hogs, a crop of corn, some household furniture, and a gun at the hands of the Creeks.[38]

Peggy Summerlin embodied the emergence of new categories of ethnic-racial identity on the southwestern frontier. The sort of property she owned and her panicked flight from the Creeks speak to her marginal status in frontier America. Although she received refuge in the world of her white ancestors, during more peaceful times she lived in the interstices of a "third race," or metis, community. As a single woman with kinship ties to nations at war with each other, yet of marginal status in both, she had more than the usual reasons for owning a gun.[39]

Summerlin's designation as a "half-breed," like that of "white Indian," "mulatto" and later, "white Negro," evidenced the need for discrete racial groups in a world where men seized the lands of Indians and enslaved (later segregated) the bodies of African Americans on grounds of white superiority. As we have seen, white attitudes about the appropriate relationship between one's race, gender, and level of power took shape during the eighteenth century and thus permeated republican ideals. At the same time, moving west allowed some people to shed their own mixed ethnic roots while enabling poorer men to assert the prerogatives of white maleness in ways not possible in the mature plantation regions of the Southeast. In Mississippi Territory, white people's sense of racial entitlement was restored at the expense of the Creeks, Cherokees, and Choctaws whose lands they eagerly appropriated, and at the expense of African Americans, whom they might purchase in the slave markets of Mobile, Natchez, and New Orleans.[40]

At the same time, however, yet another wave of interracial mixing occurred, which produced women such as Peggy Summerlin and Rachel Knight, who like Summerlin personified the mixing of peoples that occurred on the Southwestern frontier despite barriers of language, culture, war, and slavery. Rachel, a woman of African, European, and Native American ancestry who was born in Georgia in 1840, was purchased as a slave (probably in Mobile) by Jackie Knight around 1856. There are no accounts of Rachel's early life, but there are records of the social setting in which she was born. In 1936 Mandy Jones, an ex-slave, provided one of the most vivid descriptions of life in "Indian country" in the early nineteenth century. Drawing on the memories of her grandmother, whom she described as "a yaller woman" with "hair down to her shoulders," Mandy described how African American men loved watching Indian women dance "wid deir pretty long hair a hangin' down deir backs"—so much so that they tried to join the Indian "frolics" and dance with them, much to the consternation of Indian men. Thus did North Americans on the Southwestern frontier continue their long tradition of producing lines of descent that ignored political, cultural, and legal sanctions against race-mixing.[41]

Into this disorderly frontier world came itinerant preachers determined to spread the messages of the Second Great Awakening. As Norvell Robertson's career as a Baptist minister demonstrated, the growth of evangelical nationalism paralleled that of republican nationalism. Robertson's primary motive for writing his autobiography was not to recount his economic success but, rather, to provide a narrative of his conversion to the Baptist faith. All his life he struggled to bring Baptist reforms and religious order to the Mississippi frontier.

Although the Southern wing of the Baptist Church increasingly embraced slavery while the Northern wing partially embraced its abolition, both branches emerged from the nation's exhilarating victories over Great Britain twice within forty years. During the Second Great Awakening, however, the Northern and Southern halves of evangelical churches mirrored their region's developing economic structure. Thus, although backcountry Baptist preachers still emphasized the equality of souls and the purity of simple living, their earlier denunciations of the privileged and powerful faded as backcountry planters rose in power.[42]

The phenomenal post-Revolution success of Southern Baptists in organizing regional and state associations and building national Baptist networks accompanied changes in evangelical religion itself. Different classes and races of Baptists continued to worship in the same church, but slaveholders increasingly gained the upper hand. Stressing harmony rather than divisions, churches dropped the labels Separate and Regular between 1787 and 1801 and began to organize mission societies as well as church associations. In Pendleton County's Big Creek Church, for example, where Welborns, Mauldins, and Duckworths worshiped, the transition in Baptist orthodoxy was under way by the 1790s. In the church's earliest days, affairs were settled in council among all its brethren, including slaves. In addition to punishing the usual sins of drunkenness and slander, its members still practiced footwashing and, as late as 1807, enforced fair prices on goods sold by members.[43]

Radical New Light preachers, however, gave way to pro-missionary ministers who adopted a more ameliorative style that stressed harmony between unequal classes and races of people. Class conflict within Baptist ranks did not disappear, but it survived in the antimission movement that followed in the wake of Baptist unification. Still, Baptist ministers such as Norvell Robertson, who endorsed slavery and accommodated an increasingly commercialized world, guided the future of most Southern Baptist churches. In 1790 two-thirds of South Carolina Baptists owned no slaves, but many of their preachers did. Thus, although the Bush River Baptist Church was New Light in origin, by 1800 slaveholders dominated its leadership.[44]

Southern Baptists' push for unity had profound political ramifications. In South Carolina the Charleston Baptist Association unified low country and backcountry Baptist churches only after Baptist ministers put aside differences over slavery, state government, and commercial development of the backcountry. Slaveholding Regular Baptists increasingly reined in the unruly New Lights, limiting the preaching of female elders and deacons, establishing dress codes, and advocating an educated ministry. In 1790 the Charleston association excommunicated Philip Mulkey, the most powerful symbol of New Light enthusiasm, on questionable charges of adultery and the "practice of Crimes and Enormities at which humanity shudders." In Spartanburg, where Stacy Collins was born, the last ministers to express antislavery views were driven out in 1802.[45]

It was on the heels of these changes, in the winter of 1803–4, that Norvell Robertson was called to the ministry. Like Jesse Mercer of Georgia, he represented a new generation of Baptist preachers who proselytized in a new style and delivered a message different from that of the Carolinas' Great Awakening preachers. Whereas Shubal Stearns, Daniel Marshall, or Philip Mulkey would have stirred the emotions of a passive laity by thundering dire warnings of God's punishment of a wicked society, Jesse Mercer reportedly once exclaimed, "O, my congregation, I fear you are too good to be Saved!" He then burst forth with an uncontrollable torrent of tears. Seeking to build a unified, orderly movement rather than to attack entrenched, "wicked" institutions (such as slavery), Mercer's emotional sermons urged salvation through inward self-examination and outward benevolence. Thus they lacked the hard-edged social criticism of those of his predecessors.[46]

Emulating Mercer's advancement of modern missionary causes among Georgia Baptists, Norvell Robertson and Thomas Mercer (Jesse's brother) worked to facilitate that same transition in Mississippi. Becoming a frontier preacher brought Robertson respect and authority that were previously closed to him. Born in Virginia, he claimed humble origins that provided him with only a rudimentary education at the hands of "despotic" teachers who instilled in him a "deep and settled aversion to going to school." His father, he claimed, was poor. Jeffery Robertson worked as an overseer and then as a card maker, unable to purchase land until his son was thirteen years old. Although Norvell Robertson's maternal grandfather, George Norvell, was "tolerably wealthy," Robertson complained that his grandfather "never gave my Mother anything but a negro girl" because he opposed her marriage to Jeffery.[47]

Robertson's 1846 autobiography served as a pro-missionary prescription for correct moral behavior among Baptists. Confessing that neither piety nor gentility characterized his early years in Virginia, he explained that he "was raised in the time of the American Revolution, when all was bustle, confusion and distress." As a reform Baptist Robertson hoped to inspire others to follow his path of right moral action. In recounting his experience of conversion, he appropriated a familiar Christian theme, that of a life filled with degraded behavior and self-loathing before he was struck by "The Light." He attributed his youthful lack of morals to his father's having boarded him as a young man with a tavern keeper. There young Norvell worked as a blacksmith, where he met "gamblers, horse-thieves, and all manner of dissipated and abandoned characters." It was only by opening his heart to God, he assured readers, that he left such a life behind.[48]

Robertson's move west thus was intertwined with his rise to prominence as a Baptist minister. The journey was long and conflicted, however, for many frontier Baptists remained skeptical of reform-minded ministers. Between 1807 and 1817 Robertson's pro-missionary views embroiled him in a Georgia battle with "the most mischievous individual that I ever had any acquaintance with." According to Robertson, this individual almost destroyed his church by exhibiting "violent opposition to the principle of contributing anything to the support of the gospel." Furthermore, "some members" had supported this unnamed person by initiating an "uncharitable and unjust censure" of Robertson.[49]

The nasty church schism in Georgia may well have prompted Robertson's decision in 1817 to move to the new state of Mississippi, where he worked as supply minister to several Southeastern churches. After helping to found the Leaf River Baptist Church in Covington County, Robertson became its first pastor and, eventually, the most important religious figure in the community. The task before him was daunting. Unruly behavior, dissipate habits, and antimission views traveled west with the plain folk whose behavior he hoped to reform.[50]

The tireless efforts of reform-minded preachers such as Robertson continued to meet fierce opposition from stubborn folks such as Stacy Collins, who resisted evangelical discipline as well as slavery. As Collins became ever more vigilant in petitioning the government for protection of citizens' rights, he became ever less interested in being a good Baptist. Like Robertson, he sought to impose order on the frontier, but of a different sort; Collins was more interested in ideals of republican justice than of religious piety—perhaps all the more so because evangelical ministers increasingly also happened to be slaveholders.[51]

In the Zion Baptist Church of Buckatunna in Wayne County, Stacy Collins and his kinfolk regularly defied efforts by their elders to enforce pious behavior. Despite an auspicious beginning as respectable members of Buckatunna's Baptist community, the Collinses would not be "mastered" by emerging Baptist doctrine. Instead, they sinned regularly by engaging in fiddling, dancing, and drinking. For example, in May 1816, a member of the church charged Joshua Collins with having been "intockiceted." In July the church decided to exclude Joshua "from our union." The following September Stacy Collins was excluded after he accused a brother Magee of telling a lie. Stacy gained readmission only to be excluded a year later on unspecified charges of "Imorallety."[52]

In 1820 Rachel and Elizabeth Collins, the wives of Christopher and Joshua, also came "under the displeasure of the community" on unspecified charges. Soon after being reinstated, Joshua was charged with fiddling and Christopher with the "free use of ardient spirits." When called to task, Christopher defiantly boasted that he "frequently drank too much and played the fiddle for people to dance," and that he "never had any conviction nor repentance for the same." In resisting the church's numerous attempts to discipline their behavior, the Collinses revealed an unbending, fiery temperament for which the family would be renowned during the Civil War, in both Mississippi and Texas.[53]

If Stacy Collins ever considered owning slaves, his unhappy experiences in Buckatunna may have changed his mind. In fact, the problems the Collinses had with the Zion Baptist Church seemed distinctly connected to the growing popularity of slavery in Mississippi and to the desire of Christopher Collins to join the ranks of the planter class. Not only were Stacy, Joshua, and Christopher kicked out of the Zion Church, but Christopher Collins was also disgraced by the Mississippi High Court of Appeals.

Christopher's fate in the courtroom was intimately connected to the problems the Collinses had within the Zion Baptist Church. That fate was set when Christopher and another brother, Jacob, married Rachel and Lucy Hendricks, the daughters of wealthy slaveholder John Williams Hendricks. Not surprisingly, members of the Hendricks family held prominent positions of authority in the Zion Church; thus, when Christopher, Joshua, and Stacy played their fiddles and drank whiskey, they embarrassed as well as offended their well-placed in-laws.[54]

As if unruly behavior was not enough, Christopher decided after the death of Rachel's father to contest the disposition of his estate. In 1823 he risked the ten slaves he had gained through his marriage by pitting himself and Rachel against other branches of the Hendricks and Collins families. Christopher and Rachel lost their suit, and in 1830 the court ordered them to sell their slaves to satisfy court costs. Shortly thereafter the families of Christopher and Joshua Collins abandoned Buckatunna, as Stacy and Sarah had done a few years earlier.[55]

During their brief stay in Buckatunna, the Collinses—at least Stacy and Sarah—learned a valuable lesson about the politics of slavery and its connections to the power of the church and the power of the planter class. When the Collinses challenged the authority of their church elders, they were tossed out. When Christopher Collins simultaneously challenged the authority of his slaveholding father-in-law's will, he was shorn of the slaves he had gained through his marital alliance with the slaveholding class. The high-stake risks of chasing wealth in the emerging world of slaves and commerce, while refusing to accept its cultural imperatives, were demonstrated for the Collinses in both their house of worship and a court of law. Perhaps this explains why Stacy Collins raised crops and foraged herds—without ever owning slaves—in the Piney Woods of Mississippi and Texas until his death, around 1853.[56]

Economically, most settlers of the Piney Woods fell somewhere between Stacy Collins, who owned no slaves, and Norvell Robertson, who by 1850 owned seven. There was, however, a small circle of wealthy planters in Jones County as well, one that included Jackie Knight, the grandfather of Newt Knight. Born in North Carolina, Jackie moved to Georgia during the post-Revolutionary period, probably with parents who were attracted by that state's generous bounty grant system. A mania of land speculation caused the colony's white population to treble between 1775 and 1790 and its slave population nearly to double. Growing up among men on the make in Georgia's frontier society, Jackie set out early in life to make good as a planter and slaveholder.[57]

In 1798, in Richmond County, he married twenty-year-old Keziah Davis, the daughter of slaveholder John Davis and his wife, Sarah. In terms of economics, Keziah was a good catch for a man on the move, although her family background hinted at past political conflicts. The Davis family lived in Appling, Columbia County, not far from the Wrightsborough Quaker community, established in 1768 as a refuge for Regulators from North Carolina. Family tradition maintains that the Davises were Quakers, though not of the antislavery variety. Several Davises also had been Tories during the Revolution.[58] Jackie and Keziah Davis Knight apparently did not prosper in Columbia County, in part because Jackie failed to win land in the Cherokee land lotteries of 1803 and 1805. The family's fortunes would soon improve, but only by moving west yet again.[59]

Jackie and Keziah Knight reached the Leaf River sometime around 1822. They settled in Covington County, just across the Jones County line, in the community of Reddoch (later Hebron), named for settler James "Jimmie" Reddoch, who operated the river's first ferry. In 1829 both Knights and Reddochs joined Norvell Robertson in founding the Leaf River Baptist Church near the crossroads of Jones and Smith Counties. Founding members also included Giles Sumrall from the Zion Baptist Church in Buckatunna; Williams and Ruth (Welborn) Duckworth from the Big Creek Baptist Church of Anderson District, South Carolina; and William Bynum Sr., whose frontier migrations had taken him from the North Carolina Piedmont to South Carolina, Georgia, and Tennessee before he landed in Mississippi around 1817. Although Stacy and Sarah Collins lived nearby in Jones County, they did not join the church.[60]

All seemed well in 1829 in this new congregation, which included not a single Collins but did contain several rising slaveholders. By the time that Robertson and his neighbors organized the Leaf River Church, Southern evangelicals had "reformed" the earthly meaning of equality in accordance with the strict boundaries of class, race, and gender required by a slaveholding society. Orthodox Baptists had also modified or abandoned rituals and practices such as love feasts, washing of one another's feet, and lay preaching that blurred those boundaries.[61]

By the 1830s several slaveholders of the Leaf River Church were keen on instituting modern Baptist reforms. In contrast, antimission sentiments persisted among nonslaveholders, who disdained the modern mission movement as a usurpation of God's authority in the service of mortals' lust for power and wealth. Resistance to modern reforms was not limited to nonslaveholders, however. Several members of the church—including Jackie Knight and his kinfolk—would prove as unwilling as the Collinses before them to embrace the new Baptist piety. As economic divisions grew between slaveholders and nonslaveholders, disagreements deepened over appropriate standards of godly behavior. The familiar tensions between the imposition of order from above and resistance from below flashed once again, planting the seeds of yet another national crisis.[62]

There is a story that a dark skinned, curly haired
family moved to Ellisville about the time that
the county was being organized. They were
seized and sold as slaves, and the money was
used to build the first court house.—Sue Boyd
Neill, WPA writer, 1936

[The farmers of South Mississippi] hate slavery
and slaveowners almost as much as they hate
Yankees.—James Street, *Taproots*, 1943

Chapter Three
Piney Woods Patriarchs
Class Relations and the
Growth of Slavery

Although there is no evidence that any seizure of a dark-skinned, curly-
haired family ever occurred in early Jones County, that legend marks a
pivotal moment in the history of Piney Woods Mississippi. Jones County
was founded in 1826 in response to the influx of settlers from the Southeast into Mississippi after the War of 1812. Although Jones's farmers could
never have duplicated the realm of the vastly more fertile plantation belt,
they did build a world similarly divided between white freeholders and
black slaves. The legend thus seems to have purged Jones County of the last
vestiges of free people of color, who, it claimed, were immediately sold
into slavery. The cash from the sale of these mixed-race people, who had
curly, not kinky, hair—and dark, not black, skin—was used to build the
county courthouse. For nineteenth-century whites the courthouse was the
ultimate symbol of law and order, but the seizure and sale of these dark-
skinned people also underlay a "creation myth" crucial to a slave-based
society. According to this myth, people of color were only the slaves of
whites, not their ancestors or intimates.[1]

Between 1820 and 1860, Mississippi emerged as a preeminent slave-holding state and leading cotton producer. Jones County's legend thus heralded its own transition from a frontier society of mixed ethnicities, races, and economies to a slave-based community based on commercial agriculture and trade. As we shall see, however, not all whites in Jones welcomed this transition, nor was the commercial transformation complete on the eve of the Civil War. In fact, economic and social changes sowed the seeds of conflicts that divided communities well before the Civil War. Economic interests, intertwined with kinship, friendship, and local politics, later influenced significantly one's position on the Confederacy.[2]

In 1820, six years before Jones County was created, 2,230 people lived in Covington County, including 406 slaves, who constituted 18.2 percent of the population. Although that percentage was the lowest of any county in the state, it would soon change. Over time, slaveholders' numbers and the size of their holdings increased. By 1840 the number of slaves had risen to 31.5 percent of Covington's total population, and to 35.5 percent by 1860. Jones County, in contrast, remained the domain of nonslaveholders and small slaveholders throughout the antebellum period. In 1860 slaves comprised only 12.2 percent of its total population, the lowest of any county in the state.[3]

Despite the growth of a commercial slaveholding culture in the Jones County region, and the accompanying rise of a small planter-merchant elite, a distinct nonslaveholding yeoman political economy persisted. In 1860 yeoman farmers still comprised the overwhelming majority of the population. Furthermore, in Jones County 77 percent of slaveholders owned four or fewer slaves; in more fertile Covington County, 53 percent did.[4]

Most members of the band of Civil War deserters headed by Newton Knight belonged to this nonslaveholding yeomanry, while the strongest supporters of the Confederacy belonged to the county's small slaveholding/commercial elite. Of the approximately ninety-five men who joined the Knight Company, the overwhelming majority owned land but no slaves. Eleven were small slaveholders or lived in slaveholding households of families divided in their support for the Confederacy.[5]

Complicating matters for many families were the different economic paths taken between 1820 and 1860 by separate branches of the same families. The rough equality shared by white Piney Woods settlers before 1830 also brought intermarriages between families whose levels of wealth were soon to diverge. This meant that by 1860 many nonslaveholders, small slaveholders, and large slaveholders shared kinship ties. Thus, although the Collinses, Knights, Sumralls, Bynums, Welches, Welborns, and

Map 3.1. Nonslaveholding Population of Mississippi, 1860

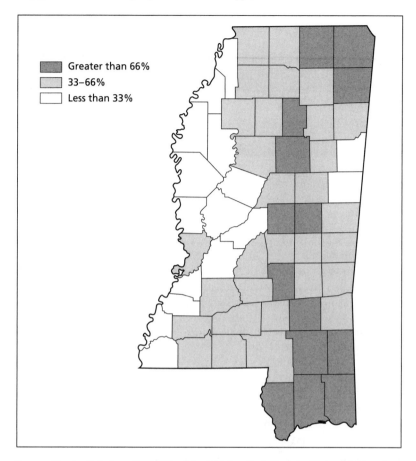

Source: Charles C. Bolton, *Poor Whites of the Antebellum South: Tenants and Laborers in Central North Carolina and Northeast Mississippi* (Durham: Duke University Press, 1994). Copyright 1994 Duke University Press. All rights reserved. Reprinted with permission.

Valentines who joined the Knight Company came from nonslaveholding households, they all had slaveholding relatives—some of whom were quite wealthy. By the same token, those families that actively supported the Confederacy, including the Robertsons, Showses, Duckworths, Baylises, and McLemores, had kinfolk among the nonslaveholding yeomanry.

In particular, the Knight and Welborn families divided into nonslaveholding and slaveholding branches, thus causing them to support opposite sides during the Civil War. For the Knights, these divisions were carried into the twentieth century by the competing narratives of Tom Knight and Ethel Knight. In the final analysis, whether or not an *individual* family held slaves was the strongest determinant of its support or opposition to the

Table 3.1. Growth of Slavery in Jones County Compared with Surrounding Counties and the State, 1820–1860

| | 1820 | | | | | | |
	Jonesᵃ	Covington	Jasper	Perry	Smith	Wayne	State
Total slave population	—	406	—	491	—	1,065	32,814
Percentage of total population	—	18.2	—	24.1	—	32.0	43.5

| | 1840 | | | | | | |
	Jones	Covington	Jasper	Perry	Smith	Wayne	State
Total slave population	164	855	1,255	454	419	979	195,211
Percentage of total population	13.0	31.5	31.7	24.0	21.4	46.2	51.9

| | 1860 | | | | | | |
	Jones	Covington	Jasper	Perry	Smith	Wayne	State
Total slave population	407	1,563	4,549	738	2,195	1,947	436,631
Percentage of total population	12.2	35.5	41.3	28.4	28.7	52.7	55.2

Source: ICPSR Archive, Study 3, Historical, Demographic, Economic, and Social Data, the United States, 1790–1970, University of Virginia Geospatial and Statistical Data Center, Internet, http//fisher.lib.Virginia.edu/.
ᵃJones became a county in 1826.

Confederacy. Families with the widest networks of nonslaveholding kinfolk exhibited the most consistent opposition.

Even in 1860 the people of Piney Woods Mississippi lived in a region peripheral to national markets and participated only marginally in political decision making in the South. They were essentially small farmers and herders who built strongly kin-based, church-centered communities and who made annual or biannual trips to Mobile to sell their livestock, wool, and small amounts of cotton and rice. In the ensuing years, however, many men had bought slaves and sacrificed economic independence in service to greater profits, growing too little corn to be truly self-sufficient in order to graze more cattle and devote more acres to cash crops. Some even aspired to achieve planter status.[6]

Before 1830, however, Piney Woods settlers seemed united in purpose and goals as they founded churches and built courthouses. In December 1822 eighty-nine men from Covington County petitioned the Mississippi State Assembly to divide their county into two so that its residents might reasonably conduct their public affairs. Their pleading that it was "not for the sake of private interest, but for the general good of the county" led to the formation of Jones County on January 24, 1826, carved from the eastern half of Covington County.[7]

Table 3.2. Distribution of Slaves in Jones County Compared with Surrounding Counties and the State, 1860

	Jones	Covington	Jasper	Perry	Smith	Wayne	State
Total number of households	482	473	1,059	313	870	390	63,015
Total number of slaveholders	116	204	503	95	331	92	30,943
Percentage of slaveholders with 1–4 slaves	77.5	53.0	48.2	40.0	53.6	31.5	42.0
Percentage of slaveholders with 5–9 slaves	16.3	18.2	24.0	35.8	24.2	27.1	22.8
Percentage of slaveholders with 10–19 slaves	4.3	19.7	15.8	15.8	17.0	16.3	18.2
Percentage of slaveholders with 20 or more slaves	1.7	8.9	12.0	8.4	5.2	9.2	16.7

Source: ICPSR Archive, Study 3, Historical, Demographic, Economic, and Social Data, the United States, 1790–1970, University of Virginia Geospatial and Statistical Data Center, Internet, http//fisher.lib.Virginia.edu/.

Note: ICPSR lists two slaveholders who owned twenty or more slaves in Jones County, 1860. While I have used their figures to compute percentages, my own count of the manuscript slave schedules indicates that there were three.

The petition calling for the creation of a new county freezes in time a moment of unity among the ancestors of several individuals who forty years later would bitterly quarrel over the Confederacy. Norvell Robertson Sr., Norvell Robertson Jr., George Baylis, Daniel Windham, John Shows Sr., and Adam Shows bore surnames of families that would remain staunchly pro-Confederate throughout the Civil War. In contrast, kinfolk of Zachariah Blackledge, Calvin Summeril (Sumrall), John Nite (Knight), Albert Nite (Knight), and Jesse Lee would fight against the Confederacy.[8]

To understand why families with similar backgrounds, experiences, and goals in the 1820s would oppose—even murder—one another during the Civil War, we must examine the communities that they built. Settlers arriving in frontier Mississippi, particularly the Long Leaf Pine Belt in which Covington County is located, found an environment similar to that of the Carolina backcountry of the Revolutionary era. In an area filled with wild animals, tall pine forests, and canebrakes, its earliest white inhabitants hunted deer much as their Carolina forebears had done, burning the forests to flush out the animals or running through dark forests with torches that illuminated deer's eyes. Early Piney Woods settlers supplemented hunting with herding livestock and planting crops. Over time they reversed the order; herding and farming became their primary economic

Table 3.3. Cash Value of Farms in Jones County Compared with Surrounding Counties and the State, 1860

	Jones	Covington	Jasper	Perry	Smith	Wayne	State
Total number of farms	361	347	779	218	583	148	37,007
Median cash value of farms[a]	$974	$1,234	$2,769	$961	$1,890	$2,350	$5,155

Source: ICPSR Archive, Study 3, Historical, Demographic, Economic, and Social Data, the United States, 1790–1970, University of Virginia Geospatial and Statistical Data Center, Internet, http//fisher.lib.Virginia.edu/.
[a]Numbers are rounded off to the nearest dollar.

mainstay, and the hunting of wild game was an important supplement. Herders still burned the pine forests, but now they did it to eliminate brushy undergrowth and encourage the growth of grasses that provided forage for livestock. Such a life dictated a monotonous diet heavy in meat, especially venison and pork. Once settled, they planted corn, their other dietary mainstay. Gradually fruit orchards and fields of vegetables appeared, adding equally "Southern" foods such as peaches, sweet potatoes, and turnips to the meager fare of frontier Mississippians.[9]

The benefits of settled agriculture encouraged some Piney Woods farmers to purchase slaves. The Mississippi descendants of Tom Sumrall, for example, demonstrated varying responses to the growth of slavery. Tom, the son of Jacob Summerall, left South Carolina before 1794 and settled in Wayne County, Mississippi, around 1808. In 1820 his descendants headed eight households in four southeastern counties of Mississippi; by 1830, at least fifteen households in seven counties. Among these Sumralls were large, small, and nonslaveholders. Tom himself made the transition from hunter to slaveholding farmer and herder before his death in 1821. Aided by his distribution of seven slaves, many of his heirs followed suit.[10]

By 1830, after six decades of restless migration stimulated by sporadic political upheavals, cyclical evangelical revivals, and the uneven but steady growth of plantation agriculture, most of the ancestors of the Knight band had settled in the southeastern portion of Mississippi. Settlers in Covington and Jones Counties shared a rough equality of wealth, most owning few or no slaves, but among them were signs of a rising slaveholding class. According to the 1830 federal population census, John Shows Sr. owned ten slaves; Norvell Robertson, seven; George Baylis, six; and Jackie Knight, five. By 1850 Robertson, the only one who did not substantially increase his holdings, owned eight slaves; Baylis owned fifteen, and Knight owned

Table 3.4. Farm Size in Jones County Compared with Surrounding Counties and the State, 1860

	Jones	Covington	Jasper	Perry	Smith	Wayne	State
Percentage of farms with 3–49 acres	72.6	51.0	49.3	65.1	54.0	52.7	37.9
Percentage of farms with 50–99 acres	19.9	23.9	22.2	21.5	25.2	18.2	24.8
Percentage of farms with 100–499 acres	7.4	24.8	26.4	13.3	20.5	27.0	30.8
Percentage of farms with 500–999 acres	—	0.3	19.2	—	0.2	1.4	5.0
Percentage of farms with 1,000 or more acres	—	—	0.1	—	—	0.6	1.3

Source: ICPSR Archive, Study 3, Historical, Demographic, Economic, and Social Data, the United States, 1790–1970, University of Virginia Geospatial and Statistical Data Center, Internet, http//fisher.lib.Virginia.edu/.

twenty-two. John Shows Sr. was now dead, but his son James owned fourteen slaves.[11]

Among such men the Jeffersonian ideal of an independent, virtuous yeomanry became ever more compatible with participation in a market economy. Mississippi's Piney Woods farmers remained Jeffersonian in their conviction that free men who tilled the earth were God's special children, but they also believed that respectability (as a landowner) and prosperity (gained from participation in the marketplace) enabled virtuous living. Accordingly, Piney Woods farmers visited Mobile regularly to sell their products. Before 1850, however, their major products were not cash crops but livestock.[12]

Norvell Robertson's life sheds light on the evolving political culture of slaveholding yeoman farmers. As we saw in Chapter 2, he was driven west by the same economic and social forces that drove most white Southerners who settled in the Jones County region, including those whose descendants later would oppose the Confederacy. The economic and social status that Robertson achieved before his death in 1855, however, predisposed his descendants to be pro-Confederate. His eventual success as a slaveholder, miller, and pro-missionary Baptist preacher enabled his children to become part of the cultural elite of Piney Woods Mississippi. Building on his legacy, some sons and grandsons became Baptist elders, preachers, and slaveholders who intermarried with the children of other slaveholders.[13]

Although Piney Woods farmers produced far fewer cash crops than did their Black Belt counterparts, they clearly operated in a world of slaves and

Map 3.2. Mississippi, 1820

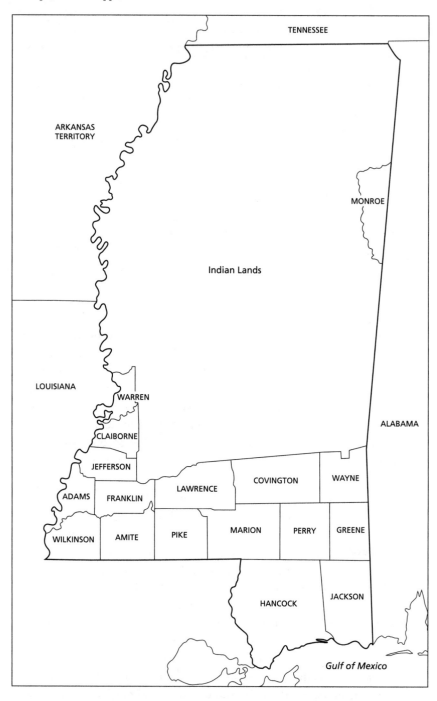

Source: Adapted from William Thorndale and William Dollarhide, *Map Guide to the U.S. Federal Censuses*, 1790–1920 (Baltimore: Genealogical Pub. Co., 1992).

Note: Mississippi became a state in 1817.

Map 3.3. Mississippi, 1840

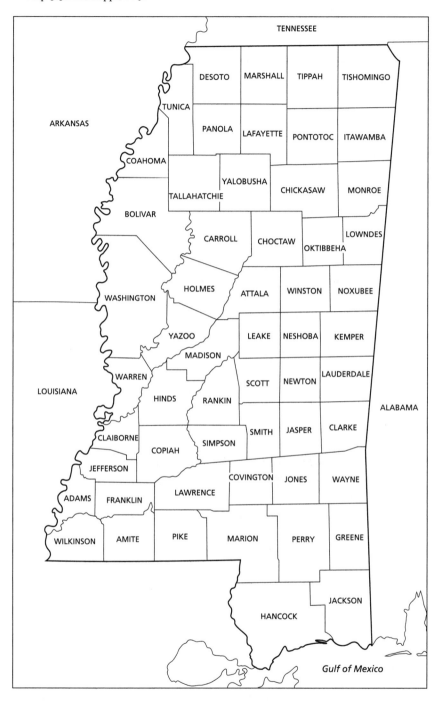

Source: Adapted from William Thorndale and William Dollarhide, *Map Guide to the U.S. Federal Censuses*, 1790–1920 (Baltimore: Genealogical Pub. Co., 1992).

commerce. For those who did not own slaves, producing for the market often meant living close to the edge. In 1850 many of them produced barely enough corn, sweet potatoes, peas, and oats to be counted as self-sufficient. By 1860, however, slaveholders and nonslaveholders alike had significantly increased their unimproved acreage, providing more land on which to forage livestock or to grow corn, cotton, or rice. Some non-slaveholding farmers achieved greater self-sufficiency during this decade, while others, particularly those who bought slaves, traded self-sufficiency for increased production of cash crops.[14]

By the Civil War, most of the families that opposed the Confederacy had achieved self-sufficiency *without* purchasing slaves and *without* growing surplus cotton. Perhaps this self-sufficiency, combined with modest market profits from the sale of surplus livestock and foodstuffs, encouraged them to believe that they were independent of the South's slaveholding cotton regime. If so, Mississippi's secession from the Union, its entry into the Confederacy, and Confederate conscription of able-bodied white Southern men would prove how precarious that independence was.

At separate community meetings held in Jones County in 1926, a number of old-timers recalled their lives during pre–Civil War days, providing descriptions of market production that hinted at a growing divergence of economic behavior among slaveholders and nonslaveholders. Several men, including seventy-five-year-old A. G. Shows, commented that the earliest pioneers settled on the creeks and rivers because "they couldn't live out in these piney woods because they had no fertilizer." He nevertheless emphasized that most families raised livestock and fowl for the market. Once or twice a year, mostly men and boys made this two- to three-week trip to Mobile. "Everybody had their own meat," remembered seventy-seven-year-old S. W. Patrick. "Wasn't nothing for a man to drive hogs to Mobile and sell $100 worth."[15]

Despite the importance of livestock to the Southern economy, increasing numbers of Piney Woods farmers raised less of it between 1840 and 1860, converting much of their lands from grazing cattle to growing crops. Profits earned from the sale of livestock were used to buy more land and slaves and, eventually, to grow more cash crops. The memories of two slaveholders' sons suggest the increasing importance of cotton in the Piney Woods economy. John M. Knight, son of Jesse Davis Knight, recalled that "we carried cotton, beef cattle, turkeys, lots of meat" to Mobile. Benjamin D. Graves, son of Robert Graves Jr., reminisced that his family needed "three or four heavy yoke of oxen" to make the journey, for they "would sometimes take six bales of cotton. They would bring the money back to buy negroes to make more cotton."[16]

Map 3.4. Mississippi, 1860

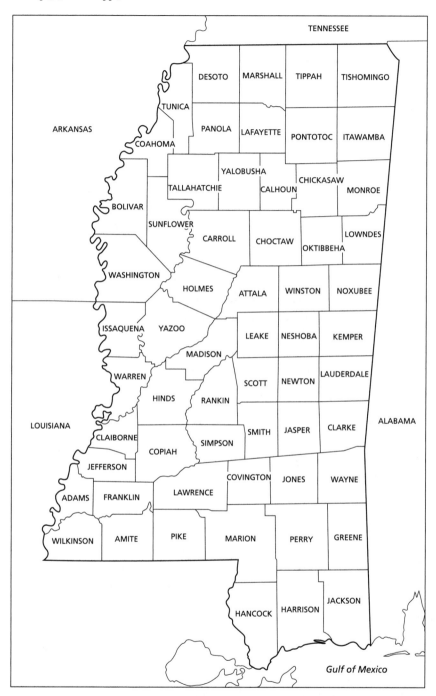

Source: Adapted from William Thorndale and William Dollarhide, *Map Guide to the U.S. Federal Censuses*, 1790–1920 (Baltimore: Genealogical Pub. Co., 1992).

Hunting and fishing remained enormously important to nonslaveholders' achievement of economic self-sufficiency. The amount of corn needed was further lessened by allowing livestock to forage on mast and grass rather than grain. "The hogs fattened themselves in the swamps," remembered Dan Pitts, the son of a nonslaveholder. The sons of small farmers emphasized as well the importance of wild game in their family's diet. "We killed all the game we wanted," said Pitts, "deer, turkeys, squirrel . . . ." S. W. Patrick echoed his remarks, describing "droves and droves" of deer, turkeys, geese, and ducks. "I have seen twenty-five squirrels on one beech tree," he exclaimed. Hunting remained so important a source of food before the Civil War that beef often replaced bread on the dinner table. Biscuits were particularly rare because "nobody grew wheat. We had corn, vegetables, and such as that, but [we] didn't try to grow wheat."[17]

The crucial role that women played in the South's agricultural economy contributed far more to yeoman self-sufficiency than is apparent from reading agricultural statistics or the words of Southern economists. At a meeting before the Daughters of the American Revolution (DAR) in 1912, Madison "Maddie" Prescott Bush remembered that when grain fell too short, Piney Woods farmwives made bread from dried turkey breast or dried clabbered milk instead of grain. Several men remembered home production of sugar, medicines, shoes, soap, candles, and cloth that surely relied on the labor of their mothers and sisters.[18]

Although white women enjoyed privileges denied enslaved or mixed-ancestry women, they, too, labored for "masters" in households and fields that relied on the labor of all family members. With the passage of time, descendants—particularly males—tended to remember women's work within neat categories deemed appropriate to a middle-class image of male breadwinners and female homemakers. Descendants of the Smith County Sullivans, for example, recalled a staunchly patriarchal society in which a "woman's worth was determined by the caliber of her tiny even rows of stitches," especially on the quilts she made after spending long winter nights "cutting and sewing scraps of clothes into designs for quilt tops." Sewing was indeed women's work, but it seemed not to occur to twentieth-century descendants that women sewed all night by candlelight because they worked in gardens, barnyards, and fields for much of the day.[19]

Although Maddie Bush, like most Jones County men, described women's work within the appropriately gendered sphere of cooking and clothmaking, he implicitly rejected bourgeois images of white womanhood when he told the DAR, "Times [before the war] weren't like they are now; ladies would sit up at night and card and spin to make clothes for their children, instead of reading their Bibles as they do now." He went on to describe how his own mother carded and spun the "few stalks" of cotton grown on his family's farm. Similarly, S. W. Patrick remembered that "Mother would spin it and weave it. . . . That was our clothes."[20]

The memories of Bush and Patrick indicated how vital women's labor was to the capacity of nonslaveholding farmers to feed and clothe their families and still produce surplus for the market. As Bush and Patrick explained, when Jones County's nonslaveholding farmers grew cotton at all, they typically produced only a bale or two, which they then passed into the hands of women, not the market. Most nonslaveholders, they insisted, marketed surplus wool, rice, corn, and sweet potatoes rather than cotton.[21]

Whether a woman made her family's clothes from homespun or commercially produced cloth provided a visual image of that family's class status. Slaveholders' wives were periodically treated to "store-bought" cloth when their husbands sold raw cotton in Mobile, whereas plain farm-wives converted that raw cotton into cloth. John M. Knight, whose father owned slaves, recalled that "a barrel of whiskey was the first thing we bought" in Mobile. He added, "We always bought a bolt of calico for the gals." Whiskey was consumed across class lines, but the purchase of cloth for wives marked one's rising economic and social status and was not typical of nonslaveholders. One farm wife recalled that "calico was fifty cents a yard, and if you wore a calico dress you were dressed up."[22]

Although cotton production increased in the Piney Woods throughout the antebellum period, the poor quality of the region's soil made it problematic even for slaveholders. Dan Pitts claimed that "people didn't make any cotton to amount to anything" before the war. Ben Graves pointed out that a farmer without fertilizer could produce "thirty or forty bushels of corn an acre" but "hardly . . . a half bale of cotton to the acre." Perhaps this explains why, in 1860, Jones County's largest slaveholder, Isaac Anderson, chose corn over cotton as his major cash crop.[23]

Both the raising of cotton and the purchasing of slaves were rejected by Stacy Collins and his sons, who exemplified the yeoman basis for opposition to the Confederacy. Though Stacy died some seven years before the outbreak of the Civil War, his sons became Jones County's staunchest, most vocal supporters of the Union. Simeon, Riley, and Jasper Collins were central figures in the formation of the Knight Company, despite its election of Newton Knight as captain. Furthermore, they were linked through marriage to many of the company's core members, including Sumralls, Bynums, Welches, Walters, and Valentines (see Appendix 5). The Collinses were so united in their support for the Union that even Ethel Knight, who expressed contempt for Newton Knight's professed Unionism, admitted that "if any person wants to get into a fist fight, just let him insinuate that the Collinses fought for any other than the Federal Union."[24]

By 1850 Stacy Collins had become a successful farmer who grew corn and raised hogs. Although he remained a nonslaveholder throughout his life, several of his children, including sons Vinson and Jasper, married into slaveholding families. Significantly, although these sons married daughters of small slaveholders, neither ever owned slaves.[25] Even more significantly, most of the Collins children married into nonslaveholding branches of the Bynum, Sumrall, Valentine, Walters, and Welch families. Intermarriage with the Collinses proved particularly significant to certain branches of the Bynum family. Whereas the slaveholding branch of that family would later support the Confederacy, those allied with the Collinses would oppose it. A prime example was Benjamin Bynum, who married Stacy and Sarah Collins's daughter Peggy. During the Civil War, Benjamin and Peggy's son, Prentice M. Bynum, would join the Knight Company alongside his Collins cousins.[26]

In 1850 none of the families allied by marriage with the Collinses produced significant amounts of cotton. The households headed by Vinson, Simeon, and Stacy Collins Jr.; Benjamin Bynum; and George W. Walters (first husband of Sally Collins) instead produced surpluses of hogs and rice. All of the households, except those of Stacy Jr. and Riley Collins, maintained sufficient fields of corn and forage to feed families and livestock. Stacy Collins Jr.'s poor economic standing perhaps influenced his decision in 1853 to move to Texas, where land was cheap and plentiful.[27]

Several members of the Collins family, including Stacy Sr. and Sarah, followed Stacy Jr. and his wife, Allie, to Hardin County, Texas. One descendant of this Texas branch later recalled hearing his folks describe how they had "picked out their own settlement and built their own log cabins and settled down to the life in the 'Wild West' where they could roam the forest and kill wild game." True to their ancestral traditions, the Collinses raised corn before all else and herded livestock on "the best stock range in the country at that time." Stacy Collins's son Warren was described by his own son as a "very poor business man and indeed a bad manager," suggesting that he had little interest in maximizing profits through market production.[28]

In the 1850s, however, the Collinses who remained in Jones County became prosperous yeoman farmers who chose not to own slaves. In 1860 Simeon Collins operated a farm valued at $6,000 and owned a personal estate assessed at $2,000. He owned no slaves but raised livestock valued at $1,200 and 600 pounds of rice. His older brother, Vinson, operated a farm valued at $1,500 and claimed personal assets worth $1,071. Like their older brothers, by 1860 Riley and Jasper had increased their farm acreage. Each operated farms assessed at $2,000 and claimed personal estates of nearly $1,000; both raised less livestock and more corn than in 1850. They produced no rice, only small amounts of cotton and surpluses of wool, peas, sweet potatoes, and butter. Jasper Collins's prosperous yet simple way of life is suggested by a WPA reporter's description in 1936 of the home that he built around 1864 near the community of Moselle. Constructed from twenty-four-foot-hewn logs, it contained one central room, an overhead loft for sleeping, and a "stick and dirt" fireplace.[29]

At least two Collins sisters prospered during the 1850s as well. The value of Peggy and Benjamin Bynum's farm increased dramatically during that decade—from $350 to $4,300—despite the fact that they owned no slaves. In 1860 they produced two bales of cotton, twenty pounds of wool, and surpluses of hogs and corn. Another Collins brother-in-law, George W. Walters, died shortly after 1850, leaving Sally Collins Walters a widow. Sally quickly regained economic security in 1852 by marrying tavern keeper and slaveholder James Parker, but her fortunes faltered when the marriage failed. In 1860 she headed her own household and claimed real estate valued at only $100, reflecting the degree to which a woman's fortunes depended on marriage. She still possessed $2,717 in personal assets, however, and with the help of her nineteen-year-old son and hired hands, she raised livestock worth $940 and sheared sixty pounds of wool.[30]

The above families clearly constituted a sturdy yeomanry, resistant to the temptation of owning slaves and growing cotton as a cash crop. In 1861 from Mississippi to Texas, these intermarried and solidly yeoman families would conclude they had much to lose if their respective states seceded from the Union. A twentieth-century descendant of Warren Jacob Collins, who led his own band of deserters in the Big Thicket of East Texas, recalled that Grandpa Warren "didn't believe in slavery but he didn't think the North ought to force the South to abandon it." In other words, the Collinses personally disapproved of slavery but did not believe that the federal government could constitutionally force its end. By the same token, they did not believe that the election of Abraham Lincoln provided constitutional grounds for secession.[31]

Between 1848 and 1855, as the nation's sectional crisis heated up, Peggy Bynum and Vinson, Simeon, and Jasper Collins all named sons after Southern Whigs (Henry Clay was a particular favorite) who offered compromises on the volatile issues of territorial and slavery expansion that increasingly divided North and South. Despite their naming practices, they were Democrats rather than Whigs. Mississippi's Whigs were too closely associated with Natchez planters for Jones County farmers to join that party, no matter how much they might admire Henry Clay and certain other Whigs.[32]

Although Mississippi's Piney Woods remained overwhelmingly Democratic in its voting patterns, divisions grew between Union Democrats and old-line Democrats who led the charge toward secession throughout the 1850s. Across the county line in Smith, Sheriff Joseph D. W. Duckworth represented the old line wing of the party. In 1845 he wrote to his Texas cousin, Frances Smith, that he supported James K. Polk over Henry Clay for the presidency. Facetiously, he expressed hope that Frances was not a Whig. Support among Piney Woods farmers for Polk's expansionist policies motivated Jones County slaveholder Daniel M. Shows to name a son born in 1847 James K. Polk Shows. In contrast to nonslaveholding Union Democrats like the Collinses, the Duckworths and Showses clearly emulated Mississippi's rising slaveholding class.[33]

The Welches and Valentines headed households similar in composition and wealth to those of the Collinses, with whom they were allied by marriage long before the Civil War erupted. Like Stacy Collins, patriarchs Bryant Welch and Allen Valentine were part of the post-Revolutionary generation that migrated to Mississippi Territory early in the century. Also like their Collins kin, the nonslaveholding Valentines and Welches would contribute numerous sons and grandsons to the Knight Company.[34]

Like the Collinses, Valentines, and Welches with whom he allied during the war, Harmon Levi Sumrall owned no slaves. On the eve of the Civil War, Harmon, the great-grandson of Tom Sumrall Sr., raised livestock on most of his four hundred acres of land and grew corn, peas, and sweet potatoes on the remaining forty acres. In 1860 his twenty-year-old unmarried brother, William Wesley Sumrall, shared his family's household. William Wesley would become Newt Knight's second lieutenant during the war; during Reconstruction both he and Harmon remained staunch supporters of Newt.[35]

If ever there was a man in southeastern Mississippi who might have been expected to raise sons and grandsons loyal to the Confederacy, it was Jackie Knight. Around 1817 Jackie, Keziah, and their seven children had migrated from Georgia to Mississippi, where Keziah gave birth to four more children. Jackie's ascent toward planter status included a verbal agreement between him and his mother, Mary, that "I was to take care of her during her lifetime and at her death." In return, upon Mary Knight's death on August 9, 1818, Jackie inherited her sole property, "one Negro girl named Huldy." By 1850 he owned twenty-two slaves. That year he produced 28 bales of cotton and 750 pounds of rice. In addition, he raised livestock valued at almost $1,000, all without sacrificing self-sufficiency in corn production. Jackie had become one of the wealthiest men in the Covington-Jones County area.[36]

By 1860 Jackie had increased his landholdings from 290 to 680 acres, cut his production of cotton by one-half, and more than doubled his output of rice. With twenty-two slaves, real estate valued at $3,000, and personal property worth $23,000, the eighty-seven-year-old patriarch had built an impressive fortune since his struggling days in Georgia. In contrast to the modest home of Jasper Collins, he lived in a much more substantial structure described by Martha Wheeler, his former slave, as "a double-pen log house with two enormous rooms on the front and two slightly smaller ones on the back . . . with a very large kitchen quite a distance back of the house." On this well-managed, busy plantation, slaves made shoes, spun cloth, ran a blacksmith shop, and worked the fields.[37]

How could so successful a slaveholder and planter as Jackie Knight be the ancestor of so many members of the Knight band, including its captain, Newton Knight? It appears, in fact, that Jackie himself may have opposed secession. Ex-slave Martha Wheeler emphasized again and again to a WPA interviewer in 1936 that her former master "grieved terribly" over the sectional crisis before his death on February 9, 1861, exactly one month after Mississippi seceded. "Sitting on the porch, moving his head from side to side," remembered Martha, he "had one song and he sang it all day, 'I am ruined, I am ruined.'"[38]

Whether or not Jackie himself opposed secession, slave ownership and marital partners were important factors in determining the positions of several Knight families on the Confederacy.[39] Significantly, the household that reared the Knight Company's most notorious member—Capt. Newton Knight—was without slaves in 1861. Other Knight relatives who joined the company were reared in yeoman households as well, where few or no slaves were owned. Noel, John Thomas, and Daniel Whitehead, for example, later executed as deserters during the war, were the sons of Jackie and Keziah's daughter Mary Ann, who married John Whitehead, a nonslaveholder. John and Mary Ann Whitehead owned no slaves until December 1858, when eighty-five-year-old Jackie Knight deeded an aging slave couple, Lewis and Cate, to Mary Ann. Considering Jackie's and the slaves' advanced ages, this "gift" to Mary Ann seemed motivated by practical rather than monetary concerns.[40]

Albert Knight, the father of Newt Knight and oldest son of Jackie, more than any of his siblings followed an economic path different from that of his father. Author Ethel Knight insisted that Newt came from a home of "culture and refinement" that included slaves and an "elaborate mansion" and that his father was deeply ashamed of Newt's Civil War behavior. In fact, however, Albert Knight was a barely self-sufficient farmer who raised corn and a small surplus of hogs. Nor could he have criticized Newt's wartime behavior, as Ethel claimed, for he died at least one year before his son deserted the Confederacy.[41]

With much greater accuracy, Knight descendant Kenneth Welch later described Albert as a shoemaker and tanner who was once given a slave by his father, but who did not keep that slave. Welch also pointed out that Albert was the only child not bequeathed a slave in his father's will. Another Knight descendant, Earle Knight, went even further, claiming that Albert rebuked the Confederacy before his death in January 1862. Earle speculated that Albert and Mason might even have opposed slavery, since none of their children, including Newt, owned slaves.[42] In the final analysis, there is no evidence that either Albert or Mason, his wife, opposed slavery. Nevertheless, this nonslaveholding branch of the Knight family provided a distinct contrast with most other Knight households.[43]

That contrast was especially evident in the memories of Ben Graves, who in 1926 described Newt as a simple dirt farmer, despite the fact that Newt was the grandson of one of Covington County's wealthiest slaveholders. Graves, whose own grandfather owned ten slaves, made clear that his family disdained men like Newt. "Why if a girl's parents owned negroes, she didn't recognize Newt Knight any more than she would a negro," he said. When a young woman announced her plans to marry, he further explained, his own folks would always ask of the fiancé's family, " 'Have they any negroes?' If they didn't . . . they weren't no account."[44]

Newt's marriage to Serena Turner, as well as his own yeoman status, may also have influenced his Civil War behavior. It linked him to the Welborn family, which like the Knights, was divided between slaveholding and nonslaveholding branches. Serena was the daughter of John Henry Turner, a nonslaveholding yeoman farmer. Her mother, Elizabeth Duckworth, was a granddaughter of Aaron Welborn of South Carolina and thus descended from several prominent North Carolina Regulators. In 1818 Serena's grandparents, Williams and Ruth Welborn Duckworth, moved from the South Carolina Pendleton District to Covington County, where Williams became constable of the newly formed county the following year. His and Ruth's successful settlement encouraged other Welborns and Duckworths to migrate to Mississippi. Aaron Welborn arrived in Jones County before 1827; around 1832 brothers William "Billy" and Younger also migrated to Jones County from Pendleton District, South Carolina.[45]

Like the Knights, during the Civil War the Welborns divided over slaveholding. Gerald W. Johnson, a descendant of Younger Welborn Sr., remembered in 1999 hearing that although "all the Welborns were on speaking terms," certain branches never "invited the other over for Sunday dinner after church." Specifically, brothers Billy and Younger Welborn, both non-slaveholders, viewed their slaveholding kin, Aaron Welborn and Joel E. Welborn, with a "certain amount of suspicion and awe."[46] Furthermore, several of Billy and Younger's children intermarried with the nonslave-holding Mauldin, Sims, and Dykes families, who would join these Welborns in opposing the Confederacy.[47]

In contrast, Aaron Welborn owned four slaves by 1840 and became judge of the probate court by 1843. The wealthiest branch of the family, however, was headed by Joel E. Welborn, whose fortunes escalated rapidly after he began speculating in lands during the mid-1840s. Welborn's prof-its soared in the 1850s as he continued selling land to his neighbors. The 1860 census enumerator listed his occupation as "trader," assessing the value of his real estate at $36,000 and his personal estate (including five slaves) at $13,000.[48]

Clearly, the years between 1847 and 1860 were busy ones for Joel Wel-born—so busy, in fact, that in 1859 the county's Board of Police charged him with having abused his position as swampland commissioner by fraudulently selling lands to his neighbors. The board may have responded to the actions of men such as Isaac Anderson, a wealthy slaveholder who won an ejectment suit against Welborn in 1855 to recover possession of his land. Amos J. Spears also purchased land from Welborn and became enraged when he learned that Welborn had somehow maintained legal title to it. Convinced that Welborn had swindled him, Spears tore down the house, some outhouses, and a fence that he had built on the land. Wel-born retaliated by suing Spears for damages, and in 1856 the state su-preme court affirmed a lower court decision granting Welborn damages of $250.[49]

Accusations against Welborn were still being lodged in 1867, when sev-eral citizens again charged him with having used his position as swamp-land commissioner to cheat them out of 25,000 acres. Welborn's fast and loose land deals made him an unpopular man in Jones County, even among some of his slaveholding peers, but they nonetheless made him rich. His rapid rise to wealth increasingly alienated him from his non-slaveholding cousins, widening the economic gap that would cause dif-ferent branches of Welborns to assume opposite stances on the Confed-eracy during the war.[50]

In contrast to several of her Welborn kin, none of Serena Knight's Duck-worth relatives joined the Knight Company or the Union Army. This is not surprising, given that by 1860 most of them had moved into the ranks of the wealthiest slaveholders in Jones and Covington Counties. Yet, like so many other settlers, the Duckworths only gradually became slaveholders. In 1820, when a "caravan" of thirty-nine relatives reportedly traveled from South Carolina to join Williams and Ruth Duckworth in Covington County, Williams owned 161 acres but no slaves. Although he had barely moved into the ranks of slaveholders by 1830, he owned nineteen slaves by 1850.[51]

Although the Duckworths were in-laws of Newton Knight, their economic and political prominence anchored them within the social class that was most likely to support secession and the Confederacy. By the time Newt and Serena married, around 1858, neither moved in the circles of Serena's more elite kinfolk. Two of her cousins held political offices in Smith and Jones Counties. Joseph D. W. Duckworth was elected sheriff of Smith County in 1844, and by 1850 his brother Benjamin was justice of the peace in Jones County. In 1854 Benjamin served as Jones County's state house representative.[52]

Several letters written by Smith County sheriff Joseph Duckworth during the mid-1840s demonstrated his commercial aspirations. Writing to his Texas cousin, Frances Smith, during a long slump in cotton prices, he complained that being sheriff brought too few profits, especially since "times are very hard in this part of the country at this time; a man cannot make money here—or but very little, though he may use ever so much industry." In September of that same year, 1846, Duckworth reiterated that "times in this county are very oppressive" and cited the scarcity of money, the "shortness" of cotton crops, and the "great ravages" of a wet season and caterpillars. Mississippians were "very anxious to sell their place here," he wrote. " 'Texas fever' is high." Joseph clearly looked to the marketplace for peace of mind, and in 1846 he found it wanting.[53]

Duckworth also alluded to a litigious society when he complained to Frances that being sheriff was particularly "troublesome" because of "the way the laws are arranged at this time." He himself was engaged in an ongoing court battle (which he did not mention in his letter) with Uriah Milsaps after being charged by the chancery court with failing as sheriff to administer a judgment rendered by the circuit court. Duckworth appealed the decision, and happily for him, in November 1846 the state supreme court overturned the lower court's decision.[54]

As a member of Mississippi's rising slaveholding class, Duckworth did not represent the average farmer who lived in the Leaf River area. Although expanding markets and better roads encouraged small farmers and herders to produce cotton, rice, and wool for the market, the great majority remained nonslaveholders. Joseph Duckworth's economic anxieties and legal squabbles do affirm, however, that despite the peripheral position of

Piney Woods counties in the South's burgeoning cotton economy, market-oriented, slaveholding farmers shared the goals and concerns of Black Belt planters.[55]

Amos McLemore, the Confederate officer believed by many to have been murdered by Newton Knight during the Civil War, followed a route to wealth and status somewhat different from that of Joseph Duckworth. Like most Jones County residents, the McLemores can be traced back to South and North Carolina. Amos's grandfather (also named Amos) had steadily increased his land and slaveholdings as he moved west. When the older Amos's son John (father of the younger Amos) died in 1854, he left three slaves, 400–500 head of cattle, and 880 acres of land to be divided among his heirs.[56]

John McLemore's sons, Abraham and Amos, continued the family's upward climb. Both men owned property in Perry County but conducted their business in Jones, where Abraham owned a hotel, store, and grist-mill. For a time Amos worked as a schoolteacher in Jones County, but during the 1850s he increased his wealth and status by becoming a land speculator, merchant, and Methodist minister. Sometime before 1860 he joined Dr. John M. Baylis, the son of wealthy slaveholder and Methodist minister George Baylis, to operate a mercantile business on the west side of the Leaf River.[57]

McLemore and Baylis were closely associated with another merchant, Amos Deason, whose antebellum home is a museum today because of its architectural beauty, and because it was the site of Amos McLemore's murder during the war. Built in the 1840s, the Deason place had several rooms and was constructed from sawed pine panels purchased in Mobile. Its wooden weatherboards were painted and sanded to resemble stone. The Deasons' spacious, modern home, a gathering place for local merchants and politicians, provided a distinct contrast to the homes of farmers such as Jasper Collins and Newton Knight, most of whom lived in single-room split-log homes that perhaps contained an attic or a loft. Some antebellum farmhouses had separate kitchens, but most simply had huge fireplaces inside the home.[58]

With their professions intimately connected to the slave economy, Joel E. Welborn, Amos and Abraham McLemore, John M. Baylis, and Amos Deason comprised Jones County's rising entrepreneurial class. In a 1936 WPA interview, Roy E. McLeod remembered that the county's "traders" were important middlemen in the Piney Woods trade with Mobile. They "came and went from Ellisville to Mobile carrying produce of the county to the city and returning with necessities and luxuries." Other WPA inter-viewees in 1936 remembered Abraham McLemore's hotel as a gathering place for "lawyers from other counties" and, like the courthouse, the "scene of many political gatherings." Even though most farming families sold livestock and crops in the marketplace regardless of whether they owned slaves, few individuals other than large slaveholders matched the wealth or status of these men.[59]

Thus, this tiny group of merchants joined the nine farmers in Jones County who owned ten or more slaves to form a small but distinct elite. By the time the Civil War erupted, Amos McLemore owned at least seven hundred acres of land in Perry and Jones Counties, as well as half-interest in the business he shared with Baylis. With wealth came status, and in 1856 McLemore achieved the highest position possible in his freemasonry lodge, that of worshipful master. By 1861 he was poised, with Joel Welborn and John M. Baylis, to become part of the county's Confederate military elite. His friend and fellow merchant Amos Deason would become his district's representative to the Mississippi Confederate legislature.[60]

How rapidly the political economy of Jones County was reshaped by men such as these between 1840 and 1860 is evident in the writings of Mississippi historian and Democratic politician John F. H. Claiborne. In 1841 and 1842 the Natchez Free Trader and Gazette published Claiborne's most famous sketch, "A Trip through the Piney Woods," in which he addressed the effects of economic changes sweeping his state by unabashedly celebrating life outside the cotton belt. In describing Jones and Covington Counties, he depicted a Jeffersonian fantasy land where farmers lived in peaceful harmony with the environment, the market, and one another.[61]

Ironically, Claiborne invited commercial development of the Piney Woods by describing a world barely touched by it. Attacking stereotypical images of the region, he firmly denied that "East Mississippi is poor and barren, and therefore destitute of resources." In truth, he asserted, Jones County was "literally a land of 'milk and honey,'" where inhabitants obtained lands at cheap government prices, lived in "comfortable cabins," and dieted on liberal supplies of beef, fowl, eggs, cheese, and butter. He marveled that the selling of cattle, chickens, and surplus foodstuffs in Mobile provided such a life of "comfort and abundance" for Piney Woods families that they had little need for courthouses. He claimed that Wayne County contained "neither lawyer, judge, justice, sheriff, clerk, nor constable," and that in Jones, "the courts scarcely deserve the name as the [court] term seldom lasts more than one day. Happy people!"[62]

By the time Claiborne's essay appeared in print, an "ordering" of Piney Woods society, similar to that which occurred in the eighteenth-century South Carolina backcountry, was already under way. Despite his exaggerated image of a simple paradise, he recognized the inevitability of change by invoking a wistful nostalgia for a fading world in the person of Tom Sumrall Jr. Much as one might lament a lost world of "noble savages," Claiborne lamented the decline of "Mr. Sumrall" of Perry County, one of the region's oldest pioneers. It was as though old Tom's decline paralleled that of the pastoral paradise in which he lived. Described by Claiborne as one of the "oldest and worthiest men in the State" and a "genuine Democrat," he was now an old man approaching death. His wife dead and his children gone to "distant settlements," Tom now lived alone with an old dog in a "weather-beaten and decayed" home, surrounded by "gnarled and mossy" trees and a "stunted and decayed" garden. This metaphor of decay expressed Claiborne's sadness that a backwoods way of life was passing.[63]

In truth, Claiborne's portrait of upright men, beautiful women, and rosy-cheeked children living in peaceful harmony failed to convey the reality of backwoods life in which violence occurred frequently and slavery was on the rise. Just a few years after Claiborne's sketch appeared, in fact, the notorious outlaw band headed by James Copeland attempted to rob and murder Tom Sumrall Jr., an incident that dramatized the region's potential for violence.[64] Simultaneously, evangelical minister Norvell Robertson struggled to enforce piety among these "happy" people as he and other slaveholders reshaped and strengthened the boundaries of race, gender, and class that separated people.

From 1820 to 1860 Mississippi's Piney Woods was a world in flux. In their "anxious pursuit" of prosperity, settlers who gambled and lost packed up frequently and moved on to new frontiers. Many, however, stayed put, raised livestock and crops, and marketed surpluses in Mobile. Moreover, most farmers never bought slaves, even as they increased their participation in the market. Thus the gulf between this region's nonslaveholding yeomanry and a rising class of slaveholding farmers, planters, and merchants steadily grew wider. Simultaneously, the nation's rapid geographic and economic expansion stimulated divisions among national politicians, journalists, and religious leaders. Within rural evangelical churches, as we shall see in Chapter 4, cultural and class antagonisms were expressed in members' resistance to church discipline and opposition to the burgeoning missionary movement. Under the strain of the Civil War, these conflicts would explode in late 1863, pitting neighbor against neighbor and even kin against kin.[65]

Those were the happy days never to be forgotten.—Ethel Knight, *Echo of the Black Horn*, 1951

Religion here appears to be at the lowest ebb
possible. . . . Splits, Schisms, & Divisions appear
to mar the peace of all sects, orders & denominations in this county at this time.
—Joseph D. W. Duckworth to Frances Smith, 1846

Chapter Four

Antebellum Life
on the Leaf River

Gender, Violence,
and Religious Strife

By the time John F. H. Claiborne took his whimsical "trip through the
Piney Woods" in 1841, the twin rise of slavery and evangelical piety had
begun to reshape people's lives in the Jones County region of Mississippi.
So intertwined did the goals of the churches and slaveholders become that
in 1861 evangelical ministers were in the forefront of calls for the South to
secede from the Union. Try as evangelical ministers might, however, they
failed in the decades preceding the Civil War to institute fully the norms of
race and gender behavior deemed appropriate to a kingdom of God anchored in a slave-based market economy. Even among the slaveholding
class, many men continued to prove their masculine prowess through
drinking, fighting, and fornicating. Likewise, some women drank "like
men," while others hosted parties where liquor flowed, cards were dealt,
and dancing was enjoyed until all hours of the night.[1]

Among those who most offended morally upright Baptists were two families who had pioneered in the settling of the region and had inter-married with each other: the Knights and Colemans of Covington County. Like the Collinses before them, members of these families had difficulty obeying the new rules of Christian deportment for gentlemen and ladies. Significantly, their children and grandchildren would also be resistant to Confederate authority during the Civil War.[2]

Most resistant to evangelical discipline were the Colemans, who did not even join the Leaf River Church before the Civil War, although several of their kinfolk and slaves did. Stories about this family's wealth, scandalous behavior, and penchant for violence followed its members well into the twentieth century. During the 1930s one old-timer of the Hebron commu-nity recalled stories about Mary Coleman, whom he described to WPA writer Addie West as a "well-to-do woman" who "had a good many slaves and some money." After Mary's husband, Sam, died, around 1842, she allegedly kept about $600 in gold and silver buried on her land and did not trust even her grown children with her wealth. She and her daughter Elizabeth, who was married to Jackie Knight's son Daniel, reportedly put on a "good little play" for the community when mother accused daughter of having stolen her treasure, only to discover later that her hogs had dug it up.[3]

But it was this rich woman's failure to adhere to feminine standards of behavior that most impressed the WPA interviewee, who told West that Mary regularly furnished her Knight in-laws with "still water" from her whiskey still and "got drunk and lay out in the woods just like the men did." Abusing alcohol may have helped Mary to dull the memories of a life punctuated by violence and untimely deaths of kinfolk. In 1858, after the death of Sam and several of her children, she endured the loss of her son Thomas Jefferson Coleman, whose murder was later recounted by Ben Graves in another WPA interview conducted by Addie West. Once again, gender behavior loomed large in the memory of the narrator as Graves described Tom's inappropriate style of masculinity. It seemed that wealth without Christian piety had left Tom a foppish "gay young widower" and "very much a dandy." Graves allowed that Tom was handsome and well educated but emphasized his "meanness" and his reputation as a braggart.[4]

Furthermore, when Jones County deputy sheriff Matt Kilgore attempted to arrest Tom for illegal (and sinful) gambling, Tom revealed himself to be a liar, one mark of a man without honor. Under the guise of seeking to borrow money in order to post bond, Tom persuaded Sheriff Kilgore to take him to the home of his kinsman, Jackie Knight, who lived just across the Jones County line in Covington. Once they arrived at Jackie's home, however, Tom taunted the sheriff, insisting that he could not arrest him now that they were standing outside Jones County. A violent melee followed that ended when the sheriff plunged a knife so far into Tom's neck that it severed his jugular vein.[5]

Again Graves described the scene in gendered terms that expressed his disdain for Tom Coleman. Having been humiliated by Coleman, Sheriff Kilgore and deputy Joe Gunter restored their masculine authority by horsewhipping him; Tom, appropriately for a "dandy," then attacked Kilgore with a "lady's pen knife." Tom's final disgrace was his ignoble death at Kilgore's hands. Jackie Knight's slave child, Martha Wheeler, allegedly described to Graves how he "bounced about on the porch like a chicken that had just had its head cut off" before landing in the yard. There he lay dead, "in the broiling hot sun," until an inquest could be performed.[6]

No doubt Ben Graves's memories of Tom Coleman were shaped by his own family's low regard for the Colemans and the Knights. Still, Tom's death must have left his Coleman and Knight kinfolk seething with anger, particularly after Sheriff Kilgore was tried for murder and found innocent. During the same court term in which Kilgore was tried, Tom Coleman's brother-in-law Daniel Knight was prosecuted for two assault and batteries and for participation in an affray against unnamed enemies. In a third case Knight was fined for damages caused to Joel E. Welborn. Whether connected to one another or not, these court cases reveal that "bad blood" existed between the Knights and the Colemans, on one side, and Matt Kilgore and Joel E. Welborn, on the other.[7]

And so it would remain during the Civil War. Welborn would become one of Jones County's highest-ranking Confederate officers, while Tom Coleman's orphaned sons, Silman and Noble "Nobe," would join the Knight band. In 1864 Sil and Nobe would be executed for treason by Confederate cavalry, but so also would Matt Kilgore die that same year—at the hands of the Knight band.[8]

Most court records from Jones County were destroyed by fire in 1887, but the minutes of the Leaf River Baptist Church reveal much about the roots of personal enmity between families. They also suggest the connection of personal feuds and local squabbles to national conflicts leading to the Civil War. Although this region might appear isolated from the larger world, and its battles little more than personal vendettas, those battles were connected to larger economic, religious, and cultural changes sweeping the state and the nation.[9]

For more than two decades, pro-missionary ministers struggled to direct the course of worship in the Leaf River Church. Although Norvell Robertson implied in his autobiography that he immediately became pastor of the newly independent Leaf River Church in 1829, "in compliance with the unanimous call" of its members, he and Giles Sumrall jointly presided over church meetings as elders rather than pastors throughout most of the 1830s. Together the two men baptized new members and visited those suspected of backsliding. In 1831 it was Sumrall, not Robertson, who took the lead in proposing that the church annually hold a three-day meeting for the purpose of preaching, washing one another's feet, and partaking of the Lord's Supper. Sumrall's call for footwashing placed the Leaf River congregation somewhat outside the mainstream of evolving Baptist orthodoxy, an indication of the congregation's reluctance to embrace modern Baptist practices. In 1837, however, the congregation, increasingly concerned with decorum and order, passed a resolution (after Sumrall had left the church) "that the duty of washing the saints' feet should be performed in a private capacity only."[10]

Participation in missionary activities became the test of how orthodox the church would become. Within four years after its founding, the church entertained motions from the Robertson faction to engage in benevolent missions and Sabbath schools and to establish a paid ministry. In February 1839 Norvell Robertson's son Asaph nudged the Leaf River Church toward a modern, orthodox stance by proposing that it join the Baptist State Convention. Membership would require payment of a $10 fee and sending a delegate to yearly convention meetings. The congregation debated Asaph's resolution in August but declined to pass it. To join the convention would signal Leaf River's official entry into the mainstream of Baptist worship, and in 1839 not all members were ready to do that.[11]

Despite slow progress, throughout the antebellum years Norvell Robertson and his allies persistently introduced "modern" Baptist practices to the Leaf River Church. They scored a decisive victory on November 27, 1841, when Robertson was appointed as the church's first salaried pastor. Antimission Baptists had long strenuously opposed a paid ministry, but in March 1841, after Robertson threatened to resign on grounds of ill health, the congregation finally officially decreed him "minister of pastoral care" and agreed to pay him $60 per year.[12]

Robertson's appointment as minister strengthened his faction's efforts to reform the church. In November 1844 Pastor Robertson asked the church to consider whether sitting instead of kneeling or standing for public prayer would be proper. "No," the members answered. But on September 6, 1845, after agitated discussion, the congregation did approve joining the Pearl River Association, signaling its acceptance of a more centralized hierarchy within the Baptist Church.[13]

The doctrinal schisms within the great evangelical churches revealed people's uncertainty over the nation's course of development, particularly in regard to the expansion of slavery. Religious schisms did not merely anticipate the coming of the Civil War; they hastened it. In the Leaf River communities of Mississippi, uncertainty over the future manifested itself in both church squabbles and courthouse litigation. In March 1846 Norvell Robertson complained that the church was in a "state of declension and moral darkness." Less than twenty years after the church's founding, "removals, exclusions, and deaths" had reduced its membership by about two-fifths of its highest number. Six months after Robertson wrote these dismal words, Joseph Duckworth similarly lamented to his Texas cousin, "Religion here appears to be at the lowest ebb possible. . . . Splits, Schisms, & Divisions appear to mar the peace of all sects, orders & denominations in this county at this time."[14]

Robertson's and Duckworth's unhappiness emanated not from debates over slavery but from people's failure to behave according to Christian doctrine, much of which centered around emerging genteel norms of gender behavior. A product of the Second Great Awakening, Robertson linked the very essence of his own manhood to religious sanctification. Conversion, he counseled readers of his autobiography, had given him the "true" courage to be a man. Using his father as a metaphor for the sinful past, Robertson insisted that the true man of God was responsible for his own as well as others' behavior. Explaining that he did not wish to "disparage" or "censure" his father, he nonetheless accused him of having treated his own son as an "inferior," "scarcely worth attention." As a result, the young Norvell had "imbibed a low and contemptible opinion" of himself and for a long time lacked the "manly boldness" essential to engaging respectably in society.[15]

Becoming an itinerant Baptist preacher in the unsettled world of frontier society enabled Robertson to experience a distinctly masculine version of success. The journey west brought him not only economic prosperity but also a surrogate father in God, the "gracious providence" who watched over him as he struggled against his biological father's world of sin and vice. Robertson found a mission in life, one that provided him with a new personal identity and a strong sense of his own importance as a man. Yet in 1846 the "dark" state of religion caused him to question his success, even to "doubt my call to the ministry."[16]

Joseph Duckworth struggled so hard to become the sort of Baptist modeled by Robertson that he, too, at times despaired over the bitter divisions among so many of his neighbors and kinfolk. As a member of the Leaf River Baptist Church, a slaveholder, and the sheriff of Smith County, Duckworth knew that churches were an important stabilizing force in backwoods societies. He lived near Sullivan's Hollow, which lay between the Okatoma and Cohay Creeks that flow into the Leaf River. Although the hollow's reputation for murderous feuds did not reach its peak until after the Civil War, it was well known during the antebellum period for bare-knuckled bouts over masculine honor, including competition over land, women, and physical prowess. The patriarch of the hollow, Tom Sullivan, was said to be its champion bare-fisted fighter.[17]

Perhaps what particularly vexed Sheriff Duckworth were the violent outbursts that occurred among his own male kin despite their church membership. In August 1836 his great-uncle Williams Duckworth (grandfather of Serena Knight) defended himself against a rumor that he had murdered his kinsman John Duckworth. No more was mentioned of this charge in church minutes, but the following month Williams admitted that he lacked Christian deportment, blaming his frequent absences from church on his being "unwilling to [share] company with those who walk upright." He promised to do better and was accepted back on those terms.[18]

Despite Williams's expressions of humility, relations among the Duckworths deteriorated further during the decade that followed. By 1840 many of them, including Williams, belonged to the Clear Creek Baptist Church, just across the Covington County line in Smith County. On July 17, 1840, the Leaf River and Clear Creek Churches formed a joint committee to reconcile Elnathan Duckworth of Leaf River with Williams Duckworth's son-in-law, John Mayfield, of Clear Creek. Elnathan admitted that he had assaulted Mayfield but refused to repent his actions. The church responded on August 15 by excluding him on a charge of unjustifiable assault.[19]

In October 1841, three months after Sheriff Duckworth joined the Leaf River congregation, family tempers flared again, this time between the sheriff's father, Patrick C. Duckworth, and Patrick's Uncle Williams, now a member of the Clear Creek Church. Nine months later Williams lodged four unspecified charges of misconduct against Patrick, and the church ordered an investigation. Despite these ongoing battles, Sheriff Duckworth seemed genuinely shocked when an unidentified assailant shot his Uncle Elnathan as he sat beside the fireplace of his own home. The wound proved superficial but created quite a stir in the community.[20]

The violence that frequently erupted among the Duckworths included the slave community and may have been an extension of Duckworth conflicts with the Craft family. In 1831 Whitmell Craft's slave Henry allegedly murdered Jacob Duckworth's slave Peter and then ran away to escape punishment. The Leaf River Church treated Henry's actions more as a management problem between slaveholders than as an abomination before God. Despite evangelical leaders' search for order, the church seemed content to leave Henry's fate to his slave master, merely excluding him from further fellowship with themselves.[21]

It was clearly risky to interfere with relations between master and slave, and neither courts nor churches were inclined to do so. Defining slaves as members of private families, modern evangelicals counseled slaveholders to treat them with familial benevolence. The dangers of extending that benevolence beyond one's own household, however, were demonstrated in yet another conflict over slaves between the Craft and Duckworth families. During the 1930s an unidentified former slave told WPA reporter Ruby Huff the story of Jessie, a slave who belonged to Bryant Craft, the son of Whitmell Craft. According to the ex-slave, Jessie's master beat him almost senseless for having sneaked his whiskey and sold it to other slaves. A Mr. Duckworth subsequently found the beaten Jessie lying by the side of the road and reportedly took him to his home, greased his mangled back with warm tallow, and then returned him to his master and tried to "reconcile" them. Bryant Craft reportedly responded to Duckworth's paternalistic intervention by delivering the slave a fatal blow and by warning Duckworth, "Let that be an example for you." Duckworth's misunderstanding of the limits of Christian benevolence had left one man dead and himself humiliated.[22]

Noninterference in master-slave relations helped the Leaf River Church to avoid potential arguments over slavery itself. Instead members argued over appropriate personal behavior, performance of church rituals, participation in missions, and the proper relationship between local, state, and national branches of the Baptist Church. Backsliders, of course, were an early issue of church concern. On July 16, 1831, less than two years after the church's founding, church secretary William P. Carter, Norvell Robertson's son-in-law, complained that too many members "manifested a lamentable degree of indifference to the duties of religion—frequently absenting themselves from the church meetings." The church directed Giles Sumrall and Williams Duckworth (a curious choice) to visit the backsliders and admonish them to do better.[23]

The Knights were likely among the backsliders, for several Knight men were soon cited for immoral behavior. Sometime in April 1833 Elders Giles Sumrall and Norvell Robertson confronted Jackie Knight with reports of his drunkenness—drunkenness perhaps exacerbated by the death earlier that year of Jackie's twenty-five-year-old son John. After Jackie expressed "a high degree of abhorrence for the Scandal he had brought upon the cause of religion by his conduct," the congregation voted unanimously on May 14 to retain him. Matters might have ended there had William Carter not proposed two months later that the church label as "drunkards" "those persons who indulge in the use of ardent spirits so as frequently to deprive themselves of their natural senses." Clearly aimed at humiliating members who abused alcohol, it also drove a wedge between tipplers and their more temperate brethren. So many members opposed the resolution that it was reworded to allow the church only to offer its "opinion" that an individual was a drunkard.[24]

In September 1835 the church cited Jackie's son Albert for undisclosed "scandalous" behavior. Albert, like his father before him, expressed contrition, and the church voted to retain him. Repentance wore thin for the Knights, however. On October 17, 1835, Jackie and another son, William, were forced to respond to undisclosed charges of misconduct. This time Jackie requested expulsion by the church, persisting until "he was finally cut off from the fellowship." To make matters worse, the church soon thereafter brought charges of gambling against Jackie's son-in-law John Whitehead. On February 20, 1836, Amos McLemore (uncle of the Amos McLemore later murdered during the Civil War) reported that Whitehead had admitted his guilt "but refused to attend conference and make satisfaction; and furthermore [he] requested . . . to be expeled [sic] from the church, which was accordingly done on the charge of gaming." Four months later several men, including William Knight, Williams Duckworth, Elnathan Duckworth, and William Bynum, were cited for neglecting to attend conference meetings.[25]

There is no record of how Williams Duckworth's brother-in-law, Younger Welborn Sr., and Younger's wife, Elizabeth, responded to the behavior and punishment of their Knight and Duckworth brethren. Unlike the Duckworths and Knights, no charges against the Welborns for sinful conduct appear in church records. Doctrinal rather than personal conflicts with the church are suggested, however, by descendant Gerald W. Johnson, who described Younger, Elizabeth, and Younger's brother, Billy, as devoutly Primitive (antimission) in their Baptist beliefs. Perhaps Younger and Elizabeth's beliefs influenced their decision to leave the church in April 1838 to join some dozen other members at the newly constituted and more conveniently located Clear Creek Baptist Church.[26]

Over time, most of the Knights also fell away from the Leaf River Church. Albert Knight was excluded for "repeated intoxication" on January 20, 1838. In December 1846 William Knight was cited a second time for habitual absences. In response he and his wife, Mary, requested and received exclusion. Ali Whitehead, kin to the Knight family through her brother-in-law John Whitehead, was excluded on May 10, 1847, on charges of fornication. Reinstated, she was expelled once and for all on October 13, 1855, after giving birth to a bastard.[27]

Only Keziah Knight continued to retain membership in the Leaf River Church, but in a manner that hinted at struggles within the family. Confronted early in 1849 for her many absences from church, she offered reasons "weighty" enough to "induce the church to bear with her." Perhaps the church was patient because her allusion to burdensome family problems conformed nicely to the duties of the true Christian woman. By the 1840s both secular and religious elites were trumpeting the tenets of "true womanhood": purity, piety, submissiveness, and domesticity.[28]

In defining the parameters of women's behavior within patriarchal evangelicalism, churches mirrored secular society. White men were the governors of this society; blacks and women were the governed. Stricter enforcement of racial and gender boundaries underscored this assumption and also obscured differences in class among white men. Religious and political leaders argued that sex and race determined one's natural characteristics and proper sphere, and that the special attributes shared by white men meant that they all might be masters. It hardly mattered that women's supposedly natural qualities had limited relevance to their actual lives, for those qualities determined what women could not be—masters—rather than who they truly were. Like those of blacks, women's inferior abilities necessitated the superior strengths of white men.[29]

John F. H. Claiborne demonstrated these assumptions when he turned from extolling the virtues of Piney Woods men to those of women in his 1841 essay. Gushing forth with sentimental images of femininity, he described Piney Woods women who lived not in rude log cabins but in whitewashed cottages, where "jessamine, honeysuckles, and grape vines twined their tendrils on porch and tree." There was no hint that frontier life might have produced women with weathered faces, strong backs, or muscled arms, let alone women who smoked pipes or chewed tobacco. Claiborne's women spent their days planting flowers, which he deemed a perfect expression of their natural attraction to that which is "most fragile and dependent." Sturdy men built communities while women, "at times timid as a startled fawn," nurtured and beautified their surroundings. Men faced the struggles of the forest; women inspired and endured. Slowly but surely, rhapsodies such as Claiborne's pushed dynamic women such as Martha Stearns Marshall, Peggy Summerlin, Polly Harper, and Rachel Knight to the back pages of history.[30]

Norvell Robertson's 1846 autobiography infused Claiborne's images of true womanhood with Baptist piety. Transporting modern ideals of womanhood backward in time, into a story set in the 1790s, Robertson told how he had encountered "Mrs. Haynes," a "Baptist professor," when he was young, unmarried, and a "wretched, lost, and ruined sinner." A sprinkling of sexual tension enlivened the story of a pious woman's spiritual ministering to a troubled man. During an evening visit to her and Mr. Haynes's home, Robertson recalled, Mr. Haynes "retired to bed, leaving me and his wife alone." In awkward silence Robertson and Mrs. Haynes sat together "mute," until she proposed that he make himself a "bed on the floor before the fire" and encouraged him to lie down and rest. As he prepared to do so, he discovered a little book titled "Grace Abounding to the Chief of Sinners," which Mrs. Haynes graciously lent to him.[31]

Although the evening had begun with Robertson feeling "a delicacy under the circumstances in entering into conversation with her," it ended not in sexual intimacy but romantically nonetheless. In lending Robertson her book, this pious, chaste woman pointed him toward the sweet path of salvation. Through his remembrance of Mrs. Haynes, Robertson jettisoned the forceful evangelical women of the Revolutionary era. This was no Martha Stearns Marshall, exhorting and converting men through sheer force of conviction and personality. Rather, with the barest hint of seduction, Mrs. Haynes instinctively nurtured and sweetly inspired Robertson to find his own salvation. It was the book that she possessed, not the force of her own words, that ultimately saved him.[32]

Neither the secular angels of Claiborne's essay nor the saintly wife of Robertson's memoir spoke to the lives of most ordinary women, who had little time for beautifying backwoods yards or instilling piety in spiritually troubled men. Nevertheless, as political and economic dependents of men, women had little choice but to accept their assigned place. Limits on their public behavior had not always been so stark, however. Before the turn of the nineteenth century, when evangelical churches met under more spontaneous and democratic conditions, some women had challenged traditional gender hierarchies. As we have seen, orthodox ministers regularly condemned churches that permitted women any level of authority as elders, deacons, or committee members. By the 1830s, mainstream Baptist churches seldom allowed women to initiate charges of misconduct against other members, particularly not against male members. More seldom did women serve on disciplinary committees empowered to investigate such charges.[33]

The Leaf River Church's own path toward greater enforcement of norms of true womanhood may be traced in its records. Under the guiding influences of Norvell Robertson and his sons, the church moved toward greater Baptist orthodoxy in matters of gender as well as missions. Certainly the church never countenanced women's authority over men, but neither during its earliest years did it treat them like hothouse flowers or helpless clinging vines. In fact, Sarah Hill initiated the church's first recorded disciplinary action on December 18, 1830, against a male member, Jesse N. Roberts. Deeply "grieved" by Roberts's undisclosed misbehavior, Sister Hill "unsuccessfully interviewed" him about his conduct. When she received no satisfaction from his response, she appealed to the church, which directed Elders Sumrall and Robertson to accompany Sister Hill to Brother Roberts's home. When Roberts refused to cooperate with the committee, the church excommunicated him by "unanimous voice." Since the nature of Roberts's offense went unrecorded, it is difficult to assess the significance of his expulsion; still, Sarah Hill's open confrontation of him *and* her participation in the church's disciplinary actions were distinctly unorthodox by 1830.[34]

Changes in gender arrangements were evident, however, on December 17, 1834, when the church plainly asserted the prerogatives of white men by declaring that whereas a man could remain a church member even if he "put away a wife for the cause of fornication and married another woman," a woman could not. Signs of a strengthened patriarchy were further suggested on June 18, 1836, when the church directed its elders to visit "several *male* members," but no female members, for "neglecting to attend conference meetings." This action implicitly assumed that male participation in church matters was more crucial than that of females.[35]

Parallel with the church's movement toward pro-mission activities, however, leaders began to punish unchaste female behavior. On August 18, 1838, the first charges of sexual misbehavior in the Leaf River Baptist Church were lodged against a woman when Catherine "Kitty" Burkhalter's "moral character" was called into question. Until then the church had never charged a woman with the typical female sins of fornication, bastardy, dancing, or gossiping. In response to a visit by Norvell Robertson, Kitty, the white, middle-aged wife of Jones Burkhalter, "manifested no penitence for her conduct and refused to attend conference." If Kitty doubted that the church would actually take action against her, she soon learned otherwise when its members voted unanimously to cut her off from membership.[36]

Synthia Rush also defied the church when it charged her with misbehavior. Her husband claimed in 1842 that she taunted him with threats to have "criminal intercourse" with Bentonville Taylor, their boarder, "if he desired it." Like Kitty Burkhalter, Synthia Rush at first was "unrepentant" of her guilt. Unlike Burkhalter, however, she reflected on her situation after the church cut her off. She later professed penitence and was restored to fellowship.[37]

Although a few white women continued to run afoul of church rules after 1845, the church's harsh treatment of Kitty Burkhalter and Synthia

Rush chastened them. When Rhoda Bullock's moral character was questioned in 1846, she quickly confessed and was forgiven; likewise, when the church charged Ali Whitehead with fornication in 1847, she apparently offered no defense and simply accepted her punishment.[38]

Some women who were stamped as deviant, notably Mary Coleman and Ali Whitehead, would have special connections to the Knight Company during the war. In a wider sense, however, the deserter band provided a patriarchal structure counter to that of the Confederacy for several families. This would be the case for Frances Ates, the mother of five sons and, in 1850 and 1860, the head of her own household. Like Burkhalter, Rush, and Whitehead, Frances and her daughter-in-law Matilda Ates ran afoul of the Leaf River Church. In 1855 fifty-year-old Frances hosted a dance party in her home, then scrambled to gain an honorable dismission from the church before elders discovered her sin. She failed to hide her behavior from the church, however, which promptly voted to withhold her letters of dismission. Little more than two years later, Matilda Ates was also charged with the offense of dancing. She admitted neither guilt nor expressed penitence, and the church excluded her.[39]

The Ates family may have suffered the twin stigmas of unruly behavior and ethnic mixture. Oral family tradition maintains that Frances Ates married a Choctaw named Langford, but she never took his name because of Indian custom. If so, she did not live with him. Whether she married a Native American or never married at all, Frances's lack of a husband left her socially and economically vulnerable in both her church and her community. In 1850 two of her sons worked as laborers in the homes of others, which in turn connected her to the Knight and Coleman families. Twenty-two-year-old Jim Ates worked and lived in the household of Jackie Knight's youngest son, Daniel. Also sharing Daniel and Elizabeth Knight's household was Elizabeth's mother, the infamous Mary Coleman. Like the grandsons of Mary Coleman, Jim Ates and his brother Tom would join the Knight band during the Civil War.[40]

Fragile domestic arrangements also later contributed to Tapley Bynum's decision to join the Knight band during the war. Tapley's father and mother, William and Sarah, had married in 1836 when William had already reached the advanced age of seventy-three. Sarah died in childbirth in 1839, leaving two-year-old Tapley and his newborn sister in the care of a father too old to tend to them properly. That same year the aging William applied for dismission from the Leaf River Church. William's grown children assumed increasing responsibility for their young siblings, which put Tapley in frequent company with his brother Benjamin and sister-in-law Peggy (Collins) Bynum. It is thus not surprising that during the war he would cast his lot with the Knight band, alongside Benjamin and Peggy's son Prentice and his Collins in-laws.[41]

A fractured family life would also later encourage Alzade Courtney to form close ties to the Knight band during the war. Although a number of Courtneys lived in the region, Alzade did not live within a nuclear family. At age nine in 1850 she lived in the home of an aged couple, Tobias and Rebecca Smith, who were probably not her biological parents. In January 1859, at age eighteen, she married James McGee of Jones County. The marriage appeared over by 1860, for in that year Alzade lived with Wiley Courtney, perhaps her older brother, and his family. Although she lived apart from her husband, in 1862 she gave birth to a son, John D. McGee. During the war the Knight Company would provide a kind of fictive kin network for Alzade, who had no visible means of support.[42]

It is not surprising that a brutal civil war would drive marginal members of the community into the company of a well-armed, organized band of men. It must be stressed, however, that most men who joined the company were not marginal members of their communities, and neither were most of the women who sheltered and fed them. The majority of women who supported the Knight Company were mothers, wives, and daughters of the mostly yeoman farmers who joined the band. In this local civil war, yeoman farm women defended themselves by defending their men.[43]

A prime example was Sally Parker, who was kin to at least fifteen members of the Knight Company. A Collins by birth, she had reasons other than simple loyalty or affection for protecting her male kin against capture by the Confederacy. Sally knew from personal experience that a woman's fate in the community was indivisible from the fate of her kinfolk, and that female submissiveness had no place in a struggle against powerful foes. She surely understood this in 1857 when her estranged second husband sued her for divorce. She had married slaveholder and tavern keeper James Parker in 1853, but the marriage had foundered within a year. Now James sought a divorce by destroying her reputation, claiming that she had "voluntarily abandoned her bed" and committed adultery with Drew Gilbert, her hired hand. Sally fought back by launching a sensational countercharge that James not only had brutalized her but also had committed adultery himself "by haveing carnal intercourse with a certain mare."[44]

Had Sally been either passive or without respectable kin, she could not have prevailed against her slaveholding husband. James Parker failed to win his divorce, and although he and Sally never again lived together, Sally's marital status returned to that of a respectable widow. She could afford to be bold in her countercharges because her brothers, Vinson, Simeon, Riley, and Jasper Collins, were not likely to ignore insults hurled against one of their own. This may explain why even the state's witnesses, Joshua Holifield and William Bush, testified that Sally's character was considered "good" by her neighbors. In regard to Sally's alleged adultery, Bush admitted only that he had "surprised" Drew and Sally one day when they were shelling corn from the same basket, causing Sally to blush.[45]

Living apart from her husband had made Sally Parker fair game for neighborhood gossip, but her respected yeoman background and deep roots in the community protected her against social degradation and poverty. In a world of forced female dependency, her most precious resource was her strong family network, not the "feminine" nature ascribed to her by society. During the Civil War she and numerous other women would defend their male kinfolk with the same boldness she had displayed in the Ellisville courthouse.[46]

No such power accrued to black women, whose family ties had neither social nor legal legitimacy among whites in the slaveholding South. Instead, the convergence of race and gender norms dictated black women's social control and left them vulnerable to sexual exploitation by white men. In June 1849, for example, the church excommunicated Rhoda, a slave, for slander when a white man charged that she was "fabricating and circulating slanderous falsehoods" about him and his family. Coming after two decades of growing sectionalism over slavery, and only four years after creation of the Southern Baptist Convention, the church's harsh discipline of Rhoda reflected whites' growing conviction that slaves who impudently disregarded boundaries between themselves and whites must be swiftly returned to their "place."

The church had difficulty reconciling the property rights of slaveholders with the unspoken right of white men to the bodies of black women. E. B. Harvey, a white man, was found guilty of engaging in "criminal intercourse" with another man's slave. Responding to demands from unnamed members that Harvey be punished, yet reluctant to challenge the personal behavior of a wealthy white male, the church decreed that Harvey voluntarily withdraw from membership, given the "scandal he was lying under." Almost three years later, however, on October 7, 1854, Harvey was reinstated. He then quickly requested and received dismission papers, making him eligible to join another Baptist church.[47]

Although little is known about the childhood of Newton Knight, we know that he grew up in this world of slavery, violence, and social strife. Raised on the modest farm of his shoemaker father, he was the grandson of Jackie Knight, one of the county's richest slaveholders. Newt, as a child, observed the impious drinking of his father, Albert, his grandfather Jackie, and his Uncle Daniel, all of whom were publicly accused of drunkenness.[48] Although Newt inherited his male kin's aversion to authority, he rejected their habit of taking refuge in the bottle.[49]

Newt, of course, was also influenced by his mother, Mason, but her influence has been shrouded by legends that have grown over the years. Some accounts suggest that it was she who developed Newt's intellect and taught him to be sensitive to the suffering of others. For example, Earle Knight claimed that Mason taught her children to read and write although her husband could do neither. Ex-slave Martha Wheeler described her as "quite a doctor," who "looked after the sick in all the surrounding country."[50]

By all accounts, mother and son were emotionally close. The most curious tale about their relationship is Tom Knight's story of how Mason changed Newt's birthdate on family records from 1830 to 1833 in order to protect him against prosecution for having "shot a negro boy." Ethel elaborated on Tom's story, claiming that Newt was born in 1829 rather than in 1830. She described how Newt, "during a fit of temper . . . murdered one of the slaves on his father's plantation." Mason, she agreed, changed Newt's birthdate to 1833 so that he would appear to be a minor child. In Ethel's version, however, Tom's allusion to a "shooting" was transformed into a "murder"; the "negro boy" had become one of Albert Knight's plantation slaves, although Albert owned no plantation and, at most, only one slave.[51]

Given the world in which Newton was raised, it is not difficult to imagine that he might indeed have shot, even murdered, a slave. It is important to emphasize, however, that no evidence other than Tom Knight's and Ethel Knight's undocumented claims exist. Significantly, Martha Wheeler never mentioned the story, despite her encyclopedic recital in 1936 to her WPA interviewer of virtually every legend and scandal associated with the Knight family. Nor did Ben Graves mention it in his 1926 interview, although he condemned Newt for deserting the Confederacy and for committing miscegenation. The story seems to have originated with Tom Knight, who was profoundly ashamed of his father's interracial connections. Deeply racist, writing in an era scarred by racial segregation and lynchings, Tom may even have manufactured the story, which did not explicitly accuse his father of murder, in order to counter images of Newt as a "Nigger-lover." Whatever its origins, the story became putty in the hands of Ethel, who shaped it to fit her image of Newt as a demented, violent murderer.[52]

Tom and Ethel's claim that Mason Knight lied about her son's age to protect him against prosecution is neither corroborated nor plausible.[53] If, as Ethel claimed, Newt murdered a slave who belonged to his father, the likelihood of Newt's being prosecuted would have been rather remote. Antebellum courts seldom interfered in matters of domestic violence, particularly in cases in which whites assaulted blacks. A gruesome example occurred in 1851 when a Jasper County mob seized a slave who they believed was guilty of rape and murder, tied him to a tree, and set him afire while over two hundred people watched and did nothing. If Newt Knight did shoot a slave belonging to his father, his punishment would likely have been left to his father.[54]

Slaves were certainly common figures in Newt's daily world, even if his parents avoided owning them. One slave whom Newt was likely to have noticed was Rachel, a sixteen-year-old mulatto woman purchased by his grandfather in 1856, probably in Mobile, Alabama, or Augusta, Mississippi. Newt and Rachel were only a year apart in age, but she was already the mother of a small daughter, Georgeanne, at the time of her arrival in Covington County. The physical appearances of both Rachel and Georgeanne clearly indicated that they were of mixed black and white ancestry.[55]

Through encounters with women such as Rachel, Newt knew that white men regularly crossed the color line despite laws and social taboos that forbade interracial liaisons and marriages. Rachel, light-skinned and physically attractive, was the sort of slave after whom many white men lusted. The fact that she had a white-skinned daughter announced to interested men that she had already been "initiated" into the world of interracial sexual relations. Before the Civil War, Rachel gave birth to two sons, Jeffrey (born about 1857) and Edmund (born about 1858). She apparently did not give birth to another child until March 1864, suggesting that the chaos of war at least brought her a respite from the unremitting sexual attentions of white men.[56]

The white-skinned children born to Rachel before the Civil War contradicted Ethel Knight's romantic portrait of the institution of slavery in Echo of the Black Horn. Ethel portrayed Jackie Knight as the quintessential paternalistic gentleman who "had as carefully reared his slaves as he had his own children." Denying that he ever traded in slaves, much less debauched slave women, she blamed all the evils that plagued the institution, including race-mixing, on slave traders. "From this type of men," she wrote, "sprang the first Mulattoes. In many instances," she admitted, "the females, were bred, unwillingly, like beasts."[57]

Establishing the villainy of the trader allowed Ethel to acknowledge the sexual vulnerability of enslaved women. For all her identification with the South's white master class, as a woman she deplored the rape of black women by white men. Obviously uncomfortable with discussing who the rapists were, she wrote evasively that "sometimes even the best master would be forced to sell off a slave for an objectionable reason. . . . Many of the objectionable reasons were never mentioned, such as rape." Ethel denounced this "practice" as "horrible, since these unfortunate people were victims of circumstance, treated without any consideration whatsoever."[58]

Perhaps because Ethel was close to suggesting that slaveholders, too, molested slave women, she turned abruptly to describing the horrors that awaited slaves at the hands of evil slave traders. As always, they, not the institution itself, debased otherwise contented slaves. Slavery, Ethel insisted, was a benevolent institution in which kindly masters such as Jackie Knight cared for and civilized a race "whose ancestors boiled and ate their sons."[59]

It was not enough for Ethel to shift the blame for race-mixing from slaveholder to slave trader. Lest readers sympathize or identify too closely with the light-skinned Rachel and her white-skinned progeny, Ethel insisted that Rachel also gave birth during the 1850s to a black-skinned child named Rosette. Through this alleged daughter, whose name does not appear on a single document, Ethel established Rachel's Africanness as negatively as possible. Employing common white stereotypes and images of blacks, she described Rosette's father as "a full-blooded, blue-gummed African" from whom Rosette "inherited her negroid features . . . even to that little odor peculiar to the full-blooded black race." Borrowing from the demeaning images of black children popularized by various white media during the first half of the twentieth century, she further described Rosette as a "banjo-bellied, spindle-legged waif" who "rolled her big eyes, and scratched her kinky head."[60]

Ethel's cruel caricatures of Rosette and her father revealed her revulsion for African Americans, notwithstanding her honeyed praise for those who "loved their white folks and were in turn loved by them, as members of families." These caricatures further enabled her to assure readers that Rachel and her children were, after all, "just another Negro family" and to emphasize that Rachel had multiple sexual partners.[61]

Like the New South writers who preceded her, Ethel judged Rachel's sexual behavior outside the historical context of slavery, in effect blaming the victim. She claimed that Rachel, because of her African roots, did not know or care who had fathered her children, during or after slavery. In Africa, Ethel assured readers, "parentage was as varied and uncertain as that of the beasts of the forests." She also claimed that "it was the custom for slave women to bear children of different fathers," and she suggested that Rachel simply continued this "custom" after gaining her freedom. Missing from Ethel's Old South were white men familiar in Newt Knight's world—slaveholders (not just slave traders) who treated black women as property to be bred like cattle, and white men who regarded sexual access to African American women as a simple right of manhood.[62]

Missing, too, from Ethel's romanticized view of slavery and antebellum life was any discussion of slave resistance. Even in the Piney Woods, where slaves were few and free blacks were practically nonexistent, black resistance to white authority occasionally found expression. Although most court records for antebellum Jones County were destroyed by fire, the Leaf River Church recorded a few instances of such resistance. In 1838, for example, a slave named Archer defended his innocence against charges of drunkenness until the committee admitted that it lacked proof of his guilt. Archer then successfully applied for dismission as a member in good standing. In 1856 another slave, Lemuel, admitted guilt on unspecified charges but refused to express penitence even though it meant his expulsion from the church.[63]

Slaves such as Archer and Lemuel risked personal well-being to maintain a measure of personal autonomy. Other slaves gambled much more, sometimes risking their very lives to obtain freedom. Outlaws such as John A. Murrel, the infamous 1820s' Mississippi "land pirate," and James Copeland, who terrorized the Piney Woods during the 1840s, were known to steal slaves or encourage them to run away from or even murder their masters. In a "confession" dictated shortly before he was hanged, Copeland recalled how a "very nice mulatto girl about seventeen years old" absconded with him after he promised to "take her for a wife and deliver her to a free state." The couple lived together for only a short time before Copeland sold her to a "rich planter" for a thousand dollars and headed off to Mobile.[64]

This young slave woman's effort to achieve freedom at enormous personal cost resembled Rachel Knight's risks in forming a common cause with Confederate deserters during the Civil War. The war offered Rachel the most powerful societal role she had ever known. Less than ten years earlier she had arrived in the Mississippi Piney Woods as a teenager, pregnant, powerless, and alone except for her child. Until the war came, she had no reason to anticipate that she would ever be free of slavery or the bearing of slave children. Her newfound power resulted directly from undercurrents of conflicts among whites that finally boiled over in the heat of war.[65]

Within the Leaf River Church, conflicts among whites became more muted in the 1850s after pro-missionary members gained control over the church. Although the road to modernization was not smooth, the church adopted explicitly pro-mission practices. On August 29, 1851, for example, it assigned white members annual dues of ten cents to support the Indian Mission Association and the Bible Cause. Throughout the South pro-missionary Baptist leaders would soon lead the charge in support of secession. On October 12, 1861, the Leaf River Baptist Church officially took its stand with the Confederacy when Asaph Robertson, the church's delegate to the Ebenezer Association, initiated a collection drive to raise money for the purchase of Bibles and testaments for Confederate volunteers.[66]

The internal divisions that plagued the Leaf River Church between 1830 and 1860 provide a window on the social and religious strife that divided people throughout the antebellum South. Although many such conflicts emerged out of personal hatreds and resentments between families and individuals, they were nonetheless connected to larger economic, religious, and cultural changes reflecting the growth of slavery and the cotton South during these years. Many members of the church would sacrifice their sons to build a separate Southern nation. But so also would ten men and boys from nearby neighborhoods be executed for committing treason against the Confederacy; nine of them were descendants of men and women who had either left or been ejected from the Leaf River Baptist Church.[67]

In 1861, as in 1775, war would draw into its vortex a multitude of local resentments, both political and personal, that would set families against families in a brutal inner civil war. As debates over secession and war heated up, long-simmering tensions, combined with personal fears, provided people with powerful motives to defy the Confederacy. As the Confederate cause consumed ever more resources and lives, several branches of the Collins, Bynum, Knight, Sumrall, Valentine, Walters, Welborn, and Welch families took not a rebel's stand but a rebellious stance, one that by 1863 was aimed straight at the Confederacy.

Part Two

Civil War, Reconstruction, and the Struggle for Power

If, in this story, you miss the oft-told tale of the
Civil War of Gettysburg and Lee, then I am glad.
—James Street, introduction to *Tap Roots*, 1943

I was no secessioner, I will tell the truth about
it.—M. P. Bush, speech before the DAR, 1912

Chapter Five

The Inner Civil War

Birth of the Free
State of Jones

In *Tap Roots* James Street indicated a weariness with Civil War histories that
told only of great battles and brave generals. He shifted his lenses from the
battlefield to the community and from the soldier to the soldier's father,
mother, sister, slave, and neighbor. In so doing he not only deepened our
understanding of the war but also exposed the narrow limits of 1940s
Civil War historiography. Street's characters might be fictional, but Southern unionists and guerrilla warfare on the Civil War home front surely
were not. Implicitly, he reminded readers that women, blacks, and a good
portion of the Southern white yeomanry had been robbed of their memories of the war.[1]

Since the publication of *Tap Roots* in 1943, historians have dramatically
expanded and revised our interpretation of the Civil War, and a much
more complex picture of the war's significance has emerged. We know
that Northern and Southern white men did not simply battle over rival
notions of freedom and economic principles while dependents passively
awaited the outcome. We also know that Southern white men fought

among themselves as well as with Yankees, and that they did not fight alone. Jones County's guerrilla war revealed with searing clarity the interdependence of men, women, children, and slaves in this struggle. The common wartime stereotype of men protecting women was turned on its head as deserters' wives and daughters protected them. Similarly, the deserters' need to enlist the aid of slaves replaced the white masters' need to govern slaves.[2]

No mere war among men, the bloody battles fought in Civil War Jones County emerged from economic, religious, and social strife that had long simmered between rival families. Disparate, unorganized resistance to local authority exploded into full-scale rebellion by late 1863, when a number of Jones County deserters organized and armed themselves into a deadly fighting force. Many more local men were absent from their Confederate units, however, than joined the band. The 7th Battalion, Mississippi Infantry, from which most Knight band members deserted, reported many of its soldiers as AWOL at some point, but most men rejoined the Confederate Army when threatened with arrest. In contrast, those who joined the Knight Company intended desertion to be permanent. Drawing on the crucial support of civilians, they refused to "skulk" in the woods as dishonored men but instead declared war on the Confederacy.[3]

Throughout the state (indeed, the South) similar home front conflicts erupted, engaging not only soldiers on battlefields but entire communities. In separate letters written in 1864, Judge Robert S. Hudson of Leake County complained bitterly to President Jefferson Davis and Governor Charles Clark about disloyal civilians in central Mississippi. Hudson recommended to President Davis that "the most radical and severe treatment" be meted out to anti-Confederate "women and noncombatants." Deserters who were not put to death should at least be transferred to military service "most remote from their homes."[4]

Lest women's support for deserters legitimize their disloyalty to the Confederacy, Judge Hudson depicted disloyal women in the most degraded terms possible to Governor Clark. Describing them as "rotten hearted," he insisted that those in his judicial district—which included Yazoo, Holmes, Attala, Madison, and Leake Counties—were "far worse than the men" and "responsible" for most of the deserters' brazen conduct. Hudson's harsh denigration of anti-Confederate women reflected the extent to which male honor—indeed, male identity—was confirmed by the loyalty of a man's community and, most especially, by that of his dependents.[5]

The involvement of women in deserter activities also underscored the merging of political and personal motives in white Southerners' opposition to the Confederacy. Women who shared the antisecession views of their fathers, sons, and husbands often encouraged them to desert at the first opportunity. But women who suffered from hunger, illness, or abuse at the hands of Confederate soldiers also provided men with ample personal reasons to desert and return home. Whether or not men and women initially opposed the Confederacy itself, the seamless blending of political and personal motives for desertion demonstrated plain people's growing awareness that the war threatened to destroy their lives. For many, personal awareness bred political resistance.[6]

Maddie Bush expressed one nonslaveholder's perspective on the Civil War in his speech before the Jones County DAR in 1912. Confessing frankly to his patriotic audience that "I was no secessioner, I will tell the truth about it," Bush belittled dominant images of masculinity, describing some men and boys as eager to go to war because "they thought it was big to get the big guns on." Although Bush offered no explanation of why he opposed secession, he conveyed a clear sense of how masculine notions of honor led many other men, even in the slave-poor county of Jones, to march off to war. Personal suffering and resentment of Confederate policies, he might also have noted, eventually led many of these same men to join their neighbors in deserting the Confederate Army.[7]

Although the history of the Free State of Jones offers an alternative Southern vision of the Civil War, it does not follow that the memories of its participants can be accepted at face value. Such memories, rarely written down before the twentieth century, are more accurately understood as constructions of the past that allow descendants to justify or take pride in their ancestors' legacy, rather than as strictly factual accounts. As a defender of anti-Confederate behavior, Maddie Bush was unique in his refusal to defend the actions of deserters beyond implying that secession and the new Confederate nation did not serve the interests of ordinary people like himself.[8]

In contrast, most descendants of pro- and anti-Confederate participants in the Jones County inner war were fiercely partisan, often telling the same ancestral tales but with crucial details added or omitted to support their family's position. Predictably, both sides depicted their ancestors as men and women of honor. Yet despite factual errors and obvious biases, individual narratives, when used in conjunction with military, legal, and governmental records, help us to understand why an organized band of men, with strong support from their respective communities, took the law into their own hands and fought their own war against the Confederate Army.

Between 1935, when Tom Knight published his romantic account of Newt Knight and the Free State of Jones, and 1951, when Ethel Knight's

Echo of the Black Horn appeared, the voices of those who approved of the Knight Company's Civil War stance prevailed. Tom's book was immediately followed in 1936 by interviews with local citizens by the WPA. Ruby Huff, a Jones County WPA writer, seized the opportunity to write a brief essay about the Knight Company in which she exulted that sometimes "this spirit of the South gets so unsouthy as to want to clap my hands and say three cheers for the most daring troop that ever tramped the Southern soil—the Deserters." Huff applauded the desertions that followed the Confederate defeat at Vicksburg, insisting that they vindicated the men who had "dared" to desert earlier.[9]

Defenders of the Knight Company took their cue from the band itself, which appropriated dominant symbols of masculinity and honor during and immediately following the war. "After the damnable siege and slaughter at Vicksburg," Huff wrote, "many officers, privates, and younger recruits left the lines of battle to join a rank of men who dared to rebel." She then transferred the label of "rebel" from Confederate soldiers to the Knight band—thereby appropriating its Lost Cause association with honor—by explaining that "these rebels were termed deserters."[10]

Denying that their ancestors had shirked military service or dishonored themselves with acts of treason, twentieth-century defenders of the Knight Company also laid claim to the principles of American republicanism by insisting that the company had resisted an ill-begotten and illegitimate government. Benjamin R. Sumrall, grandson of both Harmon Levi Sumrall and Riley Collins, told his WPA interviewer in 1936 that Knight Company men were not deserters "because in the first place their country [county] did not vote to ceceed [sic]." Proud of his kinship to the company's core members, he boasted that it was made up of "the best men in Jones County." He cited the fact that most Jones County residents did not own slaves, and then he paraphrased Lincoln to argue that those opposed to secession believed that "a house divided against itself cannot stand." Anti-secessionists feared that if the South seceded, "England would take the advantage of their discension [sic] and we would be again under the British yoke." The Knight Company, he emphasized, required members to repeat the phrase "I am of the Red, White, and Blue" before entering camp.[11]

Like Tom Knight, Sumrall downplayed any suggestion that the Knight Company was an outlaw band by justifying rather than denying its use of force against the Confederacy. He emphasized that Newt Knight instructed his men "not to destroy the property of anyone, not even their enemies, and not to kill anyone except in the protection of their lives or the lives of their company or families." Tom Knight agreed but conceded that his father's policy was necessarily one of "kill or be killed." To reinforce his father's claim to honor, he also invoked memories of mothers, grand-mothers, and aunts who risked torture, even death, to nurture husbands, sons, and fathers temporarily forced to become outlaws.[12]

The claims made by Tom Knight, Ruby Huff, and Ben Sumrall—which were followed in the 1940s by the novel and movie *Tap Roots*—infuriated Ethel Knight. To deny the Knight Company moral agency, she vehemently denied that any but a few of its men were unionists. "In fact," she claimed, "the Knight Company hated the Union as much as did any Rebel." She correctly pointed out that several deserters came from slaveholding fami-lies, but she simultaneously characterized the others as "riff-raff." Rather than a community of dissenters, Ethel described a band of misguided, fearful dupes of a demented Newt Knight.[13]

The notion that most Jones County deserters were riff-raff was rein-forced by professional historians, most of whom doubted whether a band of backwoods white farmers truly challenged the legitimacy, as well as the authority, of the Confederacy. In 1943 John K. Bettersworth described Jones County deserters as fierce unionists who, during the war, "banded together under the Federal flag, set patrols along the roads, and proceeded to destroy ginhouses and ferries." Conceding that the county "was cer-tainly in the hands of outlaws" during the war, he dismissed the notion, however, that ideological principles underlay Piney Woods unionism, attributing desertion to poverty and a "persistently independent back-woods spirit." Referring to the Piney Woods as the "real demesne of the poor white," he claimed that ideologies "meant little" to its people, who whether fighting for states' rights or the Union, "bandied words that their darkness comprehended not." Although Bettersworth stuck to the facts and stopped short of dismissing deserters as desperadoes, he nonetheless viewed Piney Woods farmers as ignorant poor whites. His Free State was inhabited by hothead rebels who reflexively defied all authority within and outside the South.[14]

Ethel gained the greatest support for her views of the Knight band in 1984 from historian Rudy Leverett. The great-grandson of Confederate major Amos McLemore, Leverett produced the third full-length book about the Free State of Jones and the first to be published by an academic press. More than any previous author, he tested the various tales about the Free State against documented facts. Although he barely mentioned Ethel Knight's book, he, like her, characterized the Knight Company as a band of mostly criminals. Ignoring altogether the involvement of women and slaves, he cast the struggle as a contest between law-abiding and law-breaking males. With the civilian population erased altogether, Confeder-ate soldiers appeared as God-fearing, hardworking, loyal citizens in Leverett's book; deserters were ignorant outlaws bent on plunder and murder.[15]

This insistence that banditry motivated the men of the Knight Company is not corroborated by the 1926 narrative of Ben Graves, a descendant of pro-Confederate slaveholders and no admirer of Newt Knight. Graves grudgingly conceded that political motives underlay Knight's opposition to the Confederacy. "I believe in giving the devil his due," he said. "Newt was a mighty sorry man. . . . But he was a poor man and didn't own any negroes. . . . He felt that the [Twenty Negro] law wasn't fair; that it enabled the rich man to evade service and that it wasn't right to ask him to risk his life for people who rated themselves so far above him." After the war, Graves pointed out, Newt "called himself a Union man and was a full-fledged Republican."[16]

Judging from extant records and people's memories, it appears that Newt gradually developed a unionist stance born of personal experiences during the war that in turn stimulated his growing political consciousness. His own memories of the war, shared in 1921 with journalist Meigs Frost of the *New Orleans Item*, suggest as much. Newt told Frost that he and his men felt justified in deserting the Confederate Army because the majority of Jones County's voters had opposed secession. On December 20, 1860, he explained, the county's cooperationist candidate, John H. Powell (father-in-law of Jasper Collins), defeated the pro-secession candidate, merchant-slaveholder John M. Baylis, to become a delegate to the Mississippi state convention. Powell then betrayed his antisecessionist constituents. On January 9, 1861, after swift defeat of several ordinances that offered alternatives to secession, he joined the overwhelming majority of delegates and voted to secede from the Union. "Then next thing we knew," said Newt, "they were conscripting us. The rebels passed a law conscripting everybody between 18 and 35. They just came around with a squad of soldiers [and] took you." But, he maintained, "if they had a right to conscript me when I didn't want to fight the Union, I had a right to quit when I got ready." To Newt's way of thinking, support for the Confederacy was entirely voluntary because the delegate Powell had failed to honor his constituents' position on secession.[17]

Newt's words do not clearly describe a unionist, although they suggest that he was a staunch believer in representative government and individual liberty (consistent with his father's and grandfather's resistance to evangelical discipline). Ben Sumrall's description of his grandfather Riley Collins, however, left no doubt of Collins's unionism. In the aftermath of secession, according to Sumrall, he "called a meeting at old Union church in Jones County where he made a great speech" condemning the "injustice" of secession. Collins urged the men of Jones to "not fight against the union," said Sumrall, "but if they had to fight [to] stay at home and fight for a cause in which they believed."[18]

Despite Riley Collins's admonitions, military records reveal that the vast majority of men enlisted for service after passage of the first Confederate conscript law. Maddie Bush explained that he and others did so "rather than be conscripted and be put in companies where we didn't want to go," a statement supported by the fact that many of the men listed on the Knight Company roster served together in the 7th Battalion; fifteen alone came from Company F.[19]

Numerous Collinses, Valentines, Welches, and Knights were among the men who joined the 7th Battalion. Because of their ages, Riley, Simeon, and Vinson Collins were exempt from service under the terms of the first conscript act. But their younger brother Jasper and two of Simeon's sons, James Madison "Matt" and Thomas Jefferson "Jeff," joined on May 13, 1862. When the age of conscription was raised to forty-five in September 1862, however, Riley Collins refused to join, not only because he was a unionist but also because his wife had died that very month, leaving several minor children in his care.[20]

Other Jones County men ignored conscription as well. Prentice Bynum never joined the Confederate Army nor, according to Welborn descendant Gerald Johnson in 1998, did the sons of Younger Welborn Sr., William E. and Tolbert, and their cousin-in-law, Berry Sims. Not only were these men from nonslaveholding families, but this branch of Welborns also held antimission (or Primitive) Baptist views that fed their suspicions of the Confederacy. Johnson described them as "skeptical of most politicians, lawyers, and law enforcement officers." According to him, they believed the parable that it was "easier for a camel to pass through the eye of a needle than for a rich man to pass through the gates of heaven." These Welborns applied their religious creed to the war. When they looked at the Confederacy, they saw a rich man's government; on the battlefields they saw a poor man's fight.[21]

Unlike several Welborns and Collinses, Newt Knight did not resist military conscription; in fact, he voluntarily enlisted for service on July 29, 1861, almost a year before passage of the first Confederate conscript law. Although like most Jones County citizens he probably opposed secession, he seemed to relish military service (which may explain why he was elected captain of the Knight Company). He quickly achieved the rank of fourth sergeant and was also detailed as provost guard. On January 2, 1862, however, he was discharged by special order, perhaps because of his father's impending death, which occurred only a few days later. On May 13, 1862, after passage of the conscript law, Newt enlisted in the Confederate Army again, this time in Company F of the 7th Battalion of the Mississippi Infantry alongside many of his neighbors and acquaintances, including Jasper Collins.[22]

Personal hardships plagued Newt during the first year of the war. His grandfather Jackie Knight died early in 1861, two years after the death of his grandmother Keziah. His father, Albert, died less than a year later. The deaths of Jackie, Keziah, and Albert spared those elders the agony of a fratricidal war, but combined with Newt's conscription into the army, they left Newt's mother, wife, and sister to share a household that included only one male adult, Bill Morgan, whom his teenaged sister had only recently married.[23]

In Newt's absence, Bill Morgan, described by Ben Graves in 1926 as "a regular outlaw" and a "desperado," supplanted him as family patriarch. According to Tom Knight, Morgan frequently whipped Newt's children; Ethel Knight even claimed that he had slipped into Serena's bed. Morgan may also have had ties to local Confederate officials. According to Tom Knight, Newt received a letter from Serena complaining that Confederate cavalrymen had appropriated the only horse available to the Knights for making trips to the nearest mill. Further fueling Newt's anger were allegations that his brother-in-law had cooperated with the Confederate authorities who seized the horse.[24]

According to Ethel and Tom Knight, Newt's decision to desert the army was influenced by the presence of Morgan in his household. Once he went AWOL, however, he worried that Morgan would turn him in to Confederate officials or even harm him. Morgan "was one man Newt was afraid of," remembered Ben Graves, "he was afraid Morgan would slip up on him."[25]

Newt allegedly shot Morgan through the head as he sat rocking a child on the Knight family's front porch. Word of the shooting spread quickly, prompting fourteen-year-old Graves to run to the Knight home and gawk at the murder scene. According to him, Mason, Serena, and Martha all swore that they did not see who shot Bill Morgan. But, recalled Graves, "everybody thought Newt did it because they were afraid of Morgan, and Newt was too."[26]

Newt's decision to desert the Confederacy resulted from more than just personal problems. He was part of the first major round of desertions by Jones County men after the battles of Iuka and Corinth in northern Mississippi. To make matters worse, Newt explained to Meigs Frost, in that same month, October 1862, "the rebels passed the Twenty-Negro Law, up there at Richmond, Virginia, the capital." The fact that this law allowed men who owned twenty or more slaves, but not nonslaveholding farmers, to return home to raise crops disturbed Newt.[27]

The Twenty-Negro Law clearly disturbed the Collinses as well. After learning of its passage in the wake of having survived Corinth, Jasper Collins promptly deserted the 7th Battalion. He never rejoined and later collaborated with Newt in organizing the Knight Company.[28] According to Gerald Johnson, many soldiers also deserted because they suffered such shortages of tents and other supplies after the 7th Battalion's retreat to Camp Rogers, near Holly Springs, that they "decided they would just up and go home for the winter, and the Confederate Army did very little to stop them."[29]

Other survivors of Corinth could not immediately desert because they were hospitalized. Soon after their release, however, Jim Ates, Tom Ates, Maddie Bush, Tapley Bynum, Jeff Collins, Alpheus Knight, Ben Knight, Dickie Knight, and James Morgan Valentine were all reported AWOL. Their brush with death seemed to convince them of the folly of remaining Confederate soldiers. Twenty-three-year-old Tapley Bynum, for example, ill and hospitalized in Saltillo by late September, deserted his unit in January 1863. Less than a year earlier he and his eighteen-year-old nephew, Benjamin Franklin Bynum Jr., had together joined the 7th Battalion. But Ben was taken prisoner during the battle of Iuka, hospitalized for illness in Jackson, and dead before the year was over. Not only did Tapley desert, but he and his nephew Prentice (Ben Bynum Jr.'s brother) subsequently joined the Knight band. John H. Harper was similarly affected by his brother's death in November 1862, one month after being admitted to the hospital at Enterprise. Disabled by wounds in both feet as a result of Corinth, Harper somehow made his way home and later joined the Knight Company.[30]

Unlike Bynum and Harper, most Jones County soldiers eventually returned to the Confederate Army. James O. Reddoch of the 7th Battalion, for example, sustained a gunshot wound to his jaw during the battle of Corinth and was hospitalized until late March 1863. He was then released and, like so many others, reported AWOL. Although James's uncle, Daniel Reddoch, deserted and joined the Knight Company, James was eventually granted a leave by the Confederacy (perhaps because of the severity of his wound) and reentered the army's good graces. William A. Bynum Jr. was reported AWOL from the Mississippi 8th Infantry Regiment even earlier than James Reddoch, but he reentered the army after three months. In these men's cases, the personal suffering that caused them to take unofficial leaves from the army did not result in their opposing the Confederacy.[31]

Slaveholding was the defining factor in Reddoch's and Bynum's loyalty to the Confederacy; otherwise they shared similar backgrounds with Newt Knight. Together the grandfathers of the three men, Jimmie Reddoch,

James O. Reddoch, Civil War veteran of the 7th Battalion, Mississippi Infantry, and grandsons, ca. 1908. James supported the Confederacy, but his uncle, Daniel Reddoch, joined the Knight Company. Photograph courtesy of Robert Cavendish.

William Bynum Sr., and Jackie Knight, had pioneered in settling Covington County and founding the Leaf River Baptist Church. Jimmie Reddoch and Jackie Knight had lived on adjoining lands, and their kinship lines had crossed over the years; but even though James O. Reddoch, like William A. Bynum, had kinfolk who joined the Knight band, the fact that he and Bynum lived in slaveholding households influenced them to cast their fate with that of the Confederacy.[32]

By late 1862 opposing attitudes toward the Confederacy were apparent among slaveholding and nonslaveholding soldiers. For one thing, as Maddie Bush realized, few plain men could expect to assume leadership roles or gain heightened prestige by strapping on the "big guns." And unlike more highly placed men, they had few opportunities to escape the battlefield except through desertion. In contrast, rising businessman Amos McLemore, whose friend and fellow merchant Amos Deason was elected to the 1862 Confederate state legislature, carved out a distinguished, though short, Confederate military career.[33]

McLemore initially opposed secession, but he quickly came to support the Confederate cause. On August 10, 1861, he received permission to raise his own regiment, the Rosinheels (officially designated Company B,

27th Mississippi Infantry, in December 1861). His first and second lieutenants, Joel E. Welborn and John M. Baylis, both of whom rose quickly within the ranks of the Confederacy, seemed handpicked from his circle of friends and business associates. In June 1862 Welborn and Baylis resigned from McLemore's unit to become commander and surgeon, respectively, for Company E of the 7th Battalion of the Mississippi Infantry.[34]

These men became the local enforcers of the Confederacy's increasingly hard line on desertion. In late 1862, as desertion rates mounted, Major Commander Welborn urged the assistant adjutant general of the Mississippi Confederate Headquarters at Jackson to take a more aggressive stance toward Jones County deserters. In a letter dated November 1, 1862, Welborn reported that many of the soldiers hospitalized or missing after the battles of Iuka and Corinth had returned home and "say they will never return to camp." He warned authorities that deserters were so numerous and so determined that "one man has no business in trying to collect these men." Furthermore, he emphasized that the deserters' movement was becoming increasingly organized: "I am well acquainted with that section of the country & am satisfied that there is some of the citizens that is encouraging these things."[35]

Welborn did not provide the names of citizens giving such counsel, but among them were many of his own kinfolk. He may also have referred to the Collinses, whose influence Newt Knight admitted in 1921 when he told Meigs Frost that Jasper Collins had convinced him in late 1862 that the Twenty-Negro Law exposed the Confederate cause once and for all as a "rich man's war and poor man's fight." Along with Benjamin F. Dykes, Newt deserted the 7th Battalion following its retreat to Fort Sloan near Abbeville in early November 1862, very near the date that Joel Welborn alerted Confederate authorities about Jones County's deserters.[36]

Maj. Gen. Dabney H. Maury responded to Welborn's letter by recommending to the commanding general at Jackson that the "most energetic measures be taken at once" against army absentees. On November 19 the major general responded by recommending the arrest of "all men belonging to the army who can be found who have no authority to be absent from their commands." Local Confederate officials were accordingly instructed to take firmer measures toward AWOL soldiers.[37]

In early 1863 Jones County's provost marshal, John H. Powell, received orders that county marshals were now responsible for taking charge of deserters. This new duty disturbed Powell, whose unpopularity with pro-Union citizens dated back to his pro-secession vote at the Mississippi state convention. It did not help that he was also the father-in-law of Jasper Collins, perhaps the proudest and most defiant deserter in Jones County.

Powell implored Governor J. J. Pettus "to give me some instructions [on] what to do, whether I am in authority or no, and Tell me whether I am in titled to Any pay for my servises or not."[38]

Whether it was Powell or other Confederate authorities who confronted the county's deserters is uncertain, but many of the men awol from the 7th Battalion, including Newt Knight, were forced to return to their companies in early 1863. In Newt's case, force was applied sometime between January and February when Confederate authorities arrested him. Several of his friends later testified to Congress that Rebels "got holt of him and they tyed him and drove him to prison." So determined were Confederate soldiers to "make him fight or kill him" that they "destroyed all his effects[:] Horses and Mewls and his household . . . and they left his family destitute." Newt's allies further testified that Confederate officials treated Newt "cruelly" "for some length of time" until May 1863, when he escaped the army once and for all.[39]

Like other soldiers, Newt became increasingly frustrated with the Confederacy as personal hardships collided with political policies. As his hatred for the Confederate Army grew, contact with the militantly pro-Union Collins family strengthened his political opposition to the Confederacy. Economic distress, fears of death, and resentment of those who benefited from exemptions encouraged Newt and other men less ideologically driven than the Collinses to turn their backs on the army. Again, Newt deserted his unit, just before the 7th battalion moved on to Vicksburg.[40]

On June 1, 1863, Second Lieut. Harmon Mathis of the 8th Mississippi Regiment reported that seventy-five to one hundred deserters were lying out in the swamps of Jones County, "prowling from house to house stealing everything they can." Their numbers would soon be augmented by the next crisis faced by Confederate soldiers: the siege of Vicksburg, which lasted from May 18 until July 4, 1863. As part of Hebert's Brigade, the men of the 7th Battalion never forgot Vicksburg, where they held on like caged, half-starved animals until their surrender by Gen. J. C. Pemberton to Gen. Ulysses S. Grant.[41]

The horrors of Vicksburg once and for all destroyed the grudging allegiance of many men of the 7th Battalion to the Confederacy. John Ellzey remembered surviving the ordeal by eating rats, parched corn, and soup made from boiled leather shoestrings. A letter written from "many Soldiers" to General Pemberton captured the men's desperation: "If you can't feed us, you had better surrender us, horrible as the idea is, than suffer this noble army to disgrace themselves by desertion. I tell you plainly, men are not going to lie here and perish." Maddie Bush reminisced that although he had participated in the great siege, he said, "I hope I didn't kill anybody. I had to go, but I didn't want to go."[42]

Many men deserted their units, regardless of their political stance on the war, after Vicksburg. Even secessionist John M. Baylis was reported AWOL from the 7th Battalion on June 30, 1863, shortly after his brother, Captain Wyatt T. Baylis, died from wounds sustained at Vicksburg. John M. Baylis returned to his unit in November 1863, but many others did not. More than ever, economic suffering and fears of death overrode many men's anxieties about being labeled cowards or being arrested. Instead they went home, citing the oaths of loyalty they had signed as a condition of parole by General Grant at Vicksburg as justification for refusing to rejoin the Confederate Army.[43]

As increasing numbers of ordinary soldiers deserted their posts, Maj. Amos McLemore was assigned responsibility for restoring order in Piney Woods Mississippi. In August 1863 Gen. Braxton Bragg ordered him back to the Jones County area to enlist resisters and return stragglers to the Confederate Army. McLemore quartered his force at Augusta, in Perry County. According to his descendant historian Rudy Leverett, Amos's brother Abraham was appointed Jones County ranger in 1863, and his wife's uncle, Baptist minister William H. Fairchild, was appointed collector of Confederate taxes-in-kind. By this time Joel Welborn had been officially granted a medical retirement, but John M. Baylis was still AWOL following the siege of Vicksburg.[44]

Amos McLemore's new assignment soon brought him face-to-face with an enemy force as deadly as Yankees. On October 5, 1863, as he sat with several Confederate officers gathered in the home of Representative Amos Deason, an assailant shot him to death. The Confederacy's concerted effort to round up deserters in the Jones County region, and Major McLemore's particularly zealous search for delinquent conscripts, had aroused the ire of men like Newt Knight. "We stayed out in the woods minding our own business," Newt later told Meigs Frost, "until the Confederate Army began sending raiders after us with bloodhounds. . . . Then we saw we had to fight."[45]

No one was ever charged with McLemore's murder, but today most people believe that Newt Knight killed him. Legend has it that Newt and two other men, one of whom was his cousin Alpheus Knight, sneaked up to Deason's house and then drew straws to decide who would shoot McLemore. When Alpheus drew the short straw, Newt allegedly took the gun anyway because he did not trust the younger man's aim. Tom Knight did not confirm that his father pulled the trigger, but he defended the murder of McLemore on grounds that he was a "news-toter" for the Confederacy and had been warned by the Knight band to stop. According to Ethel Knight, McLemore was a "hot-headed young fellow" who had been "warned that he was treading on dangerous ground but he refused to heed the warning."[46]

Like so many of the explosive events triggered by the Civil War, Mc-Lemore's murder achieved legendary status in Jones County. In fact, to-day McLemore is Jones County's most famous martyr to the Lost Cause. The old Deason house, now a museum, is rumored to be haunted, and McLemore's spilled blood allegedly rises to the surface of its wooden floors during rainy weather, despite servants' efforts to scrub it away. Ethel Knight insisted that on each anniversary of McLemore's death, at 11:00 P.M., "the door to the doorway in which Newt Knight stood swings open and promptly closes, as if by an unseen hand."[47]

Ongoing public fascination with the murder reflects not only the ghastly nature of McLemore's death but also recognition that it precipitated the creation of the Knight Company and ignited Jones County's inner civil war. Newt recorded fourteen separate battles fought between his company and Confederate forces between October 13, 1863, and January 10, 1865. The first occurred at Smith's store, two miles east of Soso, eight days after McLemore's murder. On that date the guerrillas set up camp "at a bat-tleground known as Salsbattery" and formally organized the Knight Com-pany. According to Newt, "We knew we were completely surrounded by the rebels, but we [also] knew every trail in the woods." The company would engage in six battles between November 1, 1863, and February 1, 1864, four during the infamous "Lowry raids" of April 1864 and four between November 1864 and January 10, 1865.[48]

This inner war drew women, children, and slaves onto fields of battle that occasionally included their homes. Just as surely as pro-Confederate women urged sons to perform their duties as soldiers, women from the anti-Confederate side actively assisted men in eluding Confederate capture. Newt, Tom, and Ethel Knight all pointed out that Jones County farmwives blew horns either to warn deserters away or to summon them to their side. At least two women maintained homesteads that fronted strategically lo-cated deserter camps within the area. Widow Sally Delancy's small farm on Horse Creek, near Soso, shielded Salsbattery from view, while Sally Parker's home, located near the swamps of Tallahala Creek, provided an alternate shelter for members of the Knight Company. Both women cooked meals and provided places of rest for wounded or weary deserters.[49]

These two "Aunt Sallies," both age fifty in 1860, personified the intri-cate ties of kinship and friendship that bound women and men together in this struggle. Newt alluded to the crucial support he received from one widow when he described how she provided fifty pounds of lead for the deserters' use as ammunition. "One of my men was courtin' her daugh-ter," he explained, "so of course she gave us what we needed. The ol' hen flutters when you come 'round the lone chick, you know." Certainly, Sally

Amos Deason Home, Ellisville, Mississippi, built around 1845. On October 5, 1863, this home was the site of Newton Knight's alleged murder of Maj. Amos McLemore. Author's photograph.

Parker's personal connections to the Knight band were clear. Although her oldest son died a Confederate soldier, her brothers, nephews, and cousins were members of the band. So, too, was Drew Gilbert, the man with whom her second husband had accused her of committing adultery in 1857.[50]

But loyalty to the Knight Company entailed more than romance in the midst of war; sometimes it put women in the line of fire. On December 23, 1863, Sally Parker's home on Tallahala Creek became the site of a pitched battle between Confederate soldiers and Jones County deserters. Company F of the 26th Mississippi Infantry, stationed in Ellisville since the previous August for the purpose of "arresting and guarding deserters, stragglers, absentees, and conscripts," engaged in several skirmishes with deserters and "Torys" during its stay. By far the worst occurred between fifteen Confederate soldiers and thirty or forty "armed and organized" deserters at Parker's farm. Military reports confirm Tom Knight's statement that one soldier was killed and two others "severely wounded" during that battle.[51]

Ethel Knight did not criticize the "good women" of "wide repute" who assisted the Knight band, but she did neglect to mention that Sally Parker was a member of the Collins family. Identifying Parker's family ties would have reminded Ethel's readers that entire neighborhoods, not individual

The Leaf River, intersection of Covington and Jones Counties. This was the site of
Deserters' Den, hideout of the Knight Company during the Civil War. Author's
photograph.

outlaw men, opposed the Confederacy. Although Ethel recognized that the
Knight Company provided a government of sorts for people living in war-
ravaged communities, she blamed it for inflicting most of the devastation.
Whereas Tom Knight linked the band to the community by emphasizing
its protection of women and children from pillaging Confederate cavalrymen, Ethel insisted that the deserters themselves were the worst pillagers of
the good citizens of Jones County.[52]

Women's support for the Knight Company reinforced Tom Knight's
image of its men as brave defenders of innocent dependents. Thus, for the
opposite reason that Ethel erased Sally Parker's family connections from
Echo of the Black Horn, so also did Tom alter Alzade Courtney's marital status
in his book. After interviewing ninety-seven-year-old "Mrs. Courtney," he
assured readers that she remembered Newt Knight, Jasper Collins, and
William W. Sumrall as "good men" who protected poor women against
the depredations of Confederate cavalry. Perhaps Tom did not know that
Courtney was Alzade's maiden name and that she had given birth to three
children after separating from her husband in 1862 (she divorced James
McGee in 1868; by 1880 she had returned to using the surname Courtney). If he did know, he dared not share that information with readers.
Female allies of the Knight band must appear only as widows, wives, and
mothers, not as single women like Alzade who lived outside the traditional
family setting. If Sally Parker's support raised the status of deserters to that
of respectable family men, Alzade Courtney's threatened to lower it.[53]

Thus where readers might have gained insight into the war's impact on a woman who lived outside the boundaries of a nuclear household, they were encouraged instead to focus on the heroism of the deserter band. Yet, eager to present his father as a friend of the poor, Tom nevertheless revealed the depth of Courtney's suffering during the war. She had "plowed and hoed many a day to make an honest living," he wrote, and once endured the harassment of a cavalryman who demanded to know "where is the man that has been plowing here?" Only after the soldier walked the grounds and inspected her footprints did he accept that she had no man to care for her.[54]

Like Alzade Courtney, Cornelia Coleman, daughter of the murdered Tom Coleman, shared company with the Knight band during the war. By 1860 she and her brothers lived with their aging grandmother Mary Coleman. Although seventeen-year-old Sil and thirteen-year-old Nobe Coleman were too young for military service, they enjoyed the excitement and male comradery that the Knight Company offered. In later years Cornelia would regale her grandchildren with stories of how she ministered to the Knight band as a teenager. She especially remembered riding her horse across the Leaf River to the deserters' camp, holding food prepared for her brothers high above her head as the horse swam.[55]

White women such as Cornelia Coleman, Alzade Courtney, Sally Parker, and Sally Delancy were the most obvious allies of Confederate deserters, but the more clandestine networks of deserters included slaves, who proved to be invaluable sources of food and information. In one of many fanciful conversations in Echo of the Black Horn, Ethel had Newt Knight's pro-Confederate uncle shame him for "bein' fed by the Niggers." She praised "faithful" slaves like Willis Dixon and "Uncle" Isom Benson for being "thrilled" to serve as substitutes for "their white friends" in the Confederate Army, but she dismissed those who collaborated with Newt as fearful or "too stupid to understand the purpose he had in mind." In Ethel's world of fatherly, benevolent slaveholders, it was unthinkable that the "noble gentlemen of the colored race" would identify their interests with deserters.[56]

When questioned about the Civil War by WPA interviewers, however, many former slaves recalled their ties to deserters. Jeff Rayford described a scene on the Pearl River that could as easily have occurred on the nearby Leaf River. "I cooked and carried many a pan of food to these men in Pearl River swamp," remembered Rayford. One deserter became a regular customer, in fact. As the slave walked after dark along a path beside the swamp, the deserter "would step out from behind a tree and say: 'Here Jeff,' and I would hand it to him and run back to the house."[57]

The WPA interviewer of Henri Necaise, a Creole slave from Pass Christian, was confused when Necaise described communities of men, women, and children at war among themselves instead of patiently awaiting the return of warring men from distant battlefields. When he described how he had delivered food during the war "to feed the womens and chilluns dat was fightin'," the interviewer interjected with "you mean their men [that] were fighting?" The interviewer's ignorance of the home front amused Necaise, who replied, "You make me laugh! . . . Some of [the men] was fightin' an' some was a runnin' and hidin'."[58]

The slave of most importance to the Knight Company, of course, was Rachel Knight. To erase the specter of interracial mixing, Tom Knight ignored her role altogether, but Ethel Knight reveled in bringing it before the public. Drawing on common white stereotypes about black women—particularly light-skinned women—she turned Rachel into the female counterpart of the beastly black male rapist of white Southern lore, the Jezebel who reduced white men to their basest levels of instinct. Titillating her readers with a kind of racist "folk pornography," Ethel claimed that Newt urged Rachel to "satisfy the evil pleasures" of his men. She then described "orgies, ghastly in obscenity, where Rachel and another black slave woman writhed and twisted their naked bodies in eerie dances, to the applause of the Deserters. Where fiddling and dancing went on for hours, undisturbed, . . . where there was feasting, drinking and pleasure. Where booze-crazed, prurient, sex-mad men indulged in fornication, and evil pleasures of a hideous nature." Passages such as this contributed mightily to Ethel's subversion of Tom's tale of white male heroism into a saga not only of murder and mayhem but also illicit interracial sexual relations.[59]

It is true that Rachel engaged in sexual relations with at least one white man during the war, for in March 1864 she gave birth to white-skinned Fannie. The fact that sexual relations occurred between white men and black women during the Civil War (and long before), however, should not obscure other important aspects of collaboration between slaves and deserters in Jones County. Ethel Knight blamed Rachel for infecting the slave quarters with dreams of liberation and claimed that Newt made Rachel an ally after learning from other slaves that she possessed "great powers" as a conjure woman. Certainly he valued her access to food and information. The two allegedly struck a bargain: she would spy for the deserters and supply them with food in return for his promise to work for the freedom of all African Americans.[60]

The assistance of women and slaves became ever more crucial to the Knight Company in 1864, when the Confederacy sent special troops into the Piney Woods region. The first deaths of band members at the hands of Confederate cavalry occurred early that year. Newt Knight recorded that

Reputed to be Rachel Knight, accomplice of the Knight Band and companion to Newt Knight. Photograph courtesy of Dorothy Knight Marsh.

Tapley Bynum was killed "on picket" at Tallahoma Creek, but family members recall that he was shot in his own front yard on January 10, 1864, after he had slipped home to visit his wife and newborn daughter. Also killed between January and February 1864 was John H. Harper, whose maimed feet made him an easy mark for Confederate soldiers. His military records note that he was "killed by Captain Bryan's Cavalry in Jones County, Mississippi."[61]

The inner civil war rapidly escalated during the early months of 1864, and documents support Ethel Knight's assertion that during this period, "the Company made elaborate plans to take over Jones County." On January 28 ten citizens from southeastern Smith County advised Governor Clark that there were at least three hundred well-armed deserters in neighboring Jones County. The petitioners pleaded for imposition of a "strong force" from outside to prevent their being "plundered" of all "moveable property."[62]

Interviewed by the WPA during the 1930s, J. C. Andrews, who operated a mill and a gin near the Jasper and Jones County border during the war, recalled that early 1864 was a time when "deserters brought terror into the hearts of people who sympathized with the Confederacy." In a letter to Confederate secretary of war James Seddon dated March 3, 1864, Dabney

Maury emphasized that Jones's deserters were well armed and five hundred strong. "They have been seizing Government stores," he wrote, "killing our people, and have actually made prisoners of and paroled officers of the Confederate army." That same day Lieut. Gen. Leonidas Polk complained to Gen. Samuel Cooper of the "weakness and inefficiency exhibited by the agents of the Bureau of Conscription," citing the bands of conscripts and deserters gathered in Jones and surrounding counties as evidence of the bureau's failure to keep order. Estimating the number of deserters in that region at several hundred, he reported that they had "killed the officer in charge of the work of conscription and dispersed and captured his supporting force." These reports explain why, around March 1864, Jasper Collins's father-in-law, John H. Powell, left Jones County once and for all.[63]

Officials who attempted to enforce tax-in-kind laws were especially targeted by deserters during March. In an obvious reference to the Knight Company, Polk described the deserters' recent "raid into Paulding," the county seat of Jasper, where they looted the government's tax-in-kind warehouse. In 1921 Newt Knight proudly admitted to Meigs Frost that his men loaded five wagons with corn, some of which they distributed among Paulding's poor Irish population before returning to Jones County. On March 21 Jones County court clerk E. M. Devall proclaimed the county incapable of collecting taxes, explaining to Governor Clark that deserters had held a meeting, and "they resolved not to pay any tax neither state, county, nor confederate."[64]

A few days later Capt. W. J. Bryant, post quartermaster of the seventh district, echoed Clerk Devall's complaints to Maj. James Hamilton, controlling quartermaster for tax-in-kind policies, when he described how deserters had chased the tax officials out of Jones County. Not only had deserters stopped "government agents from driving stock out of the county," but, reported Sheriff Devall to the governor, they had "ambushed, shot, and killed dead" two men assigned to collect stock to meet tax-in-kind demands.[65]

At this point Confederate officials determined that local units were inadequate to the task of controlling deserters. In March and April 1864 the families of Jones, Covington, and Smith Counties would find themselves the subject of an intense campaign—the first led by Col. Henry Maury, the second by Col. Robert Lowry—during which the Confederacy delivered its most devastating attacks on the region's communities of deserters.

For now, these were heady times for the Knight Company. Jones County Confederate officials William Fairchild, Nat "Matt" Kilgore, and William McGilvery were all reported murdered by deserters in early 1864. By late

March Confederate leaders themselves realized that they were battling intricate community networks, not merely "treasonous" men. But Maddie Bush remembered the Knight Company's near-takeover of the county with fondness: "These fellows that cried to secede were afraid that the others [deserters] would kill them; so they left," he said. "There was no sheriff, assessor, or tax collector." Perhaps it would "go down in history," mused Bush, "that Newt Knight declared this the 'Free State of Jones.' "[66]

[Lowry] pursued a vigorous policy, but the
condition of the community required it. Terror
was struck among them.—Anonymous
Confederate officer, May 3, 1864

[Lowry] hanged some of my men he had no
right to hang.—Newt Knight, March 20, 1921

Chapter Six

The Free State
Turned Upside Down

Colonel Lowry's
Confederate Raid
on Jones County

In the days surrounding April 15, 1864, several deadly confrontations erupted on the borders of Jones and Covington Counties, near the Leaf River, as the Knight Company clashed with cavalry led by Col. Robert Lowry. By the time the skirmishes ended, one cavalryman had been killed and ten deserters "summarily executed" by the cavalry. Although all of the deaths have been described in various accounts of the clash, the gruesome killing of Newt's cousin Benjamin Franklin Knight has become legendary. The story of Ben's death is yet another of many folktales and ghost stories that grew out of the inner war that divided neighbors and families in Piney Woods Mississippi during the Civil War. Contrasting versions of his death represent competing views about the Free State of Jones itself.[1]

The infamous Lowry raids of April 1864 delivered the strongest blow yet against the Knight Company. Furthermore, they came on the heels of a similar raid led by Col. Henry Maury of the 15th Confederate Cavalry Regiment of Mobile. Confederate leaders first sent Colonel Maury into Jones County after learning that deserters there controlled county government by a combination of consent and terror. On February 7, 1864, Lieutenant General Polk advised Gen. Dabney H. Maury that the "lawless banditti" of Jones must "be dealt with in the most summary manner" and directed him to send his kinsman Henry Maury and five hundred troops into the county. Colonel Maury left Mobile for Jones County on March 2, 1864, and began his assault on deserters there three days later in a battle with the Knight Company at Big Creek Church.[2]

Although Colonel Maury found the Jones County deserters "in open rebellion" and "defiant at the outset," he reported on March 12, 1864, that his men had restored order. Deserters were under control, he insisted, but he acknowledged that "some few scattered outlaws are still lurking about in the swamps and will have to be hunted out with dogs." He estimated that the total number of "resident deserters" was never higher than 150, but he admitted that they were occasionally augmented by deserters from Perry and Covington Counties who wanted to "help to whip the cavalry." He claimed that his raid had left fewer than twenty men lying out in the woods of Jones, although deserters "brag that they will get Yankee aid and return."[3]

On March 17 Lieutenant General Polk reported to Gen. Samuel Cooper that Colonel Maury had succeeded in quashing the deserters of Jones County. Indeed, J. C. Andrews remembered a Saturday morning when he witnessed the execution of several deserters in Jones County. Recalling that several members of the Knight band "were all loaded on a wagon and driven to a large oak tree near Erratta [Errata] on the old St. Stevens Trade Road," he described how a detachment of Confederate cavalry tied the men to the tree limb, then ordered the wagon driven away, leaving the men's bodies swinging in air. They hung there for days, said Andrews, until their wives came and cut them down.[4]

Despite the confident assurances of Confederate officers that they had put an end to anti-Confederate resistance, the self-proclaimed Southern Yankees remained defiant. On March 29 Capt. W. Wirt Thomson lamented the "deplorable" state of affairs in southern and southeastern Mississippi to Secretary of War James Seddon, describing the region's deserter bands as "so perfect" in their organization that "in a few hours large bodies of them can be collected at any given point prepared to attempt almost anything." Ben Sumrall later boasted that the cavalry failed to defeat the deserters because the deserters could attack Confederate camps and then melt back into the swamps, "where they could not be followed."[5]

The men and women of Jones County had barely recovered from Colo-
nel Maury's raid on their communities when they faced the forces of Col.
Robert Lowry of the 6th Mississippi Infantry. On March 22, in the wake of
Maury's failure to quell desertion in the Piney Woods, Polk reported to
President Davis that Lowry and his troops had been sent into Smith County
"to break up an organization . . . which has held three public meetings."
Lowry's men would conduct raids in Jones County as well, perhaps in
response to Capt. W. Wirt Thomson's report to Secretary of War Seddon
that Jones County deserters had boldly raised a federal flag over the courthouse. Thomson also informed Seddon that organized squads of forty to
fifty men were working one another's fields in Jones County, swearing to
"raise crops and defend themselves from cavalry this season." He predicted
that the cavalry would never dislodge these men without sending in "well-
drilled infantry troops in large forces."[6]

Growing fears of collaboration between deserter bands and the Union
Army also influenced Confederate authorities' decision to send Colonel
Lowry into the region. Members of the several bands of deserters in the
Jones County region apparently had frequent contact with one another and
moved back and forth between bands when convenient. On March 29
W. Wirt Thomson reported rumors that "Yankees are frequently among"
the Jones County deserters. Nine days later, and only one week before the
Lowry raids, Daniel P. Logan warned Provost Marshal Major J. C. Denis that
"large numbers" of Jones County deserters "have gone down Pearl River to
and near Honey Island where they exist in some force . . . openly boasting
of their being in communication with the Yankees."[7]

According to Newt Knight, during this period his company continually
sought connections with the Union Army. He recounted how Jasper Collins
had traveled without success to Memphis and Vicksburg to seek the company's recruitment into the Union Army. Newt also recalled that "Johnny
Rebs busted up the party they sent to swear us in," explaining that a
company of Union forces sent to recruit men of the Knight Company was
waylaid by Confederate forces in Rocky Creek. After that, he said, "I sent a
courier to the federal commander at New Orleans. He sent us 400 rifles.
The Confederates captured them." Newt concluded that "we'll all die guerrillas, I reckon. Never could break through the rebels to jine the Union
army."[8]

There is no direct evidence to support Newt's claim that the Knight
Company sought to join the Union, but there are numerous corroborating
statements. On February 29, 1864, just days after Union general William T. Sherman's successful campaign in Meridian, Mississippi, and just
as Lieutenant General Polk prepared to send Colonel Maury into Jones

County, Sherman informed Maj. Gen. Henry Halleck that "a declaration of independence" had been issued "by certain people who were trying to avoid Southern conscription, and lie out in the swamps. I promised them countenance, and encouraged them to organization for mutual defense."[9]

In 1904 Jasper Collins confirmed to Goode Montgomery that Newt had sent him to Memphis to seek Union recognition of their company. Furthermore, during the war Confederate leaders themselves described Jones County deserters as both outlaws and unionists. Lieut. Gen. Leonidas Polk reported to President Jefferson Davis that Jones's deserters called themselves Southern Yankees. Polk seemed to accept the label at face value, but what Confederate leaders did not accept was the legitimacy of unionist claims. Just as surely as deserters did not accept the legitimacy of the Confederate government, Confederate leaders considered deserters guilty of treason.[10]

Colonel Lowry considered the Knight Company's punishment of Confederate soldiers with "death or banishment from home" to be outright murder as well as treason. Shortly before crossing from Smith County into Jones, he told Lieut. Col. T. M. Jack that the "most rigid and summary punishment is necessary to correct these evils." He and his men lost no time in arresting and executing deserters. Just as surely as Confederate leaders considered deserters guilty of treason, the Knight Company and its supporters considered Lowry's executions of its soldiers to be murder.[11]

In a letter published in the Mobile Evening News on May 3, 1864, less than a month after the raids, one of Colonel Lowry's men described the series of executions carried out in the Jones County region. Explaining that the "condition of the community required it," the officer proudly proclaimed that "terror was struck" on the borders of Covington and Jones Counties. Among those executed were Ben Knight and Sil Coleman, who, he claimed, had participated in an ambush on "another party of our boys" near the home of Newton Knight, just days after a sniper attacked three of Lowry's men in neighboring Covington County.[12]

On April 15, according to the officer, Lowry's men "promptly executed" Daniel Reddoch, whom they identified as the sniper who had ambushed them. When his companion, Tucker Gregg, turned and ran from them, they shot him to death. They then unleashed their hounds on Ben Knight and Sil Coleman, who were run down and hanged from the same tree. The officer expressed no regret over executing Sil, despite referring to him as a "lad," and did not mention his thirteen-year-old brother Nobe, although the cavalry allegedly hanged him as well. Seventy-six-year-old Mary Coleman's reaction to the brutal deaths of her grandsons went unrecorded, although they lived with her in 1860. A descendant remembered hearing that the boys' sixteen-year-old sister Cornelia assumed the task of cutting their lifeless bodies from the hanging tree.[13]

The death of Ben Knight has been invested with religious meaning over the years. In an article published by the *Jackson Daily News* in 1974, Ruby Jordan recalled the story of his death as related by her uncle, Ben Graves. Jordan remained true to her uncle's version of Ben's death, told almost fifty years earlier at a community meeting in Hebron, Mississippi. At that gathering seventy-five-year-old Graves recalled his Civil War experiences. His memories were not those of a soldier, however, but of a twelve-year-old boy living in a war-torn community near the Leaf River.[14]

Graves remembered awakening one morning to his brother's insistence that he had heard guns firing in the night. Later that day he learned that twenty-seven-year-old Ben Knight, a neighbor, upon hearing a noise had arisen from bed to find a group of Confederate cavalry gathered near his home. Panic-stricken, Ben ran "out through them with his night clothes on." A cavalryman shot at him as he ran down the road to Newton Knight's house. Breathlessly Ben crossed the bridge that separated his home from Newt's, only to find his cousin gone. Instead Ben found another cousin, seventeen-year-old Sil Coleman, asleep at Newt's house. He woke Sil up, and together they ran to nearby Mason's Creek, where they hid in the swamp.[15]

Graves then described the cavalry's capture of Ben, who after being run down by bloodhounds, was "torn up pretty bad" and craved water "like wounded men always do." When Ben begged his captors for water, they refused and instead prepared to hang him. He then called on a merciful God to fill his grave with cool water. Graves swore that "when they dug the grave right up on top of the hill from where they hung him and Sil Coleman, water run into the grave. I have heard people who saw it say so."[16]

The horrified community of mostly Baptists and Methodists converted Ben's burial into a sacred baptism that gave meaning to the otherwise senseless loss of a young life. A decade after Graves told the story, it had become ever more vivid and detailed, and Ben ever more Christlike. In 1936 WPA writer Addie West reported that when the cavalry denied Ben water before they executed him, he prayed to the Lord, "Forgive them, for they know not what they do." Former Knight slave Martha Wheeler told West that when her husband helped the family bury him, he witnessed firsthand the water that "gushed up. . . . Two men could not keep it dipped as fast as it ran in." As West noted, "All old people knew this for a fact," and there "is awe in each voice that repeats the story."[17]

Ethel Knight disputed Martha Wheeler's claim that her husband, a slave, helped to bury Ben. It was important to Ethel that slaves not bury Ben Knight, whom she insisted was not even a deserter. She instead applied Jim Crow principles to the Civil War scene: white folks alone prepared the grave of the "innocent soldier," soon to be baptized by a regenerative spring of clear water. "The Negroes were too superstitious to be of much assistance," she wrote, "and it took persuasion to get any help out of them."[18]

Hoping to banish forever the notion that Newt Knight's rebellion had widespread community support, Ethel reshaped Ben Knight into a loyal Confederate soldier. In her version Ben was merely taking an afternoon walk to visit relatives in another neighborhood, not furtively darting through cavalry in the middle of the night to reach Newt's home. Nor did Ethel place Ben in the company of his cousin Sil Coleman at the time of his capture, claiming instead that Ben was ignorant of skirmishes between deserters and Confederate cavalry. Most importantly, she claimed that he was "home on furlough, and carried his credentials in his pocket" on the afternoon of April 15, 1864. Her Ben Knight was killed only because the cavalry mistook him for his lawless cousin, Newton Knight, to whom he bore an "unfortunate resemblance." In essence, she portrayed Newt as Ben's evil twin, ultimately responsible for his tragic death.[19]

Having established Ben's innocence, Ethel described his hanging, building on earlier accounts to create her own version of events. She elaborated on Graves's description of Ben's torture, describing how bloodhounds "bit and tore his legs as the soldiers dragged him mercilessly by the neck to the place of hanging." But she reshaped the story to present the Confederacy in the best light possible. In Ethel's version Colonel Lowry silenced soldiers who jeered the captured Ben, granted Ben a last chance to pray, and removed the rope from his neck just before he died. Finally, Lowry and his men became "ashy-faced and silent" when they discovered furlough papers in the dead man's coat pocket.[20]

By placing furlough papers in Ben's pocket, Ethel enabled "loyal" white Mississippians, especially loyal Knights such as she, to mourn his death yet deplore and disown the outlaw Newt Knight. There is solid evidence, however, that Ben Knight deserted the 7th Battalion and was a member of the Knight Company at the time of his death. The Confederate cavalry certainly had no doubts that he was in cahoots with the band of deserters they sought to vanquish.[21]

One day after executing Ben Knight and Sil Coleman (and possibly Nobe Coleman), Lowry's cavalry captured Jim and Tom Ates, sons of Frances Ates, and Tom and Daniel Whitehead, sons of John and Mary Ann (Knight) Whitehead. The Ates brothers had deserted the 7th Battalion, and all four men had joined the Knight Company. All were hanged the day after their capture in the village of Gitano. Col. William Brown, one of Lowry's raiders, explained to Governor Clark that "two brothers named Ates and two others named Whitehead" were found "guilty of desertion and armed resistance and were sentenced to death by hanging before a military court." In the Jones County region, wrote Brown, their deaths "made ten who have forfeited their lives for treason." About a week later the cavalry visited the Whitehead home and seized a third brother, Noel, as he lay sleeping. They "carried him over to Mount Carmel and hung him," remembered Ben Graves; "I saw them as they passed on their horses."[22]

These were now perilous times for the Knight band, and they required ever more vigilant support from slaves and women. According to Dickie Knight's descendants, Colonel Lowry seized Dickie's father, William H. Knight, and William's slave Joe Hatten, while they were grinding corn at Knight's Mill in the village of Gitano. As was common, the cavalry detained the aged father in order to force the deserter son in from the swamps. Old William was then forced to send his slave Joe to find Dickie and tell him that if he did not surrender, Lowry would hang his father. Until the end of his long life, Joe Hatten enjoyed telling the story of how Dickie sat silently on a fence rail for a long time, contemplating what to do after he gave him the message. Finally he told Joe, "You go back and tell the officer to just go ahead and hang Pap. He's getting to be an old man now, and they won't knock him out of many years. But they may knock me out of a good many! We are building a boat to go to New Orleans to join the Yankees." Joe decided not to deliver Dickie's message to Colonel Lowry. "I did not go back," he said. "I just went home!" William Knight was not hanged, and Dickie eventually made it to New Orleans.[23]

As did slaves, white women increasingly participated in life-and-death confrontations between deserters and cavalry. Both Tom Knight and Ethel Knight described how the Knight Company ambushed a group of cavalry by arranging a dance to be held for the soldiers at old Levi Valentine's home. The cavalry expected to hear good fiddling and to dance with pretty girls, but at a prearranged moment the Knight band sneaked in while the young women ran out the back door. Killed in the confrontation that followed, according to Tom and Ethel, were two Confederate soldiers and one Knight band member.[24]

According to Ben Sumrall's memory in 1936, community support for the deserters was so great that "many more of the Confederate Soldiers [than deserters] were killed in trying to capture them." Col. William Brown, who was in Jones County in May 1864, also called attention to the strong community support for the deserters. In a letter to Governor Clark, he took note of women's important role in the uprising that he and Lowry's men sought to quell. In remarkably sympathetic words, he explained to the governor that "among the women," who feared starvation and were tired of working the fields without the help of their menfolk, "there is great reluctance to give up their husbands and brothers." That reluctance was especially noticeable among several women who headed their own households. Frances Ates, Lucinda Todd, Susannah Valentine, Catherine Welch, and Ali Whitehead all harbored sons who deserted the Confederate Army. Sally Parker's son, George W. Walters, had died serving the Confederate Army. Sally Delancy's son Howell was briefly AWOL after the siege of Vicksburg but returned to service and received special detail as a nurse at French's Division Hospital at Lockart Station, Mississippi.[25]

Despite Newt's alleged murder of his sister Martha's husband, she too became an ally of the band during the war and married one of its members, Joseph Richard "Dick" Yawn, in 1867. In later years Martha remembered her encounter with a group of Confederate soldiers while taking a basket of food, hidden beneath corn shucks, to the Knight Company's hideout. She successfully deflected the soldiers' suspicions by scattering the shucks on the ground while calling out to the hogs. On yet another occasion, she told her children, she and Newt escaped approaching soldiers when he directed her to hide in a corncrib while he fled. Ordered by her brother to remain hidden until he returned for her, she was stuck in the corncrib for most of the day.[26]

According to Ethel Knight, at least one Confederate widow, Ellafair Chain, shifted her support to the Knight Company after her husband's death. Unfortunately Ethel provided no clues about the source of Ellafair's alliance with the band, but she may have been the widow described by Newt Knight in 1921 as having provided ammunition to the Knight band because her daughter was being courted by one of his men. Ethel revealed nothing about Ellafair's family connections, instead describing an almost mythical figure who had fought beside her Confederate husband on Civil War battlefields, carrying "ammunition in her checkered apron" until he was killed. After the death of her husband, she supposedly walked back to her home on Big Creek and provided aid to deserters. Ethel told one story in which Ellafair braved the swamps to warn deserters of an impending cavalry attack. Confronted by a cavalryman, she quickly dissembled. "Have you seen anything of my stray heifer?" she asked the soldier. When the soldier replied that he had not, Chain turned in the other direction and then headed straight for the deserters' camp to warn them that cavalry were in the area.[27]

After meeting several women of Jones County, Colonel Brown concluded that women's disloyalty emanated from abuse by the Confederate Army. In sympathetic yet condescending language, he described the suffering that caused Piney Woods women to "doubt" that the Confederacy was a true government. Praising them as "the working part of the population," he described one widow's desperate need of cotton and woolen cards and even enclosed a sample of her homemade cards in his letter. Her "workmanship" and "ingenuity," he said, compared favorably to that of the Yankees.[28]

Brown attributed abuse of women to "several small commands of cavalry sent into their country" earlier. Citing previous cavalries' "improper shooting, robbing, stealing about the houses, cutting cloth from the looms, taking horses, etc.," Brown assured the governor that Colonel Lowry and his men had conducted themselves "properly and all have endeavored to be civil and kind to citizens." He thought the women could be brought around by delivery of "a few wagonloads of corn."[29]

When Colonel Brown described Confederate abuses of women, he might have been thinking of Nancy Walters, whose story later appeared in Tom Knight's book. Nancy and her husband, Daniel, had two sons, Archibald and Merada, who joined the Knight band and, later, the Union Army in New Orleans. Like most wives during wartime, Nancy was home alone when Confederate cavalry paid her a visit, more than likely because they knew that she was the mother of two deserters.[30]

The Walters's youngest son, Calvin, only four or five years old in 1864, recalled to Tom that the cavalry—"the most men he ever saw"—rode up one day and hitched their horses to his family's shade trees. With his father gone, he and his mother watched fearfully from inside the house while the men looted the family's corncrib, killed and cleaned their chickens, and then raided the smokehouse for meat "and sliced it up and left big chunks of it in the lane, wollered up in the dirt." For Nancy the final insult came when a cavalryman saddled up the family's best mare as the men prepared to leave. Few abuses were resented more by farm people than the cavalry's impressment of their horses. Nancy allegedly burst from the house, grabbed a fence rail, and knocked the man down. Brandishing the rail over the dazed man, she threatened to kill him if he did not leave. Calvin remembered that "he took her at her word and left."[31]

Despite the obvious value of Nancy Walters's story for Tom Knight as anti-Confederate propaganda, it also demonstrated that women were frequently forced to defend their homes without the aid of any man. Furthermore, as often as not they were forced to defend the men. Newt Knight, for example, praised women for poisoning Lowry's bloodhounds. "Those ladies sure helped us a lot," he told Meigs Frost. "They had 44 bloodhounds after us, those boys and General Robert Lowry's men. But 42 of them hounds just naturally died. They'd get hongry and some of the ladies, friends of ours, would feed 'em. And they'd die. Strange, wasn't it?" The women further confounded the hounds by sprinkling polecat musk and red pepper on the trails leading to deserters' hideouts. No reference to Rachel Knight appeared in Frost's interview of Newt, but Ethel Knight claimed it was Rachel who taught white women how to throw off the scent of bloodhounds, suggesting that she learned the practice from slaves active in the Underground Railroad.[32]

By the end of May 1864, in the aftermath of Lowry's raids, deserters had either retreated to the swamps, floated down the Mississippi River to New Orleans, or rejoined the Confederate Army. Those who fled to New Orleans included Prentice Bynum, William Holifield, Willis B. Jones, Dickie Knight, Elijah Welborn Laird, Archibald Walters, Merada Walters, Richard T. Welch, William E. Welborn, and Tolbert Welborn, all of whom joined the Union Army's 1st Regiment of the New Orleans Infantry.[33]

Deserters who were captured by Colonel Lowry's men escaped execution by enlisting in or returning to the Confederate Army. According to Newt Knight's 1870 roster, most of the captured men were from the Collins, Valentine, Welch, and Welborn families. They included Simeon Collins and sons, Matt, Ben, and Morgan; brothers John Ira and Richard Valentine and their cousins, Patrick and Martin Valentine; brothers Timothy and Harrison Welch and their cousin, William M. Welch; and two Welborn brothers, Younger Jr. and William Turner.[34]

Only months after fighting Confederate forces in an inner civil war, the captured men were now forced to fight Yankees. Those who reenlisted in the Confederate Army were soon marching with Gen. Joseph E. Johnston's Army of Tennessee in its Georgia campaign, about to participate in the Confederate Army's greatest setback since Vicksburg. On July 3, 1864, Merida Coats, Simeon Collins, Matt Collins, James Eulin, Drew Gilbert, Martin Valentine, Patrick Valentine, and William M. Welch were captured again, this time by General Sherman's army near Kennesaw Mountain. All were transferred to Yankee prisons, where they remained for the duration of the war.[35]

Lowry's raid convinced even several noncaptive members or friends of the Knight band to rejoin the Confederacy. William Bryan Valentine rejoined the 7th Battalion and was captured along with his cousins, Martin and Patrick Valentine, at Kennesaw Mountain. Jesse and Francis M. Herrington, who also served General Johnston's forces in Georgia, were captured on June 19, 1864, near Marietta, then transferred to Camp Morton, Indiana. First Lieut. Thomas J. Huff rejoined the 7th Battalion only to desert a final time while attached to Sears's brigade of the Army of Tennessee near Atlanta. Huff was reported AWOL on September 16, 1864, and was subsequently dropped from the rolls of his company and regiment by a Confederate examining board.[36]

Several Jones County POWs who were sent to Northern prison camps attempted to gain their freedom by proclaiming loyalty to the Union, but only Francis Herrington and Wilson L. Jones succeeded. William M. Welch, William Bryan Valentine, and Martin Valentine told their Yankee captors that they were loyal citizens forced to join the Rebel Army, but they remained prisoners until the war ended.[37] Perhaps the most unusual POW experience was that of deserter Steven R. Whitehead, son of widow Ali Whitehead. Steven, a cousin of the three executed Whitehead brothers, was arrested in Covington County, probably during the Lowry raids. Although apparently forced back into the 7th Battalion like other captured deserters, he was discharged on August 6, 1864, by Capt. S. E. Jones, who ordered that Whitehead be released North of the Ohio River on his oath to remain there.[38]

Many men who joined the Union or Confederate armies after Lowry's raid on Jones County died from the effects of ill health. The Collins family was hit especially hard. In August 1864 forty-year-old Riley died while serving the Union Army in New Orleans. His forty-six-year-old brother Simeon died soon after his release from Camp Morton prison in May 1865, perhaps from the lingering effects of a wound sustained during Lowry's raid. Peggy Bynum, sister of Riley and Simeon Collins, lost her son-in-law, William H. Mauldin, as well as her brothers. Others from the Jones County region who died as Union soldiers in New Orleans included Archibald and Merada Walters, Younger Welborn Sr.'s son Tolbert, and James W. Lee. Among those captured by Yankees in Georgia, forty-four-year-old Drew Gilbert and twenty-five-year-old James Eulin died of disease before the war ended.[39]

Despite the havoc wreaked by Colonel Lowry and his men, including their decimation of the Knight Company, core members Newt Knight, Jasper Collins, William Wesley Sumrall, and James Morgan Valentine were among approximately twenty deserters who remained uncaptured, unrepentant, and a potent force in Jones County. On June 14, 1864, only two months after Lowry's raid, conscript officer Benjamin C. Duckworth described to Governor Clark a county so lawless that "if a man is found dead the Civil authorities pays no attention to it any more than if it was a dog." Deserters, though "thined out," remained undisturbed by the county's justices of the peace, constables, and commissioners, all of whom "stays at home and attends to there own business [while] public business is unobserved." Fearful himself, Duckworth implored the governor to "retain" the contents of his letter lest he face retaliation by the deserters, underscoring the continued powerful presence of the Knight Company in the Leaf River area.[40]

Despite Lowry's raids, a "free state" of lawlessness still prevailed in Jones County. On July 12, 1864, the *Natchez Courier* reported that "the county of Jones, State of Mississippi, has seceded from the State and formed a Government of their own, both military and civil."[41] As late as August 14, 1864, Brig. Gen. W. L. Brandon reported to Gen. Dabney Maury that a "Yankee lieutenant is now in Jones, entertained and protected by deserters." Two weeks later, with October elections of county officials approaching, Representative Amos Deason and four other prominent Confederate citizens petitioned Governor Clark to maintain Capt. M. H. Barkley's company of home guard because loyal "citizens, their families and property would be in eminent danger [from deserters] in their absence."[42]

During those elections, the Knight Company later charged, "rebel cavalry" guarded the ballot boxes in northwestern Jones County to prevent pro-Union citizens from voting. Local Confederate leaders admitted that cavalry guards arrested four deserters who attempted to vote, but they insisted that pro-Confederate candidates would have won anyway. In any case the three new officers shared important ties with other pro-Confederate families. William Hood, elected probate judge, was distantly kin to Amos McLemore and married to the daughter of Willis Windham, one of Jones's largest slaveholders and a staunch supporter of the Confederacy. Hansford D. Dossett, elected sheriff, was a wealthy land speculator who had served in the 27th Mississippi Infantry with Amos McLemore. Allan P. McGill, elected clerk of the court, was a thirty-three-year-old bachelor who lived with his parents in a household that included four slaves, one of whom Allen owned in his own name.[43]

In the months following the elections, Confederate cavalry were back in Jones County hunting for deserters. Newt recorded that his company encountered "A Lot of Rebels" sometime in November 1864 at Reddoch's Ferry on the Leaf River and that, in fact, they captured and paroled twenty-one of the Confederates.[44] In December the Knight Company battled cavalry at both Big Creek and Allen Gunter's farm near the Leaf River. Before the day ended, Samuel G. Owens, the grandson of old Tom Sullivan of Sullivan's Hollow, had been badly wounded. Joe Gunter, Alpheus Knight's brother-in-law and a member of the Knight band, was captured and hanged or, as some Gunter descendants claim, shot in front of his wife, Selena, and his children. One descendant further reported that after the soldiers killed Joe, they forced Selena to "build a fire under the wash pot, killed all her chickens, and forced her to cook for them before they made their departure."[45]

Perhaps the most frequently told story of these final six months of the Civil War is that of Alpheus Knight and Mary Powell's wedding party, which took place in late December 1864 as deserters and cavalry skirmished. On that day infant Polly Knight survived the crossfire of bullets exchanged by Confederate cavalrymen and deserters. All accounts agree that the shoot-out occurred on the day after Alpheus and Mary's wedding, as guests enjoyed a postnuptial breakfast. Alpheus and Newt's cousin, Dickie Knight, was absent from the group, but his wife, Mary; their baby daughter, Polly; and Mary's fourteen-year-old sister, Martha joined Newt, Alpheus, and Alpheus's bride, Mary, in running for their lives that day.[46]

Newt Knight described the event to Meigs Frost in 1921 when he was over eighty years old. Subsequently Tom Knight and Ethel Knight embellished Newt's story to suit their own needs, although they repeated its essential elements. According to Ethel, Confederate cavalry deliberately timed its ambush to coincide with the Knight wedding in hopes of catching the deserters off guard. She agreed with Newt that a neighborhood woman had tipped off the soldiers by sending them a note through her cook, a slave woman. From there, however, Ethel digressed. First, she invested the white mistress with moral authority by describing her as a widow whose husband had died fighting for the Confederacy. She then characterized the mistress's slave cook as disloyal, claiming she showed the mistress's note to "a pale ginger colored woman" before delivering it to the cavalry. This mulatto woman (Rachel?) in turn warned the deserters' leader, Newt Knight, of the impending siege.[47]

All accounts agree that Newt then warned the six remaining members of the wedding party of the impending attack, enabling them to flee just as the cavalry bore down on them. As they took flight, Mary Knight wailed, "I can't carry this baby so fast!" This prompted Newt to take the infant from her mother's arms. Mary offered in turn to carry his gun, but Newt's solemn reply was, "Ma'am, no one carries my gun except me." Minutes later the cavalry opened fire on the Knight family. "That baby clung tighter than ever to me when the guns went off," remembered Newt. He then returned the baby to her mother and bluffed the twenty or so cavalrymen into believing that his band of deserters was nearby. "Attention battalion! Rally on the right! Forward!" he yelled. In reality, he later mused, "there wasn't no more battalion than a rabbit." No one among the wedding party was harmed that day.[48]

Newt clearly enjoyed recalling to Frost how he had outsmarted the cavalry with his boldness and cleverness, all the while protecting the community's women and children. Tom Knight, equally determined to portray his father as a brave, humane soldier, added new details to his story. In the days following the wedding crisis, he wrote, Newt and his men skinned and tanned the hide of a cavalryman's dead horse to "make shoes for the poor women and children to wear in the winter time." For Ethel, of course, it would not do for honorable Confederate soldiers to have attacked helpless women and children. She thus attributed the cavalry's retreat during the fracas to its determination "to avoid killing the women and the child" rather than to Newt's cunning trickery.[49]

Despite endless efforts by both sides to defend their masculine honor, the final battle of Jones County's inner civil war included one incident in which humor prevailed over valor. On January 10, 1865, less than two weeks after Alpheus and Mary Knight's wedding, Confederate troops allegedly returned, looking for Alpheus. When he learned that troops were en route to his home, he "crawled up the chimney fast and told Mary to make a fire fast and put the skillet on to cook." Mary did just that but became so nervous after the cavalry arrived that she continued to put "more and more wood on the fire." Meanwhile, the soldiers searched for Alpheus "under beds, all through the rooms, out in the barn, and all over the place." They did not find him, but by the time they left and Alpheus could crawl out of the fireplace, "his rear was cooked." Not only that, but once again a woman was forced to face the enemy within the confines of her own home.[50]

Perhaps it was the failing fortunes of the Confederacy in the larger war that sustained the fragmented deserter band during these final battles. In the space of only one year, Jones's pro-Union citizens moved from mourning the execution of ten of their men to learning that Mobile, one of the last Confederate cities, had surrendered to Union forces on April 12, 1865. Five days later, and despite the assassination of President Lincoln, Union general William T. Sherman met with Confederate general Joseph E. Johnston in Durham, North Carolina, to negotiate an end to the fighting. From there, events moved quickly. On April 26 General Johnston surrendered his troops. On May 10, 1865, Union forces captured Confederate president Jefferson Davis, prompting President Andrew Johnson to proclaim that the armed resistance of the "insurrectionary states" was "virtually at an end." The war was finally over.

In the first years of peace, few people used terms like "noble," or "lost cause" to describe the war. Citing the deaths of numerous Duckworth men to a Texas relative, R. C. Duckworth complained that "the war was ceartainly [sic] a curse on the American People." A political war, moreover, soon followed in its wake, as pro- and anti-Confederates vied for power during Reconstruction. Newt Knight would be at the center of this post-war struggle, for the Civil War had irrevocably reshaped his personal and political behavior.[51]

Nor did that political war ever end for some men of the Knight Company. In later life, Prentice Bynum proclaimed to his granddaughter that "no one made me do what I did. I did it because I felt that men should not be treated that way." In 1921, shortly before Newt's death, he bitterly denounced Colonel Lowry as "rough beyond reason. He hanged some of my company he had no right to hang." Newt's old unionist mentor, seventy-seven-year-old Jasper Collins, even had more chilling words for the man who had since served as Mississippi's governor but who never again visited Jones County. In 1904 he told Goode Montgomery that he would "get up on the coldest night he ever saw to kill Lowry if he knew he was passing through Jones County."[52]

We stood firm to the union when secession
swept as an avalanche over the state. For this
cause alone we have been treated as savages
instead of freemen by the rebel authorities.
—Newton Knight et al., July 15, 1865

The name of our county has become notorious
if not infamous at least to sensitive ears and
the public-spirited.—J. M. Baylis et al.,
October 16, 1865

Chapter Seven

Reconstruction and
Redemption

The Politics of Race,
Class, and Manhood
in Jones County

Although Jones County's uprising against the Confederacy was later trivial-
ized to reinforce the Lost Cause principle of a solid (white) South, it was
clearly rooted in class, kinship, and cultural conflicts that were regularly
framed by participants as a contest over honor and true manhood. This
contest continued for several years after the Civil War ended, as pro-Union
and pro-Confederate men squared off against one another on yet another
battlefield: Reconstruction politics.[1]

Although a Republican-dominated Congress forced changes in the racial and class composition of Southern political leadership during this era,
these changes were only partial and short lived. Throughout the 1870s,
Democrats such as Col. Robert Lowry, who became Mississippi's governor
in 1882, exploited white racism to deflect attention away from the economic and political issues that deeply divided whites. At the same time,

postwar Democrats condemned Civil War deserters as "bushwhackers," "Tories," and during Reconstruction, "scalawags." Furthermore, widespread poverty among plain white Southerners encouraged both Southern Democrats and Northern Republicans to view them as backward and illiterate. Like blacks, poor whites were stereotyped as barriers to progress. Finally, after Democrats had successfully "redeemed" Mississippi's government from Republican rule, they dismissed Jones County's yeoman uprising as little more than poor white mischief.[2]

The decade following the Civil War, however, brought hope to families who had supported the Knight Company during the war. In fact, the company's former "soldiers" wasted no time capitalizing on the Union Army's victory over the Confederacy. On July 15, 1865, they and their supporters petitioned provisional governor William L. Sharkey to overturn Jones County's elections in October 1864 on grounds that "rebel cavalry" had denied "loyal men" the right to vote and treated them as "savages instead of freemen."[3]

The petition, headed by the name of Newton Knight and followed by a virtual roster of men connected to the Knight Company, exhibited language reminiscent of earlier frontier yeomen of Mississippi Territory. Proclaiming their loyalty to the federal government, the petitioners assured Governor Sharkey that "we stood firm to the union when secession swept as an avalanche over the state." As "loyal American citizens and freemen," they urged the replacement of rebel candidate William Hood as probate judge by staunch unionist Vinson Collins.[4]

Governor Sharkey, a Whig unionist during the war, responded to the requests of the Knight Company by allowing dual appointments of Hood and Collins as probate judge and of Hansford D. Dossett (also elected in 1864) and Thomas J. Huff as sheriff. Sharkey's actions infuriated Jones County's former Confederate vanguard, who implored him to reconsider. In a letter dated July 26, 1865, Court Clerk Allan P. McGill disputed charges of fraud and intimidation during the 1864 elections. Two separate petitions of protest followed on July 29. Suggesting that cowardice rather than loyalty motivated the Knight Company's wartime actions, Confederate petitioners cited Sheriff Thomas J. Huff's status as an "absentee" officer and condemned the Knight Company's petition as the product of "absentee" rather than unionist influence.[5]

In the face of the Confederate Army's defeat, deserters appeared as heroes who had rebelled against an illegitimate maverick government, but as former Confederates struggled to regain their power in the postwar South, they attacked that heroic image. In a personal letter to Governor Sharkey, John M. Baylis protested the county's political shake-up by invoking an image of Knight Company men as bandits. To counter the Knight Company's image of itself as a band of brave unionist soldiers, Baylis focused on Sheriff Huff, whose desertion as an officer of the Confederate Army made him particularly vulnerable to charges of having disgraced himself. Merging images of dishonorable behavior, banditry, and anarchy, Baylis complained that Huff had "deserted from the Confederate Army in which he was an officer, returned to Jones County and united with a band of outlaws who have been engaged in murder and Pillage during the war, and who have stated frequently that they would not submit to authority of any kind."[6]

Baylis linked Judge Vinson Collins to banditry by virtue of his kinship with numerous Knight Company members. Conceding that Collins was "exempt by age from military service, nor so far as I know has he actually taken part in any of the outrages committed upon the lives and property of the citizens of Jones County," Baylis emphasized that Collins was nonetheless "by relationships and sympathy . . . heart and hand with those who have been guilty of such acts of outlawery." This emphasis on the band's lawlessness and violence further enabled Baylis to differentiate between the behavior of Knight Company members and that of many other Jones County men, including himself, who were reported AWOL during the war.[7]

Attempts by Jones County's pro- and anti-Confederate factions to smear one another dramatized the high stakes politics of the postwar South. Throughout 1865 these factions continued their inner civil war over who would control county politics. Pro-Confederate citizens seethed with anger at the initial political successes of their wartime enemies. The military appointment in 1865 of none other than Newton Knight as "commissioner to procure Relief for the destitute in a part of Jones County" no doubt galled them. After all, here was the leader of the county's most notorious band of deserters, a group dedicated to all-out war against the Confederacy, being "Mistered" and "Sired" by federal military authorities.[8]

Newt's postwar position as relief commissioner contributed to his son Tom's later representation of him as a paternalistic protector, a sort of Robin Hood of the county. As commissioner, Newt received foodstuffs from the U.S. Army station at Meridian for distribution in one of the most destitute counties in Mississippi. On July 16, 1865, Capt. and Assistant Quartermaster O. S. Coffin ordered the transfer of 2,400 pounds of bacon, 2,000 pounds of flour, 1,250 pounds of white bread, and supplies of soap, salt, and molasses from Meridian to Shubuta at government expense for pickup by "Mr. Newton Knight" or his representative. On July 21 Capt. J. Fairbanks of Raleigh asked Newt to check on the condition of a Mrs. Davis, who had been reported to Fairbanks as "being in a very destitute condition."[9]

Newton Knight, leader of the
Knight Company. Photograph
courtesy of Earle Knight.

Official letters between Newt and his superiors indicate that he was a
powerful local figure whose responsibilities had distinctly political ends.
For example, three days after Captain Fairbanks requested Newt's aid on
behalf of Mrs. Davis, he "impowered" him to rescue two children of a
freedman whose white employer (and apparent former master) was about
to leave the county with the freedman's children in his custody. Fairbanks's
order came on the heels of a report issued to Col. Samuel Thomas, assistant
commissioner of Mississippi's Freedmen's Bureau, by J. A. Hawley, subcommissioner of Mississippi's Southern District, in which Hawley detailed
the virtual reenslavement of freedpeople by their former masters. Attempt-
ing to rectify such injustices, Fairbanks in turn told Newt, "It is right that
the families be kept together and as there is no written contract between
them it is best that the two children be retained with their father."[10]

Even Tom Knight, who preferred not to publicize his father's sympathies
with blacks, made an exception when it furthered Newt's image as benevolent patriarch. He noted that Newt had once returned a freed boy "who
had belonged to Tom Mayfield" to his parents after Mayfield refused to
relinquish custody. Tom carefully explained that the legal abolition of
slavery left Newt no choice but to respect a black father's right to his own
son. Tom's description of Mayfield as "very much disappointed" by Newt's
actions probably understated the anger that many former slaveholders felt
toward him and the military government that he served.[11]

In August 1865 Commissioner Knight confronted the county's most prominent wartime rebel, former Confederate representative Amos Deason, whose home was the site of the wartime murder of Maj. Amos McLemore, allegedly by Newt himself. On July 31, 1865, Capt. H. T. Elliott ordered Newt to "sease a certain lot of wool & cloth that is in Jones Co., said to be confederate property," from Deason, a dry goods merchant. Deason apparently challenged Newt's right to impound his wool and "jeans cloth," for on August 19 Capt. A. R. M. Smith of the federal army post of Ellisville directed Newt to delay further action until "the right of property is desided by a properly authorized agent of the Treasury Department or otherwise leagly disposed of." Less than two weeks later, military authorities upheld Newt's seizure of Deason's cloth.[12]

Newt's victory humiliated Deason and must have enraged former Confederates, who struck back less than three months later. On October 16, 1865, ninety-nine citizens petitioned the Mississippi legislature to change the name of Jones County to Davis County and of Ellisville to Leesburg in honor of Confederate president Jefferson Davis and Gen. Robert E. Lee. The petitioners expressed hope that the new names would bury "so deep that the hand of time may never reserect it" Jones County's "notorious if not infamous" wartime reputation as a deserters' haven. They further requested that their individual names be recorded in the Senate and House journals of the state legislature so that future generations would be "disabused of any [notion of] participation on our part of any of its dark deeds." Heading the petition were the names of John M. Baylis and his brother, William Baylis. As one would expect, most signers came from staunchly pro-Confederate families; many, however, such as John M. Knight, Joel E. Welborn, James Gunter, and William Bynum Sr., bore the surnames of families that were divided in their loyalties during the war.[13]

The increasingly conservative caste of the Mississippi legislature emboldened former Confederates to initiate such action. Although Whigs overwhelmingly defeated secessionist Democrats in the election of delegates to Mississippi's constitutional convention in August 1865, the convention was dominated by former slaveholders determined to restore as much of the old antebellum social order as possible. Delegates even ignored advice from President Andrew Johnson that they bestow at least nominal voting rights on some black citizens. Instead they re-created a new white man's government that denied blacks voting rights altogether. In the process they demonstrated how racism could submerge class and party differences among Mississippi's white men in the struggle to codify rights of freedom and citizenship in the new government.[14]

John M. Baylis and his associates successfully banked on the acquiescence of the conservative new legislature to their plan to shame their unionist neighbors. They timed the petition to change the name of Jones County to reach the legislature just after the October seating of newly elected state and local officers. The new officers dutifully passed the measure on December 1, 1865. Looking back on the event, Maddie Bush recalled years later that "a few of the secession party" had changed the names of Jones County and Ellisville during Reconstruction "just for a slur on so many union people living here."[15]

Bush also recalled that the change of names "didn't last any longer than when the northern people got hold of it," for Congress soon imposed military reconstruction on Mississippi. The state legislature's failure to grant suffrage to freedmen, followed by its passage of the notorious Black Codes, left Congress little choice but to invalidate the state's 1865 constitution and institute military rule from March 1867 until March 1870. In the meantime, state politicians struggled to draft a new constitution acceptable to both the federal government and their white constituents. It would be almost three more years before the original names of Jones County and Ellisville were restored; meanwhile, factionalized Republicans, old line Whigs, and Conservative Democrats fought for control over the terms by which Mississippi would reenter the union.[16]

As politicians jockeyed for power, desperate poverty and confusion over whether military or civil authorities held the reigns of government stimulated violence and bred anarchic conditions in many parts of the state. Ben Graves remembered that after the war "there was nothing here; we were absolutely poverty-stricken." A twentieth-century descendant of Jones County farmers remembered hearing grim stories about children eating dirt and green corn, and families who sent twelve- and thirteen-year-old children "down the road with the clothes on their back to fend for themselves." As elsewhere, local conflicts degenerated into neighborhood feuds that would later be remembered only as tragic eruptions of violence among outlaws or between families divided by "bad blood."[17]

Violence was both politically and personally motivated. According to Gerald Johnson, former Knight Company member Richard Hinton murdered Jim Gunter in 1866 for debauching the wife of a Confederate conscript who had close ties to the Knight Company. Gunter, who never married, reportedly had a reputation as a "dandy," or ladies' man. Unlike his brother Joe, who was killed during the war for joining the Knight band, Jim Gunter was a close associate of Joel E. Welborn, which may have gained him a choice guard duty assignment at nearby Enterprise in April 1863. That assignment and his desertion of the 7th Battalion in 1862 and again in December 1863 kept Gunter close to home throughout the war and presumably free to engage in sexual mischief. For Richard Hinton, the murder of Gunter, which added one more death to a community that had seen little else since 1862, restored honor to his cuckolded friend and meted out personal justice as no court of law could.[18]

In the summer of 1871, similar folk justice prevailed among the feuding Sullivan, Gibbons, Craft, and Chain families in the Battle of Shiloh Church in Covington County. A melee erupted after Gabriel "Gabe" Chain was accused of trying to "steal" Neace Sullivan's wife. It ended with Frank Gibbons's murders of Gabe Chain and James Dykes. Frances Ates, a witness to the killings—and whose own sons had been killed in Lowry's 1864 raids—expressed a mother's horror at men's unremittingly deadly contests over honor and justice when she reportedly yelled, "God save we'erns for Frank Gibbons has done . . . kilt James Dykes and Gabrel Chain and we ain't [n]airy a nother [man] ter spair jist now."[19]

Alongside murderous family feuds, horse thieves and cattle rustlers stimulated vigilante violence during this period. The White family of Myrick, Jones County, comprised a colorful cast of thieves. In 1860 the White men had been ordinary yeoman farmers. Sam White, his wife, Susie, and eight-year-old John lived on a farm valued at $1,500. Sam's younger brother Van and Van's wife, Mandy, lived on the farm of elder members of the White family who were probably the brothers' parents. According to Jim Bingham Walters, interviewed in 1936 by Addie West of the WPA, the White brothers and their wives, who were sisters, after the war joined the notorious Dawson Holly Ring, a gang of thieves named for its leader. The gang stole horses, cattle, hogs, and sheep for their own consumption and to sell. Walters described how the men would "bunch" the stolen horses and leave it to Mandy to "run them through the swamps to some market." When outraged citizens formed a posse to shut down the gang, Mandy's gender lent her no protection. According to Walters, the posse shot her to death as she and sister Susie sat on her front porch.[20]

The deep poverty that helped engender such violence during Reconstruction is revealed by families' declining farm values. Despite the often-cited flaws of the 1870 census, its figures suggest the desperate struggle waged by farmers to make a living from the soil. The cash value of Newt Knight's farm fell from $300 in 1860 to $90 in 1870. Farms of older, more established men, such as Benjamin Bynum, Jasper Collins, Vinson Collins, and Allen Valentine, showed even steeper declines in 1870. Widows eked out livings as best they could. Simeon Collins's widow, Lydia, operated a farm valued at $70; Daniel Knight's widow, Elizabeth, former slaveholder and daughter of Mary Coleman, claimed a farm valued at $150. John M. Baylis remained one of Jones County's wealthiest men, but the cash value of his farm was less than half of its previous level.[21]

In this male-dominated society, women had few options beyond struggling to make ends meet in households that were, literally, their life's work. An old ritual remembered in 1954 by Jones County journalist Bill Hilbun spoke to the deeply ingrained custom of female subordination that was yet so vital to a family's survival. "When a hen crowed," wrote Hilbun, "it was the pot for her in short order. That was a protest against the female of the species getting out of place." Some women, of course, like Susie and Mandy White, did "get out of place" when the going got too rough. In a world in which farm women already worked hard, however, most simply worked even harder.[22]

Frances Gandy-Walsh was told by her elders that Jones County farmers worked sixteen to eighteen days a week and that women worked in the fields even when pregnant. At a Rainey community meeting on June 10, 1926, S. W. Patrick's wife recalled that as a post–Civil War wife she spun "five or six yards of cloth a day after I got it in the loom." Weaving had to wait until after dark, to be done by torchlight. "My old man would be in bed sleeping," she said, "and I would be up working making him some breeches and shirts." She added that when families sheared their sheep, "the women did it too. I have sheared sheep myself." During the same year, at a separate community meeting, Grandma Smith remembered working in the fields all day and spinning, weaving, and sewing all night. She claimed to have constructed entire dresses in a single night on more than one occasion.[23]

Not surprisingly, a woman's honor centered around her ability to make ends meet. Hilbun remembered the time that his mother sent him to borrow a cup of sugar from a neighbor. Along with the sugar the neighbor sent back a reminder that his mother should pay it back in "full measure." Upon hearing these words, Hilbun's indignant mother immediately returned the unused sugar. Among women as well as men, "honorable people just did not lecture one another on rules of conduct."[24]

But living by the rules was difficult in this war-ravaged land for women who lacked the financial support of husbands or fathers. Among the single women who had supported the Knight band during the war, in 1870 Sally Delancy lived with her grown son, Alzade Courtney (McGee) lived with her brother and his family, and Ellafair Chain lived with her daughter and son-in-law. In 1880, however, Alzade and Sally Parker headed their own households. Thirty-five-year-old Alzade lived alone with her children, two of whom were teenagers and, like her, worked as "field hands." Seventy-year-old Sally lived with three teenaged grandchildren and served as the community's midwife. Few women in Piney Woods Mississippi, however, could support households without an adult male's income or labor. The occupation of Sarah Perry was listed simply as "beggar," despite the fact that her household included four children described variously as "hired hands" and "day laborers."[25]

Even worse were the plights by 1880 of Mary and Ansebelle Dossett, ages twenty-three and twenty, who were listed, respectively, as "prostitute" and "public woman" that year by census enumerator James L. Welborn. Although the sisters' father, Thomas, was the brother of wealthy speculator and Confederate leader Hansford D. Dossett, by 1870 he barely made a living on twenty-five acres of land. After his death between 1870 and 1880, his unmarried daughters were left to make their own way. Despite their occupations, both women eventually married, suggesting an impoverished world in which some people understood and accepted the desperate measures required by others to make a living.[26]

Lawsuits provided another method by which financially strapped people alleviated economic depression and also punished their enemies. In 1866, shortly before her death, an aged Mary Coleman was successfully sued by C. W. Wood for recovery of thirty-five bales of cotton. On November 22, 1869, James Knight, administrator of Ben Knight's estate, filed a complaint against lawyer-merchant Joel E. Welborn, who had named Knight as one of his debtors in his 1867 bankruptcy petition. After Welborn claimed in bankruptcy papers that James Knight owned him $200 (presumably for the legal costs of settling Ben Knight's estate), Knight countercharged that Welborn had plundered the estate of Jim Gunter, thereby depriving Ben Knight's estate of recovering debts owed to it by Gunter. Meanwhile, in March 1868, John M. Baylis was ordered incarcerated while awaiting trial on charges of having "carved off and interfered with cattle." In 1872 twenty-three citizens sued Joel Welborn's fellow merchant and Confederate ally Amos Deason, charging that he had succeeded the discredited Welborn as swamp commissioner without proper legal title.[27]

Although the late 1860s represented hard times for merchants such as Welborn and Deason, both of whom declared bankruptcy before the decade had passed, they foreshadowed the economic order of the 1870s and 1880s, when the crop lien system converted many planters into landlords. This system created a thriving business for furnishing merchants but left farmers heavily in debt or landless. In 1867 Mississippi legislators believed that their Act for the Encouragement of Agriculture, which initiated the lien system, would aid in the rebuilding of the state's economy, not the impoverishment of a sizable number of its people. In the decades following, however, courts interpreted lien laws in a manner that left sharecroppers and tenants without regular cash wages and without the ability to make economic decisions that served their own interests rather than those of landowning employers.[28]

With economic recovery seemingly on its way in 1868, Jones County unionists were emboldened by the election of Gen. Ulysses S. Grant to the presidency, along with a Republican-dominated Congress that now directed the course of Reconstruction. Jasper Collins celebrated the changing political climate by naming a son born in 1867 Ulysses Sherman Grant. Ben Graves recalled that Newt Knight "and his crowd carried their guns" when they went to vote at Smith's old store on election day. "They got up a big argument and used pretty rough language. I thought they were going to fight," he stressed.[29]

Radical Reconstruction led to the eventual restoration of the names Jones and Ellisville to Davis County and Leesburg, but only after a series of constitutional and procedural setbacks. On January 7, 1868, a new slate of delegates began a four-month process to draft Mississippi's new constitution. Vinson Collins attended the convention as the delegate from Davis and Smith Counties, but contrary to common belief in the area, he did not directly participate in that process.[30] In fact, he participated in the "Black and Tan" convention for only seven days. There are indications that Radical Republicanism proved too radical for him, and that unlike Newton Knight, he did not support a political movement that empowered black citizens. In his absence N. B. Bridges of Choctaw County proposed on February 1 to restore the name Jones to Davis County and to rename Leesburg Jonesboro. The resolution failed to pass, perhaps because Bridges also proposed to change the name of Lee County to Lincoln County. Despite the convention's "radical" image, truly radical Republicans were a distinct minority among its delegates. The final draft of the constitution, approved by delegates on May 15, 1868, simply provided for the automatic repeal of the 1865 act that had changed the names of the county and the county seat. Voters, however, rejected the new constitution on grounds of its radical provisions for black suffrage, public schools (without a mandate for segregation), and political proscriptions against former Confederates. Failure to ratify the constitution in 1868 delayed the name changes until 1870, when Mississippi finally reentered the union.[31]

Between 1869 and 1870 the Republican governorships of carpetbagger Adelbert Ames and scalawag James Alcorn brought several political appointments to former members of the Knight Company. In 1870 Newt's second lieutenant, William Wesley Sumrall, was assistant U.S. marshal of Jones County; Thomas J. "Jeff" Collins was justice of the peace; Prentice M. Bynum was clerk of the Jones County circuit court; and B. A. Mathews, kin to band member Lazarus Mathews, served as probate judge of the county.[32]

Prentice M. Bynum, member
of the Knight Company and
Union soldier, ca. 1895.
Photograph courtesy of Wayne
and JoAnn Wingate.

Such appointments did little to ease the economic troubles of Jones County yeomen but gave them a measure of political power. Unionists' hopes were buoyed by Mississippi's reentry into the national union and by growing congressional support for creation of the Southern Claims Commission (SCC) to compensate the losses of Southern unionists. Newt Knight, who enjoyed a favorable reputation among Republican state leaders, petitioned Congress in October 1870 for financial compensation. It is not clear why he did not wait until formal creation of the SCC before filing. Filing early did put his application ahead of the rush that followed, but it also left him subject to rules that made it almost impossible for claimants from secessionist states to win awards. Nor did his petition conform to guidelines set by the SCC. Instead of listing specific economic losses suffered at the hands of the Union Army, he provided a roster of Knight Company men and asked for compensation on the basis of their military service to the Union Army.[33]

Before submitting his claim, Newt pared down his wartime company roster from more than ninety men to fifty-five, which included the ten executed by Colonel Lowry. He requested individual sums of money for each man based on his rank within the company. Not only did he omit many men's names, but he also switched the ranks of several, significantly affecting the amount of money each would receive. Added together, the individual amounts designated for each man totaled $21,150, making Newt's claim one of the few filed from outside Mississippi's wealthy river districts that amounted to more than $10,000.[34]

Newt's claims of unionism were supported in sworn testimony from several Republicans. Writing from the circuit court in Ellisville, Judge

William M. Hancock, a scalawag described by historian William C. Harris as "a battling little judge from the piney woods whose possession of a derringer when on the bench had a salutary effect on courtroom decorum," described Newt as a "Staunch Republican" and "the recognized leader of the union party in this county." Republican state senate nominee Richard Simmons, of Jasper County, praised Newt as "a true Union man and a true friend to the Federal Government." Reflecting his own direct ties to the Knight Company, Judge B. A. Mathews described Newt's battle against Colonel Lowry in heroic terms: "Knight and his men tuck shelter in the swamps & fought men & dogs day-by-day about twenty days. . . . The men that Lowery murdered was as good citizens as the county afforded," he insisted; "all they had against them was because they weare fighting for the United States & did not deny it."[35]

Newt's "bill for the relief of Newton Knight and other citizens" was read twice before the third session of the Forty-first Congress before being referred to the Judiciary Committee. The bill was reintroduced twice, first by Representative Legrand W. Perce, then by Representative Albert R. Howe, both of whom were Mississippi carpetbaggers who championed the rights of black and white laborers. Perce reintroduced Newt's bill before the second session of the Forty-second congress, which referred it to the Committee on Military Affairs. On December 18, 1873, Howe read the bill before the Forty-third Congress, which referred it to the Committee on Claims. On February 17, 1880, Sen. Blanche K. Bruce introduced Newt's bill before Congress once again; again, the bill was referred to committee. Still, Newt refused to give up. Armed with new lawyers, he filed again for compensation in 1887 and 1891, only to have the U.S. Court of Claims rule against him, once and for all, in 1900.[36]

The reluctance of a Northern-dominated Congress to trust sworn testimonies from white Southerners, many of whom had served in Confederate units despite their unionist claims, was understandable in the aftermath of secession and civil war. But it also did not help that many Northerners considered plain white Southerners to be ignorant and uncivilized. In 1866, after touring the defeated, war-raged South, Northern journalist Whitelaw Reid described Southern poor whites as so dirty and so ignorant that "no people in America, of any color, can compare with them." In a similar account published the same year, Reid's contemporary Sidney Andrews predicted that "time and effort will lead the negro up to intelligent manhood," but he doubted that "it will be possible to ever lift this [Southern] 'white trash' into respectability."[37]

Historical works such as William Sparks's *Memories of Fifty Years*, published in 1872, further reinforced images long in place. Lamenting the illiteracy and lack of refinement of Piney Woods Mississippians, Sparks perpetuated the degraded images of backcountry people offered by Charles Woodmason a century earlier. Amid tales of the Old Southwest, he described Piney Woods children who "ran wild, half naked, unwashed and uncombed, hatless and bonnetless through the woods and grass, followed by packs of lean and hungry curs, hallooing and yelling in pursuit of rabbits and opossums, and were as wild as the Indians they had supplanted." Like Woodmason, Sparks reduced class differences among Southern whites to matters of mere instinct and native intelligence, and he conflated self-sufficient farming and cattle herding with laziness and ignorance.[38]

Influenced by such images, most Northerners put little stock in the claim that nonslaveholding whites had political views, much less that they had acted on them during the Civil War. In 1876, after Conservative Democrats had wrested power from Republicans in most Southern states, one Northern satirist dubbed the scc the Rebel War Claims Collection Company of the Solid South. Yet Northerners' indifference and sometimes outright contempt ultimately encouraged white unionists to move closer to the Southern conservative coalition, which actively courted them with racist appeals to manly honor.[39]

The most violent appeals to white racism came, of course, from the Ku Klux Klan, which emerged in Mississippi in 1868. Because of relatively small black populations, the Piney Woods counties were not central areas of Klan activity. Nevertheless, there as elsewhere, the vicious campaign launched against black citizens under the banner of ending "Negro domination" threatened to eclipse power struggles between Unionists (Republicans) and Confederates (Democrats).[40]

Some whites interviewed in the twentieth century remembered the Ku Klux Klan's activities in Covington County. For example, Ben Graves recalled the death of former slave Sandy McGill, whom he described as a "leader among the negroes," who was murdered by the Klan "because he defied them and made his boasts." Jeff Craft, a white man who lived across the creek from McGill, had earlier told Graves that he watched the Klansmen ride past his house, "one horse right after another" in a "slow walk" to McGill's house. Craft also told Graves that McGill and his brother-in-law, Bill Henderson, neither fled nor hid from the approaching men but, instead, sat on their porch waiting for them. "They didn't wait for the Ku Klux to fire; they fired on them. But they got old Sandy McGill that night." McGill was beaten to death with a "mall," remembered Graves, while Henderson "made his escape."[41]

The alleged murder of Sandy McGill was recounted again in a 1937 WPA interview with a resident of Covington County. Expressing reverence for the memory of the Klan and disdain for blacks, the interviewee described McGill as a member of a "family of impudent negroes" and relayed shocking details of the murders that followed. Not only did Klansmen beat McGill to death, according to this narrator, but they also beat a "mulatto woman into a state of unconsciousness" and "kicked an infant into the yard where it was eaten by the hogs."[42]

The combined effects of racial hatred and economic depression enabled Democratic-Conservatives to unite enough white Mississippians to derail the Republican Party in the 1875 elections. Throughout 1874 and 1875, Democratic white leaguers and white-liners, so named because they openly opposed all biracial cooperation, whipped up fears of black domination among their white constituents, effectively warning that the achievement of political democracy and economic prosperity depended on instituting white supremacy. Outbreaks of racial violence, particularly in Clinton, fifteen miles west of Jackson, and a white vigilante takeover of Yazoo County prompted Governor Ames to complain to President Grant that "domestic violence prevails in various parts of this State, beyond the power of the State authorities to suppress." The national Republican Party, more worried about the fate of Rutherford B. Hayes's presidential election, refused to intervene in Mississippi with federal troops. As national reconstruction therefore floundered, a "political culture of racism" flourished in Mississippi.[43]

Unlike the vast majority of his friends and neighbors, Newt Knight defied the racial order imposed under the "redeemed" governments of the late nineteenth century. Just as his earlier opposition to the Confederate government was rooted in personal experiences of the war, so to a large extent was his rejection of racial segregation. The fact that Newt's hated foe, Robert Lowry, became governor in 1882 after conducting an intense race-baiting campaign against his opponent, Benjamin E. King, no doubt disgusted him. More importantly, after 1870 Newt's land was inhabited and worked not only by his white family but by the family of his Civil War ally, Rachel Knight.[44]

Less than twenty years after their Leaf River battle, Newt Knight and Robert Lowry were once again at political odds, this time over race. The lives of Rachel, Newt, and Serena remained intertwined until Rachel's death in 1889. Thus Rachel's children, all of whom apparently had white fathers, grew up with the nine children of Newt and Serena. Around 1878 Molly and Mat Knight, the children of Newt and Serena, married Jeff and Fannie Knight, two of Rachel's children. These marriages began the community of "white Negroes," sometimes called simply "Knight's Negroes" by local whites.[45]

Anna Knight, born in 1874 to Rachel's oldest daughter, Georgeanne, provided a rare glimpse from within the Knight community when, in 1951, the Seventh-Day Adventist Church published her autobiography, *Mississippi Girl*. "After emancipation," wrote Anna, "my grandmother and her family moved from the old slave plantation in Jones County to Jasper County." In an obvious reference to Newt, Anna asserted that "they went with one of the younger Knights who did not believe in slavery." The Knight settlement was located on the southwestern border of Jasper County, some ten miles north of Laurel, just across the Jasper line. According to Anna, Rachel and her children sharecropped on Newt's land for "several years" before Rachel bought eighty acres of land of her own.[46]

Racially, the Knights defied both social and economic conventions of the postwar South. Although Rachel farmed only 10 of Newt's 170 acres in 1870, by 1880 she owned 126 acres in her own name. Newt's son Mat and Rachel's son Jeffrey, married to each other's sisters, owned 48 and 140 acres, respectively. Newt himself had increased his landholdings to 320 acres by 1880.[47]

As the Knights struggled to rebuild their economic prosperity, however, the increasingly shrill, racist rhetoric of Southern leaders and politicians led to legal sanctions and social barriers that impeded their mobility. White descendants of the Knight family recalled, for example, that around 1870 local authorities and neighbors made it clear to Rachel that her children would not be permitted to attend a white school. According to Tom and Ethel Knight, when Rachel sent her children to a newly built school in the community, the teacher summarily dismissed them, insisting that he would not teach in a school that included black children. When the school mysteriously burned to the ground a day later, some people claimed that either Newt or Rachel had set the fire. Ex-slave Martha Wheeler may have alluded to this incident when she remarked that Newt "had a complete break with the whites because he undertook to send several of his negro children to a white school he had been instrumental in building."[48]

If Rachel and Newt did protest racial discrimination during these early years of their settlement and the waning days of Reconstruction, they soon abandoned such dangerous behavior. As white conservatives won control over state governments, racial segregation hardened. This did not prevent Rachel and Newton's children from intermarrying, but it did force their descendants to organize separate schools and, eventually, churches.[49]

As the mixed-race Knight community grew larger and individuals who had supported the Knight Company grew older, the history of the Free State of Jones became ever more blurred by New South revisionist history. The racist campaigns of Redeemer Democrats led the way in generating

Identified as Rachel and Newt Knight, this may be Newt's son, Sullivan, with wife. Photograph courtesy of Florence Knight Blaylock.

fanatical, often violent campaigns to protect "virginal" white females from sexually aggressive black men. Over and over, whites were told that emancipation and the political empowerment of black men had unleashed untold dangers and that only the white Democratic Party could restore civilized order to society.[50]

Not only blacks but politically dissident whites were attacked by Democratic leaders while economic crisis engulfed the postwar South. These attacks became nastier with the growth of the Populist Movement, which threatened to unite whites and blacks around economic interests rather than race. In 1892 Jones County voters joined the rest of the state in giving Populist presidential candidate James Weaver almost 20 percent of its popular vote.[51]

Thus, when Mississippi Populists announced plans to hold a state convention on July 31, 1895, to nominate a state ticket for the upcoming election, editors of the Democratic *Jackson Clarion-Ledger* dismissed it as "midsummer madness." A few months later they accused "the masses" of being "no doubt honest but deluded" in their support for Populism. Linking images of white degradation with interracial (and radical) political coalitions, Mississippi Democrats defeated Populism by uniting planter and plain folk around symbols of white supremacy.[52]

Fittingly, Jones County's most prominent Populists were the sons of Jasper and Riley Collins, former members of the Knight Company. Loren R. Collins and Timothy Wyatt Collins embraced their ancestors' traditional producer ethos and long commitment to a republican ideology at odds with the dominant trends of a commercial, free market society. At the Populist convention held July 31, 1895, both were elected as delegates from Jones County. Loren Collins, described by the *Clarion-Ledger* as a "farmer and stock-raiser," was also nominated as supreme court clerk on the Populist state ticket.[53]

As Populists continued to organize, the *Clarion-Ledger* accelerated its attacks. On September 12 its editors conceded that there were still "good men" within populist ranks but warned that "disgruntled and disappointed office seekers" who hoped to attract "Republicans and negroes" controlled the party. On September 28 and October 10 editors likened the Populist Party to Adelbert Ames's "radical regime" during Reconstruction. Having invoked the image of degraded blacks and poor whites empowered by Northern Republicans, they warned that "the bottom rail will never be on top again in Mississippi."[54]

Despite mounting attacks, Mississippi Populists convened again the following year. Denouncing the Democratic Party for its "manifest insincerity, intolerance, and fraud in elections," on February 19, 1896, the party declared itself in favor of free coinage of silver, abolition of national banks, and equitable taxation of all property. Elected as delegate from the sixth district to the national convention was old Jasper Collins himself. His son Loren was appointed assistant secretary of the state organization.[55]

Although Populists made promising efforts at interracial cooperation, they ultimately capitulated to racism. Propertied farmers' traditional view of themselves as independent producers reinforced the conventional white belief that blacks were inferior by virtue of their African heritage *and* because of their degradation under slavery. So fundamental was this image to Southern white men's sense of themselves and so racist were the attacks on Populists by Democrats that together they destroyed any possibility that whites might form common cause with blacks to confront the economic problems that engulfed the postbellum South.[56]

In the early twentieth century many Jones County whites merged racism with class consciousness by supporting the political campaigns of Democrats James K. Vardaman and Theodore Bilbo, both of whom combined support for progressive social legislation for poor whites with racist diatribes that rivaled those of their Redeemer predecessors. Yet another son of Jasper Collins, however, rekindled the family's tradition of political dissent by rejecting both the Democratic and Republican Parties after the demise of Populism. In 1912 Jasper Warren Collins, a fifty-one-year-old postmaster, served as delegate from Jones County to the Progressive Party's state convention.[57]

Despite the continued presence of political divisions based on class and region in Jones County, the politics of race and the Myth of the Lost Cause ultimately prevailed. In 1895 Adelbert Ames, Mississippi's Republican Reconstruction governor, lamented that "on this race issue and this alone have the 'carpetbagger' and 'scalawag' of Mississippi been denounced and vilified in unmeasured terms." As white manhood became synonymous with a commitment to Confederate ideals, many Jones County people denied or hid their ancestors' Civil War history. Ames would have been saddened but not surprised by Addie West's essay on Reconstruction, written for the WPA in 1936. Illustrating the thoroughness of her Lost Cause education, West confidently declared that politicians had failed to institute order after the war because "the Freedmen's Bureau, through the unscrupulous carpetbagger and scalawag had imbued the negro with a spirit of social equality and it was unsafe for [white] women to go out alone." Although West also wrote several essays on Newt Knight and the Free State of Jones for the WPA, she apparently perceived no connection between the county's inner Civil War and its postwar conflicts.[58]

What people should remember of the war was
"*not* the courage, the suffering, the blood, *but*
only the causes that underlay the struggle and the results that
followed from it."—Albion Tourgee, 1884

Aye, let us have our history—as it *should* be! Give
us the correct version of that unequal struggle.
. . . A record that reads more like a golden
romance, than a living breathing reality.
—Josie Frazee Cappleman, state historian for
the Mississippi United Daughters of the
Confederacy, 1900

Chapter Eight

Defiance and Domination
"White Negroes" in the
Piney Woods New South

Many Mississippi historians apparently agreed with Josie Frazee Cappleman that the history of the Confederate cause should be written as a
"golden romance"—and a golden romance it became. In the Old South
world created by New South writers, wealthy and poor whites, men and
women, and blacks and whites all shared a harmony of interests shattered
by the invading North. Following the lead of the Southern Historical
Society, the Mississippi Historical Society replaced Northern images of a
violent, backward South with those of a brave and noble civilization.
Beginning in 1898 pro-Confederate rhetoric flooded the pages of the
historical society's journal. Authors regularly blamed Northerners and African Americans for the failure of Reconstruction by caricaturing or vilifying Republicans, while praising the motives of the Ku Klux Klan.[1]

Although the stated goal of the historical society was to paint a more
truthful picture of the past, its *Publications of the Mississippi Historical Society*
proved every bit as slanted as any product of Northern abolitionist presses.
In contrast to Albion Tourgee's insistence that the causes and effects of the

war were more important than the "courage, blood, and suffering" of one's ancestors, Lost Cause historians enshrined Confederate soldiers as heroes and expressed contempt for those who had opposed or deserted the Confederacy. The story of the Free State of Jones moved from the realm of recent history into that of legend, where over time it became distorted by caricatures of ignorant, feuding poor whites, bestial black men, besieged white women, and seductive mulatto women.[2]

Southern white women were both actors and subjects in the revision of Civil War history. In the same *Publications* issue in which Cappleman counseled local and state historians of the Civil War on their mission, Mary V. Duval likewise called on them to replace Northern versions of Southern history with their own. Duval, who authored a history textbook for Mississippi schoolchildren, painted a glowing picture of slavery. She wrote of antebellum white Southerners with "gracious manners" who owned little black "pickaninnies" who "rolled and rollicked from sheer delight in living." The supposedly finer sensibilities of middle-class white women in regard to moral values and domestic life lent authority to their words, while blossoming literary opportunities in the postwar South gave them a new public voice.[3]

North and South, the greater public visibility of genteel white women made the emerging images of freed black men all the more disturbing to middle-class audiences. Alongside Duval's renditions of happy-go-lucky black children emerged those of rapacious black men empowered by corrupt white Republicans. Between 1890 and 1920 white Southern literature—especially newspapers—commonly portrayed interracial sexual relations as the product of sex-crazed black "fiends" ravishing innocent, virginal blondes, rather than as the product of white men raping black women or of blacks and whites participating in consensual sexual relations. It followed that white men such as Newt Knight who had seized power as scalawags during Reconstruction, partly through interracial political coalitions, became traitors to both their government and their race.[4]

As early as 1868 the *Meridian Mercury* provided a lurid description of a black man "skinned alive" in Jones County for having "ravished" a white woman "to the full gratification of his lustful desires." With sarcasm and condescension, the editors noted that during the war, the county had "acquired a wide notoriety for the 'lollty' of its people, many of whom could not be persuaded to be good Confederates." Connecting the unionism of Jones County with new dangers to white women, they commented that "loyalty now means to let the negroes do any sort of devilment without retribution in kind." Such articles helped to spawn a rhetoric of rape fueled by images of vulnerable white women and lustful black men—men who had been freed by the very Union leaders who in 1868 held the reins of power. The message of conservative white editors was clear: only white men, increasingly understood to be devotedly pro-Confederate, could restore honor and order to Southern society.[5]

Following the lead of the *Mercury*, Mississippi newspapers continued to entwine class politics with images of freely roaming black men threatening the purity of white women. In 1895, only one week after the editors of the *Clarion-Ledger* accused Populists of courting "Negro" support, the paper's headlines screamed that yet another "defenseless white woman" had been "MURDERED BY A NEGRO." The paper warned that if the wheels of justice moved too slowly, "peaceable and law abiding" people would resort to lynching "these negro brutes who murder innocent women and children." Southern white editors seemed to agree that black men, unless controlled by force, threatened to destroy white men's private as well as public lives.[6]

Less than two months later, editors reported that in this case the woman's own husband had hired the black man to shoot her; they did not, however, describe the white man as a "fiend" and a "brute," as they had the black man, only as a "cowardly husband." Nor was the murdered woman any longer "innocent." It now appeared that she had been "very jealous" of her husband, having accused him of "things he never did"; furthermore, her extravagant desires had forced them to live in financial "hot water." A white man's vicious scheme to murder his wife thus became transformed into a tragic story of her domestic failures.[7]

Democrats, dependent on support from plain white men, masked the politics of class behind the rhetoric of race and white womanhood. In 1898 Democrat S. Newton Berryhill, billed as Mississippi's Backwoods Poet, metaphorically portrayed white men who had opposed the Confederate cause as animals who had abandoned their own fair civilization to rape and pillage. Using sexual imagery to bind the interests and history of all pro-Confederate whites regardless of class, he characterized carpetbaggers and scalawags as a "snarling pack" of "jackals black and white" who tear at the South's "lovely form by day, and gnaw her bones by night." Not only did Berryhill delineate clear political and racial lines for all Mississippians, but his imagery also helped to encourage and justify the era's numerous lynchings of black men.[8]

During the South's "lynching era," from 1889 to 1945, nearly 13 percent of the nation's recorded 3,786 lynchings occurred in Mississippi. One of the most vicious mob murders of a black man occurred in 1919 in Ellisville, Jones County. John Hartfield, accused of raping a white woman, was pursued for ten days through three counties before finally being caught and lynched. His public murder was organized by a committee, announced in the newspapers, and attended by a multitude of white people, many of whom carried picnic baskets.[9]

Among those who attended the lynching was fourteen-year-old junior reporter and future novelist James Street. In a collection of essays, *Look Away! A Dixie Notebook*, published in 1936, Street subtly sought to convince readers of the heinous nature of such "justice." Without denying Hartfield's guilt, he juxtaposed the image of the black man's grisly death against that of white folks who simultaneously "ate their picnic on the courthouse lawn, under the Confederate monument." Street gently tugged at the mask of reverence for white female honor by noting the incongruity of the alleged rape victim's appearance on her porch, where she waved to the bloodthirsty crowd. "It seemed to me the woman should have been in seclusion," wrote Street. "I can't say she enjoyed the excitement. Her face looked drawn, but there she was leaning on a bannister and talking with her avengers." He concluded his essay by linking racial hatred to class hatred—and both to reverence for the Confederacy—by noting that Hartfield was hanged from the same sycamore tree used by the Confederacy to hang three of Newt Knight's men during the Civil War.[10]

Although Street's voice was one of reason, it did not prevail. Hysterical spectacles of violence, especially lynchings, drove the image of black men as "fiendish brutes" ever deeper into the minds of white people. In 1936, the same year that Street published his account of Hartfield's lynching, B. A. Boutwell offered his own version of the murder to a WPA interviewer. In words dripping with the sentimental treacle of New South rhetoric, Boutwell described the events that led to the pursuit of Hartfield. "Like the cave man of long ages past," he said, "a black fiend had rushed out . . . and seazed one of the most beautiful flowers in the garden of society and dragged her into a nearby woods to satisfy his own beastly desire." Clearly believing that justice was served that day, Boutwell methodically described how the crowd tortured, burned, and mutilated Hartfield's body. Presumably because his seven-page description was so approving and graphic, a WPA official wrote in the margins, "omit this story."[11]

Sixty years after the Ellisville lynching, the power of "black beast" imagery still colored the memories of Jones County's seventy-nine-year-old Hulon Myers, who had attended the incident. Although he disavowed the Klan to an interviewer in 1979, he admitted having been a member of the organization in the 1920s, when the Klan was "all right" because their actions were "the only thing that kept the raping down and all like that." When asked how law officers responded to lynch mobs back then, he replied approvingly that "they just kept hands off most of the time."[12]

So rigidly were the boundaries of race reinscribed by the segregated New South that when Meigs Frost interviewed Newt Knight in 1921, he mentioned neither Rachel Knight nor the mixed-race composition of his homestead. Given that Newt openly lived among his mixed-race kin until his death, it seems likely that Frost, not Newt, censored all mention of Rachel, and it is easy to see why. Frost sought to write a sympathetic story about "Captain Knight" and the Free State of Jones, not an exposé about miscegenation. Writing for a white audience during a decade that sanctioned violent enforcement of racial segregation and white domination over blacks, he dared not place a woman of African ancestry at the center of a legendary white uprising. Rachel thus disappeared from sight.[13]

Tom Knight's 1935 biography of Newt made only a veiled mention of Rachel, Georgeanne, and the mixed-race community and totally ignored his father's intimate connections with them. These omissions enabled him to replace painful memories of miscegenation with a glorified interpretation of his father's Civil War exploits. A product of his times, Tom did not merely fear the racist judgments of white society; the shame of being son and brother to members of a mixed-race community strained his relations with his father for most of his adult life.[14]

Ethel Knight, who was almost fifty years younger than Tom, was even more thoroughly immersed in a culture that insisted on purity of race and made the Confederate Lost Cause its dominant symbol. Embarrassed by her great-uncle Newt, she condemned him as a cold-blooded murderer and an outlaw, a man "with a warped and twisted mind, . . . almost wild in his habits." Furthermore, she insisted that Newt had stood ready to murder his own wife and children if they opposed his scheme to force marriages between his and Rachel's children. In an apparent effort to match the "blood and thunder" prose of James Street's *Tap Roots*, Ethel enlivened her stories—at times far-fetched and unsubstantiated—with unknowable details of the Knights' innermost thoughts and feelings.[15]

According to Ethel, Serena was essentially Newt's prisoner, appalled by her children's interracial marriages but powerless to thwart her husband's will. Ethel claimed that Serena had attempted to leave Newt during the late 1870s but that he forced her back home by shooting at her from behind briars and bamboo as she attempted to flee. Although Serena's life with Newt may well have been miserable, records verify only that she moved to the home of Molly and Jeffrey sometime before 1900, which hardly suggests that she opposed their marriage.[16]

Although Ethel was determined to expose Newton as an advocate of miscegenation, she also sought to deny kinship between as many black and white Knights as possible. To this end, she disputed long-standing rumors

Serena Knight and Newton Knight. The couple's aged appearance places the date of
this photograph as later than that of Rachel and Newton Knight, indicating that
Newton maintained simultaneous intimate relationships with both women.
Photograph courtesy of Frances and Marion Jackson.

that Newt had fathered children with both Rachel and Rachel's daughter
Georgeanne. To further reduce the number of her black kin, Ethel even
claimed that all but one of Molly's children—Otho, the father of Davis—
had been fathered by white men rather than by Molly's husband, Jeffrey.[17]

Though she offered not a shred of evidence, Ethel labeled Rachel, Molly,
and Georgeanne as whores, prostitutes, and even murderers to serve her
own ends. For example, although Molly married Jeffrey while still a teenager and remained his wife until her death, Ethel pronounced her a "har-
lot" who had "launched out upon a career of prostitution" even before her
marriage. Georgeanne, according to Ethel, was so craven with desire for
Newt that she had attempted to murder Serena with an axe and possibly
poisoned her own mother just to get to him.[18]

In the segregated South, black women and white women who lived
among blacks could be slandered with impunity. Societal stereotypes that
posited white women who crossed the color line as sexually promiscuous
and black women as naturally lascivious enabled Ethel to portray the
mixed-race community as deviant, dangerous, and outside the boundaries
of normal, decent society. She obviously had no direct knowledge of
any turmoil that rocked the households of Newton, Serena, Rachel, and
Georgeanne between 1870 and 1900, yet she filled readers' minds with
fantastic—and undocumented—tales of lust and murder.[19]

Grace Knight, Lessie Knight, and Georgeanne Knight, ca. 1905. Grace and Lessie were
the daughters of Georgeanne Knight and rumored to be the daughters of Newton
Knight. Georgeanne was the daughter of Rachel Knight. Photograph courtesy of
Dorothy Knight Marsh.

Until Ethel published her account, journalists and historians who wrote
about the Free State of Jones ignored Newt's interracial relationships, fo-
cusing instead on whether or not the county had formally seceded from
the Confederacy. In 1886 G. Norton Galloway, a Northerner who billed
himself as "historian of the 6th Army Corps," built on earlier newspaper
accounts of Civil War Jones County to present deserters as feuding back-
swoodsmen who created a local "confederacy," wrote their own constitution, and elected "Nathan" Knight, "one of the most illiterate citizens of
Jones County," as their president. Galloway claimed that this minirepublic

Family of Jeffrey Early Knight, son of Rachel Knight and son-in-law of Newt and
Serena Knight through his marriage to their daughter, Martha (Molly). On Jeffrey's
left is his second wife, Sue Ella Smith; seated in front is Serena. Photograph, ca. 1918,
courtesy of Frances and Marion Jackson.

attracted so many dissidents and "miscreants" that the county's population
rose from 3,323 to more than 20,000 in little more than a year. He alleged
that 10,000 of these people belonged to Knight's "army."[20]

Galloway's highly inaccurate version of the story of Jones County entertained Northerners and ridiculed Southerners with images of "bloody
butchery" among men engaged in a fratricidal war, "blood-curdling in the
extreme." Southern whites were portrayed as ignorant and illiterate brutes,
no matter on which side of the war they fought. Plainly intending to
endorse the civilizing effects of industrialization, Galloway ended by praising Northern capitalists' introduction of lumber mills into Jones County.[21]

Newt Knight, poorly educated but hardly illiterate or ignorant of the
world around him, neither fit Galloway's image of him nor celebrated the
glories of Northern progress. In an 1887 letter to his brother John in
Arkansas, he lamented the fact that missionaries, "skillet-head" doctors,
and the lumber industry had penetrated his Piney Woods. Complaining
that four steam-powered sawmills regularly interrupted the stillness of
Tallahoma Creek, he commented to his brother that "I tell you they are
slaien [slaying] them big pines."[22]

Served a steady diet of articles by authors such as Galloway, most
middle-class Americans assumed that industrialization would turn back
Southern poverty and civilize Southern poor whites. To such readers the

Knight Company's Civil War uprising merely demonstrated poor whites' penchant for violence. That image was reinforced in 1891 and 1892 when Albert Bushnell Hart and Samuel Willard drew heavily on Galloway's distorted vision of the Free State of Jones to publish separate articles on the uprising in the *New England Magazine* and the *Nation*.[23]

As the century drew to a close, it was not only Northerners who ridiculed Piney Woods folks. In 1894, as North and South clasped hands across the ruins of war to build an economically "progressive" New South, Dabney H. Maury, the same Confederate general who thirty years earlier had ordered Col. Henry Maury into Jones County, offered a Southern version of the Free State of Jones. In his memoir, *Recollections of a Virginian*, he, too, characterized the deserters as hypersecessionists, referring to the uprising as an "*imperium in imperio.*" Like Galloway, Maury portrayed deserters as degraded poor whites, but from a class-based rather than a Northern perspective. Jones County, which he explained was part of the "vast piney woods that sweep along our seaboard from Carolina to the Sabine," contained the "worst class of our population."[24]

By the close of the nineteenth century, to be Southern was to be white, and to be white was to revere the Lost Cause of the Confederacy. In light of this dictum and Galloway's inaccurate and inflammatory article, two Mississippi historians decided to correct the record in regard to Jones County's Civil War record. In 1898 University of Mississippi professor Alexander L. Bondurant dismissed the legend of Jones County's secession as a pure "fabrication" in an article published by the Mississippi Historical Society. In 1904 Goode Montgomery, a Jones County schoolteacher, attorney, and future mayor of Laurel, expanded on Bondurant's work in the same journal.[25]

Although both Bondurant and Montgomery painted a much more accurate picture of Jones County's "secession," they also displayed passion for more than the mere truth when they assured readers that Jones County was loyal to the Lost Cause. Bondurant hoped to restore the "good name of a county which rendered brave and efficient service to the Confederacy." Montgomery wrote a much more factual, straightforward account than that of Bondurant, admitting that up to 125 Jones County men deserted the Confederate Army and joined the "Newt Knight Company." Still, he emphasized that most men, even those who initially opposed secession, "enlisted early in the war and served until they were mustered out in 1865, as faithful to the Confederacy as any troops in the Southern army."[26]

Raised in Pontotoc County, Montgomery was personally connected to the Free State of Jones through his wife, Nora Herrington, whose maternal uncle was Prentice Bynum, a member of the Knight band. Montgomery did not mention this connection; instead, he interviewed fifteen

Jones County citizens who had lived during the war and who assured him that the Knight band never passed an ordinance of secession from the Confederacy.[27] Two of these interviewees were Jasper J. Collins and William Wesley Sumrall, whom Montgomery described as unrepentant members of the band. In fact, he noted, "no one of Knight's men" with whom he talked "was ashamed to be numbered with that company." Glorification of the Confederate cause seemed not to convince them that they had acted shamefully during the war. They denied the legend that they had seceded from the Confederacy, but their denial was not the product of shame and regret. They denied it simply because it was not true on procedural grounds.[28]

To provide a more civilized image of the Jones County area, Montgomery emphasized that Newt Knight went "wherever his business calls him" and lived "peaceably with his neighbors just like any other farmer." But despite Montgomery's sanguine words, he knew that a sympathetic portrayal of Newt could not include mention that he had crossed the color line. Mississippi lawmakers proscribed biracial education and interracial marriages in 1878 and 1880; the state's 1890 constitutional convention codified the laws and also disfranchised black citizens. By 1904 it was controversial enough for Montgomery merely to mention that opposition to the Confederacy existed among respectable men in Jones County; he dared not present as respectable a man who deserted the Confederate Army *and* who lived among his black kinfolk.[29]

It is difficult to know how Newt's nineteenth-century friends and associates responded to his disregard for laws that forbade interracial marriages and mandated racial segregation. His 1887 letter to his brother John contained ordinary accounts of activities and deaths among friends and relatives; it certainly did not suggest a man shunned by all white society. Several of his and Serena's children married white partners after the mixed marriages of their siblings had taken place. Given that three of them were grandchildren of Younger Welborn Sr., this suggests that distant kinship with Serena and shared bonds with Newt during the Civil War overrode some Welborns' disapproval of Newt's postwar behavior.[30]

Even if kinship ties and shared Civil War experiences forged lifelong loyalties between Newt Knight and some of his associates, he clearly paid a price for ignoring the color line, especially as time passed. In fact, Jasper County's 1900 federal census enumerator went so far as to deprive him of his white identity. A comparison of that year's census with that of 1880 reveals the reconstructed racial identity of many members of the "white Negro" community. In 1880, for example, the census enumerator listed Newton's children Molly and Mat as white and their spouses, Jeffrey and

Fannie, as mulatto. Twenty years later the enumerator listed no mulattoes and only one white family in their community: Joseph S. Knight (Sullivan), a son of Newton and Serena, was listed as white presumably because he had married a woman accepted by the community as white. Yet Sullivan's parents and sister Molly were enumerated as black, no doubt because they lived in households that included descendants of Rachel Knight. By contrast, Newton and Serena's son Mat Knight remained "white" because he had separated from Rachel's daughter Fannie, moved out of the community, and married a white cousin. Obviously "race" was no mere matter of biology.[31]

Long before Ethel wrote her book, people whispered that Newt had fathered children by both Rachel and Georgeanne. In fact, many descendants of Rachel Knight's son John Madison "Hinchie" Knight and her daughter Augusta believe that Newt is their direct ancestor. However, while it is certain that Newt and Rachel's children intermarried, the nature of Newt's relationships with Rachel and Georgeanne is speculative. Newt and Serena lived together until at least 1880, and both remained within the family's network of households until their deaths.

Fortunately there are voices far more reliable than Ethel's as to relations within the households of Newt, Serena, Rachel, and Georgeanne. A more believable source on Newt's sexual affairs is ex-slave Martha Wheeler, his contemporary, who pointed out in 1936 that "Rachel was considered [Newt's] woman." After Rachel's death in 1889, said Martha, "her daughter, Georgianne, took her place [with Newt] and separated him from his wife, who went out and lived . . . among her children."[32]

The earliest memories of Georgeanne's oldest daughter, Anna, were of a crowded household plagued by poverty and segregation. "When I was old enough to understand," she wrote, "I discovered myself living in a large family; some of its members were grown men and women, two of whom were married. All lived in the same house, and all except one of the children was older than I."[33] Anna could not attend whites' schools but remembered learning to read and write from playing with white children. Play time was scarce, however, and both girls and boys worked hard, felling trees with axes and chopping cotton all day. She emphasized that "there was no rest for women," for housework awaited their completion of fieldwork. As a child who lived in a household in which people worked "all the time," she felt that she was "always in the way" and that she was "shoved and pushed around."[34]

During the twentieth century, as segregation deepened, most whites shunned the mixed-race community, and some white branches of the Knight family hid their kinship with Newt Knight from their children.

John Madison "Hinchie" Knight, ca. 1900, son of Rachel Knight and believed to be the son of Newton Knight. Photograph courtesy of Florence Knight Blaylock.

Many believed, as did Ben Graves, that "what he did after the war was worse than deserting."[35] Paula Bolan, great-granddaughter of Newt's sister Martha Yawn, did not discover until she was in the eighth grade that she was kin to the county's most famous outlaw. She later learned that her great-grandfather Joseph Richard "Dick" Yawn had once refused to accompany his wife on a visit to her brother Newt's home, even though he had ridden with the Knight Company during the war. Lonnie Knight, a descendant of Newt's brother James (who was also the ancestor of Ethel Knight), was told by his parents, "No, we are not related to that [Newt's] bunch."[36]

Nevertheless, some white friends and relatives continued to admire Newt despite his discredited behavior. During the 1930s, when Tom Knight gathered stories and testimonials for his father's biography, he found several older Jones County folk who still admired Newt's wartime stance. George A. Valentine, whose older brothers had joined the Knight Company, extolled Newt's unionist ideals and described him as a "quiet and peaceable" man. Martha Ellzey Knight, the wife of Newt's younger brother Taylor, told Tom that "she did not know what would have become of the poor little children and women here in Jones County had it not been for Captain Knight and his company [during the war]."[37]

William Pitts, born in 1921 and descended from Newt's brother Albert, remembered that his family seldom spoke of Newt because of the "Negro thing" but nonetheless gave him the "feeling" that the Civil War was so terrible that Newt ought not be judged too harshly. Similarly, DeBoyd Knight and Earle Knight—both descendants of Dickie Knight—and Julius Huff, a descendant of Thomas J. Huff, were all raised with a certain respect for Newt Knight, despite his interracial relationships.[38]

Newt's closest white friend in later years may have been his cousin George "Clean Neck" Knight. Although Clean Neck's father, Jesse Davis Knight, died fighting for the Confederate Army, and although his mother was a Baylis, he and Newt developed a close relationship after the war, perhaps in part because their wives were also kin. Clean Neck was also closely connected to William Wesley Sumrall, who, at age sixty-eight, married Clean Neck's twenty-four-year-old daughter Mollie. Loyal to Newt until the end, Clean Neck died on his one-hundredth birthday in 1952, having lived just long enough to complain that Ethel Knight's book contained "not a shred of truth."[39]

Even had whites wanted to, however, those sympathetic to Newt could do little to change the prevailing norms of society that marked him as deviant. Much more important to the mixed-race community's ability to thrive was Anna Knight, whose conversion to Seventh-Day Adventism first transformed her own life. Anna discovered Adventism around 1890 during the church's intense campaign to evangelize the South under the leadership of the charismatic prophetess Ellen G. White. Although Anna was the granddaughter of a slave, she developed a personal sense of mission similar to that of Norvell Robertson during an earlier era (see Chap. 4). Just as becoming a pro-missionary Baptist had provided Robertson with the rationale for instituting reforms favorable to white male slaveholders, so, too, did Adventism give Anna the tools with which to educate and reform the habits of her kinfolk.[40]

Under the auspices of the Seventh-Day Adventists, Anna not only taught the "three Rs" and Adventist theology in her Sunday school, but she also convinced her relatives to accept Adventist reforms in their diet, dress, and social behavior. Although she lived outside the Knight community most of her adult life, she influenced the community's development more profoundly than did Newt Knight himself. To gain the skills and authority to redirect the course of the community, however, she had to first leave Mississippi, which she did under the sponsorship of the church.[41]

Shortly after joining the Adventist Church, Anna moved to Chattanooga at the invitation of church elder L. Dyo Chambers and his wife, who then provided for her education. In 1895 Anna moved to Battle Creek, Michi-

Family of George "Clean Neck" Knight and Elmyra Turner Knight, ca. 1900. Clean Neck is seated in the front row; daughter Nola is standing on his right. Elmyra has been rubbed out of the photograph. Standing in the back row, left to right, are daughter Mollie Olivia, who married sixty-eight-year-old William Wesley Sumrall, former member of the Knight Company, in 1909 at age twenty-four; son Daniel; and son Davis. The fourth child on the far right is unidentified. Photograph courtesy of Earle Knight.

gan, where she trained as a missionary nurse at the church's American Medical Missionary College. After graduating from its nursing program, she fulfilled the college's required self-supporting medical missionary work by establishing a school for her Mississippi kinfolk.[42]

Anna escaped Mississippi at a critical point in the life of a young African American woman in the 1890s South. To make so sudden a move (she was barely sixteen years old), she had first to reject her mother's and grandmother's lives as models for her own. Like them, she never married, but unlike them, she never had children. As a devoutly pious woman writing a church-sponsored autobiography, she did not openly discuss sexual matters but hinted at sexual tensions when she described how a raging thunderstorm once halted a dance party that she had attended against her better judgment. Convinced that the storm was God's warning, she wrote, "From that time on I never took part in any more card parties or dances. Jesus saved me from all such things."[43]

The storm occurred around 1889, the year of Rachel Knight's death. Just as Anna was reaching womanhood, her forty-nine-year-old grandmother died—from having had "too many babies," descendant Annette

Knight later remembered hearing. Two years after Rachel's death, in 1891, Anna's mother, Georgeanne, gave birth to Grace, a child fathered by either Newt or another white man.[44] The life that lay before Anna must have been made chillingly clear by the lives of her mother and grandmother. Although she eventually returned to live in the South, she escaped rural Mississippi and gained protection against sexual exploitation and poverty within the nurturing environment of Seventh-Day Adventism.[45]

As Ethel Knight's book makes abundantly clear, many whites refused to consider Rachel and Georgeanne, both unmarried black women with light-skinned children, as anything other than prostitutes or concubines of white men. When Anna returned to Jones County, around 1898, white men there were confronted by a dignified, educated missionary rather than a pretty and vulnerable woman whose "black blood" made her sexual fair game. And just in case anyone questioned the seriousness of her purpose, she packed a revolver "and sometimes a double-barreled shotgun" when she taught Sunday school.[46]

Anna was also attracted to Adventism because of the church's racial tolerance, reflective of its origins among the antebellum Millerites, who were abolitionists. Adventists challenged both gender and racial barriers in their evangelical missions, particularly in the postbellum South but, like other institutions, were eventually forced to segregate their facilities. Anna remembered that when she joined, however, "white and colored worshiped together." As the church's black membership grew, so, too, did fierce opposition to race-mixing, often from within the church itself. According to Anna, after she enrolled in the Adventist Graysville Academy in Tennessee, several students' parents protested her admission. Her sponsors then withdrew her and arranged for her to receive private tutoring.[47]

In 1898, two years before the Jasper County census enumerator designated all members within the mixed community as "black," Anna opened a private school in Soso for the Knight children under the sponsorship of the Seventh-Day Adventist Church. According to her, white neighbors burned this first school to the ground around 1902. She then traveled to India as a missionary for the church, leaving the Knight community without a school for over five years. At the urging of her relatives, she returned to Mississippi around 1908 and directed the rebuilding of the school in nearby Gitano in Jones County.

Because of the demands of Anna's work as a teacher and missionary, she educated her sister Grace, who eventually replaced her as teacher of the school. For most of her life Anna lived and worked at Oakwood College, which the Adventist Church founded for African Americans in 1896 in Huntsville, Alabama. Many mixed-race Knights received their grade school

The Knight School, Gitano, Mississippi, ca. 1908, founded by Anna Knight under the auspices of the Seventh-Day Adventist Church. Anna Knight, daughter of Georgeanne Knight, is seated front row center; directly behind her is her sister and coteacher, Grace Knight. Photograph courtesy of Minneola Dixon, Oakwood Archives and Museum, Oakwood College, Huntsville, Alabama.

education from Grace and then left the area to attend high school at Oakwood College. These two schools became their most important resources for battling against total debasement under increasingly strict racial segregation.[48]

Although Anna and Grace became two of the community's most important figures, the presence of such an imposing white male as Newt Knight enabled the community to survive and grow. Although he exercised his sexual prerogative as a white male by boldly crossing the color line, he deviated from the usual pattern of interracial relations by sanctioning his children's marriages and by openly living among Rachel, Georgeanne, and his mixed-race descendants. It would appear that his lifelong reputation as one who lived as he chose—a right he had successfully defended with arms during the war—discouraged many direct challenges to his shocking postwar behavior. As Maddie Bush emphasized in 1912, Newton still "toats [sic] his old gun."[49]

Newt's presence may have protected Rachel's oldest son, Jeffrey, from prosecution or mob violence when Jeffrey married Newt's daughter Molly. This marriage might easily have inflamed whites' fantasies about black males' lust for white women, but the fact that Jeffrey looked "almost" white may have enabled some to ignore his marriage. Most did not challenge it because Newt either had "given" his daughter to him or, as Ethel

Grace Knight, ca. 1908, daughter of Georgeanne Knight and believed to be the daughter of Newton Knight. Photograph courtesy of Dorothy Knight Marsh.

Knight would have it, forced his own daughter to marry a black man. To most whites it seemed not so much that Jeffrey had challenged white males' exclusive access to white women, but that he reaped the benefits of a white father's misuse of patriarchal authority. Indeed, racist whites did not expect a black man to refuse the "gift" of a white woman. Like Ethel, they considered Molly tainted and incapable of respectability.[50]

But Newt Knight, particularly as an old man, could not prevent all the dangers inherent in a society in which blacks were controlled through violence as well as segregation. In late November 1920, less than two years before Newt's own death, Stewart Knight, Rachel's son (and perhaps Newt's) was murdered. Sharp Welborn, a white man who reportedly lived near him, was convicted of manslaughter. Stewart, light-skinned and well dressed, may have aroused resentment for his lifestyle among his white neighbors. Although Welborn's apparent motive was robbery, some of Stewart's relatives believe that an incident involving a white woman precipitated the attack.[51]

The heightened role of the Ku Klux Klan in the Jones County area raises the question of whether Stewart's murder was racially motivated. Not only was John Hartfield lynched in Ellisville in 1919 but so, too, was an unidentified black man lynched in Estabutchie, Jones County, during the same year. Only two years after Stewart's murder, a large parade of robed Klans-

Stewart Knight, son of Rachel
Knight and believed to be
the son of Newton Knight.
He was murdered in 1920.
Photograph courtesy of
Florence Knight Blaylock.

men marched in the streets of Hattiesburg. That same year, on October 23, 1922, twenty-five klansmen warned "Mr. Letow," a black man who owned a restaurant in Hattiesburg, to move his business from the white to the black section of town.[52]

The Klan hit closer to home around that time when it intruded on two Baptist churches, one in Laurel, Jones County, and the other in nearby Moselle, Jones County. On October 20 the *Laurel Daily Leader* reported that the First Baptist Church of Laurel had received a visit from Klansmen clothed in "full regalia" who left behind a "well-filled purse" and a warning that the Klan was sworn to protect the "purity of womanhood" and "100 percent Americanism." The very next day the Klan visited the Moselle Baptist Church in Jones County. The *Daily Leader* reported that the Reverend C. F. Austin dutifully seated the men near the pulpit and "delivered a dramatic eulogy on the historical record of the Klan from the days after war strife until the present day." An approving Klan once again left money and a letter outlining its guiding principles for the accommodating minister.[53]

In this dangerous and circumscribed world, members of the Knight community made difficult personal choices. Many married their light-skinned cousins to assure that their children would be equally light-

Oree Knight, son of Hinchie
Knight, and Eddress Booth
Knight, ca. 1929. Photograph
courtesy of Florence Knight
Blaylock.

kinned. In the process they created enclaves of people who were neither
"white" nor "black," with complex and doubled lines of descent from
both Rachel and Newt Knight. Florence Blaylock, a great-granddaughter of
Rachel Knight, remembered the importance of skin shade and hair texture
within the racial system in which she grew up. The realization that many
mixed-race Knights did not consider themselves "black" was driven home
to her as a child when she heard a light-skinned, pretty cousin insist that
"if a black man ever tried to talk to me, I would slap his face!" Florence's
own racial identity was complicated, however, by her light-skinned father's marriage to brown-skinned Eddress Booth rather than to one of
his light-skinned cousins. The children of Oree and Eddress Knight inherited varying shades of skin and hair texture, which meant that some
could ignore segregation ordinances, while others had no choice but to
obey them.[54]

In 1939 black sociologist E. Franklin Frazier characterized communities
such as the Knights' as "racial islands."[55] As Mississippi's racial climate
worsened, however, many of the lightest-skinned Knights left their protec-
tive enclave to seek acceptance elsewhere as whites. Newt and Serena's son
Mat separated from Fannie and in 1895 married a white cousin (under
Mississippi's antimiscegenation laws, no divorce was necessary). Several of
Mat and Fannie's children moved to Texas before 1920 and successfully
blended into white society. Their descendants were told only that their

Florence Knight Blaylock
holding grandson, 1999.
Photograph courtesy of
Florence Knight Blaylock.

grandmother (Fannie Knight) was a "full-blooded Cherokee Indian." Similarly, several grandchildren of Jeffrey and Molly Knight moved to Arkansas
after 1920, where they explained their olive skin to their children and
neighbors by transforming Serena Knight, their white grandmother, into
an Indian, while ignoring Rachel, their mulatto grandmother. According
to their version of the family's history, Newt Knight had met Serena in
Oklahoma, where she arrived via the Cherokee Trail of Tears.[56]

Despite these Knights' erasure of their African ancestry, to say that they
passed for white is to accept a social construction of race that lacks a logical
scientific basis. Given many of the Knights' physical appearances, it is
more accurate to say that Mississippi forced them to pass for black. As
retired black Kentucky politician Mae Street Kidd commented in 1997
about her own white appearance, "It's so very obvious that I'm so much
whiter than I am black that I have to pretend to be black." Like Kidd, the
Knights knew from direct experience that the true essence of race was
socially rather than biologically determined, as demonstrated by their
ability to be white in one region of the country and black in another.[57]

Certainly, the Knights could not remain in the Jones County area and
expect to be accepted as white. In a 1914 court dispute over the estate of
the deceased Mat Knight, Fannie Knight, by then married to Dock Howze,
was interrogated by attorney Goode Montgomery as to her and Dock's true

Dock Howze, Minister of the Gospel, with second wife, Fannie Knight Howze, ca. 1905. Fannie, daughter of Rachel Knight, was earlier married to George Madison "Mat" Knight, son of Newton and Serena Knight. Photograph courtesy of Dorothy Knight Marsh.

George Monroe Knight and William Gailie Knight, sons of Mat and Fannie Knight, ca. 1910. Photograph courtesy of Florence Knight Blaylock.

Martha Ann Eliza "Molly" Knight, daughter of Newton and Serena Knight, ca. 1915. She married Jeffrey Early Knight, son of Rachel Knight. Photograph courtesy of Florence Knight Blaylock.

Chances Omar Knight, son of Jeffrey and Molly Knight, ca. 1915. Photograph courtesy of Frances and Marion Jackson.

Serena Knight, ca. 1920.
Photograph courtesy of
Frances and Marion Jackson.

racial identities. Despite Fannie's description of herself as "Choctaw and French" and of Dock as "Choctaw and Irish," Montgomery insisted that they were "Negroes," to which Fannie replied, "Well, you will have to do your own judging." When Montgomery next asked her if she was "living with niggers," Fannie conceded, "Yes sir, I stay on that side." To be "on that side" in the segregated South was, of course, evidence of Fannie's blackness, no matter how light her skin. This reality led the daughters of Fannie's sister Georgeanne—Anna, Grace, and Lessie Knight—along various paths of racial identification. Grace remained in the community, never married, and lived as a black woman despite her white appearance. Lessie married a white man and moved to Texas, where she lived as a white woman, though she frequently returned home on visits. Anna never married, lived outside Mississippi for most of her life, yet identified herself as a "colored" woman.[58]

By 1923, the Knight community's first generation had passed away. On February 16, 1922, less than a year after his interview with Meigs Frost, Newt Knight died. The editors of the *Ellisville Progress* wrote a remarkably sympathetic obituary, taking pains to explain why he had deserted the Confederate Army. Newt and "his followers," they wrote, "held that after the twenty negro law was passed . . . they had no interest in the fortunes of

Rachel Dorothy Knight,
daughter of Mat and Fannie
Knight, ca. 1910. Photograph
courtesy of Ardella Knight
Barrett.

the confederacy." The editors acknowledged that "there was a great deal of truth" in their convictions but lamented that Newt had "ruined his life and future by marrying a negro woman."[59]

Six months later Georgeanne died, followed by Serena in 1923. These deaths inevitably changed the community. Some white neighbors remember Klan harassment of Knights during the 1930s, including one instance in which a white man was beaten "because he had dated a Knight girl." Many Knights moved away during this period, but those who remained in the Jones County area looked ever more to Anna and Grace Knight and to the Adventist Church for protection against the worst effects of racial prejudice and segregation.[60]

Ardella Knight Barrett, a granddaughter of Fannie and Mat's who attended the Knight sisters' school as a child, later enjoyed a distinguished career as an Adventist schoolteacher. Born in 1908 to Peter and Dorothy Knight Castleberry, her unpublished autobiography fondly recalled a childhood that included making pets of chickens, ducks, and geese; watching as sugar cane was converted to a "delightful, golden syrup"; and the wonders of watching trains pass by. Life was not as simple as it sounded, however,

Ardella Knight Barrett,
daughter of Peter and Rachel
Dorothy Knight Castleberry,
ca. 1930. Photograph courtesy
of Ardella Knight Barrett.

for Ardella also noted that "it was during this time that my mother taught me to shoot a Smith and Wesson thirty-two pistol."[61]

Ardella was still a teenager in 1923 when her mother and her Uncle Fred died. Convinced all her life that they were poisoned, she provided in her autobiography confused details of the events that led to their deaths. She and her mother, she wrote, were awakened one night by men's voices "along the road which passed in front of the house." The men, she claimed, intended to set fire to her mother's home because she had refused to sell her property to interested white buyers. Ardella and her mother escaped by fleeing to her Uncle Fred's house by way of the railroad, "to avoid leaving footprints in the road." Although she offered no proof, she insisted that the same men who threatened to burn down her family's home subsequently poisoned her mother and uncle.[62]

The struggles faced by the mixed-race Knights during the 1920s were both racial and economic. Thus Oakwood College became increasingly more important as a source of education that enabled individual Knights to leave Mississippi and build careers elsewhere. (Many returned to their native state to live after retirement.) In 1935, after applying to Oakwood

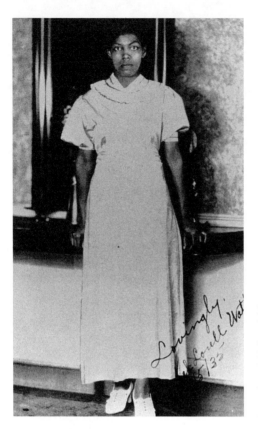

Rachel Watts, daughter of
William Watts and Augusta
Ann Knight Watts, 1935.
Photograph courtesy of
Minneola Dixon, Oakwood
Archives and Museum,
Oakwood College, Huntsville,
Alabama.

for admission, Rachel Watts sent her cousin Anna a picture of herself on
which she wrote that she was "very anxious to hear their decision." Later,
in a narrative poem, Rachel explained the events that convinced her and
her brothers to attend the black Adventist college. During the 1920s, wrote
Rachel, her debt-ridden father fled to New Orleans, leaving their mother
to raise six children alone. In 1928 two brothers, Curtis and Enoch, struck
out on their own to find work. Their adventure ended before it began,
however, when Enoch lost his grip while clambering aboard a moving
freight train and was thrown to the tracks and killed. Shortly thereafter, all
the remaining Watts children decided to attend Oakwood College rather
than to "wander."[63]

The "white Negro" community existed in defiance of every tenet of the
New South creed. Twentieth-century racism, reshaped between 1890 and
1920 by the architects of segregation, reinforced many Americans' desperate determination to deny any and all African ancestry. Perhaps with even
greater urgency, many continued to explain olive skin as the legacy of
distant Indian, Spanish, Portuguese, and even Carthaginian—but never

Augusta Ann Knight Watts, daughter of Rachel Knight and believed to be the daughter of Newton Knight, ca. 1930. On her right is son Ezra; on her left is daughter Rachel. Photograph courtesy of Olga Watts Nelson.

African—forebears.[64] White people's denial of black ancestry was certainly not surprising in a white supremacist society that claimed by the turn of the twentieth century that one drop of "African" blood overpowered all other blood in determining one's racial identity. If most planter- and yeoman-class Southern whites denied knowledge of their darker-skinned kinfolk during the nineteenth century, few Southern whites of the segregated twentieth-century South would admit even to socializing with blacks.

The belief by many that "one drop" of African blood made one black culminated in 1948 with the miscegenation trial of Davis Knight, a grandson of Molly and Jeff. That trial, however, was about much more than simply one man's racial identity. As the nation inched closer to a confrontation over segregation, many white Southerners feared what lay ahead. In opposing Davis Knight's claim to whiteness when he married across the color line, they once more took their stand, this time with the Lost Cause of segregation.[65]

A casualty of Davis Knight's battle over racial identity was Tom Knight's romanticized portrayal of the Knight Company as a band of heroic white yeoman farmers who acted in defense of liberty and the safety of women and children. Largely because of Davis's trial, Ethel Knight successfully replaced Tom's version of the Free State of Jones with her own, a tale that featured a demented white man, a manipulative green-eyed mulatto woman, and one hundred or more men who were persuaded to join a misbegotten plot to overthrow what she believed was the noblest government on earth—the Confederacy.

Segregation was the rule and always will be the rule as long as one Southerner descended from the old South lives, and as long as the teachings of the old Christian colored race are remembered by their descendants there will be no danger of a Mongrel race, as purity of race is the primary objective of segregation.

—Ethel Knight, *The Echo of the Black Horn*, 1951

As *soon* as I knew where I was, I got out.

—Van Buren Watts, grandson of Rachel Knight, 1969

Epilogue

The Free State of Jones Revisited

Davis Knight's Miscegenation Trial

Not until author David Cohn returned to his native Mississippi after an absence of two decades did he understand the complexities of the racial system in which he, a white man, had been reared during the early twentieth century. "I began to discover that this apparently simple society was highly complex," he wrote in the 1948 foreword to his memoir of Delta life. "It was marked by strange paradoxes and hopelessly irreconcilable contradictions. It possessed elaborate behavior codes, written, unwritten, and unwritable."[1]

In the same year that Cohn's words were published, Davis Knight, age twenty-three, collided with this system of paradoxes, contradictions, and codes. On June 22, 1948, the Jones County Circuit Court of Ellisville indicted Knight, who claimed to be—and certainly looked—white, for the crime of miscegenation. Two years earlier, on April 18, 1946, he had married Junie Lee Spradley, a white woman. The state claimed that even though Knight appeared white, he was in fact black.[2]

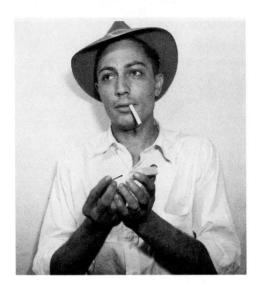

Davis Knight, age twenty-three, son of Otho and Addie Knight; great-grandson of Newton and Serena Knight; great-great-grandson of Rachel Knight, December 27, 1948. Photograph courtesy of AP/Wide World Photos.

The transcript of Knight's trial reveals the contours of the mixed-race neighborhood founded by Newton, Serena, and Rachel Knight after the Civil War. Labeled "white Negroes" by local whites, their precise racial classification varied according to who was classifying them and whether that classification reflected social custom or law. Genealogically and institutionally, these Knights defied efforts of white supremacists to identify and separate people simply according to whether they were either white or black.

Davis Knight's trial sheds light on both the community and the events that shaped the authors of the two most widely read accounts of the Free State of Jones. As we have seen, both Tom Knight and Ethel Knight lived in a segregated society steeped in Lost Cause mythology; indeed, Ethel had never known any other world. Tom, embarrassed by his father's social behavior, admitted that Newt was a Republican during Reconstruction but downplayed his interracial associations and praised the "lily white" Republicans as the more progressive branch of the party. In contrast, Ethel denounced deserters of the Confederacy and blamed corrupt carpetbaggers and scalawags (like Newt Knight) for imposing "Negro Rule" on innocent, decent whites during Reconstruction. Although both Tom and Ethel wrote within white supremacist frameworks, they agreed on little except that Newt had reached the pinnacle of his power during Reconstruction. Davis Knight's trial, however, enabled Ethel to replace Tom Knight's version of the Free State of Jones with her own.[3]

More broadly, the Davis Knight trial speaks to white Southern fears about the black civil rights movement that had steadily gained momentum

Jones County Courthouse, Ellisville, Mississippi, 1996. Author's photograph.

during the 1930s and 1940s. President Franklin Roosevelt's New Deal programs enabled Southern liberals to push for greater political democracy in the South. African American New Dealers enjoyed vigorous support from first lady Eleanor Roosevelt, who campaigned much more boldly for black civil rights than did the president. In 1938 a biracial coalition of New Deal Democrats formed the Southern Conference for Human Welfare (SCHW) as a vehicle for reforming Southern politics.[4]

Stimulated by the nation's deep depression, some white Southerners rejected agrarian romanticism and rediscovered a distant past that revealed conflicts, not harmony, between slaveholding and nonslaveholding whites of the Old South. The editors of the *Laurel Leader Call* echoed the SCHW's reformist spirit in March 1939 by proclaiming that the city of Laurel "does not belong to the Old South." Explicitly invoking the memory of the Knight Company, they reminded readers that "the natives of Jones County refused to take part in a rich man's war, which they deemed a poor man's fight." Disavowing Lost Cause principles altogether, they further noted, "This is not the sector which boasts of white-haired colonels, in wide-brimmed hats, who rode blooded steeds over plantations and counted their acres by the thousands, along with their slaves."[5]

It was at this point, writes historian Patricia Sullivan, that "the national Democratic Party implicitly challenged the political foundation of white supremacy." Moreover, during the 1940s, labor and civil rights organizations increasingly combined their efforts. In 1946 the Congress of Industrial Organizations, through its Operation Dixie campaign, built interracial labor unions in many Southern cities—including Laurel, Mississippi, in Jones County.[6]

In the face of unprecedented challenges to segregation, white supremacists responded with lynchings and Communist witch-hunts. Organizations like the SCHW, which supported both labor organizing and civil rights, were red-baited by conservative politicians. Senator Theodore G. Bilbo of Mississippi attacked the SCHW as an "un-American, negro social equality, communistic, mongrel outfit" and warned that racial "intermingling" would drag white civilization into a "maelstrom of miscegenation, interbreeding, intermarriage, and mongrelization."[7]

Here was Davis Knight, behaving just as Bilbo had warned. As African American soldiers engaged in a Double V campaign that linked the fight for democracy abroad with the fight for racial equality at home, Davis successfully enlisted in the navy as a white man and then married a white woman. If the war's encouragement of racial democracy disturbed Jones County whites, Davis's ability to become white through navy service probably outraged them. To make matters worse for segregationists, in 1948 the insurgent Progressive Party offered a pro–civil rights platform, and both the Democratic and Republican Parties endorsed greater racial equality in their political campaigns. On July 26, 1948, President Harry Truman signed Executive Order No. 9981, desegregating the U.S. military. Only the Dixiecrat candidate, Strom Thurmond, remained firmly committed to racial segregation.[8]

With the stories of Newt, Serena, Rachel, and the "white Negro" community as backdrop, Davis Knight's 1948 trial at times resembled a theater of the absurd. Lawyers attempted not only to untangle the community's complicated genealogy but also to explain how two white people could be the biological grandparents of "Negroes," or how a former slave could have white descendants. Referring to Davis Knight as "the man—the boy," prosecutor Paul Swartzfager began by introducing evidence of Davis's marriage to Junie Lee Spradley. Deputy Circuit Clerk Nell Graves identified the marriage license that she had issued the couple two years earlier, but on cross-examination, defense attorney Quitman Ross asked her to explain how she had determined whether to record the license in the white or the colored record book. "Well Mr. Ross," she replied, "we can't very well ask them [their race]." Besides, she later explained, Davis had entered the court "with a crowd of white ladies," and "the girl's mother was a white woman, and she [Junie Lee Spradley] was white."[9]

Whether intentionally or not, attorney Ross's efforts to prove that Davis was white consistently exposed the contradictions between legal and social constructions of race. Graves had merely practiced the racial etiquette taught to all genteel whites in the twentieth-century South. She considered it improper to ask Davis and Junie their race even though the law required her to practice racial discrimination. She assumed that if physical characteristics did not reveal one's race, one's behavior and associations surely would. She presumed that a crowd of white ladies would not enter a public arena with a black man in tow.[10]

Ross shrewdly based his defense of Davis Knight on the sort of assumptions exhibited by the clerk. A white Mississippian, Ross knew that most white Southerners abided by the one drop rule—that is, they considered a person with any degree of African "blood" a "Negro." Mississippi law, however, defined as "Negro" any person with one-eighth or more African ancestry. As a former slave, Rachel was the prosecution's key to proving that her great-grandson was black. Unless Swartzfager also proved that Davis had more than one black ancestor, Rachel had to be of full African ancestry in order for Davis to be black, mathematically and legally.[11]

The prosecution produced several witnesses who testified that Rachel was a "full-blooded" African. The defense countered with witnesses who just as forcefully argued that she was of mixed Indian and European, not African, ancestry. Witness after witness discussed the "blood" of Davis Knight's ancestors much as one would clinically discuss a contagious bacterium. When asked whether Davis's grandfather had "Negro" blood, for example, Wiley McHenry insisted, as though he were describing the victim of a vampire, that "Jeff had the unmistakable marks of a negro about his features, his neck . . . and all, and I think he knew it." Three witnesses, including a doctor, believed that blood tests could determine the presence and level of "African blood" in a person. Their language suggested that white and black blood were not merely different, but that European blood was "pure," and that purity was destroyed by any amount of African blood, no matter how white one's skin.[12]

Witnesses who insisted that Davis Knight was black also agreed with attorney Ross that "any person who is known or thought to have Negro blood in them, whether it is a little or much, is considered a Negro by White people in the South." McHenry sought assurances from Ross that this assumption was grounded in science, revealing all too clearly the pseudoscientific and psychological grip of Negrophobia: "I think they can tell them by blood, can't they, Quitman[?] . . . If he's got Negro blood in him he is a negro, isn't he?"[13]

D. H. Valentine, a witness for the state who claimed to have known Rachel personally, assumed a defiant tone when Ross informed him that

Rachel had died in 1889, more than a year before he was born. Valentine continued to insist that he knew Rachel when he was "a little fellow, coming up." He confidently described her as an "old midwife, an old Negro woman," a "full-blooded African." However, when pressed by Ross to elaborate on the "occasions" he had spent in Rachel's company, Valentine became entangled in the contradictions that his memories posed, not only in regard to his year of birth but also to the ethos of segregation. Unwilling to admit that he had ever socialized with a black woman, Valentine said he had only "met her on the road and would see her around the community," because "I was raised white myself."[14]

Having flustered Valentine, Ross baited him further. After Valentine had described his father and Newton Knight as close friends, Ross asked, probably with feigned surprise, "Did I understand you to say your father and Newt Knight were close associates?" Intimidated by the question's connotations, Valentine retorted, "Not so much associates—my father was a White man, altogether." Finally, when Valentine claimed to have seen Rachel at church, Ross asked whether he had seen her in a white or "Negro" church. Lamely, Valentine explained that perhaps he had seen Rachel while he was passing by one of the "Negro" churches.[15]

Valentine's erroneous claim that he knew Rachel discredited him as a witness, but his testimony was nonetheless revealing. He may genuinely have believed that he had seen Rachel as a child, for his family probably spoke of her long after her death. He might even have seen mixed-race Knights in his church during the 1890s. Wiley Jackson, a white witness who was fourteen years old when Rachel died, remembered seeing her in his family's church.[16]

Certainly Valentine's description of his father and Newt as close friends rings true, since four Valentine men rode with Newt's band of deserters during the Civil War, among them Valentine's grandfather.[17] In 1948, however, few white Mississippians would admit to associating with blacks or with whites accused of miscegenation. As Valentine illustrated in his remark that Newt Knight's "character" caused him to be buried among mixed-race people, whites knew that such contacts lowered one's status. Several witnesses insisted that whites who associated too intimately with blacks should themselves be classified as "Negroes." When attorney Ross prodded Oscar Williams to explain how he "knew" that Davis Knight's mother, Addie, was black, Williams cited as evidence "where she has been living and who she has been living with." Similarly, Mrs. Bertis Ellzey considered Addie a "Negro" because "she is living with Otho [Davis's father], so that's all I [need to] know."[18]

Not all white witnesses exhibited identical racial attitudes. Several of those born before 1880 spoke of their associations with Newt and Rachel

Knight without apparent embarrassment. Wiley Jackson, age seventy-four, casually admitted that his family and Rachel attended the same church during the 1880s. Seventy-seven-year-old Albert Gunter, whose uncles rode with Newt's band, acknowledged attending the burial of Rachel Knight's son Stewart after his murder in 1920.[19]

Sixty-nine-year-old Dr. John W. Stringer unabashedly recalled "numerous occasions" in the 1880s when his father took him to Rachel's farm to trade hogs and syrup. His memory of the Knights' participation in community bartering is reinforced by Anna Knight's description of how, as a child, she often walked six miles to town with her mother and grandmother (Georgeanne and Rachel) in order to trade eggs and chickens for sugar and coffee. Stringer further testified that he had known Otho Knight, Davis Knight's father, and Otho's parents, Jeffrey and Molly, "all of their lives, every one of them." He was Molly's attending physician in 1917 when she died of uterine cancer; during that sixteen-hour ordeal, he testified, he ate meals with the Knight family.[20]

The testimony of these witnesses reveals attitudes developed during childhood, during years when racial boundaries were fluid, when Southerners still debated appropriate black/white relations. Despite institutionalized segregation, some whites, such as John Stringer, continued to mingle with the mixed-race Knights. The deep roots of both white and black Knights in the community must also have influenced witnesses. Annette Knight recalled that Dr. Stringer was "much beloved" by the mixed-race Knights because he provided them medical care without regard for their race.[21]

In 1948 Stringer and Wiley Jackson seemed unwilling to see Newt Knight's great-grandson convicted of miscegenation. Neither indicated opposition to racial segregation, however, only to the prosecution's contention that Davis was black. Stringer testified that Davis's grandparents employed black servants who ate their meals in a side room, something that Davis's grandmother Ella Knight, also a witness, denied.[22]

In more important testimony, Stringer described Rachel as an Indian-looking woman "of a brown color, with long hair hanging down on her shoulders, long hair hanging down her back." Wiley Jackson similarly suggested that the "white Negroes" were Indians. He described Rachel as a "ginger-cake colored" woman who might have been half "Negro" but who more resembled a Choctaw Indian than an African. Perhaps Stringer and Jackson truly regarded the mixed-race Knights as Indians rather than Africans, but more likely they simply hoped to keep a young man whose family they had known all their lives from spending five years in the infamous Parchman penitentiary.[23]

Whatever their motives, Stringer and Jackson reinforced the testimonies of Henry and Ella Knight, Davis's grandparents. Henry denied unequivocally that his grandmother Rachel had African ancestors.[24] Like Wiley Jackson, he described her as the color of "ginger cake." When asked if she had kinky hair, Henry replied, "Her hair was curly, wasn't no kinky about it." He insisted that Rachel was part Creole and part Indian and that she "had no Negro blood in her at all." He described his grandfather Newton Knight as white, a "thoroughbred." The serious consequences that faced Davis Knight if he were legally classified as African American make it difficult to know whether Henry Knight truly believed—or cared—whether Rachel had African ancestry.[25]

Swartzfager, the prosecutor, next tried to prove that witness Ella Knight was black. Ella denied that she was "Negro" or that she even associated with "Negroes." When Swartzfager asked whether she attended a "Negro" school or church, she replied, "I went to our private school, with my kind of people." "In other words," asked Swartzfager, "you don't associate with colored people nor white people, just among yourselves?" Yes, she replied, "our own selves." Despite the label of "white Negroes," the Knight community had confounded the two major criteria—physical appearance and institutional affiliations—used to identify a person's race in segregated America.[26]

The Knights' tangled genealogy underscored the degree to which racism and segregation forced them to turn inward for insulation from a society that would not allow them to be white and that regarded blackness as a badge of inferiority. Although the grandparents' testimonies strengthened the defense's claim that Davis was white, they nonetheless increased confusion over who in this family was related to whom, and how. Henry and Ella, the court learned, had divorced, freeing Ella to marry Davis's other grandfather, Jeffrey, whose son Otho had married her daughter Addie. Thus Ella became her own daughter's step-mother-in-law and Davis's grandmother and step-grandmother.[27]

Although Davis's cousin Grace probably attended his trial, it is not surprising that Grace's sister Anna did not.[28] Attorney Ross surely did not want an avowedly African American Knight present, and ironically, the prosecution seemed not to know of her existence. In predominantly Baptist, Jim Crow Mississippi, Anna Knight's activities on behalf of the Seventh-Day Adventists and her own kinfolk seemed unknown to whites too young to have actually witnessed her at work. Thus the prosecution missed calling the one "white Negro" who could not, and would not, have denied that she considered herself black.[29]

Although the census enumerator for 1900 had classified all members of the "white Negro" community as black (see Chap. 8), trial witnesses in

Anna Knight. Photograph
courtesy of Minneola Dixon,
Oakwood Archives and
Museum, Oakwood College,
Huntsville, Alabama.

1948 agreed that Newt, his wife, Serena, and their children Molly and Mat
were white. Indeed, the prosecution's major witness was Tom Knight,
Newt and Serena's son, who two years earlier had published his sympathetic biography of his father. Deeply ashamed of the interracial marriages
of his sister and brother, Tom had left home at age eighteen and was
estranged from his father at the time of his death. Tom did not attend his
father's funeral and claimed never to have visited the grave.[30]

Tom Knight's racial views conformed to those of his society. He recon-
ciled with the memory of his dead father only by ignoring what he referred to during the trial as that "supposed business." The trial's revival of
old scandals shattered his hard-won peace of mind. On the witness stand,
eighty-eight-year-old Tom described Rachel as a full-blooded African with
"kinky hair, a wooly head, or whatever you want to call it." Rachel was
"just a regular Negro woman . . . she wasn't no half-mixture, wasn't no
half-mixture to it." Having suffered the humiliation of his family's miscegenation for seventy years, Tom seemed determined to prevent those
responsible for "tainting" his family's blood from becoming white, dis-

daining to recognize his mixed-race kin. One of those kin, Flo Wyatt, remembered being frightened as a child by this disheveled old man reduced to selling peanuts, chewing gum, and candy bars on the streets of Laurel.[31]

Apparently on the strength of Tom Knight's testimony as to Rachel's race, the Jones County Circuit Court convicted Davis Knight of miscegenation on December 17, 1948. Attorney Quitman Ross immediately requested a new trial, citing several procedural errors and "for the additional reason that the statute under which the defendant was tried and convicted is unconstitutional." The court denied his motion, and on December 20 Davis Knight appealed to the state supreme court. Fourteen citizens, including Wiley Jackson and John Stringer, posted his $2,500 bond.[32]

Since Ross had argued in the circuit trial that Davis was legally white and therefore had not questioned the constitutionality of Mississippi's miscegenation statutes, no issue of constitutionality was addressed by the state supreme court in Knight's appeal. On November 14, 1949, the high court reversed the lower court's verdict and remanded the case, concurring with Ross that the state had failed to prove beyond a reasonable doubt that "the party in question [Davis Knight] had one-eighth or more of Negro (or Mongolian) blood" and therefore was African American. Ross's original decision not to raise issues of constitutionality allowed the high court to base its decision strictly on laws governing racial identification, thereby circumventing criticism from civil rights groups. Since the case was not tried again, the high court, in effect, granted Davis Knight legal status as a white man.[33]

In the aftermath of their ordeal, mixed-race Knights differed in the way they racially identified themselves. For example, Davis Knight lived as a white man until his accidental death on August 8, 1959, in Houston, Texas, but his cousin Anna Knight spent twenty-six years as the president of the Seventh-Day Adventists' National Colored Association of Teachers. She died in 1972 at her beloved Oakwood College in Huntsville, Alabama. Until the very end of her ninety-eight years, she combined religious work with efforts to advance African American education and social mobility.[34]

Davis Knight's legal victory enabled his sister, Louvenia Knight, to wage a successful battle between 1960 and 1965 to have her two sons admitted to a white school. Just as Davis had collided in 1948 with a racial system of "strange paradoxes and hopelessly irreconcilable contradictions," so, too, did Louvenia in the 1960s. And, as in the case of her brother, those contradictions ultimately won her a victory. Arguing that she was legally white, she attempted in the midst of Mississippi's violent struggle over school integration to enroll her children in a nearby white school. She claimed that she did so *because* she opposed racial integration. After all, the children could not attend a "Negro" school if they were white.[35]

White members of the community insisted, however, that Louvenia's children were "Negroes." On that basis the West Jasper County School Board voted not to admit the boys, warning that violence might erupt if they did. After investigating Louvenia's case, the Mississippi State Sovereignty Commission struggled to break the stalemate between Louvenia and the school board. Commission members knew that legally the children must attend school, but they hoped to avoid press coverage of the case.[36]

Commission director Erle Johnston Jr. keenly perceived the paradox faced by the state of Mississippi. In a letter to the state superintendent of education dated December 12, 1963, he warned of the repercussions of denying enrollment of the Knight children in a white school: "Yet, if they [are] enrolled in a Negro school, because they are legally white, Jasper County would have an integrated public school—the first integration of a public school in Mississippi history." In the contradiction to end contradictions, the segregationist Sovereignty Commission supported the integration of the "white Negroes" into white schools as part of its last desperate effort to hold back the tide of racial integration in Mississippi schools.[37]

The struggles waged by Davis Knight and his sister, Louvenia, to attain legal whiteness provide fascinating examples of the unstable and shifting constructions of race in U.S. society. Equally important, they demonstrate the various strategies used by state leaders to resist the changing structure of race relations. Just as the state supreme court ruled in 1948 that Davis Knight was legally white in order to sidestep the more volatile question of whether antimiscegenation laws were constitutional, so, too, did the Mississippi State Sovereignty Commission support the enrollment of two children considered black by their white neighbors into white schools to prevent setting a precedent for racial integration.

Although the trial of Davis Knight did not directly advance the cause of black civil rights, it exposed the paradoxes of racial categorization in the segregated South. In the courtroom race was recognized as a legitimate determinant of whether Davis deserved full membership in society. Expressed in language about pure and impure blood, this discourse assumed that African Americans were the "other," a separate species of humankind who would pollute mainstream society if allowed freely to mate or roam about. Whether they believed it or not, Davis's family and friends were forced to argue that he had not a drop of African blood. Not surprisingly, most Mississippi whites continued to "know" that Davis was black, regardless of what the law said.

Automobile bumper sticker. Courtesy of DeBoyd Knight.

So deeply ingrained was the "one drop" theory of race and its accompanying assumptions about racial purity that as late as 1963 the director of the Mississippi Sovereignty Commission referred to Davis's great-
grandmother Rachel as the "villian [sic]" who "infused Negro blood into
the white blood of the descendants of Newton Knight."[38] Although Africans, Europeans, and Native Americans have long shared their ancestry as
well as their history, many people continued to deny this fact by ignoring
their own mixed-race kin and by defining mixed-race people as "Indian,"
"colored," or "black"—but rarely as "white"—even when they were of
primarily European ancestry. Reinforced by a genteel silence in regard to
interracial sexual relations, discrete racial categories continued to maintain
the fiction of distinct races.[39]

Certainly Ethel Knight did not change her racial views in light of Davis
Knight's new status as a white man. In spite of a growing number of
historical works during the 1940s and 1950s that subjected the Myth of
the Lost Cause to withering criticisms, she zealously asserted all of its chief
tenets. Publishing The Echo of the Black Horn in the same year as C. Vann
Woodward's pathbreaking Origins of the New South, Ethel successfully pack-
aged the Free State of Jones in a straitjacket of Lost Cause sentimentality
and indignation reminiscent of the publications of the Mississippi Historical Society.[40]

Ethel's version of the Free State of Jones became the story primarily of
one man: Newt Knight, a traitor not only to the Lost Cause but also to his
own race. She even gained Tom Knight's endorsement of her version of his
father's life by cleverly showcasing his bitter denunciation of his father's
interracial relations in bold letters on the book's dust jacket. With God's
help, Tom proclaimed, he had lived down "the disgrace and shame that my
father heaped upon me when he went to the Niggers!" Since Tom was
"soon to die," he authorized Ethel "to tell it all, the whole truth about my
father." The cover of Ethel's book assured readers that even old Tom agreed
that the truth must be told.[41]

Earle Knight, grandson of William Martin "Dickie" Knight, member of the Knight Company and Union soldier. Photograph courtesy of Earle Knight.

Headstone at mass grave of three men executed by Confederate colonel Robert Lowry in Jones County on April 16, 1864. Author's photograph.

Ethel achieved a difficult political and personal task when she wrote *The Echo of the Black Horn*. Perhaps nothing better demonstrated her success in pruning Newt Knight from the white branches of the family—and simultaneously defaming the Knight Company—than her version of Ben Knight's execution by Colonel Lowry (see Chap. 6). After vilifying her hated kinsman Newt with her "exposé" of Rachel, she claimed the sanctified Ben Knight for the loyal side of the family. Her rewriting of Ben's death, coupled with tales of mayhem and debauchery among the Knight

Company, disarmed many kinfolk who otherwise took a certain pride in their rebellious ancestors.

But not quite all. Until his death in 1998 at age ninety-three, Earle Knight joined his cousin DeBoyd Knight in maintaining the memory of the Knight Company. Proud of their grandfather Dickie Knight, who rode with the Knight band and later joined the Union Army, and of Dickie's more famous cousin, they replaced Newt's gravestone when it was stolen years ago. For Sil Coleman, T. H. (J. T.) Whitehead, and Thomas Yates (Ates)—three of the men executed during Lowry's raid—they erected a headstone in Jackie Knight's cemetery with an inscription proudly reminding visitors that the men "buried here in unmarked graves" were "summarily executed by the Confederate cavalry during the War Between the States because of their honest convictions."[42]

In regard to the story of Ben Knight, Earle seemed far more interested in describing to me how his great-uncle had slashed the throats of two or three Confederate bloodhounds with his knife before the cavalry brought him down than in speculating about whether Ben was carrying furlough papers in his pocket at the time. And Earle still delighted in telling how grandpa Dickie, who fled to the Union Army in New Orleans, often laughed that he would be "the only Yankee buried in Big Creek cemetery."[43]

Afterword

In the preface to the first edition of The Free State of Jones (2001), I noted that my research had "revealed a true story of the South that no novelist's fantasy could rival, one that begged to be told from a historical perspective, not to be treated as legend or gossip." I must confess, though, the image of a movie did briefly flash before my eyes. And why not? After all, this was history begging for a script, one in which a Civil War guerrilla band took up arms against the Confederacy, led by a charismatic leader, Newt Knight, who engaged in a forbidden sexual relationship with Rachel, his grandfather's slave. Before the nineteenth century ended, a community of "White Negroes" had emerged over which Newt presided until his death in 1922. Then, years after he and Rachel died, a jury convicted Davis Knight, their great-great-grandson, of the crime of marrying across the color line.

Although excited over a story brimming with controversy, I knew that Hollywood rarely buys the rights to make movies from books that historians write—no matter how dramatic the story. Moreover, I had written the history of the Free State of Jones with detailed analysis, rigorous examination of sources, and careful documentation. And in a manner distinctly unsuited to the Big Screen, I began the Civil War saga by tracing the roots of Jones County dissent back to the Revolutionary War era, and I ended it by connecting the story to the modern civil rights era.

Yet somehow the story of the Free State of Jones did capture the imagination of Hollywood. In 2005, my book *The Free State of Jones* was optioned by Outtabrooklyn Productions and Babbage Industries; in 2006, Universal Pictures purchased the option and exercised it the following year. But the movie seemed to languish until 2014, when STX Entertainment purchased the contract from Universal. At last, the movie, *The Free State of Jones*, directed by Gary Ross and starring Matthew McConaughey as guerrilla leader Newt Knight, was filmed in 2015 and is now set for release in early 2016.

My research on the Free State of Jones did not end with the 2001 publication of my book. In 2008, in anticipation of my next book, *The Long Shadow of the Civil War: Southern Dissent and Its Legacies* (University of North Carolina Press, 2010), I created the blog *Renegade South* as a forum for discussing Southern Unionism and relations of class and race from the Civil War era into the twentieth century. The blog quickly became a place for descendants and researchers nationwide to share information about Unionist communities of the South, including the Free State of Jones. Guest posts by Jones County descendants Jonathan Odell, B. T. Collins, Cindy DeVall, Nancy Stevens, and others soon enlivened the discussions of the scope and meaning of the Free State of Jones.

Thanks to guest bloggers on *Renegade South*, we now know that Unionist loyalties in Jones County were even more extensive than previously documented. In a three-part blog series, "Crossing the Rubicon of Loyalties," independent researcher Ed Payne expanded our understanding of Jones County's Unionist families, including his own Collins ancestors about whom he has published an article in the *Journal of Mississippi History*, and he showed that more than 200 men from the region joined the Union Army in New Orleans. Civil War historians Grady Howell and Jeff Giambrone likewise contributed documents that expanded our knowledge of Newt Knight and reinforced images of southeastern Mississippi as a center of Unionist sympathies.

Knight family historian and retired librarian Yvonne Bivins shared her expansive research on Rachel Knight in a three-part article published on *Renegade South*. In chronicling Rachel and Newt's connections to other mixed-race families of the area, Yvonne showed that interracial families and neighborhoods were far more common in the slaveholding and segregated South than perhaps most people realize. One of *Renegade South's* most popular articles is her riveting history of the 1966 murder of civil rights activist Vernon Dahmer, which she coauthored with his grandniece Wilmer Watts Backstrom. The multiracial "Kelly Settlement" where Dahmer lived shared close ties to the Knight community of Jones County.

Thanks to Knight family descendants who reached out to me through email, Facebook, and *Renegade South*, I understand their complicated story of race and racial identity better today than I did in 2001. The 1948 miscegenation trial of Davis Knight, I learned, is but one important milestone in more than a century and a half of controversy, confusion, and challenges as to whether the descendants of Newt and Rachel are black, brown, or white people. They are, of course, all three.

When the Mississippi State Supreme Court struck down Davis Knight's conviction on grounds the prosecution had failed to prove that enough "black blood" coursed through his veins to legally consider him black, the ruling spoke to issues of racial identity and, specifically, to the "one drop rule" of race. A mere one drop of African "blood," insisted white supremacists in the nineteenth- and twentieth-century United States, overrode European ancestry in determining one's racial identity. In fact, however, under Mississippi law one could legally have up to one-eighth African ancestry and still be categorized as white.

When it came to custom, however, people with any degree of African ancestry were expected to accept segregation and second-class citizenship. Many refused to abide by this rule, though, and since writing *The Free State of Jones*, I have had the pleasure of meeting several descendants and relatives of Newt and Rachel Knight who identify themselves racially in various ways.

Harlen McKnight, of Texas, for example, was raised as white although DNA tests confirmed several years ago that he is descended from Newt and Rachel. Delighted to learn the true history of his origins, he has since become acquainted with long lost relatives, and he recently accepted a small part in the movie *The Free State of Jones*. By contrast, Yvonne Bivins was raised black despite her white appearance. As the member of a family deeply involved in the civil rights movement in the sixties, Yvonne proudly claims her "one drop" and is critical of those Knights who chose to "pass" for white or Indian.

On the other hand, the word "pass" does not fit Dianne Walkup, who contacted me after reading *The Free State of Jones* to share her cultural upbringing as a woman of Native American ancestry. I got to know Dianne personally when she and her husband visited my husband Gregg and me at our home in Hannibal, Missouri. She is no more "passing" for Indian than Yvonne is passing for black, or Harlen for white. All are who they claim to be because race, let's remember, is a social invention and a cultural identification, not a biological reality.

Historically, people of mixed ancestry have often identified as white to escape oppression and violence, but also because they neither feel nor look "black." To insist on their "blackness" is to accept the one drop rule. Therefore, I no longer refer to persons of mixed-race ancestry as black unless, like Yvonne, they culturally identify themselves as such.

A different vision of the effect of mixed ancestry on the Knight descendants is articulated in *The State of Jones: The Small Southern County That Seceded from the Confederacy*, coauthored by journalist Sally Jenkins and Harvard professor John Stauffer and published in 2009. Jenkins and Stauffer present Newt Knight as an activist for "black equality," citing not only his actions on behalf of freedpeople during Reconstruction, but also his devotion to his "black" family and his burial in a "black" cemetery. There is, however, no evidence of Newt's own views on the "race" of his mixed-ancestry descendants. Though we know that Newt lovingly acknowledged, educated, and financially supported his mixed descendants, we don't know that he considered them black. In fact, Ethel Knight and Yvonne Bivins, local historians whose perspectives on the Knight community have often clashed, agree that Newt counseled his children to identify and marry as white.

The fact is, Newt left no record of his personal views on either racial equality or racial identity. In a sense, as novelist/memoirist Jonathan Odell points out, "Newt Knight is a kind of Rorschach. . . . His story, as well as Rachel's, has served for over a century to promote, deter, blame, inspire, include, or censure whatever personal bias we want to project onto him. If he never lived, we would have to invent him. . . . Whatever your demons or god, you can find enough 'facts' to name him 'Newt.'" Newt's protection of former slaves' rights of citizenship was his responsibility as an officeholder during Republican Reconstruction. His actions in that regard should not be conflated with a call for full racial equality, which was a hotly contested issue, even among Republicans.

For a clearer glimpse inside the walls of the "white Negro" community, I suggest we turn from Newt and Rachel and look more closely at Newt's (white) wife, Serena. Based on communications with Yvonne Bivins and Knight descendants Florence Blaylock, Olga Watts Nelson, and Dianne Walkup, and a rereading of the ex-slave narrative of Martha Wheeler, I think it is likely that Serena remained in Newt's household until the 1890s. But even when she left, she didn't go far. Until at least 1917, Serena lived with her daughter Molly and her mixed-race family. Even after Molly's death, Serena remained in the mixed-race household of her son-in-law and her grandchildren.

In other words, Serena, whose sons and daughters intermarried with the sons and daughters of Rachel, was as much a part of the mixed-race Knight community as was her husband Newt—and for far longer than Rachel, who died in 1889. The children who grew up in this community had every reason, culturally and physically, to consider themselves white—or, at least, as not black. As Ella Smith Knight testified during the Davis Knight trial, their racial associations were with those among "our own selves." To describe their community as "black" and then posit Newt Knight as a pioneer of "black equality" threatens to bury a complex history of race relations and racial identification that offers its own examples of courage and heroism, and must be approached on its own terms.

In 2010, I published new research and perspectives on the Free State of Jones in *The Long Shadow of the Civil War*. This collection of essays compares three Unionist communities in three different Southern states and assesses their impact on third-party political movements and postwar relations. Several of its chapters analyze material not used when I wrote *The Free State of Jones*.

The Long Shadow of the Civil War expands our understanding of Newt Knight's evolution from Confederate soldier to Unionist guerrilla leader who, as an old man in a moment of reflection, insisted that in retrospect the small farmers of the South should have risen up in a class revolution to destroy slavery. As for the children and grandchildren of Newt, Serena, and Rachel, we now better understand, too, that their experiences in the context of late nineteenth- and early twentieth-century America's obsession with racial "purity" shaped their decisions to identify as white or as persons of color.

I also devoted a chapter to three sisters from the mixed-race Knight community—Anna, Grace, and Lessie Knight—whose experiences shed further light on the role of mobility and opportunity, as well as on the political pressures and complexities that confronted them when it came to racial identity. Anna served as a missionary for the Seventh-Day Adventist Church; Grace was the Knight community's schoolteacher; and Lessie became the manager of a Hilton hotel in Texas. Only Lessie identified as white. Did she "pass" for white in Texas? Or is it more accurate to say that her sisters were forced to "pass" for black?

Thanks to social media, research by new scholars, and the upcoming movie, we have not heard the last of the Free State of Jones by a long shot. Given the current political climate, the timing of the movie could not be better! In the fourteen years since my book appeared, political arguments over the role of the federal government, the election and reelection of President Barack Obama, institutionalized racism, restrictive voter ID laws, and violence at home and abroad have divided the United States. Police brutality within a racially divided judicial system and struggles over issues of gun control, immigration, gay marriage, and abortion have become hot button issues. Perhaps it's not surprising, then, that political divisions have reinvigorated the United States' never-ending debate over the causes and effects of the American Civil War.

Arguments over the meaning and legacy of the Civil War exploded in the media after Dylann Roof, an avowed white supremacist, allegedly massacred nine African American men and women on June 17, 2015, in the historic Emanuel African Methodist Episcopal Church in Charleston, South Carolina. Roof is accused of taking the lives of the victims—who had welcomed him, a stranger, into their circle—for the mere fact that they were black. His favored icon for expressing his hatred for people of color? The Confederate flag.

As the nation reeled from news of this horrific crime, many pointed to the Confederate flag's popularity as a banner of white supremacy and racial segregation and called for its removal from Southern state capitols and federal buildings. Many white Southerners countered that the flag is an important symbol of heritage, one grounded not in hate, but in their ancestors' sacrifices on behalf of preserving a Southern way of life. Invoking the myth of the Lost Cause, they insisted that the Confederate cause was not about preserving slavery, but about protecting the constitutional principle of states' rights.

This Lost Cause fantasy, created by Southern journalists, novelists, and historians around the turn of the twentieth century, was sanctified by Hollywood in two landmark motion pictures: *Birth of a Nation* (1915) and the wildly popular *Gone with the Wind* (1939). Both movies entertained viewers with visions of noble slaveholders and contented slaves whose pastoral way of life was destroyed by greedy Northern industrialists intent on subjugating the South.

The Free State of Jones challenges the very core of this Lost Cause history, bringing to life white landowning, nonslaveholding families who acted aggressively in their own interests—interests that did not coincide with those of slaveholders. Dismissed by their pro-Confederate detractors as treasonous poor whites, outlaws, and cowards, the men and women who supported Jones County's Civil War insurrection in fact form a "heritage" long obscured by Confederate flags and monuments, as well as by cinematic portrayals of a mythic South.

Arguments over Southern heritage will surely be stoked by the appearance of a new movie that delves directly into the controversy. Director Gary Ross, who has read widely on the Free State of Jones, has written his own version of the story, one not based on any particular source. Even more important, he has written a screenplay, not a book. As those who revere history know, many Hollywood movies are historically based, but few are historically factual. Nor would most of the public enjoy them more if they were. A movie must appeal to our senses and emotions, and it must do so with lightning speed. It must satisfy our desire to be inspired, fired up, or just plain entertained—and it must do so with images and dialogue, not words on a page.

What does this mean to those who love history with all its nuances, complexities, unexpected turns, and sometimes unsatisfying, even inexplicable, endings? What does it mean, especially, to professional historians who painstakingly research and document every paragraph they write? Foremost, it requires that we remember the difference between a book and a movie, whose primary purpose is to entertain. Given those differences, one might conclude that moviemakers shouldn't tinker with historical topics at all. After all, scholars of history and the readers who love their books know that the movies likely won't "get it right."

Such a conclusion would be wrong in my judgment, and here's why. Movies stimulate our senses in ways that books cannot. Moreover, many people will not or cannot read books. So, even while the movie The Free State of Jones cannot tell its story with the depth and documentation expected of historians, and even while it will likely highlight the time-honored topics of battle scenes and romance, it will yet tell a vitally important story about class conflict, racial identity, and interracial cooperation, all wrapped in the cinematically unfamiliar story of Southern Civil War Unionism. In this movie, the white protagonists will be neither slaveholders nor poor whites; instead, we will meet landowning farmers with independent judgment and a strong sense of justice.

Instead of heroines reminiscent of Scarlett O'Hara, Melanie Wilkes, and the loyal Mammy of Gone with the Wind fame, in the movie The Free State of Jones, as well as in the book, farmwives, poor women, and women of color emerge as important allies of men who took to the swamps to resist Confederate authorities. Lastly, the movie will re-create the 1948 miscegenation trial of Newt and Rachel's descendant Davis Knight, after which the Mississippi State Supreme Court rendered a little-known decision that exploded the one drop rule of racial identity—not once and for all, but at least for the time that it took to keep a young man from spending five years in the Mississippi State Penitentiary (a.k.a. Parchman Farm).

Might the movie change how we think about the Civil War South in ways that historians cannot do alone? And perhaps even inspire us to read a few of the many fine books about Southern Unionism, guerrilla warfare, and the home front? That's where I'm placing my hopes.

Appendixes

Appendix 1: Selected Descendants of the Knight Family

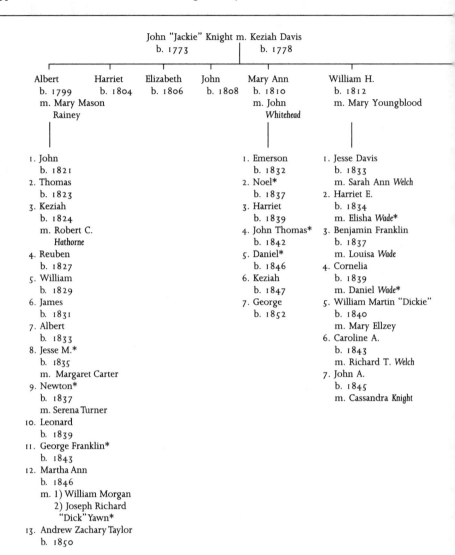

John "Jackie" Knight m. Keziah Davis
b. 1773   b. 1778

Albert	Harriet	Elizabeth	John	Mary Ann	William H.
b. 1799	b. 1804	b. 1806	b. 1808	b. 1810	b. 1812
m. Mary Mason				m. John	m. Mary Youngblood
Rainey				Whitehead	

1. John
   b. 1821
2. Thomas
   b. 1823
3. Keziah
   b. 1824
   m. Robert C.
   Hathorne
4. Reuben
   b. 1827
5. William
   b. 1829
6. James
   b. 1831
7. Albert
   b. 1833
8. Jesse M.*
   b. 1835
   m. Margaret Carter
9. Newton*
   b. 1837
   m. Serena Turner
10. Leonard
    b. 1839
11. George Franklin*
    b. 1843
12. Martha Ann
    b. 1846
    m. 1) William Morgan
       2) Joseph Richard
          "Dick" Yawn*
13. Andrew Zachary Taylor
    b. 1850

1. Emerson
   b. 1832
2. Noel*
   b. 1837
3. Harriet
   b. 1839
4. John Thomas*
   b. 1842
5. Daniel*
   b. 1846
6. Keziah
   b. 1847
7. George
   b. 1852

1. Jesse Davis
   b. 1833
   m. Sarah Ann Welch
2. Harriet E.
   b. 1834
   m. Elisha Wade*
3. Benjamin Franklin
   b. 1837
   m. Louisa Wade
4. Cornelia
   b. 1839
   m. Daniel Wade*
5. William Martin "Dickie"
   b. 1840
   m. Mary Ellzey
6. Caroline A.
   b. 1843
   m. Richard T. Welch
7. John A.
   b. 1845
   m. Cassandra Knight

Sources: U.S. Federal Manuscript Censuses, 1790–1860; Thomas et al., *Family of John "Jackie" Knight*; Sumrall and Welch, *Knights and Related Families*; Edwards and Strickland, *Who Married Whom*; Newton Knight folder, NA; Ethel Knight, *Echo of the Black Horn*; Thomas J. Knight, *Life and Activities of Captain Newton Knight*.

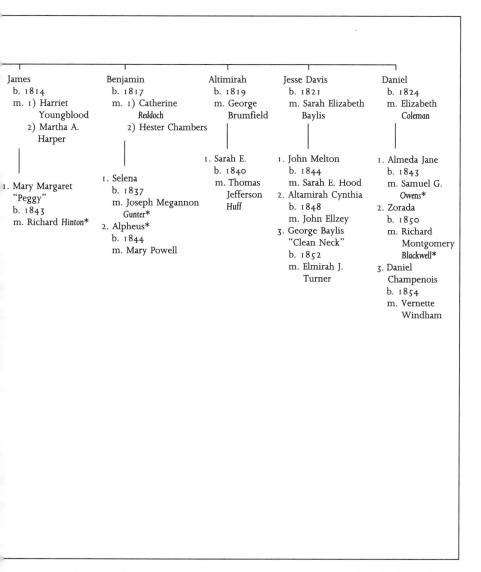

James	Benjamin	Altimirah	Jesse Davis	Daniel
b. 1814	b. 1817	b. 1819	b. 1821	b. 1824
m. 1) Harriet	m. 1) Catherine	m. George	m. Sarah Elizabeth	m. Elizabeth
Youngblood	*Reddoch*	Brumfield	Baylis	*Coleman*
2) Martha A.	2) Hester Chambers			
Harper				

1. Mary Margaret "Peggy"
b. 1843
m. Richard *Hinton**

1. Selena
b. 1837
m. Joseph Megannon *Gunter**
2. Alpheus*
b. 1844
m. Mary Powell

1. Sarah E.
b. 1840
m. Thomas Jefferson Huff

1. John Melton
b. 1844
m. Sarah E. Hood
2. Altamirah Cynthia
b. 1848
m. John Ellzey
3. George Baylis "Clean Neck"
b. 1852
m. Elmirah J. Turner

1. Almeda Jane
b. 1843
m. Samuel G. *Owens**
2. Zorada
b. 1850
m. Richard Montgomery *Blackwell**
3. Daniel Champenois
b. 1854
m. Vernette Windham

Note: All dates are approximate. Surnames of families that included individuals who supported the Knight Company are italicized. Asterisks denote men whose names appear on Newt Knight's Knight Company roster.

Appendix 2: Selected Descendants of the Coleman Family

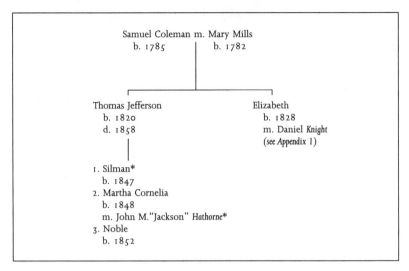

Samuel Coleman m. Mary Mills
b. 1785 | b. 1782

Thomas Jefferson
b. 1820
d. 1858

1. Silman*
 b. 1847
2. Martha Cornelia
 b. 1848
 m. John M."Jackson" *Hathorne**
3. Noble
 b. 1852

Elizabeth
b. 1828
m. Daniel *Knight*
(*see Appendix 1*)

Sources: U.S. Federal Manuscript Censuses, 1790–1860; Minnie S. Davis, *Confederate Patriots of Jones County*; Smith, Strickland, and Edwards, *Who Married Whom*; Newton Knight folder, NA; Ethel Knight, *Echo of the Black Horn*; Thomas J. Knight, *Life and Activities of Captain Newton Knight*.

Note: All dates are approximate. Surnames of families that included individuals who supported the Knight Company are italicized. Asterisks denote men whose names appear on Newt Knight's Knight Company roster.

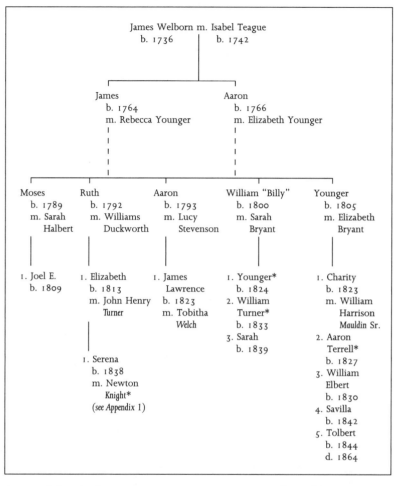

James Welborn m. Isabel Teague
b. 1736 | b. 1742

James
b. 1764
m. Rebecca Younger

Aaron
b. 1766
m. Elizabeth Younger

Moses	Ruth	Aaron	William "Billy"	Younger
b. 1789	b. 1792	b. 1793	b. 1800	b. 1805
m. Sarah	m. Williams	m. Lucy	m. Sarah	m. Elizabeth
Halbert	Duckworth	Stevenson	Bryant	Bryant

1. Joel E.
b. 1809

1. Elizabeth
b. 1813
m. John Henry
Turner

1. Serena
b. 1838
m. Newton
*Knight**
(see Appendix 1)

1. James
Lawrence
b. 1823
m. Tobitha
Welch

1. Younger*
b. 1824
2. William
Turner*
b. 1833
3. Sarah
b. 1839

1. Charity
b. 1823
m. William
Harrison
Mauldin Sr.
2. Aaron
Terrell*
b. 1827
3. William
Elbert
b. 1830
4. Savilla
b. 1842
5. Tolbert
b. 1844
d. 1864

Sources: U.S. Federal Manuscript Censuses, 1790–1860; Welborn folder, Genealogy File Cabinet, ML-USM; Gerald Johnson Genealogy Files; Sandra E. Boyd, *Benjamin Duckworth*; Newton Knight folder, NA; Ethel Knight, *Echo of the Black Horn*; Thomas J. Knight, *Life and Activities of Captain Newton Knight*.

Note: All dates are approximate. Surnames of families that included individuals who supported the Knight Company are italicized. Asterisks denote men whose names appear on Newt Knight's Knight Company roster. Broken lines of descent indicate uncertainty over which brother fathered which children.

Appendix 4: Selected Descendants of the Bynum Family

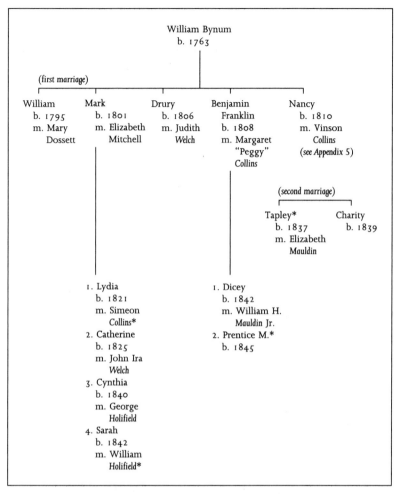

William Bynum
b. 1763

(first marriage)

William
b. 1795
m. Mary
Dossett

Mark
b. 1801
m. Elizabeth
Mitchell

Drury
b. 1806
m. Judith
Welch

Benjamin
Franklin
b. 1808
m. Margaret
"Peggy"
Collins

Nancy
b. 1810
m. Vinson
Collins
(see Appendix 5)

(second marriage)

Tapley*
b. 1837
m. Elizabeth
Mauldin

Charity
b. 1839

1. Lydia
   b. 1821
   m. Simeon
   *Collins**
2. Catherine
   b. 1825
   m. John Ira
   Welch
3. Cynthia
   b. 1840
   m. George
   Holifield
4. Sarah
   b. 1842
   m. William
   *Holifield**

1. Dicey
   b. 1842
   m. William H.
   Mauldin Jr.
2. Prentice M.*
   b. 1845

Sources: U.S. Federal Manuscript Censuses, 1790–1860; Baird, *Bynum and Baynham*; Sanders, *Bynum and Herrington Connections*; Wayne and JoAnn Wingate Genealogy Files; Newton Knight folder, NA; Ethel Knight, *Echo of the Black Horn*; Thomas J. Knight, *Life and Activities of Captain Newton Knight*.

Note: All dates are approximate. Surnames of families that included individuals who supported the Knight Company are italicized. Asterisks denote men whose names appear on Newt Knight's Knight Company roster.

Appendix 5: Selected Descendants of the Collins Family

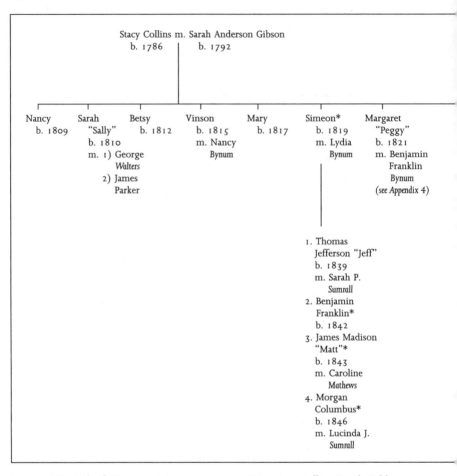

Stacy Collins m. Sarah Anderson Gibson
b. 1786   b. 1792

Nancy	Sarah	Betsy	Vinson	Mary	Simeon*	Margaret
b. 1809	"Sally"	b. 1812	b. 1815	b. 1817	b. 1819	"Peggy"
	b. 1810		m. Nancy		m. Lydia	b. 1821
	m. 1) George		Bynum		Bynum	m. Benjamin
	Walters					Franklin
	2) James					Bynum
	Parker					(*see Appendix 4*)

1. Thomas
   Jefferson "Jeff"
   b. 1839
   m. Sarah P.
   Sumrall
2. Benjamin
   Franklin*
   b. 1842
3. James Madison
   "Matt"*
   b. 1843
   m. Caroline
   Mathews
4. Morgan
   Columbus*
   b. 1846
   m. Lucinda J.
   Sumrall

Sources: U.S. Federal Manuscript Censuses, 1790–1860; Stacy Collins Family Bible (copy in possession of Mary Bess Gamero-Adams); Carr P. Collins Jr., *Royal Ancestors*; Vinson Allen Collins, *Story of My Parents*; Regina Roper Genealogy Files; Newton Knight folder, NA; Ethel Knight, *Echo of the Black Horn*; Thomas J. Knight, *Life and Activities of Captain Newton Knight.*

Stacy	Riley	Jasper J.*	Newton	Warren	Christopher	Edwin W.
b. 1823	James*	b. 1827	b. 1830	Jacob	Calhoun	b. 1840
m. Allie	b. 1825	m. Gatsy		b. 1833	b. 1835	
Walters	m. Desdemonia	Powell		m. Tolitha		
	Welch			Eboline		
				Valentine		

Note: All dates are approximate. Surnames of families that included individuals who supported the Knight Company are italicized. Asterisks denote men whose names appear on Newt Knight's Knight Company roster.

Appendix 6: Selected Descendants of the Sumrall Family

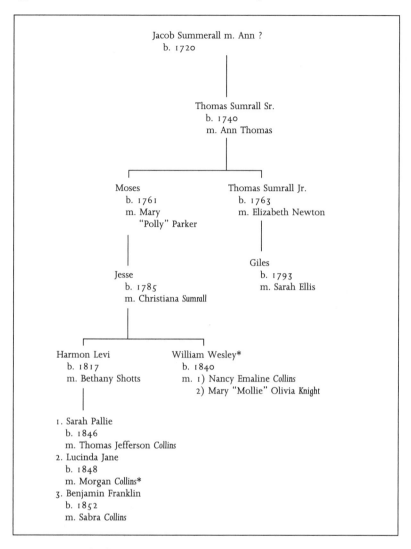

Jacob Summerall m. Ann ?
b. 1720

Thomas Sumrall Sr.
b. 1740
m. Ann Thomas

Moses
b. 1761
m. Mary
"Polly" Parker

Thomas Sumrall Jr.
b. 1763
m. Elizabeth Newton

Jesse
b. 1785
m. Christiana *Sumrall*

Giles
b. 1793
m. Sarah Ellis

Harmon Levi
b. 1817
m. Bethany Shotts

William Wesley*
b. 1840
m. 1) Nancy Emaline *Collins*
2) Mary "Mollie" Olivia *Knight*

1. Sarah Pallie
b. 1846
m. Thomas Jefferson *Collins*
2. Lucinda Jane
b. 1848
m. Morgan *Collins**
3. Benjamin Franklin
b. 1852
m. Sabra *Collins*

Sources: U.S. Federal Manuscript Censuses, 1790–1860; Hines, The Families Somerville, Somervaill, Summerall, Summerell, Summerill, Summerlin, Sumlin, Sumrall, and Sumril; Sumrall folder, Genealogy Vertical Files, MDAH; Newton Knight folder, NA; Ethel Knight, Echo of the Black Horn; Thomas J. Knight, Life and Activities of Captain Newton Knight.

Note: All dates are approximate. Surnames of families that included individuals who supported the Knight Company are italicized. Asterisks denote men whose names appear on Newt Knight's Knight Company roster.

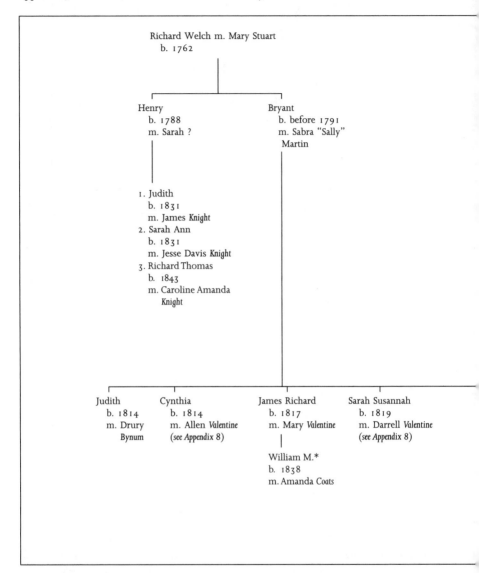

Richard Welch m. Mary Stuart
b. 1762

Henry
b. 1788
m. Sarah ?

Bryant
b. before 1791
m. Sabra "Sally"
Martin

1. Judith
  b. 1831
  m. James Knight
2. Sarah Ann
  b. 1831
  m. Jesse Davis Knight
3. Richard Thomas
  b. 1843
  m. Caroline Amanda
    Knight

Judith
b. 1814
m. Drury
  Bynum

Cynthia
b. 1814
m. Allen Valentine
(see Appendix 8)

James Richard
b. 1817
m. Mary Valentine

Sarah Susannah
b. 1819
m. Darrell Valentine
(see Appendix 8)

William M.*
b. 1838
m. Amanda Coats

Sources: U.S. Federal Manuscript Censuses, 1790–1860; Carr P. Collins Jr., *Royal Ancestors*; Vinson Allen Collins, *Story of My Parents*; Edwards and Strickland, *Who Married Whom*; Newton Knight folder, NA; Ethel Knight, *Echo of the Black Horn*; Thomas J. Knight, *Life and Activities of Captain Newton Knight*.

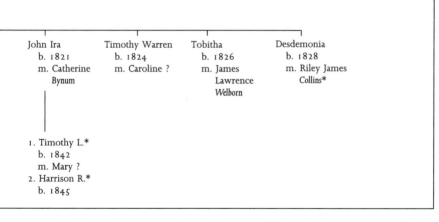

John Ira	Timothy Warren	Tobitha	Desdemonia
b. 1821	b. 1824	b. 1826	b. 1828
m. Catherine	m. Caroline ?	m. James	m. Riley James
Bynum		Lawrence	*Collins**
		Welborn	

1. Timothy L.*
   b. 1842
   m. Mary ?
2. Harrison R.*
   b. 1845

Note: All dates are approximate. Surnames of families that included individuals who supported the Knight Company are italicized. Asterisks denote men whose names appear on Newt Knight's Knight Company roster.

Appendix 8: Selected Descendants of the Valentine Family

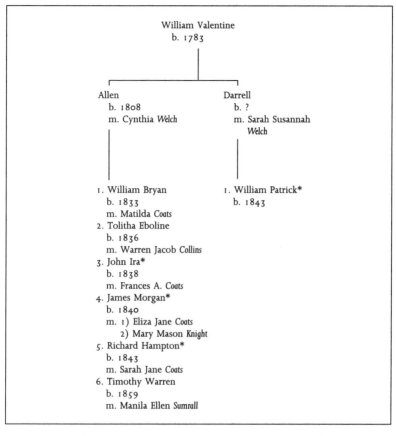

William Valentine
b. 1783

Allen
b. 1808
m. Cynthia *Welch*

Darrell
b. ?
m. Sarah Susannah
Welch

1. William Bryan
   b. 1833
   m. Matilda *Coats*
2. Tolitha Eboline
   b. 1836
   m. Warren Jacob *Collins*
3. John Ira*
   b. 1838
   m. Frances A. *Coats*
4. James Morgan*
   b. 1840
   m. 1) Eliza Jane *Coats*
      2) Mary Mason *Knight*
5. Richard Hampton*
   b. 1843
   m. Sarah Jane *Coats*
6. Timothy Warren
   b. 1859
   m. Manila Ellen *Sumrall*

1. William Patrick*
   b. 1843

Sources: U.S. Federal Manuscript Censuses, 1790–1860; Carr P. Collins Jr., *Royal Ancestors*; Vinson Allen Collins, *Story of My Parents*; Edwards and Strickland, *Who Married Whom*; Newton Knight folder, NA; Ethel Knight, *Echo of the Black Horn*; Thomas J. Knight, *Life and Activities of Captain Newton Knight*.

Note: All dates are approximate. Surnames of families that included individuals who supported the Knight Company are italicized. Asterisks denote men whose names appear on Newt Knight's Knight Company roster.

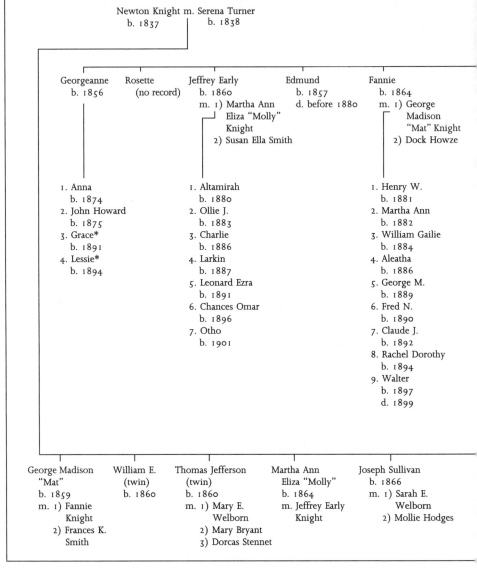

Newton Knight m. Serena Turner
b. 1837 | b. 1838

Georgeanne	Rosette	Jeffrey Early	Edmund	Fannie
b. 1856	(no record)	b. 1860	b. 1857	b. 1864
		m. 1) Martha Ann	d. before 1880	m. 1) George
		Eliza "Molly"		Madison
		Knight		"Mat" Knight
		2) Susan Ella Smith		2) Dock Howze

1. Anna		1. Altamirah		1. Henry W.
b. 1874		b. 1880		b. 1881
2. John Howard		2. Ollie J.		2. Martha Ann
b. 1875		b. 1883		b. 1882
3. Grace*		3. Charlie		3. William Gailie
b. 1891		b. 1886		b. 1884
4. Lessie*		4. Larkin		4. Aleatha
b. 1894		b. 1887		b. 1886
		5. Leonard Ezra		5. George M.
		b. 1891		b. 1889
		6. Chances Omar		6. Fred N.
		b. 1896		b. 1890
		7. Otho		7. Claude J.
		b. 1901		b. 1892
				8. Rachel Dorothy
				b. 1894
				9. Walter
				b. 1897
				d. 1899

George Madison	William E.	Thomas Jefferson	Martha Ann	Joseph Sullivan
"Mat"	(twin)	(twin)	Eliza "Molly"	b. 1866
b. 1859	b. 1860	b. 1860	b. 1864	m. 1) Sarah E.
m. 1) Fannie		m. 1) Mary E.	m. Jeffrey Early	Welborn
Knight		Welborn	Knight	2) Mollie Hodges
2) Frances K.		2) Mary Bryant		
Smith		3) Dorcas Stennet		

Sources: U.S. Federal Manuscript Censuses, 1870–1920; Thomas et al., *Family of John "Jackie" Knight*; Sumrall and Welch, *Knights and Related Families*; Ardella Knight Barrett Papers; Genealogy Files of Rhonda Benoit, Florence Knight Blaylock, Versie McKnight Frederick, Frances Jackson, Olga Watts Nelson, and Kenneth Welch.

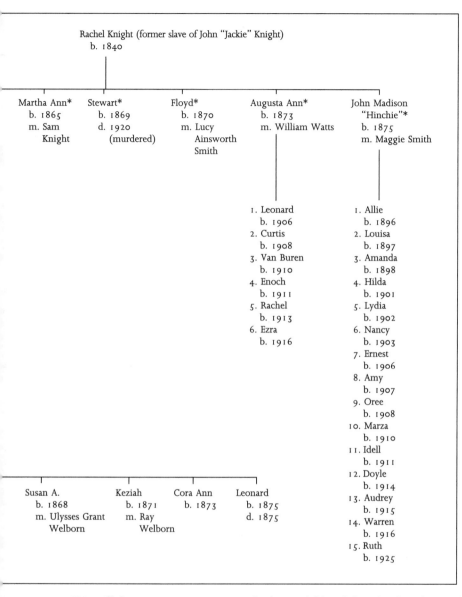

Rachel Knight (former slave of John "Jackie" Knight)
b. 1840

Martha Ann*
b. 1865
m. Sam
Knight

Stewart*
b. 1869
d. 1920
(murdered)

Floyd*
b. 1870
m. Lucy
Ainsworth
Smith

Augusta Ann*
b. 1873
m. William Watts

John Madison
"Hinchie"*
b. 1875
m. Maggie Smith

1. Leonard
   b. 1906
2. Curtis
   b. 1908
3. Van Buren
   b. 1910
4. Enoch
   b. 1911
5. Rachel
   b. 1913
6. Ezra
   b. 1916

1. Allie
   b. 1896
2. Louisa
   b. 1897
3. Amanda
   b. 1898
4. Hilda
   b. 1901
5. Lydia
   b. 1902
6. Nancy
   b. 1903
7. Ernest
   b. 1906
8. Amy
   b. 1907
9. Oree
   b. 1908
10. Marza
    b. 1910
11. Idell
    b. 1911
12. Doyle
    b. 1914
13. Audrey
    b. 1915
14. Warren
    b. 1916
15. Ruth
    b. 1925

Susan A.
b. 1868
m. Ulysses Grant
Welborn

Keziah
b. 1871
m. Ray
Welborn

Cora Ann
b. 1873

Leonard
b. 1875
d. 1875

Note: All dates are approximate. Asterisks denote children believed to have been fathered out of wedlock by Newton Knight.

Notes

Abbreviations

The following abbreviations are used throughout the notes.

GDAH	Georgia Department of Archives and History, Atlanta
ICPSR	Inter-University Consortium for Political and Social Research
MDAH	Mississippi Department of Archives and History, Jackson
ML-USM	McCain Library, University of Southern Mississippi, Hattiesburg
NA	National Archives, Washington, D.C.
NA-SE	National Archives, Southeast Region, East Point, Ga.
NCDAH	North Carolina Division of Archives and History, Raleigh
RG	Record Group
SCDAH	South Carolina Department of Archives and History, Columbia
WPA	Works Projects Administration

Introduction

1. *State of Mississippi v. Davis Knight*, Dec. 13, 1948, case no. 646, court record and transcript of the Circuit Court, Jones County, Miss. (Clerk's Office, Mississippi Supreme Court, Jackson), transcript, 4–6 (hereafter these two separately paged sections of the record of the case are cited as either *State v. Knight*, record, or *State v. Knight*, transcript).

2. *State v. Knight*, transcript, 11; U.S. Bureau of the Census, Federal Manuscript Censuses, 1880, 1900, Jasper County, Miss.; Jan Sumrall and Kenneth Welch, *The Knights and Related Families* (Denham Springs, La.: n.p., 1985), 12; Ethel Knight, *The Echo of the Black Horn: An Authentic Tale of "The Governor" of "The Free State of Jones"* (n.p., 1951), 298. Molly Knight's proper name was Martha Ann Eliza Knight; Jeffrey's was Jeffrey Early; Mat's

was George Madison; and Fannie was listed as Frances in the 1900 Federal Manuscript Census. Censuses indicate that the marriages took place in 1878, although Ethel Knight claimed that both couples married on Christmas Eve 1884.

3. On the connections between interracial sexual relations and lynching, see esp. Nancy MacLean, *Behind the Mask of Chivalry: The Making of the Second Ku Klux Klan* (New York: Oxford University Press, 1994), 141–48; LeeAnn Whites, "Rebecca Latimer Felton and the Wife's Farm: The Class and Racial Politics of Gender Reform," *Georgia Historical Quarterly* 76 (summer 1992): 354–72; and Jacquelyn Dowd Hall, " 'The Mind That Burns in Each Body': Women, Rape, and Racial Violence," in *Powers of Desire: The Politics of Sexuality*, ed. Ann Snitow, Christine Stansell, and Sharon Thompson (New York: Monthly Review Press, 1983), 328–49.

4. James Street, *Tap Roots* (Garden City, N.Y.: Sun Dial Press, 1943). On the life and career of Street, see Thomas L. McHaney, "James Street: Making History Live," in *Mississippi's Piney Woods: A Human Perspective*, ed. Noel Polk (Jackson: University Press of Mississippi, 1986), 121–33.

5. Thomas J. Knight, *The Life and Activities of Captain Newton Knight and His Company and the "Free State of Jones"* (1935; rev. ed, Laurel, Miss.: n.p., 1946).

6. The novel *Tap Roots* was made into a movie with the same name by Universal-International.

7. *State v. Knight*, record, 27–30; *Time*, Dec. 27, 1948; *Knight v. State*, 207 Miss. 564 (1949).

8. Ethel Knight, *Echo of the Black Horn*, 7.

9. Ibid., frontispiece.

10. Ibid., 7, 82–85, 90–95, 126, 142, 168.

11. Ibid., 104.

12. Mary Looram, "A Little-Known Republic," *Outlook*, Mar. 17, 1920; James Street, *Look Away! A Dixie Notebook* (New York: Viking, 1936); and Craddock Goins, "The Secession of Jones County," *American Mercury*, Jan. 1941, all perpetuated myths surrounding the legend of Jones County's secession. Newton Knight and his followers were described as principled unionists in Thomas J. Knight, *Life and Activities of Captain Newton Knight*, 17; Street, *Tap Roots*; and Jack D. L. Holmes, "The Mississippi County That 'Seceded' from the Confederate States of America," *Civil War Times Illustrated* 3 (Feb. 1965): 85–94; as hardheaded individualists in John K. Bettersworth, *Confederate Mississippi: The People and Policies of a Cotton State in Wartime* (Baton Rouge: Louisiana State University Press, 1963), 524–25; as thieves and murderers in Ethel Knight, *Echo of the Black Horn*, and Rudy Leverett, *Legend of the Free State of Jones* (Jackson: University Press of Mississippi, 1984).

13. Alexander L. Bondurant, "Did Jones County Secede?," *Publications of the Mississippi Historical Society* 1 (1898): 103–6; Goode Montgomery, "Alleged Secession of Jones County," *Publications of the Mississippi Historical Society* 8 (1904): 13–22. Jones's secession was also denied by L. R. Collins, youngest son of Jasper Collins, in a letter to the *Mobile Daily Herald* dated May 19, 1914; see typed copy of letter in unpublished files, WPA, RG 60, vol. 316, MDAH. In 1921 Newton Knight denied that Jones County seceded from either the Union or the Confederacy (*New Orleans Item*, Mar. 20, 1921).

14. Colonel Brown to Governor Clark, May 5, 1864, Governors' Papers, RG 27, vol. 56, MDAH.

15. *Mobile Evening News*, 3 May 1864, James L. Power Scrapbook, Private Manuscripts, MDAH. On plain folk democracy, see Lacy K. Ford, "Popular Ideology of the Old South's Plain Folks: The Limits of Egalitarianism in a Slaveholding Society," in *Plain Folk*

of the South Revisited, ed. Samuel C. Hyde Jr. (Baton Rouge: Louisiana State University, 1997), 225–27. On the Texas Collinses', see Campbell Loughmiller and Lynn Loughmiller, Big Thicket Legacy (Austin: University of Texas Press, 1977), 70–72.

16. On the importance of studying the local settings of unionism, see esp. John Inscoe and Robert Kenzer, eds., Enemies of the Country (Athens: University of Georgia Press, forthcoming); Daniel E. Sutherland, Unionists, Guerrillas, and Violence on the Confederate Home Front (Fayetteville: University of Arkansas Press, 1999); David Williams, Rich Man's War: Class, Caste, and Confederate Defeat in the Lower Chattahoochee Valley (Athens: University of Georgia Press, 1998); Kenneth W. Noe and Shannon H. Wilson, The Civil War in Appalachia: Collected Essays (Knoxville: University of Tennessee Press, 1997); Phillip Paludan, Victims: A True Story of the Civil War (Knoxville: University of Tennessee Press, 1981).

Chapter One

1. Although it must be used with care, the best composite source for birthplaces of the greatest number of free residents of Jones County is Patricia N. Edwards and Jean Strickland, Who Married Whom: Jones County, Mississippi (Moss Point, Miss.: n.p., 1986).

2. James Street, Oh, Promised Land (New York: Dial Press, 1940), 16–23, 410–41, and Tap Roots (Garden City, N.Y.: Sun Dial Press, 1943), 25–31.

3. On Anglo-Indian wars of the Carolina and Georgia backcountry, see esp. Tom Hatley, The Dividing Paths: Cherokees and South Carolinians through the Revolutionary Era (New York: Oxford University Press, 1995), and Louis De Vorsey Jr., The Indian Boundary in the Southern Colonies, 1763–1775 (Chapel Hill: University of North Carolina Press, [1961] 1966). On economic development and political strife in the backcountry, see Kenneth E. Lewis, "Economic Development in the South Carolina Backcountry: A View from Camden," in The Southern Colonial Backcountry: Interdisciplinary Perspectives on Frontier Communities, ed. David Colin Crass, Steven D. Smith, Martha A. Zierden, and Richard D. Brooks (Knoxville: University of Tennessee Press, 1998), 87–107; Rachel N. Klein, Unification of a Slave State: The Rise of the Planter Class in the South Carolina Backcountry, 1760–1808 (Chapel Hill: University of North Carolina Press, 1990), 9–108; and Richard Maxwell Brown, The South Carolina Regulators (Cambridge, Mass: Belknap Press of Harvard University Press, 1963). On the worldview of Regulators, see Marjoleine Kars, " 'Breaking Loose Together': Religion and Rebellion in the North Carolina Piedmont, 1730–1790" (Ph.D. diss., Duke University, 1994), 73, 74, 87, 123.

The King's Mountain and Cowpens battles of the Ninety Six District are covered in detail in Robert D. Bass, Ninety Six: The Struggle for the South Carolina Back Country (Lexington, S.C.: Sandlapper Store, 1978). On battles between Whigs and Tories, especially in the Georgia upcountry counties of Wilkes, Richmond, and Burke, see Edward Cashin, "From Creeks to Crackers," in Crass, Smith, Zierden, and Brooks, Southern Colonial Backcountry, 69–75, and Robert Scott Davis Jr., Georgians in the Revolution: At Kettle Creek (Wilkes Co.) and Burke County (Easley, S.C.: Southern Historical Press, 1986) and Georgia Citizens and Soldiers of the American Revolution (Easley, S.C.: Southern Historical Press, 1983).

4. On the concept of a "popular memory" transferred from one generation to the next, see Alfred F. Young, "English Plebeian Culture and Eighteenth-Century American Radicalism," in The Origins of Anglo American Radicalism, ed. Margaret Jacob and James Jacob (Boston: Allen and Unwin, 1983), 185–212, and Catherine McNicol Stock, Rural Radicals: Righteous Rage in the American Grain (Ithaca, N.Y.: Cornell University Press, 1996), 18–33. On the role of class conflict in yeoman uprisings against the Confederacy, see esp. David Williams, Rich Man's War: Class, Caste, and Confederate Defeat in the Lower Chattahoochee Valley (Athens: University of Georgia Press, 1998).

5. Ethel Knight, *The Echo of the Black Horn: An Authentic Tale of "The Governor" of "The Free State of Jones"* (n.p., 1951), 16.

6. Street, *Tap Roots*, 17, 43–45, 226–27.

7. Thomas J. Knight, *The Life and Activities of Captain Newton Knight and His Company and the "Free State of Jones"* (1935; rev. ed, Laurel, Miss.: n.p., 1946), 2–3. Mason Rainey married Albert Knight on December 20, 1820. Tom Knight claimed that "in some way that I have not learned, [Mason Rainey Knight] was a Griffin" and was "raised an orphan by Jackie Knight." Tom's assertions, like Ethel's, must be studied with care. He claimed, for example, that Newt was "yet a boy" when his father died, although facts show that Albert Knight died in 1862, when Newt was at least twenty-four years old. Although Martha Wheeler agreed that Jackie and Keziah Knight raised Mason Rainey, she "did not credit" the story that Jackie brought a pot of gold with him to Mississippi that allegedly belonged to his ward. See George P. Rawick, ed., *The American Slave: A Composite Autobiography*, supplement, ser. 1, vol. 10, *Mississippi Narratives*, pt. 5 (Westport, Conn.: Greenwood Press, 1972), 2265.

8. Street, *Tap Roots*, 44; Ethel Knight, *Echo of the Black Horn*, 84. Perhaps the final word should be Kenneth Welch's; he labeled Tom Knight's and Ethel Knight's tales about Mason Rainey "too far-fetched to believe." Based on 1816 and 1820 state censuses of Mississippi, which do not indicate a female of Mason Rainey's age living in Jackie Knight's household, Welch concluded that "Mason Rainey was not raised by John Knight" (Jan Sumrall and Kenneth Welch, *The Knights and Related Families* [Denham Springs, La.: n.p., 1985], 150).

9. Street, *Tap Roots*, 44; Ethel Knight, *Echo of the Black Horn*, 7, 10, 83. Although Street incorporated local gossip about the early history of the Knight family into various *Tap Roots* characters, he did so in an inconsistent manner that enabled him to create his own tale.

10. On the construction of race in the colonial and Revolutionary South, see esp. Catherine Clinton and Michele Gillespie, eds., *The Devil's Lane: Sex and Race in the Early South* (New York: Oxford University Press, 1997). On Gideon Gibson's role in the Regulator Movement, see Klein, *Unification of a Slave State*, 69–71, and Winthrop D. Jordan, *White over Black: American Attitudes toward the Negro, 1550–1812* (Chapel Hill: University of North Carolina Press, 1968), 172–74. Internet sources include Paul Heinegg, "Free African Americans of Virginia, North Carolina, South Carolina, Maryland, and Delaware," Mar. 4, 1999, http://www.freeafricanamericans.com/introduction.htm, 8–9, and WGBH/Frontline, Mario de Valdes y Cocom, "The Blurred Racial Lines of Famous Families," memo of Apr. 25, 1996, http://www.pbs.org/wgbh/pages/frontline/shows/secret/famous/april25.html.

11. Daniel Richter, " 'Believing That Many of the Red People Suffer Much for the Want of Food': Hunting, Agriculture, and a Quaker Construction of Indianness in the Early Republic," and Jon Gjerde, " 'Here in America there is neither king nor tyrant': European Encounters with Race, 'Freedom,' and Their European Pasts," both in *Journal of the Early Republic* 19, no. 4 (winter 1999): 601–28, 673–90; Edmund Morgan, *American Slavery, American Freedom: The Ordeal of Colonial Virginia* (New York: Norton, 1975), 292; Alfred F. Young, "How Radical Was the American Revolution," afterword in *Beyond the American Revolution: Explorations in the History of American Radicalism*, ed. Alfred F. Young (DeKalb: Northern Illinois University Press, 1993), 342–47.

12. On the dynamics of class and the impact of slavery on the construction of race in early North America and the nineteenth-century South, see esp. David R. Roediger, "The Pursuit of Whiteness: Property, Terror, and Expansion, 1790–1860"; Lois E. Horton, "From Class to Race in Early America: Northern Post-Emancipation Racial

Reconstruction"; James Brewer Stewart, "Modernizing 'Difference': The Political Meanings of Color in the Free States, 1776–1840"; and Lacy K. Ford Jr., "Making the 'White Man's' Country White: Race, Slavery, and State Building in the Jacksonian South," all in *Journal of the Early Republic* 19, no. 4 (winter 1999): 579–600, 629–50, 691–712, 713–38; Martha Hodes, *White Women, Black Men: Illicit Sex in the Nineteenth-Century South* (New Haven: Yale University Press, 1997), 28–31; Kathleen M. Brown, *Good Wives, Nasty Wenches, and Anxious Patriarchs: Gender, Race, and Power in Colonial Virginia* (Chapel Hill: University of North Carolina Press, 1996), 1–2, 9, 187–211, 369–70; Peter Bardaglio, *Reconstructing the Household: Families, Sex, and the Law in the Nineteenth-Century South* (Chapel Hill: University of North Carolina Press, 1995), 48–55; A. Leon Higgin-botham, *In the Matter of Color: Race and the American Legal Process: The Colonial Period* (New York: Oxford University Press, 1978), 14, 40–47; Morgan, *American Freedom, American Slavery*, 328–37; and Jordan, *White over Black*, 136–78.

13. Stewart, "Modernizing 'Difference,'" 693–96; Joan Pope Melish, "The 'Condition' Debate and Racial Discourse in the Antebellum North," *Journal of the Early Republic* 19, no. 4 (winter 1999): 651–72; Kathleen M. Brown, *Good Wives, Nasty Wenches, and Anxious Patriarchs*, 355–56; John Shelton Reed, "Mixing in the Mountains," *Southern Cultures* 3, no. 4 (spring 1998): 25–36; Edward Cashin, "From Creeks to Crackers"; James H. Dorman, "Ethnicity and Identity: Creoles of Color in Twentieth-Century South," in *Creoles of Color in the Gulf South*, ed. James H. Dorman (Knoxville: University of Tennessee Press, 1996), 166–79; N. Brent Kennedy with Robyn Vaughan Kennedy, *The Melungeons: The Resurrection of a Proud People, an Untold Story of Ethnic Cleansing in America* (Macon, Ga.: Mercer University Press, 1994); Paul Heinegg, *Free African Americans of North Carolina and Virginia* (Baltimore: Genealogical Pub. Co., 1994); Carl A. Brasseaux, Keith P. Fontenot, and Claude F. Oubre, *Creoles of Color in the Bayou Country* (Jackson: University Press of Mississippi, 1994); Enrique Eugene Gildemeister, "Local Complexities of Race in the Rural South: Racially Mixed People in South Carolina" (unpublished paper in author's possession, June 1977); Gary B. Mills, *The Forgotten People: Cane River's Creoles of Color* (Baton Rouge: Louisiana State University Press, 1977).

14. On the fluidity of racial lines in the eighteenth-century South, see Hodes, *White Women, Black Men*, 20–38; Heinegg, *Free African Americans*; Gildemeister, "Local Complexities"; Rhys Isaac, *The Transformation of Virginia, 1740–1790* (Chapel Hill: University of North Carolina Press, 1982), 20–23, 31–32, 52–53, 132–33; and Bardaglio, *Reconstructing the Household*, 55–56. Although few slaves were imported into North Carolina during the eighteenth century, persons who already held slaves, particularly in the Albemarle region, increased their holdings; see H. Roy Merrens, *Colonial North Carolina in the Eighteenth Century: A Study in Historical Geography* (Chapel Hill: University of North Carolina Press, 1964), 79–81.

15. Francis Jennings, "The Indians' Revolution," in *The American Revolution: Explorations in the History of American Radicalism*, ed. Alfred F. Young (DeKalb: Northern Illinois Press, 1976), 319–48; Gary Nash, "The Image of the Indian in the Southern Colonial Mind," *William and Mary Quarterly* 29 (Apr. 1972): 197–230; Kathleen M. Brown, *Good Wives, Nasty Wenches, and Anxious Patriarchs*, 174–85.

16. Bardaglio, *Reconstructing the Household*, 57; Hodes, *White Women, Black Men*, 147. Newt's behavior was even more threatening to whites of his era because of their decreasing tolerance of interracial relationships in the wake of black freedom.

17. Ethel Knight, *Echo of the Black Horn*, 16. On racial mixing and trade relations among Creek Indians and Anglo settlers in pre-Revolutionary Augusta, Georgia, see Edward Cashin, "From Creeks to Crackers," 69–75. Some Knight family genealogists, notably Ethel Knight, contend that Miles Knight, a Revolutionary soldier from North Carolina,

was the father of Jackie Knight. This is not credible (see also Sumrall and Welch, *Knights and Related Families*, intro., xi). There is no record that suggests kinship, nor does his name appear in any Georgia records. Furthermore, Miles Knight was alive in New Hanover County, N.C., at least until 1800, and he had a wife named Nancy, not Mary. See Alexander McDonald Walker, comp., *New Hanover Co. Court Minutes, 1794–1800* (n.p., 1962), pt. 3:63; pt. 4:51, 75, 94, 96, 98.

18. Emma Jean Ponder Wood, Annie Ponder Sarrett, and Kathleen Wood Cook, comps., *Ponder-Teague Connections* (Camden, Ark.: Dan Cook's Printing, 1988), 276–77. The experiences of Edward Teague, a direct ancestor of Jones County deserter Younger Welborn Jr., demonstrated the early migration patterns of many small landowners. Edward was the great-grandfather of Isabella Teague Welborn, the mother of Aaron Welborn and great-grandmother of Younger Welborn Jr. He typified those indentured servants transported to Maryland during the politically and economically unstable final decades of the seventeenth century. The Irish teenager arrived in 1675, transported under a headright held by Thomas Jones, a mariner and trader from Bristol. Dead by age thirty-seven, Edward lived his short life (by today's standards) in Cecil County, Maryland. As a freedman he made strides toward planting firm roots in America. He married, established a household, obtained two tracts of land equaling 290 acres, raised tobacco, and fathered three children before his death in 1697. His son, William, in turn migrated to the North Carolina Piedmont.

19. Robert D. Mitchell, "The Southern Backcountry: A Geographical House Divided," in Crass, Smith, Zierden, and Brooks, *Southern Colonial Backcountry*, 1–35. On yeoman aspirations during this era in the Chesapeake region, see Allan Kulikoff, "The Revolution, Capitalism, and the Formation of the Yeoman Classes," in Young, *Beyond the American Revolution*, 86–88; on the Chesapeake's conversion from servant to slave labor, see esp. Morgan, *American Freedom, American Slavery*, 296–315; for Maryland, see Lois Green Carr and Russell R. Menard, "Immigration and Opportunity: The Freedman in Early Colonial Maryland," in *The Chesapeake in the Seventeenth Century: Essays on Anglo-American Society*, ed. Thad W. Tate and David L. Ammerman (New York: Norton, 1979), 238–39. By 1723 settlers with the Jones County surnames of Coleman, Collins, Gilbert, Hathhorn, Lee, Ates, and Whitehead owned land in the Albemarle region. Records on these families may be found in Margaret M. Hofman, *Abstracts of Land Patents, Province of North Carolina, 1663–1729* (Weldon, N.C.: Roanoke News Co., 1979), 8–11, 13, 37–38, 42–45, 187, 189, 192, 194, 196, 197, 217–18; Hofman, *Abstracts of Deeds, Edgecombe Precinct, Edgecombe County, North Carolina, 1732–1758* (Weldon, N.C.: Roanoke News Co., 1969), 83; and Hofman, *The Granville District of North Carolina, 1748–1763: Abstracts of Land Grants* (n.p., 1986), 1:95.

In Bertie County between 1761 and 1787, land deeds were granted to men bearing the surnames of Collins, Hinton, Huff, Knight, Rawls, Reddick, Turner, and West. See Mary Best Bell, comp., *Colonial Bertie County, North Carolina*, vol. 2, *Abstracts of Deed Books, 1725–1730 and 1739* (Windsor, N.C.: Colonial Bertie, 1963), 62, 329; Edythe Smith Dunstan, comp., *The Bertie Index for Courthouse Records of Bertie Co., N.C., 1720–1875: Deeds, Land Divisions, Grants, Abstracts, of Wills and Marriage Bonds, Maps, Illustrations* (n.p., 1966); and Alan D. Watson, *Bertie County: A Brief History* (Raleigh: Division of Archives and History, North Carolina Department of Cultural Resources, 1982), 1–14.

20. Stock, *Rural Radicals*.

21. W. Stitt Robinson, *The Southern Colonial Frontier, 1607–1763* (Albuquerque: University of New Mexico Press, 1979), 226–44; Isaac, *Transformation of Virginia*, 71–87; Kathleen M. Brown, *Good Wives, Nasty Wenches, and Anxious Patriarchs*, 267–74.

22. Hugh T. Lefler and William S. Powell, *Colonial North Carolina: A History* (New York: Charles Scribner's Sons, 1973), 184; Isaac, *Transformation of Virginia*, 33–34, 43–45, 56;

Stephanie McCurry, *Masters of Small Worlds: Yeoman Households, Gender Relations, and the Antebellum South Carolina Low Country* (New York: Oxford University Press, 1995), 13–19.

23. Kathleen M. Brown, *Good Wives, Nasty Wenches, and Anxious Patriarchs*, 26, 86–87; Stephanie McCurry, "The Two Faces of Republicanism: Gender and Proslavery Politics in Antebellum South Carolina," *Journal of American History* 78 (Mar. 1992): 1246; Allan Kulikoff, *Tobacco and Slaves: The Development of Southern Cultures in the Chesapeake, 1680–1800* (Chapel Hill: University of North Carolina Press, 1986), 165–204; David Hackett-Fischer, *Albion's Seed: Four British Folkways in America* (New York: Oxford University Press, 1989), 298–306; Isaac, *Transformation of Virginia*, 31–32, 52–53; Joan Hoff-Wilson, "The Illusion of Change: Women and the American Revolution," in Young, *American Revolution*, 383–445.

24. Will of William Knight, Dec. 3, 1751, Bertie County, NCDAH. William Knight left his widow, Martha, the standard one-third of his remaining estate, plus livestock and tobacco, which she was directed to sell to pay off his debts. Although I have not established a definite link between Jackie Knight and the Knights of Edgecombe County, the preponderance of overlapping names convinces me that they are his kinfolk. The standard genealogies of the Knight family are Sumrall and Welch, *Knights and Related Families*, and Winnie Knight Thomas, Earle W. Knight, Lavada Knight Dykes, and Martha Kaye Dykes Lowery, *The Family of John "Jackie" Knight and Keziah Davis Knight, 1773–1985* (Magee, Miss.: Robert and Delores Knight Vinson, 1985).

25. Will of John Knight, Oct. 10, 1770, Edgecombe County, NCDAH. The household goods left by John Knight indicate wealth greater than two slaves, suggesting that he may have distributed other slaves as gifts before his death. Information on the Knights in Georgia is from Marie De Lamar and Elisabeth Rothstein, eds., *The Reconstructed 1790 Census of Georgia: Substitutes for Georgia's Lost 1790 Census* (Baltimore: Genealogical Pub. Co., 1989), 8, 141, 143, 155, and Robert Scott Davis Jr. and Rev. Silas Emmet Lucas Jr., comps., *The Families of Burke County, 1755–1855: A Census* (Easley, S.C.: Southern Historical Press, 1981). Nehemiah Knight was in Georgia by the 1780s and held title to land distributed from the Creek Cession of 1783. His name appears on the tax index of Richmond County in 1797. A William Knight appeared on the tax index of Burke County, Georgia, in 1798. Jackie Knight lived in both these counties during this decade. He may be connected to the John or Jonathan Knight who owned 250 acres of land in Burke County as early as 1787, when Jackie was fourteen years old. Also, a John Knight received a grant of land in Burke County, Georgia, between 1790 and 1795. This John might be the brother of Nehemiah Knight listed in the 1752 will of William Knight, particularly since a John Knight administered the deceased Nehemiah's estate in 1819. See Georgia Tax Index, 1789–1799, GDAH; Name Index, GDAH.

26. Wood, Sarrett, and Cook, *Ponder-Teague Connections*, 284; Jo White Linn, *Rowan County Deed Abstracts*, vol. 1, *1753–1762: Abstracts of Books 1–4* (n.p., n.d.), 51. Around 1759 Moses Teague obtained a grant of land from the earl of Granville. Between two wives, Elizabeth Loften and Rachel Taylor, he fathered five daughters and four sons. Regulator Thomas Welborn settled in Orange County's Sandy Creek settlement around 1756; in 1759 William Welborn lived in Rowan County on land adjoining that of Moses Teague.

27. Will of William Bynum, May 20, 1746, Edgecombe County, N.C., described in Robert W. Baird, *Bynum and Baynham Families of America, 1616–1850* (Baltimore: Gateway Press, 1983), 143; will of James Bynum, June 20, 1763, Halifax County, NCDAH. By 1761 brothers William, James, and Luke Bynum of Orange County had achieved moderate success, even a degree of refinement, by combining farming with raising livestock. The brothers are identified by most genealogists as sons of the William Bynum who settled in Bertie County (Edgecombe by 1741).

Like the Teagues, Bynums, and Knights, William Coleman of Anson County, the probable ancestor of Jones County Colemans, struggled to rise into the upper ranks of North Carolina society. In his 1750 will he left land to all five of his minor sons, William, Thomas, John, James, and Samuel. He also specified that his wife, Elizabeth, be left "provision" enough to educate their children. The will did not specify the dispersal of slaves among his heirs, but in 1763 William and John Coleman of Anson County were each taxed for one slave. See abstract of will of William Coleman, May 1, 1750, in May Wilson McBee, comp., *Anson County, North Carolina: Abstracts of Early Records* (Baltimore: Genealogical Pub. Co., 1978), 118; Brent Holcomb, comp., *Anson County, N.C., Deed Abstracts*, vol. 2, 1757–1766 and 1763 Tax List (n.p., 1975).

28. Kars, " 'Breaking Loose Together' "; James P. Whittenburg, "Planters, Merchants, and Lawyers: Social Change and the Origins of the North Carolina Regulation," *William and Mary Quarterly* 34 (Apr. 1977): 215–38; Marvin L. Michael Kay, "The North Carolina Regulation, 1766–1776: A Class Conflict," in Young, *American Revolution*, 73–123; Kulikoff, "Revolution, Capitalism, and the Formation of the Yeoman Classes," 91–92; Young, "How Radical Was the American Revolution?," 319; Joyce E. Chaplin, *An Anxious Pursuit: Agricultural Innovation and Modernity in the Lower South, 1730–1815* (Chapel Hill: University of North Carolina Press, 1993), 11–13. On the hopes and the hazards for economic success in the Old Southwest, see Charles C. Bolton, *Poor Whites of the Antebellum South: Tenants and Laborers in Central North Carolina and Northeast Mississippi* (Durham: Duke University Press, 1994), 66–83.

29. Chaplin, *Anxious Pursuit*, 11–13; Whittenburg, "Planters, Merchants, and Lawyers," 222–27; Kay, "North Carolina Regulation," 90–91. For Regulator documents that include the names and surnames of these men, see William L. Saunders, *The Colonial Records of North Carolina* (Raleigh: Josephus Daniels, 1890), 7:733–36. On the English origins of nascent yeoman ideology, see Kulikoff, "Revolution, Capitalism, and the Formation of the Yeoman Classes," 84–86. Randolph County was carved out of Rowan in 1771; Montgomery was carved from Anson County in 1779.

Among the families connected later with the Knight Company in Civil War Mississippi, the Arnolds, Ateses (or Yateses), Blackwells, Bynums, Coatses, Colemans, Collinses, Duckworths, Gilberts, Harpers, Knights, Lees, Loftins, Mauldins, Raineys, Sumralls, Turners, Valentines, Welborns, Welches, Whiteheads, and Youngbloods all descended from families directly involved in the Great Awakening and the Regulator and Revolutionary movements of the eighteenth century.

30. Gerald W. Johnson, conversation with author, July 18, 1999, ML-USM; Welborn folder, Genealogy File Cabinet, ML-USM; Jo White Linn, comp., *Abstracts of the Deeds of Rowan County, N.C., 1753–1785* (n.p., n.d.), 111; U.S. Bureau of the Census, Federal Manuscript Censuses, 1790, Ninety Six District, Pendleton County, S.C., and 1800, Pendleton County, S.C. For information on the Regulator activities of the Welborns, the Teagues, and James Younger, see William S. Powell, James K. Huhta, and Thomas J. Farnham, eds., *The Regulators of North Carolina: A Documentary History, 1759–1776* (Raleigh: State Department of Archives and History, 1971), 80, 149–50, 361, and Saunders, *Colonial Records of North Carolina*, 7:702–3, 733–37, 8:68–70, 521–22, 9:25–30. On the social classes and networks of Rowan County during this era, see Daniel B. Thorp, "Taverns and Communities: The Case of Rowan County, North Carolina," in Crass, Smith, Zierden, and Brooks, *Southern Colonial Backcountry*, 76–86.

31. Regina Roper, e-mail message to author, Feb. 1, 1999, ML-USM; A. O. Collins, *"Ole Man Moses and His Chillun": The Story of Moses Collins of South Carolina, Georgia, Alabama, and Mississippi, and His Descendants* (Aransas Pass, Tex.: Biography Press, 1974), 402. Stacy Collins was born in 1786 in Spartanburg, South Carolina, just across the state line from Anson County. In 1804 in Barnwell County, South Carolina, he witnessed the sale by

Joshua and Elizabeth Collins of land formerly belonging to Christopher Collins. Although his kinship to Jacob and Joshua Collins of Anson County is undocumented, he had brothers with the same first names (see Chap. 2).

32. Petition signed by Jacob Collins and Joshua Collins, reprinted in John Hill Wheeler, *Historical Sketches of North Carolina from 1584 to 1851: Compiled from Original Records, Official Documents, and Traditional Statements, with Biographical Sketches of Her Distinguished Statesmen, Jurists, Lawyers, Soldiers, Divines, etc.*, 2 vols. in 1 (Philadelphia, 1851; reprint, Baltimore: Regional Pub. Co., 1964), 23–24; Petition of Inhabitants of Anson County, being part of the Remonstrance of the Province of North Carolina, Oct. 9, 1769, in Saunders, *Colonial Records of North Carolina*, 7:733–37, 8:75–79. The Anson County petition signed by Jacob and Joshua Collins requested that "Benjamin Franklin or some other known patriot be appointed Agent, to represent the unhappy state of this province to his Majesty." Names appended to Orange County's "Regulators' Advertisement No. 9" of 1768 included several Gilberts, Youngbloods, Mauldins, George and Peter Cortner (Courtney), Jeremiah Duckworth, William Raney (Rainey), Henry Welch, Walter Welch, Thomas Wilborne (Welborn), Richard Wineham (Windham), Rubin Landrum, and James Younger, all of whom bore surnames of families that would later appear in Mississippi Territory.

33. Saunders, *Colonial Records of North Carolina*, 8:867, 9:39; Powell, Huhta, and Farnham, *Regulators of North Carolina*, 362; Baird, *Bynum and Baynham*, 145. Regulator James Bynum was either the cousin or the uncle of eight-year-old William Bynum of Halifax County, who migrated around 1817 to Mississippi's Piney Woods.

Although there is no proof of their kinship to the Jones County Knights, at least two Knights from the North Carolina Piedmont became Regulators. In 1768 the same Ephraim Knight who would manumit two slaves in 1789 joined sixty-six other petitioners to protest the high taxes and shortage of money suffered by inhabitants of that county. Likewise, Thomas Knight revealed sympathies for the movement by signing a petition that implored Governor Josiah Martin to pardon the notorious Regulator Ninian Beall Hamilton.

34. Leah Townsend, *South Carolina Baptists, 1670–1805* (Florence, S.C.: Florence Printing Co., 1935), 123–24, 174. On the connections between the Great Awakening and political radicalism, see Young, "How Radical Was the American Revolution?," 322; Kars, " 'Breaking Loose Together,' " 162; Christine Leigh Heyrman, *Southern Cross: The Beginnings of the Bible Belt* (Chapel Hill: University of North Carolina Press, 1997), 10–11; William L. Lumpkin, *Baptist Foundations in the South: Tracing through Separates the Influence of the Great Awakening, 1754–1787* (Nashville: Broadman Press, 1961), 75–85.

On Shubal Stearns and the connections between evangelism and commercial growth, see Randy J. Sparks, *On Jordan's Stormy Banks: Evangelicalism in Mississippi, 1773–1876* (Athens: University of Georgia Press, 1994), 2; Bill Cecil-Fronsman, *Common Whites: Class and Culture in Antebellum North Carolina* (Lexington: University Press of Kentucky, 1994), 180, 182–84; Klein, *Unification of a Slave State*, 43; Bertram Wyatt-Brown, "The Antimission Movement in the Jacksonian South: A Study in Regional Folk Culture," *Journal of Southern History* 36 (Nov. 1970): 501–29.

35. On genealogical links among the Welborn, Stearns, and Marshall families, see "Memorial Letter" of 1835, written by Dr. Samuel Scott Starnes (Stearns) Sr., abstracted by Virginia Weeks Warbington, posted on the Internet at Genforum.genealogy.com., July 2, 1999; Ann Beason Gahan, e-mail message to author, May 15, 1999, ML-USM; and Joseph T. Maddox and Mary Carter, comps., *North Carolina Soldiers, Sailors, Patriots, and Descendants* (Albany: Georgia Pioneers Publications, n.d.), 1:215–16. On the marriages between the Welborn and Younger families, see Welborn folder, Genealogy File Cabi-

net, ML-USM. On genealogical links between the Bynums, Tapleys, and Mulkeys, see JoAnn and Wayne Wingate, e-mail message to author, Oct. 12, 1999, ML-USM, and will of Philip Mulkey Sr., in Ruth Smith Williams and Margaret Glenn Griffin, *Abstracts of the Wills of Edgecombe County, North Carolina, 1733–1856* (Rocky Mount, N.C.: Joseph W. Watson, 1980), 234. William Welborn Jr., the brother of James Welborn Sr., married Hephzibah Stearns, daughter of Isaac Stearns, who was the brother of Shubal Stearns. In 1778 William and Hephzibah moved to Wilkes County, Georgia, where their son, Elias, married Mary Marshall, the daughter of Daniel Marshall and Martha Stearns Marshall. Philip Mulkey's half-sister, Martha Patterson, married Luke Bynum, James Bynum's brother.

36. John Boles, *The Great Revival, 1787–1805* (Lexington: University Press of Kentucky, 1972), 194–95; Kulikoff, "Revolution, Capitalism, and the Formation of the Yeoman Classes," 107–8; Drew R. McCoy, *The Elusive Republic: Political Economy in Jeffersonian America* (Chapel Hill: University of North Carolina Press, 1980), 251–52. On Regulator attitudes toward slavery, see Kars, " 'Breaking Loose Together,' " 156–77. James Whittenburg ("Planters, Merchants, and Lawyers," 220) estimated that 55 percent of Regulators from Orange, Randolph, and Montgomery Counties ranked among the lower-middle and poorest range of taxpayers. Among these, 22 percent were in the poorest category. Forty-five percent ranked in the high-middle to high range, but only 10 percent of these were among the wealthiest 10 percent of taxpayers.

On the connections between New Light theology and slaveholding, see esp. Rodger M. Payne, "New Light in Hanover County: Evangelical Dissent in Piedmont Virginia, 1740–1755," *Journal of Southern History* 61 (Nov. 1995): 681, and Frederick A. Bode, "The Formation of Evangelical Communities in Middle Georgia: Twiggs County, 1820–1861," *Journal of Southern History* 60 (Nov. 1994): 747. Both authors show that evangelicalism had special appeal not only to poor and marginalized members of society but also to slaveholders of considerable wealth and status.

37. Heyrman, *Southern Cross*, 25–27; Townsend, *South Carolina Baptists*, 61–77, 125, 159, 161. Biographical material on James Younger is from George Washington Paschal, *History of North Carolina Baptists*, 2 vols. (Raleigh: General Board of the Baptist State Convention, 1930, 1955), 1:290–91, and William L. Lumpkin, *Baptist Foundations in the South*, 41–43, 53. On the Abbotts Creek Baptist Church and Welborn's Meeting House, see Kars, " 'Breaking Loose Together,' " 237, 457.

38. Kars, " 'Breaking Loose Together,' " 177–83; Catherine A. Brekus, *Strangers and Pilgrims: Female Preaching in America, 1740–1845* (Chapel Hill: University of North Carolina Press, 1998), 62, 67, 96, 129.

39. *Christian Index, History of the Baptist Denomination in Georgia* (Atlanta, Ga.: James P. Harrison, 1881), 13–14.

40. Ibid., 14; Townsend, *South Carolina Baptists*, 290–91; William L. Lumpkin, *Baptist Foundations in the South*, 29, 55; Kars, " 'Breaking Loose Together,' " 179–80.

41. Klein, *Unification of a Slave State*, 43; Richard J. Hooker, ed., *The Carolina Backcountry on the Eve of the Revolution: The Journal and Other Writings of Charles Woodmason, Anglican Itinerant* (Chapel Hill: University of North Carolina Press, 1953), 112, 31–33; Townsend, *South Carolina Baptists*, 126.

42. Hooker, *Carolina Backcountry*, 31–33.

43. Heyrman, *Southern Cross*, 15.

44. Townsend, *South Carolina Baptists*, 200. For information on Welborn, Younger, Mauldin, Turner, and Teague families, see James E. Wooley, ed., *A Collection of Upper South Carolina Genealogical and Family Records*, 3 vols. (Easley, S.C.: Southern Historical Press, 1979), 1:335. On the Teagues in South Carolina, see Sara Sullivan Ervin, *South Carolinians*

in the Revolution (1949; reprint, Baltimore: Genealogical Pub. Co., 1981), 162, 173. Land transactions effected by the Teagues, Youngers, and Welborns are recorded in Linn, *Abstracts of the Deeds*, 111, 122, 190, 215.

45. Powell, Huhta, and Farnham, *Regulators of North Carolina*, 470–71; Wood, Sarrett, and Cook, *Ponder-Teague Connections*, 284. North Carolina Governor William Tryon issued a proclamation on May 31, 1771, granting pardons to repentant Regulators. Joshua Teague, however, was forbidden from applying for the pardon. Between 1792 and 1804 numerous Teagues appeared on the membership lists of the Bush River Baptist Church: Abner, Abraham, Isaac, James (a deacon), Joshua, Mary, Nancy, Sarah, and Susanna. See Townsend, *South Carolina Baptists*, 164–66.

46. Ronald Hoffman, "The 'Disaffected' in the Revolutionary South," in Young, *American Revolution*, 273–316; Hatley, *Dividing Paths*, 179–228; Klein, *Unification of a Slave State*, 37–39; Richard Maxwell Brown, *South Carolina Regulators*, 1–12. Some Regulators did not flee their neighborhoods, at least not immediately, but continued to struggle to bring orderly development to their counties. In 1777 former Regulator William Coleman joined fellow residents to urge the North Carolina Assembly to divide Anson County into two counties along the Peedee River or, that failing, move its courthouse near the center of the county. In 1779 and 1783 James Ates and Peter Ates, men who bore a surname closely associated eighty years later with the Coleman family in Jones County and with Newt Knight's band, signed similar petitions (documents reprinted in McBee, *Anson County*, 138–39).

47. Hatley, *Dividing Paths*, 179–90; Klein, *Unification of a Slave State*, 47–77; Richard Maxwell Brown, *South Carolina Regulators*, 25, 38–51, 112.

48. Mary Medley, *History of Anson County, North Carolina, 1750–1976* (Wadesboro, N.C.: Anson County Historical Society, 1976), 306; Robinson, *Southern Colonial Frontier*, 169–70. On Summerall's treatment by Regulators, see Richard Maxwell Brown, *South Carolina Regulators*, 88–89, 202, and Klein, *Unification of a Slave State*, 72–73. According to genealogist James H. Hines (*The Families Somerville, Somervaill, Summerall, Summerell, Summerill, Summerlin, Sumlin, Sumrall, and Sumril* [n.p., 1981], vii–ix, 9), the original Sumrall ancestor was merchant John Summerell, who migrated from Scotland to Isle of Wight, Virginia, on April 20, 1687. His grandson, Henry, in turn migrated to the Carolina backcountry, where he bought land in Anson County before moving to the South Carolina backcountry.

49. On Jacob Summerall, the Moderator Movement, and Laurence Rambo, see Klein, *Unification of a Slave State*, 72–73, 187; Richard Maxwell Brown, *South Carolina Regulators*, 83–95, 202, 211; letter to John Stuart, Esq., from Jacob Sommerhall, reprinted in Saunders, *Colonial Records of North Carolina*, 7:866. On Col. John Stuart's relations with Cherokees, see Hatley, *Dividing Paths*, 11, 15, 41, 102, 226. In advancing his own personal fortunes, Laurence Rambo epitomized South Carolina Regulators. According to Klein, he was from a wealthy planter family, owned four or five slaves, and received a suspect warrant for 55,543 acres of land in the Orangeburgh District.

50. Klein, *Unification of a Slave State*, 84–91; Hoffman, " 'Disaffected' in the Revolutionary South," 311–13. Philip Mulkey, for example, became a Tory.

51. Individuals' Revolutionary service may be traced in Virgil D. White, abstractor, *Genealogical Abstracts of Revolutionary War Pension Files* (Waynesboro, Tenn.: National Historical Pub. Co., 1991), vols. 1–3. On South Carolina, consult Bobby Gilmer Moss, *Roster of South Carolina Patriots in the American Revolution* (Baltimore: Genealogical Pub. Co., 1983). On Georgia loyalists, see Heard Robertson, "A Revised, or Loyalist Perspective of Augusta during the American Revolution," *Richmond County History* 1 (summer 1969): 5–24, and Robert Scott Davis Jr., *Georgia Citizens and Soldiers of the American Revolution* (Easley, S.C.:

Southern Historical Press, 1983), 18–19, 81, 198, 204. On the genealogy of the Valentine and Welch families, see Carr P. Collins Jr., *Royal Ancestors of Magna Charta Barons* (Dallas, Tex.: n.p., 1959), 293–95, and Vinson Allen Collins, *A Story of My Parents: Warren Jacob Collins and Tolitha Eboline Valentine Collins* (Livingston, Tex.: n.p., 1962).

52. Klein, *Unification of a Slave State*, 109–18; Heyrman, *Southern Cross*, 22–27; Donald G. Mathews, "The Second Great Awakening As an Organizing Process," *American Quarterly* 21 (1969): 23–43; Townsend, *South Carolina Baptists*, 70, 139, 144–45, 175; Christian Index, *Baptist Denomination in Georgia*, 27.

53. Street, *Oh, Promised Land*, 18–19, 144–45, 150.

54. Ibid., 128; Street, *Tap Roots*, 25–29.

55. On Southern farmers' development of a yeoman ideology, see Kulikoff, "Revolution, Capitalism, and the Formation of the Yeoman Classes," 90.

Chapter Two

1. Ethel Knight, *The Echo of the Black Horn: An Authentic Tale of "The Governor" of "The Free State of Jones"* (n.p., 1951), 89–90; Thomas J. Knight, *The Life and Activities of Captain Newton Knight and His Company and the "Free State of Jones"* (1935; rev. ed, Laurel, Miss.: n.p., 1946), 16–17; U.S. Bureau of the Census, Federal Manuscript Censuses, 1790, Camden, Ninety Six, and Orangeburgh Districts, S.C. In 1790 the nation's first federal census recorded a striking number of South Carolina surnames that matched those of men who later rode with Newt Knight's band. Families in the Ninety Six and Orangeburgh Districts alone displayed thirty-four of the fifty-six surnames (of ninety-three men) that appeared on Newton Knight's Civil War roster. In Orangeburgh District, South Carolina, surnames of Jones County settlers included Arnold, Blackledge, Bush, Coats, Collins, Elsey, Gunter, Rainey, Valentine, and Welch; in South Carolina's Ninety Six District were households headed by men surnamed Arnold, Blackwell, Bynum, Coats, Collins, Corley, Delany (Delancy), Dikes, Gilbert, Gunter, Holifield, Pitts, Reeves, Tucker, Valentine, Welborn, and Welch.

2. Bill Cecil-Fronsman, *Common Whites: Class and Culture in Antebellum North Carolina* (Lexington: University Press of Kentucky, 1994), 106–7; Steven Hahn, *The Roots of Southern Populism: Yeoman Farmers and the Transformation of the Georgia Upcountry, 1850–1890* (New York: Oxford University Press, 1983), 15–18; Grady McWhiney, "Antebellum Piney Woods Culture: Continuity over Time and Place," in *Mississippi's Piney Woods: A Human Perspective*, ed. Noel Polk (Jackson: University Press of Mississippi, 1986), 40–58; Frank L. Owsley, *Plain Folk of the Old South* (Baton Rouge: Louisiana State University Press, 1949), 23–77.

3. William D. Liddle, " 'Virtue and Liberty': An Inquiry into the Role of the Agrarian Myth in the Rhetoric of the American Revolutionary Era," *South Atlantic Quarterly* 77, no. 1 (winter 1978): 15–38; Drew R. McCoy, *The Elusive Republic: Political Economy in Jeffersonian America* (Chapel Hill: University of North Carolina Press, 1980), 13–47; Joyce E. Chaplin, *An Anxious Pursuit: Agricultural Innovation and Modernity in the Lower South, 1730–1815* (Chapel Hill: University of North Carolina Press, 1993), 48–53, 281–85; Harry L. Watson, *Jacksonian Politics and Community Conflict: The Emergence of the Second American Party System in Cumberland County, North Carolina* (Baton Rouge: Louisiana State University Press, 1981), 54.

4. McCoy, *Elusive Republic*, 13–47; Chaplin, *Anxious Pursuit*, 48–53, 281–85.

5. Thomas Perkins Abernethy, *The Formative Period in Alabama, 1815–1828* (Tuscaloosa: University of Alabama Press, 1990). Important works of the more recent past include Daniel H. Usner Jr., *Indians, Settlers, and Slaves in a Frontier Exchange Economy: The Lower Mississippi*

Valley before 1783 (Chapel Hill: University of North Carolina Press, 1992); Charles C. Bolton, *Poor Whites of the Antebellum South: Tenants and Laborers in Central North Carolina and Northeast Mississippi* (Durham: Duke University Press, 1994); Steven Hahn, *Roots of Southern Populism;* Eugene D. Genovese, *The Political Economy of Slavery: Studies in the Economy and Society of the Slave South* (New York: Random House, 1965).

6. Elder Norvell Robertson Sr., "An Autobiography, 1765–1846," typed copy in Virginia Historical Society, Richmond, Va., addendum, 43–44. According to Norvell Robertson's grandson, Elder N. L. Robertson, sixteen of Robertson's grandsons served the Confederacy; all but four died during the war.

7. Ibid., 17–18.

8. Ibid., 21. On the impetus of young evangelical preachers to move West, see Christine Leigh Heyrman, *Southern Cross: The Beginnings of the Bible Belt* (Chapel Hill: University of North Carolina Press, 1997), 135. For a description of yeoman farmers' economic goals in this region that conforms neatly with those of Robertson, see Bradley G. Bond, "Herders, Farmers, and Markets on the Inner Frontier: The Mississippi Piney Woods, 1850–1860," in *Plain Folk of the South Revisited*, ed. Samuel C. Hyde Jr. (Baton Rouge: Louisiana State University Press, 1997).

9. On migrants' desire for "access to markets of their own choosing," see Bond, "Herders, Farmers, and Markets," 74.

10. Stacy Collins Family Bible (copy in possession of Mary Bess Gamero-Adams). My thanks to Gamero-Adams and Judy Smith, descendants of Stacy and Sarah Collins, for calling my attention to persistent rumors that Sarah Anderson Gibson was of Indian ancestry. With no documented proof of the identity of either Sarah's or Stacy's parents, the ancestral trail ends with them.

11. Marilyn Davis Hahn, *Old St. Stephens Land Office Records and American State Papers, Public Lands* (Easley, S.C.: Southern Historical Press, 1983), 107; U.S. Bureau of the Census, Federal Manuscript Censuses, Population Schedule, 1840, 1850, 1860, Jones County, Miss.; Regina Roper, e-mail message to author, Feb. 1, 1999, ML-USM. In 1818 Stacy Collins owned land in Wayne County; by 1820 he appears on the federal manuscript census for Covington County.

12. Leah Townsend, *South Carolina Baptists, 1670–1805* (Florence, S.C.: Florence Printing Co., 1935), 164–66. South Carolina families that migrated to Mississippi behind Tom Sumrall included the Coatses, Collinses, Duckworths, Lees, Loftins, Mauldins, Pittses, Sumralls, Tuckers, Turners, Valentines, Welborns, and Welches, all of whom had descendants who joined the Knight band.

13. Harry L. Watson, " 'The Common Rights of Mankind': Subsistence, Shad, and Commerce in the Early Republican South," *Journal of American History* 83 (June 1996): 19; Cecil-Fronsman, *Common Whites*, 7–8. On eighteenth-century fence laws that favored herdsmen over planters, see Steven Hahn, *Roots of Southern Populism*, 60. In a 1791 petition from New Hanover County, North Carolina, petitioners argued that planters, rather than fence in their fields, had provided their slaves with guns and ammunition to fire on the roaming cattle and hogs of small farmers. The petitioners urged the legislature to pass stronger fence laws against the "owners of cultivated grounds" and to impose "penalties on Negroes committing such depredations." Significantly, they did not criticize the institution that enabled planters effectively to maintain private, captive military forces. See General Assembly Session Records, Dec. 1791–Jan. 1792, box 3, 13 Dec. 1791, Miscellaneous Petitions, "Petition of sundry inhabitants of the County of New Hanover," NCDAH.

14. Harry L. Watson, " 'Common Rights of Mankind,' " 42; Chaplin, *Anxious Pursuit*, 351–55; Tom Downey, "Riparian Rights and Manufacturing in Antebellum South

Carolina: William Gregg and the Origins of the 'Industrial Mind,'" *Journal of Southern History* 65 (Feb. 1999): 77–108. In Nash and Edgecombe Counties, Boykins, Collinses, Pridgens, Sullivans, Tisdales, and Tuckers, all surnames of migrants to Mississippi Territory, were among the 405 residents who petitioned the General Assembly in July 1810 to open the Great Falls of the Tar River in Nash County so that they might "Receve a part of the fish that the Almity intended for all mankind." Opposing petitioners included Matthew Whitehead, John Gilbert, James Lee, Henry E. Knight, and William Tisdial (Tisdale), who argued that opening the Great Falls at the expense of the millers would leave "hundreds of people" without the ability to have their corn and wheat ground into meal and flour. See Petitions, "The Inhabitants of the Counties of Nash & Edgecomb" concerning the flow of water and fish over a mill dam, both in General Assembly Session Records, Nov.–Dec. 1810, box 3, NCDAH.

15. See Chaplin, *Anxious Pursuit*, 280–81, and Harry L. Watson, " 'Common Rights of Mankind,' " 23, 43, on state legislators' passage of laws that favored entrepreneurial commerce over individual property rights and compelled many yeomen to move west in search of independence and prosperity. From Orangeburgh District and Big Lynches Creek in South Carolina, members of the Dykes, Turner, Vollentine, and Welch families participated in squabbles over the use of waterways; see Petitions, Inhabitants of Orangeburgh, 1787, #8; Inhabitants of Orangeburgh, 1792, #87; Inhabitants of Big Lynches Creek, 1792, #215, to the General Assembly of South Carolina, in SCDAH. Names of Orangeburgh County residents listed in the 1790 federal manuscript census that match those of settlers of Jones and Covington Counties include James Arnold, Zachariah Blackledge, Isaac Bush, Joseph Coats, Michael DeLaney (Delancey), Mary Elsey, Joshua Gunter, Joseph Guter (Gunter), John Parker, Thomas Rainey, James Valentine, Thomas Valentine, and Levi Valentine. In the Camden District, through which the Little Lynches River flows, lived Thomas Gilbert and Samuel Yates (Claremont County); John Mills, Thomas Night, James Rainey, and William Rainey (Chester County); Samuel Mayfield and John Whitehead (Fairfield County); and "Widow" Deason, Enoch Deason, James Huff, Robert Lee, and William Raney (Lancaster County). In Cheraws District, across the dividing line of the Lynches River out of which the Little Lynches flows, lived Abraham Blackwell, William Blackwell, Harmon Holloman, Kindred Holloman, Amos McLemore, Williams Walters, James Waters, Amos Windham, John Windham, and William Windham.

16. Jackson Turner Main, *The Social Structure of Revolutionary America* (Princeton: Princeton University Press, 1965), 164–96. On Piney Woods settlers' ongoing attempts to convince the federal government to implement internal improvements, see Edwin Arthur Miles, *Jacksonian Democracy in Mississippi* (Chapel Hill: University of North Carolina Press, 1960), 20–22. For a revealing case study of the convergence of evangelicalism, slavery, and property in producing Georgia's planter elite, see Alan Gallay, *The Formation of a Planter Elite: Jonathan Bryan and the Southern Colonial Frontier* (Athens: University of Georgia Press, 1989). On Anglo Americans' movement west in the wake of the War of 1812, see Owsley, *Plain Folk of the Old South*, 23–77, and Abernethy, *Formative Period in Alabama*. On the ideals and realities of Jeffersonian republicanism, see esp. McCoy, *Elusive Republic*.

17. For complaints by settlers east of the Pearl River, Mississippi Territory, about governmental neglect of their needs, see Clarence Edwin Carter, ed., *The Territory of Mississippi, 1807–1817*, vol. 6 of *The Territorial Papers of the United States* (Washington, D.C.: Government Printing Office, 1938), 569–630. On honor among backcountry yeomen, see esp. Elliott J. Gorn, "Gouge and Bite, Pull Hair and Scratch: The Social Significance of Fighting in the Southern Backcountry," *American Historical Review* 90 (Feb. 1985): 18–43; Charles C. Bolton and Scott Culclasure, eds., *The Confessions of Edward*

Isham: A Poor White Life of the Old South (Athens: University Press of Georgia, 1998); and Ann R. Hammons, Wild Bill Sullivan: King of the Hollow (Jackson: University Press of Mississippi, 1980), 47–48.

18. Chaplin, Anxious Pursuit, 281; Allan Kulikoff, "The Revolution, Capitalism, and the Formation of the Yeoman Classes," in Beyond the American Revolution: Explorations in the History of American Radicalism, ed. Alfred F. Young (DeKalb: Northern Illinois University Press, 1993), 84, 108; Ephraim Kirby to the President, May 1, 1804, in Carter, Territorial Papers, 5:322–24. On Ephraim Kirby's responsibilities as commissioner for the Mississippi Territory, see Alan V. Briceland, "Land, Law, and Politics on the Tombigbee Frontier, 1804," Alabama Review 33 (Apr. 1980): 67–92.

19. Usner, Indians, Settlers, and Slaves, 3, 112–13; Robert Scott Davis Jr. and Rev. Silas Emmett Lucas Jr., comps., The Families of Burke County, 1755–1855: A Census (Easley, S.C.: Southern Historical Press, 1981), 94, 145–46; Murtie June Clark, Loyalists in the Southern Campaign of the Revolutionary War: Official Rolls of Loyalists Recruited from North and South Carolina, Georgia, Florida, Mississippi, and Louisiana (Baltimore: Genealogical Pub. Co., 1981), vol. 1; Walter Lowrie, ed., Early Settlers of Mississippi As Taken from Land Claims in Mississippi Territory (Easley, S.C.: Southern Historical Press, Inc., 1986) (reprinted from American State Papers, vol. 1 [Washington, D.C.: Duff Green, 1834]). Many surnames of future Jones County settlers are found in loyalist records, notably Blackledge, Coates, Coleman, Collins, Courtney (Coatney), Delancy (Delany), Dikes, Elzey, Huff, Gregg, Gunter, Knight, Maulding, Reddick, Summerall, Valentine, and Welch.

20. Bolton, Poor Whites of the Antebellum South, 66–112; Chaplin, Anxious Pursuit, 131–84; Rachel N. Klein, Unification of a Slave State: The Rise of the Planter Class in the South Carolina Backcountry, 1760–1808 (Chapel Hill: University of North Carolina Press, 1990), 178–202; Steven Hahn, Roots of Southern Populism, 15–49; Alfred Glaze Smith Jr., Economic Readjustment of an Old Cotton State: South Carolina, 1820–1860 (Columbia: University of South Carolina Press, 1958); Usner, Indians, Settlers, and Slaves, 5, 149–90; Henry deLeon Southerland Jr., and Jerry Elijah Brown, The Federal Road through Georgia, the Creek Nation, and Alabama, 1806–1836 (Tuscaloosa: University of Alabama Press, 1989), 10, 14.

21. Owsley, Plain Folk of the Old South, 40–41; Southerland and Brown, Federal Road, 1–10, 32–40. On the Tensaw settlement, see Briceland, "Land, Law, and Politics on the Tombigbee Frontier," 92–124. Early landholdings for this region may be traced in Marilyn Davis Hahn, Old St. Stephens Land Office Records, and Lowrie, Early Settlers of Mississippi. In November 1805 forty-one male heads of families in the Tensaw region, including William Coleman, John and Zachariah Landrum, and Francis Huff, implored Congress to grant them preemption rights to the lands they had settled and improved. When the United States gained coveted Indian lands that same year through the first Choctaw cession, white settlers began moving into southeastern Mississippi, west of the Tombigbee River but still east of the Pearl. Here, during the next two decades, Wayne (1809), Marion (1811), Covington (1819), and Jones (1826) Counties were formed.

22. Ephraim Kirby to the President, May 1, 1804, and Petition to the House of Representatives by Inhabitants of Washington County (Nov. 15, 1805), both in Carter, Territorial Papers, 5:322–23, 442; Alan V. Briceland, "The Mississippi Territorial Land Board East of the Pearl River, 1804," Alabama Review 32 (Jan. 1979): 38–68; Briceland, "Land, Law and Politics on the Tombigbee Frontier," 92–124; "Petition to the Legislative Council by Inhabitants Living on the Chickasawhay River, 1808," printed and discussed by Richard S. Lackey in Journal of Mississippi History 37, no. 3 (Aug. 1975): 279–82. For an overview of the early settlement of this region, see Abernethy, Formative Period in Alabama, 44–63. Depending on whether Tom Sumrall junior or senior signed the petition, Giles and Calvin were his sons or grandsons.

23. Petition to the President and Congress by Inhabitants of Washington County (referred Feb. 7, 1809), in Carter, *Territorial Papers*, 5:693–96; Murtie June Clark, *Loyalists in the Southern Campaign*, 10, 11, 247, 257, 287, 326, 397, 517–18. Tom Sumrall Sr.'s father, Jacob Summerall of South Carolina, was a Tory. Petitioner William Coleman may be the loyalist of the same name from North Carolina. Likewise, John Mills and James Mills may be the men identified as loyalists from the Ninety Six District of South Carolina. Several other signers bore the surnames of South Carolina tories—Landrum, Lott, Welch, and Whitehead—but there is no evidence that they themselves were Tories.

24. Ephraim Kirby to the President, May 1, 1804, and Petition to Congress by Inhabitants of the Eastern Part of the Territory (referred Dec. 14, 1815), both in Carter, *Territorial Papers*, 5:323, 6:570; Daniel Richter, " 'Believing That Many of the Red People Suffer Much for the Want of Food': Hunting, Agriculture, and a Quaker Construction of Indianness in the Early Republic," *Journal of the Early Republic* 19, no. 4 (winter 1999): 609; James P. Ronda, " 'We Have a Country': Race, Geography, and the Invention of Indian Territory," *Journal of the Early Republic* 19, no. 4 (winter 1999): 739–56, esp. 740–41.

25. John D. W. Guice, introduction to *Frontier Claims in the Lower South: Records of Claims Filed by Citizens of the Alabama and Tombigbee River Settlements in the Mississippi Territory for Depredations by the Creek Indians During the War of 1812*, comp. Richard S. Lackey (New Orleans: Polyanthos, 1977), xi–xiii, 64. Petition to Congress by Inhabitants of the Territory [referred Dec. 26, 1815], in Carter, *Territorial Papers*, 6:625–30. James Shows gave a sworn statement in regard to the Fort Mims massacre on November 24, 1815. According to the federal manuscript census of 1820, Covington County, Mississippi, he and Adam Shows, Cornelius Shows, John Shows, and John Shows Jr. were by then living in that county. None were slaveholders that year except John Shows Jr., who owned two slaves.

26. Petition from Inhabitants of the Eastern Part of the Mississippi Territory to U.S. Congress (referred Dec. 14, 1815), in Carter, *Territorial Papers*, 6:569–74.

27. Ibid., 569–70. On the evolution of yeoman identity and class consciousness, see esp. Kulikoff, "Revolution, Capitalism, and the Formation of the Yeoman Classes," 80–119.

28. Harry Toulmin to William Lattimore, Dec. 18, 1815, in Carter, *Territorial Papers*, 6:618–22. For more on Judge Harry Toulmin, see Guice introduction, xii–xiii. In 1815 the counties within Washington District included Baldwin, Clarke, Greene, Jackson, Mobile, Washington, and Wayne.

29. Petition to Congress by Inhabitants East of Pearl River, [referred Dec. 14, 1815], in Carter, *Territorial Papers*, 6:601–3. In addition to Thomas Sumrall Sr., Thomas Sumrall Jr., Calvin Sumrall, and Giles Sumrall signed the petition.

30. Sandra L. Myres, *Westering Women and the Frontier Experience, 1800–1915* (Albuquerque: University of New Mexico Press, 1982), 48–49, 59; James Street, *Tap Roots* (Garden City, N.Y.: Sun Dial Press, 1943), 65–66.

31. Maria Crump to Joseph and Judith Michaux, June 12, 1814, Michaux-Randolph Papers, 1745–1863, NCDAH. For a gendered analysis of women's perspectives on migration to the Southwestern frontier, see Joan E. Cashin, *A Family Venture: Men and Women on the Southern Frontier* (Baltimore: Johns Hopkins University Press, 1991).

32. Fletcher M. Green, ed., *Lides Go South . . . and West: The Record of a Planter Migration in 1835* (Columbia: University of South Carolina Press, 1952), 15.

33. *Pendleton District Messenger*, Feb. 16, 1823, reprinted in "Colonial Records, Attainders, and Confiscations," Mary Bondurant Warren, *Carolina Genealogist* (1970): 166.

34. For positive images of women's perspectives on moving west, see Julie Roy

Jeffrey, *Frontier Women: The Trans-Mississippi West*, 1840–1880 (New York: Hill and Wang, 1979), and Myres, *Westering Women*, 36. On divorce in Mississippi Territory, see Donna Elizabeth Sedevie, "The Prospect of Happiness: Women, Divorce, and Property," *Journal of Mississippi History* 52, no. 1 (Feb. 1995): 189–206.

35. Evidence of Elizabeth E. Knight's separate estate is from court documents reprinted in Winnie Knight Thomas, Earle W. Knight, Lavada Knight Dykes, and Martha Kaye Dykes Lowery, *The Family of John "Jackie" Knight and Keziah Davis Knight, 1773–1985* (Magee, Miss.: Robert and Delores Knight Vinson, 1985), 336. The 1840 Federal Manuscript Census for Covington County reported that her father, Samuel Coleman, owned seventeen slaves. On Thomas Jefferson Coleman's genteel affectations, see Chap. 4.

36. Marilyn Davis Hahn, *Old St. Stephen's Land Office Records*, 14, 16; May Wilson McBee, comp., *Anson County, North Carolina: Abstracts of Early Records* (Baltimore: Genealogical Pub. Co., 1978), 59, 133–39; Beverly Fleet, *Virginia Colonial Abstracts: The Original Thirty-four Volumes Reprinted in Three* (Baltimore: Genealogical Pub. Co., 1988), 51, 55, 233, 389, 457; Lowrie, *Early Settlers of Mississippi*, 654, 758; Minnie S. Davis, *Confederate Patriots of Jones County* (Ellisville, Miss.: printed by the *Progress-Item* for Minnie Mae Davis, 1977), 3; U.S. Bureau of the Census, Federal Manuscript Censuses, 1820, 1840, Covington County, Miss. The above sources suggest that Samuel Coleman migrated from Anson County, North Carolina, around 1808 after first marrying Mary Mills, a widow with three children (the surname Mills was also common in Anson County), and that he may have been the son of Regulator William Coleman, who left Anson County for Mississippi Territory before 1812. Both Colemans were landowners in Washington County, Mississippi Territory, before the War of 1812, and both of their names appear on several of the same territorial petitions. Overlapping first and middle names also suggest kinship. William Coleman had a brother named Samuel (see Chap. 1) for whom he may have named his son; the younger Samuel's daughter Elizabeth Knight named one of her sons Champenois, or Champion, which was a recurring name in the Coleman and Terry families of Anson County. The roots of Mary Mills Coleman are more obscure. She was born in Georgia, and she may have been the Mary Mills who lived in Washington County in 1804, married to Maj. John Mills. Mary and Sam Coleman may have separated before his death, since no female from Mary's age group was listed in his household in the 1840 census.

37. Polly Harper's name appears on section 3 of Subscribers to Petition (no date) of the earlier Petition to Congress by Inhabitants of the Territory (referred Dec. 26, 1815), in Carter, *Territorial Papers*, 6:628. Mary Harper's claim is reported in Lackey, *Frontier Claims in the Lower South*, 26. Her purchase of land is recorded on Ledger 3, General Land Office, Hoole Collections, University of Alabama, Tuscaloosa, 365. For additional information on Mary Harper, see Marilyn Davis Barefield, ed., *Clarke County, Alabama, Records, 1814–1885* (Easley, S.C.: Southern Historical Press, 1983), 3), and Marilyn Davis Hahn, *Old St. Stephen's Land Office Records*, 26.

38. Lackey, *Frontier Claims in the Lower South*, 62.

39. For tales about Indian heritage among Piney Woods Mississippians, see Hammons, *Wild Bill Sullivan*, 3, 26, and Chester Sullivan, *Sullivan's Hollow* (Jackson: University Press of Mississippi, 1978), 11–12. Women of mixed ancestry like Peggy were maternal forebears of unknown numbers of Piney Woods citizens and slaves. In Jones County, William Tisdale and Stacy Collins were rumored to have married women of Indian ancestry; so was Tom Sullivan of Sullivan's Hollow in neighboring Smith County.

40. Lacy K. Ford Jr., "Making the 'White Man's' Country White: Race, Slavery, and State Building in the Jacksonian South," *Journal of the Early Republic* 19, no. 4 (winter

1999): 737. On the eighteenth-century history of Jacob Summerall and Tom Sumrall, see Chap. 1. A Summerlin's Ferry (renamed Stone's Ferry), was located on the Savannah River along the Georgia and South Carolina border; see Robert Scott Davis Jr., *Georgians in the Revolution: At Kettle Creek (Wilkes Co.) and Burke County* (Easley, S.C.: Southern Historical Press, 1986), 18, 239. On the various spellings of Sumrall and for a description of evidence that by 1794 Tom Sumrall was living as a hunter on the Alabama River in the Creek Nation, see James H. Hines, *The Families Somerville, Somervaill, Summerall, Summerell, Summerill, Summerlin, Sumlin, Sumrall, and Sumril* (n.p., 1981), ix. On the mixing of Africans, Indians, and Europeans in North America, see Martha Hodes, ed., *Sex, Love, Race: Crossing Boundaries in North American History* (New York: New York University Press, 1999); Hodes, *White Women, Black Men: Illicit Sex in the Nineteenth-Century South* (New Haven: Yale University Press, 1997); Catherine Clinton and Michele Gillespie, eds., *The Devil's Lane: Sex and Race in the Early South* (New York: Oxford University Press, 1997); and Joel Williamson, *New People: Miscegenation and Mulattoes in the United States* (New York: Free Press, 1980).

41. George P. Rawick, ed., *The American Slave: A Composite Autobiography*, supplement, ser. 1, vol. 8, *Mississippi Narratives*, pt. 3 (Westport, Conn.: Greenwood Press, 1972), 1239. On the prevalence and tolerance of sexual mixing between white immigrants and Indians on the Southwestern frontier, see Terry G. Jordan and Matti Kaups, *The American Backwoods Frontier: An Ethnic and Ecological Interpretation* (Baltimore: Johns Hopkins University Press, 1989), 87–88. On the "paucity" of laws governing interracial mixing on the Cherokee frontier, see Theda Perdue, *Slavery and Evolution of Cherokee Society, 1540–1866* (Knoxville: University of Tennessee Press, 1979), 57.

42. Bertram Wyatt-Brown, "From Piety to Fantasy: Proslavery's Troubled Evolution," in *Yankee Saints and Southern Sinners*, ed. Bertram Wyatt-Brown (Baton Rouge: Louisiana State University Press, 1985), 155–57.

43. Heyrman, *Southern Cross*, 24–27; Stephanie McCurry, *Masters of Small Worlds: Yeoman Households, Gender Relations, and the Antebellum South Carolina Low Country* (New York: Oxford University Press, 1995), 144–47; Klein, *Unification of a Slave State*, 269–302; Anne C. Loveland, *Southern Evangelicals and the Social Order, 1800–1860* (Baton Rouge: Louisiana State University Press, 1980), 188; Townsend, *South Carolina Baptists*, 144–45, 281.

44. Bertram Wyatt-Brown, "The Antimission Movement in the Jacksonian South: A Study in Regional Folk Culture," *Journal of Southern History* 36 (Nov. 1970): 502–3; Klein, *Unification of a Slave State*, n. 57, 299.

45. Heyrman, *Southern Cross*, 204–5, 225; Klein, *Unification of a Slave State*, 249–51, 280–82; Loveland, *Southern Evangelicals and the Social Order*, 68; Townsend, *South Carolina Baptists*, 142–43, 150–51, 207, 230. Alleged sexual improprieties and criticism of slavery cost other South Carolina preachers their positions, too. Following the peak revival year of 1802, during which thousands of people attended several upcountry camp meetings, Regular Baptist James Furman criticized the meetings' "enthusiasm," especially when they hosted love feasts. Three preachers who participated in the Spartanburg camp meeting, James Gilleland, William Williamson, and Robert G. Wilson, were all forced out of South Carolina by 1805, apparently because of their antislavery practices.

On the parallel reining in of Methodist women during this era, see Cynthia Lynn Lyerly, "Enthusiasm, Possession, and Madness: Gender and the Opposition to Methodism in the South, 1770–1810," in *Beyond Image and Convention: Explorations in Southern Women's History*, ed. Janet L. Coryell, Martha H. Swain, Sandra Gioia Treadway, and Elizabeth Hayes Turner (Columbia: University of Missouri Press, 1998), 53–73.

46. Heyrman, *Southern Cross*, 111–12; Loveland, *Southern Evangelicals and the Social Order*, 161; Christian Index, *History of the Baptist Denomination in Georgia* (Atlanta, Ga.: James P.

Harrison, 1881), 42. The Mercers were sons of North Carolina Baptist preacher Silas Mercer, a contemporary of Shubal Stearns, Daniel Marshall, and Philip Mulkey. According to Robertson, Mercer baptized him in March 1791 at the Baptist Church at Providence, Jefferson County, Georgia; see Elder Norvell Robertson Sr., "Autobiography," 31.

47. Elder Norvell Robertson Sr., "Autobiography," 1–2. Thomas Mercer moved to Mississippi Territory in 1800 and in 1808 helped build the newly founded Mississippi Baptist Association. Like his brother Jesse, he worked for the establishment of Baptist missions, particularly among the Creek Indians. See Robert G. Gardner, *A Decade of Debate and Division: Georgia Baptists and the Formation of the Southern Baptist Convention* (Macon: Mercer University Press, 1995), 6.

48. Wyatt-Brown, "From Piety to Fantasy," 155–82; Loveland, *Southern Evangelicals and the Social Order*, 4–11; Elder Norvell Robertson Sr., "Autobiography," 3. On the typicality of Robertson's early life descriptions, see Heyrman, *Southern Cross*, 41–43.

49. Elder Norvell Robertson Sr., "Autobiography," 34–36. After his move to Mississippi, Robertson and ten other settlers founded the Providence Church in October 1818 in Marion County. If Robertson had hoped to avoid the religious schisms he encountered in Georgia, he was doomed to disappointment. In 1823 the Providence Church hosted a session of the Pearl River Association, which initiated the creation of a Baptist state convention. The first Baptist State Convention was organized at the Bogue Chitto Baptist Church in 1824. At that time there were three Baptist associations in the state, the Mississippi, the Union, and the Pearl River. By 1828, however, "disaffection" with centralized authority was so pronounced and "opposition so determined" among the scattered churches that delegates approved its dissolution. Thus, Mississippi's Baptist State Convention, to which all three state Baptist associations belonged, was dissolved. See Jesse Laney Boyd, *A Popular History of Baptists in Mississippi* (Jackson, Miss.: Baptist Press, 1930), 38–42. On Norvell Robertson Sr.'s position during the pro- and antimission controversy in Mississippi and the formation of the Primitive Baptist Association by antimission Baptists, see Z. T. Leavell and T. J. Bailey, *A Complete History of Mississippi Baptists from the Earliest Times*, 2 vols. (Jackson: Mississippi Baptist Pub. Co., 1904), 1:126–61, 2:725–82, 1226–40.

50. See Christian Index, *Baptist Denomination in Georgia*, 40, 68, for a description of Robertson in 1881 as one of the early preachers who "universally engaged themselves devotedly in itinerant labors" in order to spread the missionary spirit throughout eastern Georgia. As a result, "for several years we find no traces of the anti-missionary spirit [in Georgia]."

51. Elder Norvell Robertson Sr., "Autobiography," 1–2.

52. Richard S. Lackey, ed., "Minutes of Zion Baptist Church of Buckatunna, Wayne County, Miss.," *Mississippi Genealogical Exchange* 19, nos. 1–4 (spring 1973): 13–21, 59–65, 85–93, 123–25 (cited material is from 61–62) (original manuscript at Mississippi Baptist Historical Commission Library, Mississippi College, Clinton). All three Collinses were nonslaveholding taxpayers in Buckatunna according to the 1812 Tax List for Wayne County, Mississippi Territory, Territorial Records, series B, Auditor's Records, vol. 19, real and personal assessments for 1812, Wayne County, MDAH. On resistance to church discipline among ordinary people, see Heyrman, *Southern Cross*, 9, 18–20, and Ted Ownby, *Subduing Satan: Religion, Recreation, and Manhood in the Rural South, 1865–1920* (Chapel Hill: University of North Carolina Press, 1990), 17–18.

53. Lackey, "Minutes of Zion Baptist Church," 61–62.

54. Collins folder, Genealogy File Cabinet, ML-USM.

55. *Christopher Collins and wife, Rachel, vs. Ann Hendricks et al., heirs of John William Hendricks,*

1825, Wayne County, drawer 115, MDAH, and *Christopher Collins and Rachel Collins* vs. *Ann Hendricks and Jacob Collins*, 1831, suit to void will of John Hendricks, drawer 65, case #6a, listed in Mary Louise Flowers Hendrix, comp., *Mississippi Court Records from the Files of the High Court of Errors and Appeals, 1799–1859* (n.p., 1950), 2, 250–51.

56. Lackey, "Minutes of Zion Baptist Church," 93–94. Typed copies of the proceedings in Christopher and Rachel Collins's suit against the Hendricks estate in the circuit courts of Wayne and Marion Counties, Sept. 5, 1825, Oct. 30, 1826, Jan. 1, 1830, are in the Collins folder, Genealogy File Cabinet, ML-USM.

57. George R. Lamplugh, *Politics on the Periphery: Factions and Parties in Georgia, 1783–1806* (Newark: University of Delaware Press, 1986), 17–42.

58. John Davis's 1826 will (reprinted in Thomas et al., *Family of John "Jackie" Knight*, 329) listed an estate that included six slaves. It also provided the names of Keziah Davis's brothers and sisters. On Wrightsborough, Georgia, see Marjoleine Kars, " 'Breaking Loose Together': Religion and Rebellion in the North Carolina Piedmont, 1730–1790" (Ph.D. diss., Duke University, 1994), 248–49, and Allen D. Candler, comp., *The Colonial Records of Georgia* (Atlanta: Franklin-Turner, 1907), 10:86, 383, 268. On the loyalist and patriot activities of the Davis family, see Allen D. Candler, comp., *The Revolutionary Records of the State of Georgia* (Atlanta: Franklin-Turner, 1908), 1:27–29, and Robert Scott Davis Jr., *Georgia Citizens and Soldiers*, 92, 119, 140–41, 143, 203.

59. Jackie Knight's failure to win Indian lands is reported in Virginia S. Wood and Ralph V. Wood, *1805 Georgia Land Lottery* (Cambridge: Greenwood Press, 1964), 197. The Abstract of Jones Co., Ga., Tax Digest, 1811, is reprinted in Carolyn White Williams, *History of Jones County, Georgia: One Hundred Years, Specifically, 1807–1907* (Macon, Ga.: J. W. Burke, 1957), 710.

On May 13, 1807, Jackie Knight sold fifty-four acres of land to Joshua Sanford; by 1811 he, his brother James, and their mother, Mary, had moved west to Jones County, Georgia. In 1811 John "Night" paid taxes on two tracts of land, each 202.5 acres, one of which had been granted to "M. Knight," his mother. In February of that same year, Mary Knight granted Jackie power of attorney so that he might return to Hertford County, North Carolina, to collect her inheritance from her recently deceased father. See Jones County, Ga., Superior Court Records, Deeds and Mortgages, book C, 1811–1812, p. 28, microfilm, Drawer 153, GDAH.

60. Addie West, unpublished WPA records, RG 60, vol. 315, MDAH; Records of the Acts and Doings of the Baptist Church of Christ at Leaf River, Covington County, Miss., private manuscripts, no. 1049m (microfilm, roll 4026), MDAH. Several of Jackie and Keziah's sons and their wives also joined the church: Albert and Mason Rainey Knight, William H. and Mary Youngblood Knight, and John Knight Jr., who was unmarried.

61. Records, Leaf River Baptist Church; Heyrman, *Southern Cross*, 159–60; Randy J. Sparks, *On Jordan's Stormy Banks: Evangelicalism in Mississippi, 1773–1876* (Athens: University of Georgia Press, 1994), 116; Jesse Laney Boyd, *Baptists in Mississippi*, 43.

62. Wyatt-Brown, "Antimission Movement," 504–7.

Chapter Three

1. Sue Boyd Neill, unpublished WPA records, 1936, RG 60, MDAH.

2. W. Todd Groce similarly finds that many of the Confederate military leaders from East Tennessee were "town-based merchants and lawyers" ("Social Origins of East Tennessee's Confederates," in *The Civil War in Appalachia: Collected Essays*, ed. Kenneth W. Noe and Shannon H. Wilson [Knoxville: University of Tennessee Press, 1997], 30–54); so also does Phillip Paludan, *Victims: A True Story of the Civil War* (Knoxville: University of Tennessee Press, 1981), 7, 59.

For studies that emphasize factors that encouraged Southern yeoman support for the Confederacy, see esp. Stephanie McCurry, *Masters of Small Worlds: Yeoman Households, Gender Relations, and the Antebellum South Carolina Low Country* (New York: Oxford University Press, 1995), 277–304, and Eugene Genovese, "Yeoman Farmers in a Slaveholders' Democracy," *Agricultural History* 49 (Apr. 1975): 331–42. In one of the earliest works to address the subject of yeoman-planter relations, Frank Owsley underestimated the degree of class conflict that existed between slaveholders and nonslaveholders because he separated the expansion of agriculture from that of slavery. This led him to argue that the simple expansion of agriculture, rather than the rise of a Piney Woods elite, destroyed plain folks' way of life. He claimed that plain folk did not harbor class resentments but respected the "character and judgement of individual planters." Bradley Bond recognizes class tensions but finds that "race-conscious politics prevailed over class-conscious politics." See Frank L. Owsley, *Plain Folk of the Old South* (Baton Rouge: Louisiana State University Press, 1949), 24–27, 39–41, 51, 75–77, 90–91, 139, and Bradley G. Bond, *Political Culture in the Nineteenth-Century South: Mississippi, 1830–1900* (Baton Rouge: Louisiana State University Press, 1995), 82. Works that emphasize class tensions among slaveholders and nonslaveholders include Charles C. Bolton, *Poor Whites of the Antebellum South: Tenants and Laborers in Central North Carolina and Northeast Mississippi* (Durham: Duke University Press, 1994), 135–36, 160–64; Bill Cecil-Fronsman, *Common Whites: Class and Culture in Antebellum North Carolina* (Lexington: University Press of Kentucky, 1994), 86; Fred Arthur Bailey, *Class and Tennessee's Confederate Generation* (Chapel Hill: University of North Carolina Press, 1987); Paul D. Escott, *Many Excellent People: Power and Privilege in North Carolina, 1850–1900* (Chapel Hill: University of North Carolina Press, 1985); J. William Harris, *Plain Folk and Gentry in a Slave Society: White Liberty and Black Slavery in Augusta's Hinterlands* (Middletown, Conn.: Wesleyan University Press, 1985); Steven Hahn, *The Roots of Southern Populism: Yeoman Farmers and the Transformation of the Georgia Upcountry, 1850–1890* (New York: Oxford University Press, 1983), 84–85; Harry L. Watson, *Jacksonian Politics and Community Conflict: The Emergence of the Second American Party System in Cumberland County, North Carolina* (Baton Rouge: Louisiana State University Press, 1981), 320–23; Peter W. Bardaglio, "Power and Ideology in the Slave South: Eugene Genovese and His Critics," *Maryland Historian* 12 (fall 1981): 23–39; and Paul Goodman, "White over White: Planters, Yeomen, and the Coming of the Civil War: A Review Essay," *Agricultural History* 54 (July 1980): 446–52.

3. On the profitability and rising rate of slavery in Mississippi between 1830 and 1860, see Edward Countryman, "The Price of Cotton: The Human Cost of Slavery in Mid-Nineteenth-Century Mississippi," paper prepared for the Milan Biennial Conference on Early American History, June 19–23, 1992 (copy in author's possession), and Charles S. Sydnor, *Slavery in Mississippi* (1933; Baton Rouge: Louisiana State University Press, 1966), 131–202.

4. ICPSR, Study 00003: Historical Demographic, Economic, and Social Data: U.S., 1790–1970 (Internet, http://fisher.lib.Virginia.edu).

5. For additional statistics on slaveholding, see Bradley G. Bond, "Herders, Farmers, and Markets on the Inner Frontier: The Mississippi Piney Woods, 1850–1860," in *Plain Folk of the South Revisited*, ed. Samuel C. Hyde Jr. (Baton Rouge: Louisiana State University Press, 1997), nn. 90–91.

6. On social, economic, and geographic characteristics of the Southern plain folk, see esp. Owsley, *Plain Folk of the Old South*, and Hyde, *Plain Folk of the South Revisited*.

7. Petition to the Mississippi General Assembly for the division of Covington County, Dec. 1822, Petitions and Memorials, 1817–1839, RG 47, No. 17, Legislative Records, MDAH.

8. Ibid.

9. ICPSR census data, 1820, 1840, 1860. On hunting, herding, and farming in frontier Mississippi, see Bond, Political Culture in the Nineteenth-Century South, 14–21. On the economic practices and food supply of Mississippians during the settlement years, see Sam Bowers Hilliard, Hog Meat and Hoe Cake: Food Supply in the Old South, 1840–1860 (Carbondale: Southern Illinois Press, 1972), 33–34, 38–40. On agricultural trends in Mississippi over time, see Herbert Weaver, Mississippi Farmers, 1850–1860 (Nashville: Vanderbilt University Press, 1945; reprint, Gloucester, Mass.: Peter Smith, 1968), 85–105. On deer hunting in the colonial South Carolina backcountry, see Rachel N. Klein, Unification of a Slave State: The Rise of the Planter Class in the South Carolina Backcountry, 1760–1808 (Chapel Hill: University of North Carolina Press, 1990), 55.

10. James H. Hines, The Families Somerville, Somervaill, Summerall, Summerell, Summerill, Summerlin, Sumlin, Sumrall, and Sumril (n.p., 1981), ix; U.S. Bureau of the Census, Federal Manuscript Censuses, 1820, 1830, Miss. Thomas Sumrall was reported as a landowner in Wayne County, Mississippi Territory, on December 23, 1811; see Marilyn Davis Hahn, Old St. Stephens Land Office Records and American State Papers, Public Lands (Easley, S.C.: Southern Historical Press, 1983), 14. Typed copies of Thomas Sumrall's deeds of gifts of slaves are in the Sumrall folder, Vertical Files, MDAH. On factors impelling men like him to leave South Carolina, see Klein, Unification of a Slave State, 51–52, 81–86, 178–202, and Tom Hatley, The Dividing Paths: Cherokees and South Carolinians through the Revolutionary Era (New York: Oxford University Press, 1995), 188–90. After the second Choctaw cession of 1820, more profit-minded Sumralls moved from Marion and nearby counties of Wayne, Perry, and Covington to those of Simpson, Hinds, and Copiah. One of the wealthiest was Henry Sumrall of Copiah County, who in 1860 owned twenty-four slaves.

11. Joyce E. Chaplin, An Anxious Pursuit: Agricultural Innovation and Modernity in the Lower South, 1730–1815 (Chapel Hill: University of North Carolina Press, 1993), 352–53. Names of Mississippi territorial settlers are from Walter Lowrie, ed., Early Settlers of Mississippi As Taken from Land Claims in Mississippi Territory (Easley, S.C.: Southern Historical Press, Inc., 1986) (reprinted from American State Papers, vol. 1 [Washington, D.C.: Duff Green, 1834]). Information on individuals' slaveholding status is from U.S. Bureau of the Census, Federal Manuscript Censuses, Population and Slave Schedules, 1830, 1850, Covington and Jones Counties, Miss.

12. Bond, Political Culture in the Nineteenth-Century South, 3–7. Percy Rainwater claimed in 1938 that "until about 1835, Mississippi regarded slavery as an evil and hoped to see the institution abolished in the indefinite future" (Mississippi: Storm Center of Secession, 1856–1861 [Baton Rouge: Otto Claitor, 1938], 12).

13. Anne C. Loveland, Southern Evangelicals and the Social Order, 1800–1860 (Baton Rouge: Louisiana State University Press, 1980), 10. Robertson recorded his birthdate as May 22, 1765; see Elder Norvell Robertson Sr., "An Autobiography, 1765–1846," typed copy in Virginia Historical Society, Richmond, 5–6.

14. Bond, "Herders, Farmers, and Markets," 73–99. On the remarkable increase of unimproved lands owned by Piney Woods farmers between 1850 and 1860, see also Weaver, Mississippi Farmers, 63–84. For the argument that most yeoman farmers practiced "safety-first" methods by growing enough corn to maintain their households before engaging in production of cash crops, see Gavin Wright, The Political Economy of the Cotton South: Households, Markets, and Wealth in the Nineteenth Century (New York: Norton, 1978), 62–74.

15. A. G. Shows, Johnson School Community Meeting, July 1, 1926, and S. W. Patrick, Rainey Community Meeting, June 10, 1926, Lauren Rogers Museum of Art, Laurel, Miss.

16. Bond, "Herders, Farmers, and Markets," 93–98; J. M. Knight, Rainey Commu-

nity Meeting, June 10, 1926, and B. D. Graves, Hebron Community Meeting, June 17, 1926, Rogers Museum. John M. Knight was sixteen years old in 1860. His father, Jesse Davis Knight, claimed $3,000 in real estate and $8,450 in personal estate. Although he is not listed as a slaveholder in the 1860 census, he inherited three slaves in 1861 from his father, Jackie Knight. Benjamin Graves's father was dead by 1860, and nine-year-old Benjamin lived with the W. K. Foreman family, next door to his grandfather, Robert Graves Sr., who owned ten slaves. See U.S. Bureau of the Census, Federal Manuscript Census, Population and Slave Schedules, 1860, Jones County, Miss., and will of John "Jackie" Knight, Probate Minutes, book 1, 1854–1861, p. 374, Collins, Miss.

17. Daniel Pitts and S. W. Patrick, Rainey Community Meeting, June 10, 1926, and Brown Shows, Historical Events in Whitfield Community, Jones County, Miss., June 4, 1926, Rogers Museum. On livestock foraging and small farmers' production of corn and wheat in the Old South, see Wright, *Political Economy of the Cotton South*, 57 n. 26, and Hilliard, *Hog Meat and Hoe Cake*, 157–65.

18. Address of M. P. Bush before the Meeting of the DAR, Feb. 17, 1912, and J. M. Knight and S. W. Patrick, Rainey Community Meeting, June 10, 1926, Rogers Museum.

19. McCurry, *Masters of Small Worlds*, 75–85; Ann R. Hammons, *Wild Bill Sullivan: King of the Hollow* (Jackson: University Press of Mississippi, 1980), 33.

20. Address of M. P. Bush, Feb. 17, 1912, and S. W. Patrick, Rainey Community Meeting, June 10, 1926, Rogers Museum.

21. Address of M. P. Bush, Feb. 17, 1912, and S. W. Patrick, Rainey Community Meeting, June 10, 1926, Rogers Museum.

22. J. M. Knight, Rainey Community Meeting, June 10, 1926, and Mrs. S. E. Weeks, Historical Events in Whitfield Community, Jones County, Miss., June 4, 1926, Rogers Museum.

23. Dan Pitts, Rainey Community Meeting, June 10, 1926, and B. D. Graves, Hebron Community Meeting, June 17, 1926, Rogers Museum; U.S. Bureau of the Census, Agricultural and Manufacturing Census, 1860, Jones County, Miss.; Countryman, "Price of Cotton," 7–8; Bond, *Political Culture in the Nineteenth-Century South*, 53–80. Bond's argument continues that advanced by Chaplin (*Anxious Pursuit*, 330–55) for an earlier period of economic development in the South.

24. Ethel Knight, *The Echo of the Black Horn: An Authentic Tale of "The Governor" of "The Free State of Jones"* (n.p., 1951), 82; U.S. Bureau of the Census, Federal Manuscript Census, Population Schedules, 1850, 1860, Jones and Jasper Counties, Miss.; Vinson Allen Collins, *A Story of My Parents: Warren Jacob Collins and Tolitha Eboline Valentine Collins* (Livingston, Tex.: n.p., 1962), 1–9. Riley Collins is variously referred to as James Riley and Riley James on official documents. On kinship ties among members of the Knight Company, see Appendixes 1–8.

25. Vinson Allen Collins, *Story of My Parents*, 1. The William Bynum who migrated to Mississippi Territory was reportedly born in 1763 in Halifax County, North Carolina. The Federal Manuscript Census of 1820 for Covington County, Mississippi, reported him without slaves. On the genealogy of the Jones County Bynums, see Ruby Bynum Sanders, comp., *The Bynum and Herrington Connections* (Ellisville, Miss.: n.p., 1994). On kinship ties between the Collinses and Bynums, see Appendixes 4 and 5.

26. U.S. Bureau of the Census, Federal Manuscript Censuses of 1830, 1840, 1850, 1860, for Covington and Jones Counties, Mississippi, show that William Bynum Jr., born 1795 and the oldest son of William Bynum Sr., headed the slaveholding branch of Jones County Bynums.

27. U.S. Bureau of the Census, Agricultural and Manufacturing Censuses, 1850, Jones, Jasper Counties, Miss.

28. Vinson Allen Collins, *Story of My Parents*, 4–5, 11–13.

29. U.S. Bureau of the Census, Federal Manuscript Population Census, 1850, Jones, Jasper Counties, Miss. The description of Jasper Collins's home is from unpublished WPA records, Jones County, Miss., RG 60, vol. 315, MDAH. Comparison of the 1850 and 1860 federal manuscript censuses indicates so great an increase in the property values of the nonslaveholding Collins and Bynum families as to cast some doubt on the accuracy of the 1850 census. For example, although Stacy Collins's oldest son, Vinson, held a position as president of the Board of Police from 1846 to 1848 and headed a family that included a wife and three children, the 1850 census attributed no property value to his household. Furthermore, deed records show that Stacy Collins Sr. purchased 80 acres of land in Jones County from Isaac Anderson in 1828; in 1836 he purchased 160 acres from John Stricklin in Jasper County. They also indicate that throughout the 1840s, he, his sons, and his sons-in-law bought and sold land. In regard to Benjamin Bynum, court deeds show that in 1843 he; his wife, Peggy; and his father, William Bynum Sr., sold 160 acres to Drury Bynum. See U.S. Bureau of the Census, Federal Manuscript Census, Population, Agricultural, and Slave Schedules, 1850, 1860, Jones and Jasper Counties, Miss., and Ben Strickland and Jean Strickland, *Records of Jones County, Mississippi: Deed Book A & B, 1827–1856* (Moss Point, Miss.: n.p., 1981), 13, 14, 26, 32, 34, 36, 55, 67, 75, 106.

30. U.S. Bureau of the Census, Federal Manuscript Censuses, Population, Agricultural and Manufacturing, and Slave Schedules, 1850, 1860, Jones County, Miss. James Parker sought and failed to obtain a divorce from Sally; see Chap. 4 and *James Parker v. Sarah Parker*, 1857, Jones County Chancery Court, Final Records, 1st District, 1857–1890 (microfilm), MDAH. Benjamin Bynum's economic gains are noted in Weaver, *Mississippi Farmers*, 121.

31. Quoted passage on the political views of Warren Collins is from Bud Overstreet, "The Jayhawkers," in *Big Thicket Legacy*, by Campbell Loughmiller and Lynn Loughmiller (Austin: University of Texas Press, 1977), 72. The Collinses' viewpoint was consistent with that of the Great Compromiser, Henry Clay. Although Clay advocated secession if the North *imposed* slave emancipation, he also stated in 1850 that "if my own state . . . contrary to her duty, should raise the standard of disunion, . . . I would go against Kentucky" (William W. Freehling, *Road to Disunion: Secessionists at Bay, 1776–1854* [New York: Oxford University Press, 1990], 359, 506).

32. U.S. Bureau of the Census, Federal Manuscript Censuses, 1850, 1860, Jones and Jasper Counties, Miss. Vinson Collins was identified as a Democrat by B. D. Graves, Hebron Community Meeting, June 17, 1926, Rogers Museum. On the political divisions between Piney Woods and Natchez District voters during the 1920s, see Edwin Arthur Miles, *Jacksonian Democracy in Mississippi* (Chapel Hill: University of North Carolina Press, 1960), 16, 20–22. For evidence that the majority of Jones County voters supported Democrats in every presidential contest, see Rainwater, *Mississippi*, 15.

Benjamin and Peggy Collins Bynum named a son born in 1848 Zachary Taylor. In honor of both Henry Clay and John J. Crittenden, Vinson and Nancy named one Clay Crittenden in 1852; Simeon and Lydia Bynum Collins, who named their first three sons Thomas Jefferson, Benjamin Franklin, and James Madison, named a son born in 1854 Millard Fillmore. In 1855 Jasper and Gatsy Collins named their new son Henry Clay. On the political stances of these politicians between 1848 and 1854, see Freehling, *Road to Disunion*, 467–77, 490–93, and Robert V. Remini, *Henry Clay, Statesman for the Union* (New York: Norton, 1991), esp. 687–786.

On May 21, 1845, the *True Democrat* of Paulding announced the candidacy of Drury Bynum (reputed to be the brother of Benjamin) for reelection as representative of Jones County, a "truly democratic county" (reprinted in Richard S. Lackey, ed. *East Mississippi Source Material*, vol. 1, *Newspaper Abstracts* [Forest, Miss: n.p., 1968], 1).

33. Joseph D. W. Duckworth to Jourdan Smith and Frances Elizabeth Smith, May 31, 1845, and Sept. 5, 1846, Duckworth-Smith-McPherson Family Papers, Center for the Study of American History, University of Texas, Austin; U.S. Bureau of the Census, Federal Manuscript Census, 1850, Jones County, Miss. On Democratic voting patterns in Piney Woods Mississippi, see Miles, *Jacksonian Democracy in Mississippi*, 9. On divisions between Mississippi's Union and old-line Democrats, see Bond, *Political Culture in the Nineteenth-Century South*, 99–109, and Bolton, *Poor Whites of the Antebellum South*, 161–62.

34. Vinson Allen Collins, *Story of My Parents*, 5; Carr P. Collins Jr., *Royal Ancestors of Magna Charta Barons* (Dallas, Tex.: n.p., 1959), 293–94; U.S. Bureau of the Census, Federal Manuscript Censuses, Agricultural, Population, and Slave Schedules, 1860, Jones County, Miss. For genealogical links among the Collinses, Valentines, and Welches, see Appendixes 5, 7, and 8. In 1860 Allen Valentine owned a farm valued at $1,200 and livestock worth $410. He and his wife, Cynthia Welch, produced two hundred bushels of corn, thirty-five pounds of wool, and enough peas and sweet potatoes to be deemed self-sufficient. They also produced small surpluses in hogs, wool, and butter. During the same year, Catherine Bynum Welch, widow of John Ira Welch and sister-in-law to Allen and Cynthia Valentine, claimed $2,000 in real estate and $500 in personal property. Twenty-three-year-old William M. Welch claimed $300 in real estate and $250 in personal property. Among the Valentines, twenty-two-year-old John Ira Valentine claimed $500 in real estate and $175 in personal property, and nineteen-year-old James Morgan Valentine claimed $150 in real estate and $250 in personal property. Like the Collinses, the Valentines and Welches who joined the Knight Company did not own slaves despite the fact that several of them married daughters of slaveholder Daniel Coats. Daniel Coats himself may have opposed secession, for his son, Merida M. Coats, also joined the Knight Company.

35. U.S. Bureau of the Census, Federal Manuscript Censuses, Population, Agricultural and Manufacturing Censuses, 1850, 1860, Jones County, Miss. The Federal Manuscript Census of 1840 for Covington County, Miss., shows that Harmon Levi Sumrall's father, Jesse Sumrall, also owned no slaves. For a genealogy of the Sumrall family, see Appendix 6. The combined worth of Harmon Levi Sumrall's cattle, sheep, and swine was $676. In addition to four hundred acres of land, in 1860 he owned seventy-five hogs, six milch cows, six "additional cattle," six sheep, and two oxen in Jones County. His largest crop was three hundred pounds of Indian corn, but he also produced two bales of cotton and five pounds of wool.

36. Winnie Knight Thomas, Earle W. Knight, Lavada Knight Dykes, and Martha Kaye Dykes Lowery, *The Family of John "Jackie" Knight and Keziah Davis Knight, 1773–1985* (Magee, Miss.: Robert and Delores Knight Vinson, 1985), 25, 332, 341–42. Either because Jackie Knight needed cash, preferred to own male slaves, or was a slave trader as some descendants claim, he sold his mother's slave, Huldy, for $800 in 1820. Jackie and Keziah's children Albert, Harriet, Elizabeth, John, Mary Ann, William H., and James Knight were born in Georgia; Benjamin Franklin, Altimirah, Jesse Davis, and Daniel Knight were born in Mississippi. Names and births of Knight children; Jackie Knight's sworn statement of military service during the War of 1812, Dec. 7, 1850; and his statement in regard to his economic arrangement with his mother to T. R. White, Clerk of Probate Court, Oct. 13, 1860 (this document reports Mary Knight's year of death as 1818, although her tombstone reports 1817), are reprinted in Thomas et al., *Family of John "Jackie" Knight*. Although Jackie's oldest son, Albert, born in 1799, signed the 1822 petition alongside his father, the two did not always reside in the same county. Albert was living in nearby Marion County in 1820 when he married Mary Mason Rainey. In 1830 he was listed as a taxpayer in Pike County. In 1832 he and wife Mason reappeared

in Covington County. See Jan Sumrall and Kenneth Welch, *The Knights and Related Families* (Denham Springs, La.: n.p., 1985), 150.

37. George P. Rawick, ed., *The American Slave: A Composite Autobiography*, supplement, ser. 1, vol. 10, *Mississippi Narratives*, pt. 5 (Westport, Conn.: Greenwood Press, 1972), 2263–64.

38. Ibid., 2268. On rural isolation as a factor in some wealthy mountaineers' opposition to the Confederacy, see Paludan, *Victims*, 30, 61.

39. See J. M. [John Melton] Knight, Rainey Community Meeting, June 10, 1926, Rogers Museum, for an example of the influence of marriage on one's political views. John Melton's father, Jesse Davis Knight, married Sarah Elizabeth Baylis from the slave-holding Baylis family and also supported the Confederacy during the war. John Melton confirmed the influence of his mother's family in his statements that "all my people owned slaves, both sides," and that "all my mother's people were Methodists and I have been one ever since." (Slaveholder George Baylis was a Methodist preacher.)

40. U.S. Bureau of the Census, Federal Manuscript Censuses, 1820, 1830, 1840, Covington County, Miss.; Minutes, Jan. 16, Dec. 18, 1830, Records of the Acts and Doings of the Baptist Church of Christ at Leaf River, Covington County, Miss., private manuscripts, no. 1049m (microfilm, roll 4026) MDAH; U.S. Bureau of the Census, Federal Manuscript Censuses, Slave Schedules, 1860, Jones, Covington Counties, Miss.; Janet Smith, Jean Strickland, and Patricia N. Edwards, *Who Married Whom: Covington County, Mississippi* (Moss Point, Miss.: n.p., 1991), 183; will of John "Jackie" Knight; see also Thomas et al., *Family of John "Jackie" Knight*, 337–38. John Whitehead's father was non-slaveholder Daniel Whitehead, who pioneered alongside Tom Sumrall Sr. in the settling of Mississippi Territory (see Chap. 2). In 1830 John Whitehead headed his own nonslaveholding household. With the receipt of Jackie Knight's gift of slaves, John and Mary Ann became the only Whiteheads in Jones and Covington Counties who owned slaves. By 1860 neither was reported as owning slaves, indicating perhaps that Lewis and Cate had died.

41. For Ethel Knight's description of Albert Knight as a wealthy slaveholder, see her *Echo of the Black Horn*, 61.

42. Will of John "Jackie" Knight. Neither Albert nor Newton Knight were reported as slaveholders in the slave schedules of U.S. Bureau of the Census, Federal Manuscript Censuses, 1850, 1860, Jones, Covington, Jasper Counties, Miss. Benjamin D. Graves recalled in 1926 that Albert Knight owned one slave and that Newton owned none; see B. D. Graves, Hebron Community Meeting, June 17, 1926, Rogers Museum. Kenneth Welch claims that Jackie Knight gave Albert a slave named Jordan in 1859 but that Albert seems not to have kept the slave. Welch points out that, unlike in the case of other children, Jackie Knight left money but no slaves to Albert in his will and that none of Albert's sons owned slaves. See Sumrall and Welch, *Knights and Related Families*, 151.

43. James Street, *Tap Roots* (Garden City, N.Y.: Sun Dial Press, 1943), 30–31, 65. The legends and gossip that swirled around the Knight family well into the twentieth century provided raw material for Street's characters, but only he knew exactly when and where fact and fiction merged. Albert and Mason Knight's pro-Union views are suggested by their naming their last son, born in 1850, Andrew Zachary Taylor. Earle Knight's description of Albert Knight's antislavery views resembles James Street's description of Hoab Dabney as an abolitionist. Street reinforced the resemblance between Albert Knight and Hoab Dabney by describing Hoab's wife, Shellie, as an orphan raised by the Dabneys, similar to the legend that Albert's wife, Mason, was raised by the Knights.

44. B. D. Graves, Hebron Community Meeting, June 17, 1926, Rogers Museum.

45. Leah Townsend, *South Carolina Baptists*, 1670–1805 (Florence, S.C.: Florence Print-

ing Co., 1935), 200; James E. Wooley, ed., *A Collection of Upper South Carolina Genealogical and Family Records*, 3 vols. (Easley, S.C.: Southern Historical Press, 1979), 1:335; Sandra E. Boyd, comp. and ed., *Benjamin Duckworth: His Descendants and Related Families* (Hattiesburg, Miss.: n.p., 1989), 433, 452. Information on Aaron Welborn from 1827 Tax Roll, Jones County, and 1837 State Census, Jones County, both reprinted in Strickland and Strickland, *Records of Jones County*, 67, 96. For a genealogy of the Welborns, see Appendix 3. In 1850 Serena's father, John Henry Turner, was barely self-sufficient and grew corn and sweet potatoes and raised hogs and sheep; see U.S. Bureau of the Census, Federal Agricultural and Manufacturing Census, 1850, Jones County, Miss.

46. Gerald W. Johnson, e-mail message to author, Feb. 7, 18, 1999, ML-USM.

47. Ibid., Jan. 12, 1999. Younger Sr. and Elizabeth Welborn moved from South Carolina to Mississippi around 1832. By 1839 the family had moved across the border into Jasper County. According to family sources and documents, Turner and Younger Welborn Jr., sons of William (Billy) and Sarah Welborn, and their cousins, William Elbert and Tolbert, sons of Younger Sr. and Elizabeth Welborn, all joined the Knight Company during the Civil War. William Elbert and Tolbert later joined the Union Army in New Orleans. See "Union Army Pension Records," in *Miscellaneous Records of Jones County, MS*, comp. Jean Strickland and Patricia N. Edwards (Moss Point, Miss.: n.p., 1992), 155, 157, 186.

Knight Company rosters vary in their listings of Welborns. Ethel Knight, for example, listed a W. T. Welborn (William Elbert?) and a Turner Welborn. She does not list Tolbert Welborn at all. The full name of the man she listed as Elijah Welborn was Elijah Welborn Laird. See Thomas J. Knight, *The Life and Activities of Captain Newton Knight and His Company and the "Free State of Jones"* (1935; rev. ed, Laurel, Miss.: n.p., 1946), 17, and Ethel Knight, *Echo of the Black Horn*, 89–90.

In 1850 in Jones County, the Welborns were struggling farmers who raised surplus hogs but appeared to produce too little grain to be deemed self-sufficient. By 1860 in Jasper County, their grain production was sufficient, but they had minimal surpluses for the market. Billy and Sarah Welborn fared somewhat better. In 1850 they produced sufficient grain and surpluses in sweet potatoes, hogs, and wool. In 1860 they produced surplus wool and two bales of cotton. See U.S. Bureau of the Census, Federal Agricultural and Manufacturing Censuses, Jones, Jasper Counties, Miss.

48. U.S. Bureau of the Census, Federal Manuscript Census, 1840, Jones County, Miss.; Strickland and Strickland, *Records of Jones County*, 27; Appendix 3. In the 1850 census forty-year-old Joel Welborn was reported without slaves and possessing $800 in real and personal property. That amount seems low considering his successful purchase in 1847 of almost 430 acres of land seized from various owners for nonpayment of taxes by the Jones County sheriff. Welborn's rise to wealth may be traced through U.S. Bureau of the Census, Federal Manuscript Censuses, Population and Slave Schedules, 1850, 1860, Jones County, Miss., and in Strickland and Strickland, *Records of Jones County*, 52, 63–111, passim.

49. "Final Records of the Chancery Court," in Strickland and Edwards, *Miscellaneous Records of Jones County*, 94–95; *Joel Welborn v. Amos J. Spears*, 32 Miss. 138–42 (1856); *J. E. Welborn v. Isaac Anderson* 37 Miss. 155–64 (1859). In 1850 twenty-nine-year-old Amos J. Spears and his wife, Frances Parker, lived with her parents, tavern keeper James Parker, Parker's wife Mary, and the couple's seven children. (Mary Parker presumably died soon after, freeing James to marry widow Sally Collins Walters.) In 1850 Isaac Anderson owned nineteen slaves; in 1860 he owned twenty-three slaves. See U.S. Bureau of the Census, Federal Manuscript Censuses, Population and Slave Schedules, 1850, 1860, Jones County, Miss.

50. Gerald W. Johnson, e-mail, Feb. 18, 1999. Details of the suits are from "Final Records of the Chancery Court," in Strickland and Edwards, *Miscellaneous Records of Jones County*, 59.

51. U.S. Bureau of the Census, Federal Manuscript Censuses, Population and Slave Schedules, 1820, 1830, 1840, 1850, 1860, Covington, Jones Counties, Miss. Williams Duckworth's older brother, Benjamin, and his nephews, Zabud and Joseph, made similar progress as slaveholders. By 1840 Benjamin owned eleven slaves; Zabud, six; and Joseph, two. Patrick C. Duckworth, a nephew of Williams and Benjamin, married Benjamin's daughter Sarah (his first cousin) and owned five slaves in 1830. By 1860 Patrick and Sarah's son, Benjamin Cass, owned twenty slaves, making him Jones County's second largest slaveholder after Isaac Anderson, who owned twenty-three slaves.

52. U.S. Bureau of the Census, Federal Manuscript Censuses, Population and Slave Schedules, 1830, 1840, 1850, 1860, Jones County, Miss. Genealogical information from Sandra E. Boyd, *Benjamin Duckworth* 2, 294, 295. Both men were sons of Patrick and Sarah Duckworth.

53. Wright, *Political Economy of the Cotton South*, 15; Joseph D. W. Duckworth to Jourdan Smith and Frances Elizabeth Smith, May 31, 1845, and Sept. 5, 1846, Duckworth-Smith-McPherson Family Papers. Francis E. Smith was the daughter of Jacob Duckworth, a brother of Joseph D. W. Duckworth's mother, Sarah. Both Jacob and Sarah were children of Benjamin and Mary Duckworth. J. D. W. Duckworth served only one term before going to work for John G. Blackwell, Clerk of the Smith County Probate Court. On cotton prices in antebellum Mississippi, see Bond, *Political Culture in the Nineteenth-Century South*, 69–71; Douglass C. North, *The Economic Growth of the United States, 1790–1860* (New York: Norton, 1966), 122–34; and Sydnor, *Slavery in Mississippi*, 181–202.

54. Joseph D. W. Duckworth to Jourdan Smith and Frances Elizabeth Smith, May 31, 1845, Duckworth-Smith-McPherson Family Papers. The chancery court filed a writ of injunction against Duckworth for his failure to administer a court judgment; see J. D. W. Duckworth et al. v. Uriah Millsaps, 15 Miss. 308 (1846).

55. Eugene D. Genovese, *The Political Economy of Slavery: Studies in the Economy and Society of the Slave South* (New York: Random House, 1965), 3–10; Wright, *Political Economy of the Cotton South*, 37–39, 70–74.

56. Amos McLemore's grandparents, Amos and Equilla McLemore, moved from Duplin County, North Carolina, to Darlington County, South Carolina, before 1790. In South Carolina they lived on 400 acres of land (officially granted to Amos Sr. by the state in 1793) and belonged to the Lynches Creek Baptist Church. By 1800 the McLemores had left South Carolina. In 1830 Amos's widow, Equilla, and several of their children lived in Covington, Jones, and Perry Counties, Mississippi. Information from Rudy Leverett, "Ole Rosinheels: A Genealogical Sketch of the Family of Major Amos McLemore, 27th Mississippi Infantry Regiment, C.S.A." (unpublished manuscript, 1988, in author's possession).

57. Information on Abraham McLemore is from "An Incident in Old Ellisville," unpublished WPA records, RG 60, vol. 315, MDAH. Amos McLemore was born in 1823. Around 1850 he married his cousin Rosa Lavinia McLemore, whose mother, Sarah Fairchild McLemore, was the daughter of Robert Fairchild. Like Amos, Sarah's brother, William H. Fairchild, was murdered by deserters during the Civil War. Amos McLemore's business connections with the Baylis family may have influenced his decision to join the Methodist Church, for his mother and several other relatives were Baptists. See Leverett, "Ole Rosinheels," 13–17, 21–23.

58. Description of the Deason home is from Roy E. McLeod, unpublished WPA

records, Jones County, RG 60, vol. 315, MDAH. In 1860 the Federal Manuscript Census reported Amos Deason as a merchant who possessed $3,000 in real estate and $3,000 in personal property. For a description of the typical farmhouse in antebellum Jones County, see Ben Hilbun, "Cracker's Neck," *Mississippi Quarterly* 7 (Jan. 1954): 68.

59. Statements of Roy E. McLeod and Sue Boyd Neill, student volunteers, unpublished WPA records, Jones County, RG 60, vol. 315, MDAH.

60. U.S. Bureau of the Census, Federal Manuscript Censuses, Population, Slave, and Agricultural Schedules, 1860, Jones County, Miss. On McLemore's budding social status, see Leverett, "Ole Rosinheels," 21–22. The 1860 census enumerator listed thirty-four-year-old Amos McLemore's occupation as merchant and reported his real estate as worth $2,000 and his personal worth at $4,098. He was not listed as owning slaves. His business partner, Dr. John M. Baylis, was one of Jones County's wealthiest citizens in 1860. I have counted him among the nine citizens who owned ten or more slaves because he owned seven in his own name and held four in trust for members of his household. Baylis claimed real estate valued at $11,000 and personal worth of $8,300. Other slaveholders claiming ten or more slaves were Elijah Graves (10), Robert Graves Sr. (10), B. J. Rushton (15), Margaret Ferguson Smith (11), and Willis Windham (13). Three men owned twenty or more slaves: B. C. Duckworth (20), James Shows (20), and Isaac Anderson (23).

61. J. F. H. Claiborne, "A Trip through the Piney Woods," 1841–42, reprinted in *Publications of the Mississippi Historical Society*, 9 (1906): 487–538. Claiborne served in the Mississippi House of Representatives from 1836 to 1840. In 1841 he became an editor for the *Mississippi Free Trader*, an organ of the Democratic Party. See Franklin L. Riley, "Life of Col. J. F. H. Claiborne," *Publications of the Mississippi Historical Society* 7 (1903): 220–27. A similar image of life in the Piney Woods by a present-day historian is offered in Grady McWhiney, "Antebellum Piney Woods Culture: Continuity over Time and Place," in *Mississippi's Piney Woods: A Human Perspective*, ed. Noel Polk (Jackson: University Press of Mississippi, 1986), 40–58.

62. Claiborne, "Trip through the Piney Woods," 516 (second and fifth quoted phrases), 522 (third quoted phrase), 524 (first quoted phrase), 529 (fourth quoted phrase).

63. Ibid., 517. Tom Sumrall (Jr.) was reported as a landowner in Perry County on July 26, 1821; see Marilyn Davis Hahn, *Old St. Stephen's Land Office Records*, 23.

64. Dr. J. R. S. Pitts, *Life and Confession of the Noted Outlaw James Copeland*, introduction by John D. W. Guice (Jackson: University Press of Mississippi, 1992 [facsimile of 1909 edition]), 78, 100.

65. Klein, *Unification of a Slave State*, 44–46, 271–72, 276–84; Bond, *Political Culture in the Nineteenth-Century South*, 133–34. For additional studies of the interplay between economic growth, expansion of slavery, and politics in regions of the South outside the plantation belt, see esp. Harry L. Watson, *Jacksonian Politics and Community Conflict*; Steven Hahn, *Roots of Southern Populism*; and John Inscoe, *Mountain Masters: Slavery and the Sectional Crisis in Western North Carolina* (Knoxville: University of Tennessee Press, 1989). On the development of evangelicalism in the nineteenth century, see esp. Christine Leigh Heyrman, *Southern Cross: The Beginnings of the Bible Belt* (Chapel Hill: University of North Carolina Press, 1997); McCurry, *Masters of Small Worlds*; Randy J. Sparks, *On Jordan's Stormy Banks: Evangelicalism in Mississippi, 1773–1876* (Athens: University of Georgia Press, 1994); and Loveland, *Southern Evangelicals and the Social Order*. On the roots of the antimission movement, see Bertram Wyatt-Brown, "The Antimission Movement in the Jacksonian South: A Study in Regional Folk Culture," *Journal of Southern History* 36 (Nov. 1970), 502–3.

Chapter Four

1. Christine Leigh Heyrman, *Southern Cross: The Beginnings of the Bible Belt* (Chapel Hill: University of North Carolina Press, 1997), 9, 214–17; Ted Ownby, *Subduing Satan: Religion, Recreation, and Manhood in the Rural South, 1865–1920* (Chapel Hill: University of North Carolina Press, 1990), 1–18; Bertram Wyatt-Brown, "The Antimission Movement in the Jacksonian South: A Study in Regional Folk Culture," *Journal of Southern History* 36 (Nov. 1970), 510–21. Although Piney Woods people were affected by the cotton economy and slavery, they were increasingly marginalized in the wake of larger changes sweeping the South's cotton belt. For descriptions of a similar process in the South's mountain regions, see Phillip Paludan, *Victims: A True Story of the Civil War* (Knoxville: University of Tennessee Press, 1981), 3–11.

2. Records of the Acts and Doings of the Baptist Church of Christ at Leaf River, Covington County, Miss., private manuscripts, no. 1049m (microfilm, roll 4026), MDAH.

3. Addie West, "Hogs Nose in on Treasure," Unpublished WPA Papers, Jones County, RG 60, vol. 315, MDAH; Records, Leaf River Baptist Church; U.S. Bureau of the Census, Federal Manuscript Census, 1850, Covington County, Miss.; Unpublished WPA Papers, Jones County, RG 60, vol. 315, MDAH. In 1850 the widowed Mary Coleman lived with daughter Elizabeth and son-in-law Daniel Knight and was not reported as owning slaves. In 1860 seventy-eight-year-old Mary Coleman headed her own household and was reported owning five slaves. These slaves may have been transferred to her at her son Tom's death in 1858. See U.S. Bureau of the Census, Federal Manuscript Censuses, Population Schedules, 1840, 1850, 1860, Covington, Jones Counties, and Slave Schedules, 1850, 1860, Covington, Jones Counties, Miss.

4. Ben Graves interview by Addie West, "The Killing of Tom Coleman," Unpublished WPA Papers, Jones County, RG 60, vol. 315, MDAH.

5. Ibid.; Kenneth S. Greenberg, *Honor and Slavery: Lies, Duels, Noses, Masks, Dressing As a Woman, Gifts, Strangers, Humanitarianism, Death, Slave Rebellions, the Proslavery Argument, Baseball, Hunting, and Gambling in the Old South* (Princeton: Princeton University Press, 1996), 8, 12–16.

6. Ben Graves interview by Addie West, "Killing of Tom Coleman"; Greenberg, *Honor and Slavery*, 35–36.

7. Circuit Court Minutes, Book 2, 1858–1866, Office of the Chancery Clerk, Covington County, Collins, Miss. The murder trial of M. T. G. Kilgore is recorded in the circuit court minute book without details; it does, however, list Joe Gunter as a witness for the state.

8. On the influence of local feuds and geographic isolation on anti-Confederate sentiments, see Paludan, *Victims*, 61–63.

9. For a similar conclusion about the links between local and national events, see ibid., xi.

10. Elder Norvell Robertson Sr., "An Autobiography, 1765–1846," typed copy in Virginia Historical Society, Richmond, 37; Records, Leaf River Baptist Church; Anne C. Loveland, *Southern Evangelicals and the Social Order, 1800–1860* (Baton Rouge: Louisiana State University Press, 1980), 81; Randy J. Sparks, *On Jordan's Stormy Banks: Evangelicalism in Mississippi, 1773–1876* (Athens: University of Georgia Press, 1994), 108, 116. On January 27, 1833, Elder Robertson alone was reported to have baptized Synthia Rush. He was not addressed as "pastor," however, until November 27, 1841. According to Suzanne Spell ("History of Jones County," master's thesis, Mississippi College, 1961), there were 18 churches of the following denominations in Jones County in 1860:

Baptist (6), Primitive Baptist (1), Congregational Methodist (4), Methodist (6), and Presbyterian (1).

11. Records, Leaf River Baptist Church.

12. Ibid.; Elder Norvell Robertson Sr., "Autobiography," 35–36. Before his appointment, Norvell Robertson's official title seems to have been supply pastor, one who traveled once or twice a month from his own church to preach at a church that had no settled pastor. See Loveland, *Southern Evangelicals and the Social Order*, 47.

13. Records, Leaf River Baptist Church.

14. C. C. Goen, *Broken Churches, Broken Nation: Denominational Schisms and the Coming of the American Civil War* (Macon, Ga.: Mercer University Press, 1985), 4–13; Elder Norvell Robertson Sr., "Autobiography," 37; Joseph D. W. Duckworth to Jourdan Smith and Frances Elizabeth Smith, Sept. 5, 1846, Duckworth-Smith-McPherson Family Papers, Center for the Study of American History, University of Texas, Austin.

15. Elder Norvell Robertson Sr., "Autobiography," 3.

16. Ibid., 6, 38.

17. Tom Sullivan died in 1855. On the history of the hollow, see Chester Sullivan, *Sullivan's Hollow* (Jackson: University Press of Mississippi, 1978), 12–13, and Ann R. Hammons, *Wild Bill Sullivan: King of the Hollow* (Jackson: University Press of Mississippi, 1980), 24, 35–36. On masculine honor in the Old South, see esp. Greenberg, *Honor and Slavery*, and Bertram Wyatt-Brown, *Southern Honor: Ethics and Behavior in the Old South* (New York: Oxford University Press, 1982). On ritualized violence among backcountry men, see esp. Elliott J. Gorn, "Gouge and Bite, Pull Hair and Scratch: The Social Significance of Fighting in the Southern Backcountry," *American Historical Review* 90 (Feb. 1985): 18–43, and Charles C. Bolton and Scott Culclasure, eds., *The Confessions of Edward Isham: A Poor White Life of the Old South* (Athens: University Press of Georgia, 1998). On the connection between antebellum feuds and Civil War divisions in local communities, see Paludan, *Victims*, 29, 62.

18. Records, Leaf River Baptist Church. I have not ascertained the identity of John Duckworth, identified also as John Moore, or the circumstances under which he died. A likely possibility is that he was a stepson to Benjamin C. Duckworth, who married Sarah A. Moore. See Sandra E. Boyd, *Benjamin Duckworth*, 294.

19. Records, Leaf River Baptist Church. John Mayfield was married to Williams Duckworth's daughter, Anna; see Sandra E. Boyd, *Benjamin Duckworth*, 433.

20. Sandra E. Boyd, *Benjamin Duckworth*, 452; J. D. W. Duckworth to Jourdan Smith and Frances Elizabeth Smith, Sept. 5, Dec. 30, 1846, Duckworth-Smith-McPherson Family Papers.

21. Records, Leaf River Baptist Church. The next charge of slave misconduct was not issued until February 18, 1837, when Amos McLemore reported "Brother Lewis" guilty of drunkenness. The church expelled Lewis in June of the same year. That same month they expelled another male slave (Henry) for adultery. Such charges were more often reserved for whites, however. Between 1829 and 1865 only two slaves were charged with drunkenness and one with adultery. The literature on master-slave relations among men is voluminous; see esp. Greenberg, *Honor and Slavery*, 46–50; Bertram Wyatt-Brown, "The Mask of Obedience: Male Slave Psychology in the Old South," *American Historical Review* 93 (Dec. 1988): 1228–52; Theodore Rosengarten, *Tombee: Portrait of a Cotton Planter* (New York: McGraw-Hill, 1987), 149–67; John Blassingame, *The Slave Community: Plantation Life in the Antebellum South* (Oxford University Press, 1972); 223–322; and Eugene Genovese, *Roll, Jordan, Roll: The World the Slaves Made* (New York: Pantheon, 1974).

Piney Woods Baptists pronounced enslaved African Americans to be children of

God, but by the 1820s most churches segregated them in adjoining rooms built onto the churches. On August 14, 1830, as the leaders of the Leaf River Church planned the building of their new meetinghouse, they directed that "a certain portion . . . be separated by a banister partition for the use of the colored part of the congregation" (Records, Leaf River Baptist Church). On evangelical churches' segregation of blacks from whites, see also Heyrman, *Southern Cross*, 68–69, and Randy J. Sparks, *On Jordan's Stormy Banks*, 134–35.

22. The story of Jessie is from George P. Rawick, ed., *The American Slave: A Composite Autobiography*, supplement, ser. 1, vol. 7, *Mississippi Narratives*, pt. 2 (Westport, Conn.: Greenwood Press, 1972), 529–31. On the courts' reluctance to interfere in master-slave relations, see Heyrman, *Southern Cross*, 249–52, and Greenberg, *Honor and Slavery*, 37–40.

23. Records, Leaf River Baptist Church. Throughout the 1830s and 1840s evangelical battles over personal and doctrinal issues paralleled growing national schisms among Presbyterians, Methodists, and Baptists, whose rupture into sectional factions preceded that of the federal government by fifteen years. See Goen, *Broken Churches, Broken Nation*, 4–13.

24. Records, Leaf River Baptist Church; Elder Norvell Robertson Sr., "Autobiography," 43.

25. The charges against Whitehead were introduced in January 1836 (Records, Leaf River Baptist Church); Amos McLemore of Leaf River Baptist Church is identified in Rudy Leverett, "Ole Rosinheels: A Genealogical Sketch of the Family of Major Amos McLemore, 27th Mississippi Infantry Regiment, C.S.A." (unpublished manuscript, 1988, in author's possession), 13.

26. Records, Leaf River Baptist Church; Gerald W. Johnson, e-mail messages to author, Dec. 8, 1998, ML-USM. Younger Sr. and Elizabeth Welborn joined the Leaf River Church in 1833. Supporting the possibility that they may have departed because of antimission sentiments was the church's resolution in August 1837—eight months before the Welborns left—to ban footwashing except in a "private capacity only." One church officially designated Primitive was founded in Jones County before the Civil War.

27. Records, Leaf River Baptist Church. Ali Whitehead, born Agnes Allis Robertson about 1818, married William Whitehead, brother to John, before 1840. In 1850 six children ranging in age from two to fifteen years lived with them. In 1860 William was gone, and Ali headed her own household, which included four adults (probably her and William's children) and three children between sixteen and five. Five-year-old Mary was likely the illegitimate child for which Ali was punished by the Leaf River Church. See U.S. Bureau of the Census, Federal Manuscript Censuses, 1840, 1850, 1860, Covington County, Miss.

28. Records, Leaf River Baptist Church; Barbara Welter, "The Cult of True Womanhood: 1820–1860," *American Quarterly* 18 (summer 1966): 151–74.

29. LeeAnn Whites, *The Civil War As a Crisis in Gender: Augusta, Georgia, 1860–1890* (Athens: University of Georgia Press, 1995), 10–11; Stephanie McCurry, *Masters of Small Worlds: Yeoman Households, Gender Relations, and the Antebellum South Carolina Low Country* (New York: Oxford University Press, 1995), 6–7.

30. J. F. H. Claiborne, "A Trip through the Piney Woods," 1841–42, reprinted in *Publications of the Mississippi Historical Society*, 9 (1906): 525–27; Chester Sullivan, *Sullivan's Hollow*, 60. On conventions of white womanhood in the antebellum South, see Heyrman, *Southern Cross*, 161–205; Brenda E. Stevenson, *Life in Black and White: Family and Community in the Slave South* (New York: Oxford University Press, 1996), 37–62; McCurry, *Masters of Small Worlds*, 208–38; Victoria E. Bynum, *Unruly Women: The Politics of Social*

and *Sexual Control in the Old South* (Chapel Hill: University of North Carolina Press, 1992), 35–57; Elizabeth Fox-Genovese, *Within the Plantation Household: Black and White Women of the Old South* (Chapel Hill: University of North Carolina Press, 1988), 192–241; Catherine Clinton, *The Plantation Mistress: Woman's World in the Old South* (New York: Pantheon, 1982); and Anne Firor Scott, *The Southern Lady: From Pedestal to Politics, 1830–1930* (Chicago: University of Chicago Press, 1970).

31. Elder Norvell Robertson Sr., "Autobiography," 27, 29.

32. Ibid., 30.

33. Heyrman, *Southern Cross*, 161–205; Rachel N. Klein, *Unification of a Slave State: The Rise of the Planter Class in the South Carolina Backcountry, 1760–1808* (Chapel Hill: University of North Carolina Press, 1990); Cynthia Lynn Lyerly, "Enthusiasm, Possession, and Madness: Gender and the Opposition to Methodism in the South, 1770–1810," in *Beyond Image and Convention: Explorations in Southern Women's History*, ed. Janet L. Coryell, Martha H, Swain, Sandra Gioia Treadway, and Elizabeth Hayes Turner (Columbia: University of Missouri Press, 1998), 55, 68–72. Uneasiness over whether gender distinctions were becoming too blurred surely prompted the following query, issued on October 6, 1804, to the Black Creek Church of Cheraws District, South Carolina: might women "speak even for their own defense in the church?" The church offered a qualified yes, but only if the woman was careful "so as not to use authority over the man" (quoted from Leah Townsend, *South Carolina Baptists, 1670–1805* [Florence, S.C.: Florence Printing Co., 1935], 94).

34. Records, Leaf River Baptist Church; McCurry, *Masters of Small Worlds*, 180; Randy J. Sparks, *On Jordan's Stormy Banks*, 160; Klein, *Unification of a Slave State*, 279, 293–95. The Leaf River Baptist Church clerk designated Sarah Robertson, the wife of Elder Norvell Robertson, as "deaconness" upon her death in 1853. The fact that he did so after her death, however, indicated that the title was honorific rather than customary. The congregation voted collectively on matters of admissions, dismissions, and disciplinary actions, but exactly *who* voted was not recorded.

35. Ben Hilbun, "Cracker's Neck," *Mississippi Quarterly* 7 (Jan. 1954): 67–71; Records, Leaf River Baptist Church, June 18, 1836. On the gradual strengthening of patriarchal authority in evangelical churches between 1810 and 1830, see Heyrman, *Southern Cross*, 117–252.

36. Records, Leaf River Baptist Church.

37. Ibid.

38. Ibid. Rhoda Bullock appears elsewhere in the church minutes as Rhoda Ballard. Bentonville Taylor, the object of Synthia Rush's desires, may have particularly shocked her husband and the church since he was a native New Yorker (i.e., a stranger) whom some already suspected of being a con artist. Though listed as a lawyer possessing real estate worth $5,000 and personal worth of $3,200 in the 1860 census, according to gossip still remembered in 1936, during the 1850s Taylor allegedly moved to Ellisville, Jones County, where he boarded at James Parker's hotel and identified himself as a Yankee schoolteacher. There he supposedly claimed that his female companion was his sister, although citizens of Jones discovered otherwise. See U.S. Bureau of the Census, Federal Manuscript Census, 1860, Covington County, Miss.; unpublished WPA records, RG 60, vol. 315, MDAH. In 1857 Taylor was accused of trying to prevent the conviction and execution of the notorious outlaw James Copeland; see Dr. J. R. S. Pitts, *Life and Confession of the Noted Outlaw James Copeland*, introduction by John D. W. Guice (Jackson: University Press of Mississippi, 1992 [facsimile of 1909 edition]), 196–99. On Southern suspicions of strangers as men of "stealth and trickery," see Greenberg, *Honor and Slavery*, 144.

39. Records, Leaf River Baptist Church.

40. Ibid.; U.S. Bureau of the Census, Federal Manuscript Censuses, Population Sched-ules, 1850, 1860, 1870, Covington County, Miss.; Janet Smith, Jean Strickland, and Patricia N. Edwards, *Who Married Whom: Covington County, Mississippi* (Moss Point, Miss.: n.p., 1991), 3–4. Frances Ates and her sons were born in Louisiana. In 1850 Frances headed a household that included two of her sons, William, age twenty-two, and John W., age seventeen. Living in nearby households of their own were sons Calvin Ates, age twenty-five; James Ates, age twenty-two; and Thomas Ates, age twenty-one. I have not found Matilda Ates in the federal manuscript censuses and suspect that she is the Martha Ann Sullivan who married Thomas Edward Ates in 1851, especially since the couple named a daughter born in 1854 Martha Matilda. Calvin Ates married Eliza Jane Sullivan in 1850. Evidently there were two Thomas Ateses in Covington County, one of whom married Angelina Sullivan. Thomas and Angelina Ates were both alive in 1870; the Thomas Ates who married Martha Ann Sullivan was hanged as a deserter during the Civil War. Sarah Elizabeth Ates, daughter of John Ates and granddaughter of Frances Ates, married Julius Evander Sullivan of Sullivan's Hollow. From this branch came the rumors that Frances Ates had married a "full-blooded Choctaw Indian named Lang-ford." For this and other information on marriages between Sullivans and Ateses, see Hammons, *Wild Bill Sullivan*, 85, 115, 117, 125.

41. Records, Leaf River Baptist Church; Ruby Bynum Sanders, comp., *The Bynum and Herrington Connections* (Ellisville, Miss.: n.p., 1994), 35–37. William Bynum replied in July 1836 to charges that he was neglecting his religious duties by citing "circum-stances" that were "unfavorable" for his attendance. Several pages of his family Bible chronicle the upheavals that occurred in his personal life between 1837 and 1841. Son "Tapleigh" was born May 1, 1837; daughter Charity was born September 10, 1839; wife Sarah died on the same day that she gave birth to Charity. In June 1843 eighty-year-old William Bynum Sr. applied for dismission from the Leaf River Church. He died in 1858 at age ninety-five.

42. U.S. Bureau of the Census, Federal Manuscript Censuses, Population Schedules, 1850, 1860, 1870, 1880, Smith, Jones Counties, Miss. Evidence that Alzade Courtney worked in the fields is from Thomas J. Knight, *The Life and Activities of Captain Newton Knight and His Company and the "Free State of Jones"* (1935; rev. ed, Laurel, Miss.: n.p., 1946), 55–57, and the 1880 federal census enumerator for Jones County, who listed her occupa-tion as "field hand." Rebecca Smith's age, sixty-six, makes it highly improbable that she was Alzade's mother. In 1868 Alzade and James McGee officially divorced after James McGee sued her on grounds that she had abandoned their household. See *James McGee v. Alzade Courtney*, May 2, 1868, Final Records of the Chancery Court, 133–35 (micro-film), MDAH. Alzade lived in the household of Wiley and Mary Courtney until at least 1870. By 1880 she had returned to using the surname Courtney, as did her children.

43. On poor white women of the Southern backcountry, see Victoria E. Bynum, "Mothers, Lovers, and Wives: Images of Poor White Women in Edward Isham's Auto-biography," in Bolton and Culclasure, *Confessions of Edward Isham*, 85–100.

44. Whites, *Civil War As a Crisis in Gender*; Drew Gilpin Faust, *Mothers of Invention: Women of the Slaveholding South in the American Civil War* (Chapel Hill: University of North Carolina Press, 1996); McCurry, *Masters of Small Worlds*.

45. *James Parker v. Sarah Parker*, 1857, Jones County Chancery Court, Final Records, 1st District, 1857–1890 (microfilm), MDAH.

46. Ibid. Sarah Parker's marital status was reported as "widow," and her occupation as "midwife" in U.S. Bureau of the Census, Federal Manuscript Census, Population Schedule, 1870, Jones County, Miss.

47. Records, Leaf River Baptist Church. On churches' punishment of slave women,

see Stevenson, *Life in Black and White*, 37–62; on their failure to enforce reciprocal punishment of slave masters, see McCurry, *Masters of Small Worlds*, 201.

48. Ex-slave Martha Wheeler recalled that Newton's Uncle Daniel wasted much of his inheritance paying court fines for drunkenness; see Rawick, *American Slave*, pt. 5, 10:2262–63, 2265.

49. *New Orleans Item*, Mar. 20, 1921. No author, including Ethel Knight, has suggested that Newt Knight abused alcohol. In his 1921 interview Newt himself claimed that he strictly forbade the use of alcohol among his men during a raid on a government storehouse.

50. Earle Knight, conversations with author, June 28–30, 1994, ML-USM; Jan Sumrall and Kenneth Welch, *The Knights and Related Families* (Denham Springs, La.: n.p., 1985), 150; Rawick, *American Slave*, pt. 5, 10:2265. Tom Knight claimed that Newton Knight joined the Zora Primitive Baptist Church around 1885–86; see Thomas J. Knight, *Life and Activities of Captain Newton Knight*, 14.

51. Neither Tom Knight nor Ethel Knight presented evidence that Newton Knight had shot or murdered a slave, or that his mother changed his age; see Thomas J. Knight, *Life and Activities of Captain Newton Knight*, 2, and Ethel Knight, *Echo of the Black Horn*, 85. Nevertheless, despite the lack of evidence, Newton Knight is described in a college survey textbook as a "staunch Baptist given to fits of violence" who "once killed a black." See Gary Nash, Julie Roy Jeffrey, John R. Howe, Peter J. Frederick, Allen F. Davis, and Allan M. Winkler,, eds. *The American People: Creating a Nation and a Society*, vol. 1, 3d ed. (New York: HarperCollins, 1994), 363–64.

52. For Martha Wheeler's remarks, see Rawick, *American Slave*, pt. 5, 10:2262–71. On whites' use of violence to control slaves, see Greenberg, *Honor and Slavery*, 37; Stevenson, *Life in Black and White*, 194–205; Paul D. Escott, *Slavery Remembered: a Record of Twentieth-Century Slave Narratives* (Chapel Hill: University of North Carolina Press, 1979) 40–43; Blassingame, *Slave Community*, 249–83; Kenneth M. Stampp, *The Peculiar Institution: Slavery in the Antebellum South* (New York: Random House, 1956), 141–91.

53. Sumrall and Welch, *Knights and Related Families*, 156–57. Contradicting both Tom Knight's and Ethel Knight's claims that Mason Knight changed her son's birthdate is the 1900 census enumerator's report that Newton Knight was born in November 1837. This date conforms to every census report taken between 1850 and 1920. Finally, as Kenneth Welch pointed out, if Mason Knight had changed her son's birthdate, she would also have had to change the birthdates of the children born before and after him, which she did not do.

54. Joseph Benjamin Lightsey Diary, Feb. 21, 1851, MDAH. The lynched slave, whose name was Haley, was alleged to have raped and murdered his slave master's wife, Mary Dixon, and to have murdered their son.

55. Ethel Knight, *Echo of the Black Horn*, 34, 39–45.

56. U.S. Bureau of the Census, Federal Manuscript Censuses, 1870, 1880, 1900, Jasper County, Miss.

57. Ethel Knight, *Echo of the Black Horn*, 24, 29.

58. Ibid., 31.

59. Ibid., 250.

60. Ibid., 37, 262–63. The documentary film *Ethnic Notions* (San Francisco: Resolution Inc./California Newsreel, 1987) provides an excellent overview of negative media stereotypes of African American adults and children. No Rosette Knight appears in the federal manuscript censuses for Jasper, Jones, or Covington Counties between 1860 and 1920, nor is she mentioned in Jackie Knight's will. Although several witnesses at Davis Knight's trial recalled the names of various children of Rachel, not one men-

tioned a Rosette. Nor has a single Knight descendant interviewed by myself offered evidence that this Rosette Knight existed.

61. Ethel Knight, *Echo of the Black Horn*, 30, 262.

62. Ibid., 250 (second quoted phrase), 261 (first quoted phrase). Between 1854 and 1875 Rachel gave birth to at least nine children. They included Georgeanne, Jeffrey, Edmund, Fannie, Martha, Stewart, Floyd, Augusta Ann, and John Madison "Hinchie." Ethel Knight added Rosette but omitted Edmund (who apparently died before 1870) and Augusta Ann. See U.S. Bureau of the Census, Federal Manuscript Censuses, 1870, 1880, Jasper County, Miss.

On the history of enslaved African American women in the antebellum South, see esp. Patricia Morton, ed., *Discovering the Women in Slavery: Emancipating Perspectives on the American Past* (Athens: University of Georgia Press, 1996); Darlene Clark Hine and Barry David Gaspar, eds., *More Than Chattel: Black Women and Slavery in the Americas* (Bloomington: University of Indiana Press, 1996); Deborah Gray White, *Ar'n't I a Woman: Female Slaves in the Plantation South* (1985; rev. ed, New York: Norton, 1999); Stevenson, *Life in Black and White*, 159–327; Melton A. McLaurin, *Celia, a Slave* (Athens: University of Georgia Press, 1991); and Fox-Genovese, *Within the Plantation Household*, 242–333, 372–96.

63. Records, Leaf River Baptist Church.

64. On John A. Murrel and slave stealing, see Robert M. Coates, *The Outlaw Years: The History of the Land Pirates of the Natchez Trace* (New York: Macauley Co., 1930; reprint, Lincoln: University of Nebraska Press, 1986), 181–86, and Lightsey Diary, Apr. 11, 1852. On James Copeland, see Pitts, *Life and Confession*, 38–43.

65. U.S. Bureau of the Census, Federal Manuscript Censuses, 1870, 1880, 1900, Jasper County, Miss.

66. Records, Leaf River Baptist Church. In Georgia, for example, Jesse Mercer's entire career was devoted to building a united association of Baptists. Like most nineteenth-century Southern Baptists, he also vigorously defended slavery against Northern Baptist abolitionism. On Baptist support for the Confederate cause, see Heyrman, *Southern Cross*, 248–49; on Mississippi Baptists' support for secession, see Z. T. Leavell and T. J. Bailey, *A Complete History of Mississippi Baptists from the Earliest Times*, 2 vols. (Jackson: Mississippi Baptist Pub. Co., 1904), 1:109, 2:732–33.

67. U.S. Bureau of the Census, Federal Manuscript Censuses, Population Schedules, 1850, 1860, Jones, Covington Counties, Miss.; Records, Leaf River Baptist Church. The kin relationships between men executed by the Confederacy and members of the Leaf River Baptist Church were as follows: Benjamin Knight, son of William H. and Mary (Youngblood) Knight; Noel, John Thomas, and Daniel Whitehead, sons of John and Mary Ann (Knight) Whitehead; Sil Coleman, nephew of Elizabeth Coleman and Daniel Knight; Thomas and James Ates, sons of Frances Ates; Tapley Bynum, son of William Bynum Sr.; and Daniel Reddoch, son of James Reddoch.

Chapter Five

1. Historians who pioneered before 1943 in producing monographs on the Civil War from the perspective of the Southern home front and Southern dissenters include Ella Lonn, *Desertion during the Civil War* (New York: Century, 1928; reprint, Lincoln: University of Nebraska Press, 1998), and Georgia Lee Tatum, *Disloyalty in the Confederacy* (Chapel Hill: University of North Carolina Press, 1934; new ed. with an introduction by David Williams, Lincoln: University of Nebraska Press, 2000). The attraction of women scholars to this topic perhaps reflects the extent to which Lost Cause versions of the war spoke mainly to masculine ideals of Confederate honor and dishonor

(embodied by Confederate deserters) and almost wholly neglected the experiences of women, who did more than stoically endure the deaths or await the return of their men.

For thoughtful essays on the effects of Lost Cause history in burying or reshaping personal and collective memories of the Civil War, see David W. Blight, " 'For Something beyond the Battlefield': Frederick Douglass and the Struggle for the Memory of the Civil War," and Robert E. McGlone, "Rescripting a Troubled Past: John Brown's Family and the Harpers Ferry Conspiracy," both in *Journal of American History*, Memory and American History: A Special Issue, 75 (Mar. 1989): 1156–78, 1179–1200.

2. For an excellent theoretical overview of why so many historians of the Civil War have focused so narrowly on white men and battlefields, even after the Myth of the Lost Cause was dismantled, see LeeAnn Whites, *The Civil War As a Crisis in Gender: Augusta, Georgia, 1860–1890* (Athens: University of Georgia Press, 1995), 1–11.

3. Compiled Service Records of Confederate Soldiers Who Served in Organizations from the State of Mississippi, 7th Battalion, Mississippi Infantry, M269, NA (microfilm).

4. R. S. Hudson to Jefferson Davis, President, Confederate States of America, Mar. 14, 1864, U.S. War Department, *War of the Rebellion: A Compilation of the Official Records of the Union and Confederate Armies* (Washington, D.C.: Government Printing Office, 1880–1901), ser. 1 (hereafter referred to as *Official Records*), 32 (3):626; R. S. Hudson to Governor Clark, June 25, 1864, Governors' Papers, RG 27, vol. 56, MDAH.

5. R. S. Hudson to Jefferson Davis, President, Confederate States of America, Mar. 14, 1864, *Official Records*, 32 (3):626; R. S. Hudson to Governor Clark, June 25, 1864, Governors' Papers, RG 27, vol. 56, MDAH; Drew Gilpin Faust, *Mothers of Invention: Women of the Slaveholding South in the American Civil War* (Chapel Hill: University of North Carolina Press, 1996), 9–18; Whites, *Civil War As a Crisis in Gender*, 6–7.

6. Faust, *Mothers of Invention*, 30–35; 51–52; Whites, *Civil War As a Crisis in Gender*, 61–63; Victoria E. Bynum, *Unruly Women: The Politics of Social and Sexual Control in the Old South* (Chapel Hill: University of North Carolina Press, 1992), 120–50; George C. Rable, *Civil Wars: Women and the Crisis of Southern Nationalism* (Urbana: University of Illinois Press, 1989), 50–90.

7. Address of M. P. Bush before the Meeting of the DAR, Feb. 17, 1912, Lauren Rogers Museum of Art, Laurel, Miss. In 1860 twenty-four-year-old Madison P. Bush was a nonslaveholding farmer with real estate valued at $200 and personal worth of $247. He and his wife, Margaret, were the parents of two children. Although Bush is not listed on any of Newt Knight's rosters, he clearly supported the Knight Company. His military records show that he served in Company C, 7th Battalion, alongside many of its future members; was a POW at Vicksburg; was reported AWOL in January 1864; was a POW at Citronelle, Alabama; and was paroled at Mobile, Alabama, on June 1, 1865. At the time of his parole he was described as twenty-nine years old and six feet tall, with light hair and blue eyes. His brother, Scott Bush, was listed on the Knight Company roster. See U.S. Bureau of the Census, Federal Manuscript Census, 1860, Jones County, Miss.; Compiled Service Records, Madison P. Bush, 7th battalion, Mississippi Infantry, NA.

8. On the subject of how history, politics, and individuals' personal experiences have converged to shape memories of the nineteenth-century South, see Whites, *Civil War As a Crisis in Gender*, 133–59. Also see Edward L. Ayers, "Memory and the South"; Scot A. French, "What Is Social Memory?"; Maurice M. Manring, "Aunt Jemima Explained: The Old South, the Absent Mistress, and the Slave in a Box," all in *Southern Cultures* 2, no. 1 (fall 1995): 5–44; Richard D. Starnes, "Forever Faithful: The Southern Historical

Society and Confederate Historical Memory," *Southern Cultures* 2, no. 2 (winter 1996): 177–94; and David Thelen, "Memory and American History," *Journal of American History* 75, no. 4 (Mar. 1989): 1120.

9. The quoted passage is from Ruby Huff, "A Skirmish—Cavalry versus Deserters— Where in Newt Knight's Men Raid Lowrey's Raiders," unpublished WPA records, Covington County, RG 60, vol. 272, MDAH. Lieut. Thomas Jefferson Huff, a commissioned officer, failed to report to parole camp after being wounded at Vicksburg; see Compiled Service Records, Thomas J. Huff, 7th Battalion, Mississippi Infantry, NA. In 1860 Thomas J. Huff was married, thirty-two years old, and the father of two children. His real estate was valued at $1,000; his personal worth, at $2,400. He owned one slave. See U.S. Bureau of the Census, Federal Manuscript Census, Population and Slaveholding Schedules, 1860, Jones County, Miss. See also Addie West's "Brief History of Jones," unpublished WPA records, RG 60, vol. 315, MDAH, which includes a lengthy discussion of Newt Knight and the Free State of Jones based largely on Tom Knight's book.

10. Huff, "A Skirmish." Rudy Leverett characterized the Knight Company's unionism as mere expediency yet conceded that "for some of the civilians in the region, no doubt, the coming of Sherman was viewed as a liberation from an illegitimate Confederate regime" (*Legend of the Free State of Jones* [Jackson: University Press of Mississippi, 1984], 105). I believe this sentiment was far more widespread than does Leverett.

11. Interview with B. R. Sumrall, Aug. 31, 1936, unpublished WPA records, RG 60, vol. 316, MDAH. Benjamin R. Sumrall was the son of Benjamin Franklin Sumrall, the son of Harmon Levi Sumrall (see Appendix 6). Benjamin Franklin Sumrall married Sabra Collins, the daughter of Riley James Collins. See U.S. Bureau of the Census, Federal Manuscript Censuses, Population, 1850, 1860, 1900, Jones County, Miss., and James H. Hines, *The Families Somerville, Somervaill, Summerall, Summerell, Summerill, Summerlin, Sumlin, Sumrall, and Sumril* (n.p., 1981), 51, 107. Historians who stress the economics of the Piney Woods revolt against the Confederacy include Charles C. Bolton, *Poor Whites of the Antebellum South: Tenants and Laborers in Central North Carolina and Northeast Mississippi* (Durham: Duke University Press, 1994), 178, and Bradley G. Bond, *Political Culture in the Nineteenth-Century South: Mississippi, 1830–1900* (Baton Rouge: Louisiana State University Press, 1995), 133–34.

12. B. R. Sumrall, unpublished WPA records, Jones County, RG 60, vol. 316, MDAH; Thomas J. Knight, *The Life and Activities of Captain Newton Knight and His Company and the "Free State of Jones"* (1935; rev. ed, Laurel, Miss.: n.p., 1946), 20, 24.

13. Ethel Knight, *The Echo of the Black Horn: An Authentic Tale of "The Governor" of "The Free State of Jones"* (n.p., 1951), 82, 96–112.

14. John K. Bettersworth, "The Home Front, 1861–1865," in *A History of Mississippi*, ed. Richard Aubrey McLemore (Hattiesburg: University and College Press of Mississippi, 1973), 1:519, 521, 524–25. This essay is a condensation of material originally published in John K. Bettersworth, *Confederate Mississippi: The People and Policies of a Cotton State in Wartime* (Baton Rouge: Louisiana State University Press, 1963).

15. Leverett, *Legend of the Free State of Jones*, 34–36, 62–66, 75–85. On the murder of Amos McLemore by Newton Knight, see also Ethel Knight, *Echo of the Black Horn*, 168, and Thomas J. Knight, *Life and Activities of Captain Newton Knight*, 74–75.

16. B. D. Graves, Hebron Community Meeting, June 17, 1926, Rogers Museum. Ben Graves's father, Robert Graves Jr., was reported as owning ten slaves; see U.S. Bureau of the Census, Federal Manuscript Census, Slave Schedule, 1860, Jones County, Miss. He may be the Robert P. Graves who died in a hospital at Mobile, Alabama, shortly after his parole following the siege of Vicksburg; see Compiled Service Records, Robert Graves, Company F, 7th Battalion, Mississippi Infantry, NA.

17. *New Orleans Item*, Mar. 20, 1921. According to Percy L. Rainwater, Jones County cast 166 votes for the cooperationist candidate and 89 for the secession candidate. See his *Mississippi: Storm Center of Secession, 1856–1861* (Baton Rouge: Otto Claitor, 1938), 198–200; see also Leverett, *Legend of the Free State of Jones*, 38–39. On the secession crisis in Mississippi, see Bolton, *Poor Whites of the Antebellum South*, 161–85, and Bond, *Political Culture in the Nineteenth-Century South*, 111–23. For a New South, pro-secession version of events at the convention, see Mississippi judge Thomas H. Woods's essay, "A Sketch of the Mississippi Secession Convention of 1861—Its Membership and Work," *Publications of the Mississippi Historical Society*, 11 (1902): 91–104.

18. B. R. Sumrall, unpublished WPA records, Jones County, RG 60, vol. 316, MDAH.

19. Ibid.; Address of M. P. Bush, Feb. 17, 1912, Rogers Museum.

20. Compiled Service Records, Jasper J. Collins, James Madison Collins, and Thomas Jefferson Collins, Company F, 7th Battalion, Mississippi Infantry, NA. On Confederate conscription laws and their unpopularity among the yeomanry, see James M. McPherson, *Ordeal by Fire: The Civil War and Reconstruction* (New York: Knopf, 1982), 181–83. Desdemonia Collins's death is reported in the pension application filed by descendants of Riley James Collins; see "Union Army Pension Applications," in *Miscellaneous Records of Jones County, MS*, comp. Jean Strickland and Patricia N. Edwards (Moss Point, Miss.: n.p., 1992), 148–49.

21. Gerald W. Johnson, e-mail message to author, Nov. 11, Dec. 8, 1998, Jan. 12, 1999, ML-USM; Newton Knight File, RG 233, box 15, HR 1814, NA; Strickland and Edwards, *Miscellaneous Records of Jones County*, 155, 157–58. For kinship connections among the Welborns, Bynums, and Mauldins, see Appendixes 3–4. Like his brother-in-law, Prentice Bynum, William Mauldin eventually joined the Union Army at New Orleans. Aaron Terrell Welborn and William Turner Welborn enlisted in Company F of the 7th Battalion after passage of the Conscription Act; William Elbert and Tolbert Welborn refused to do so.

22. Newton Knight first served as a private in Company K, 8th regiment, Mississippi Volunteers (later, Company E, 8th Mississippi Infantry). On May 12, 1862, he enlisted in Company F, 7th Battalion, Mississippi Infantry. He claimed in 1921 that he avoided the battlefield by enlisting as a hospital orderly, but there is nothing on his military records to bear this out. Benjamin R. Sumrall buttresses Newt's claims with his remark that, after conscription laws were passed, pro-Union men "said that they would go [into the Confederate Army] and work among the sick but they would not fight for a cause in which they did not believe" (unpublished WPA records, Jones County, RG 60, vol. 316, MDAH).

Soldiers from this unit who appear on at least one of the three Knight Company rosters include Jasper J. Collins, James Madison Collins, William W. Sumrall, Tapley Bynum, Richard H. Hinton, Merida M. Coats, Morris W. Kervin, James Eulin, John H. Harper, Benjamin Franklin Dykes, Martin B. Valentine, James Morgan Valentine, John Ira Valentine, Aaron Terrell Welborn, and William M. Welch (Compiled Service Records, Company F, 7th Battalion, Mississippi Infantry, NA). For comments on Newton's performance in the Confederate Army, see Jan Sumrall and Kenneth Welch, *The Knights and Related Families* (Denham Springs, La.: n.p., 1985), 157–58.

23. The deaths of Jackie, Keziah, and Albert Knight are recorded in Sumrall and Welch, *Knights and Related Families*. Martha Knight Morgan was reported as an unmarried fourteen-year-old living in the household of her parents, Albert and Mason Knight, in the 1860 federal manuscript census for Jones County. Serena Knight's name appears on an undated list of 318 destitute families in Jones County (Confederate Records, RG 9, vol. 56, MDAH). Thus Leverett is correct when he states that Newton Knight's desertion was originally motivated by "economic necessity" and "family loyalties" (*Legend of the*

Free State of Jones, 85). I would also argue, however, that his political views were reshaped by his personal experiences.

24. B. D. Graves, Hebron Community Meeting, June 17, 1926, Rogers Museum; Thomas J. Knight, *Life and Activities of Captain Newton Knight*, 22, 37–38. Bill Morgan was allegedly exempted from service because he was a blacksmith; see Earle Knight, conversations with author, June 28–30, 1994, ML-USM. No record of either Bill Morgan's marriage to Martha Knight or his murder has been found. His identity is something of a mystery as well, since there were two Bill Morgans, father and son, in the area. The father was married to Elizabeth Rayborn and was about forty years old in 1860. Though his marriage to Martha Knight is highly unlikely, this Bill Morgan did die in the 1860s and was from Louisiana, as described by Ben Graves. The younger Morgan, age eighteen in 1860, is more likely to have married the teenaged Martha Knight, but he did not die until 1926 (information from Kenneth Slade, e-mail message to author, Mar. 30, 2000, ML-USM).

Perhaps because Ethel Knight preferred to portray Newt as a jealous husband rather than an outraged father, she accused Serena of having an affair with Bill Morgan. That accusation is not corroborated, nor does it jibe with Serena's complaints about her brother-in-law in letters to her husband. Nonetheless, gossip about Serena's alleged sexual improprieties may have indeed embarrassed Newt and inflamed his hatred of Bill Morgan. See Ethel Knight, *Echo of the Black Horn*, 63–69.

25. B. D. Graves, Hebron Community Meeting, June 17, 1926, Rogers Museum.

26. Ibid. Tom Knight stated that Morgan was shot through an open window; see Thomas J. Knight, *Life and Activities of Captain Newton Knight*, 37–38. Accounts passed down to descendants of Martha Knight Morgan and her second husband, Joseph Richard "Dick" Yawn, correspond to that of Ben Graves, however (Paula Bolan, e-mail message to author, Apr. 19, 2000, ML-USM). No definite date for the murder is recorded, but it probably occurred before the formal organization of the Knight Company.

27. *New Orleans Item*, Mar. 20, 1921. Despite Newt's rationale for desertion, candidates to the 1861 convention were not pledged to any specific vote; see Rainwater, *Mississippi*, 176). The movements of the 7th Battalion, Mississippi Infantry, may be traced in U.S. War Department, *Supplement to the Official Records of the Union and Confederate Armies*, ed. Janet B. Hewett (Wilmington, N.C.: Broadfoot Pub. Co., 1996), pt. 2, *Record of Events*, vol. 33, ser. 45 (hereafter cited as *Supplement*), 101–13.

28. For further confirmation of Jasper Collins's objection to the Twenty-Negro Law, see Goode Montgomery, "Alleged Secession of Jones County," *Publications of the Mississippi Historical Society* 8 (1904): 14. Ethel Knight claimed that the Knight Company was not pro-Union, yet elsewhere she admitted that the Collinses were staunch supporters of the Union (*Echo of the Black Horn*, 82, 115). In Texas the three Collins brothers who moved to Hardin County in 1853 with their parents, Stacy and Sarah, headed their own band of pro-Union deserters in the Big Thicket region. See Campbell Loughmiller and Lynn Loughmiller, *Big Thicket Legacy* (Austin: University of Texas Press, 1977), 70–72.

29. Gerald W. Johnson, e-mail, Nov. 15, 1998. On the battles themselves, see Peter Cozzens, *The Darkest Days of the War: The Battles of Iuka and Corinth* (Chapel Hill: University of North Carolina Press, 1997); Richard Beringer, Herman Hattaway, Archer Jones, and William N. Still Jr., *Why the South Lost the Civil War* (Athens: University of Georgia Press, 1986), 133–34, 176–77; McPherson, *Ordeal by Fire*, 292; and Edwin C. Bearss, *Decision in Mississippi: Mississippi's Important Role in the War between the States* (Jackson: Mississippi Commission on the War between the States, 1962), 1–103.

30. U.S. Bureau of the Census, Federal Manuscript Censuses, 1850, 1860, Jones County, Miss.; Compiled Service Records, Co. F, 7th Battalion, Mississippi Infantry, NA.

The listed men were all reported hospitalized on October 13, 1862. Tapley Bynum was reported AWOL in January–February 1863. Benjamin Franklin Bynum was the son of Benjamin and Peggy (Collins) Bynum. In 1860 thirty-year-old John H. and nineteen-year-old H. T. Harper lived in the household of their father, Josiah Harper, a fifty-eight-year-old nonslaveholder with real estate valued at $1,000 and personal wealth valued at $630. See U.S. Bureau of the Census, Federal Manuscript Census, Population and Slave Schedules, 1860, Jones County, Miss.

31. James Reddoch was reported AWOL from June until late October 1863. See Compiled Service Records, James Oliver Reddoch and Daniel Reddoch, Co. G, 7th Battalion, Mississippi Infantry, NA, and William A. Bynum, Co. K, 8th Mississippi Infantry, vol. 4B, folder 25, Confederate Records, RG 9, MDAH.

Many Southern soldiers who took unapproved leaves, such as James O. Reddoch and William A. Bynum, did not consider themselves disloyal to the Confederacy. For an analysis of local factors that contributed to their greater sense of loyalty to community, see Ralph Mann, "Ezekial Counts's Sand Lick Company: Civil War and Localism in the Mountain South," in The Civil War in Appalachia: Collected Essays, ed. Kenneth W. Noe and Shannon H. Wilson (Knoxville: University of Tennessee Press, 1997), 78–103.

32. For evidence that William A. Bynum supported the Confederacy, see Petition to Governor William Sharkey, July 29, 1865, Governors' Papers, RG 27, vol. 61B, and Senate Journal, Nov., 29, 1865, RG 47, vol. 88, MDAH. Reddoch's loyalty to the Confederate cause, despite his suffering a horrific wound at Corinth, is indicated in his letter of March 27, 1863, written to his parents from Enterprise Hospital. (My thanks to his descendants, Dorothy Bradley Cavendish and Robert John Cavendish Jr., for sharing Reddoch's letter with me.) In 1860 James O. Reddoch owned three slaves; his father, John, owned five. William A. Bynum lived in his father's household, which contained three slaves, in 1860. See U.S. Bureau of the Census, Federal Manuscript Censuses, Slave Schedules, 1860, Covington and Jones Counties, Miss. James O. Reddoch's mother, Dicey Hathorne, and William Bynum's mother, Mary Dossett, both came from slaveholding families.

33. Address of M. P. Bush, Feb. 17, 1912, Rogers Museum.

34. Leverett, Legend of the Free State of Jones, 38, 125; Supplement, 7th Battalion, Mississippi Infantry, and 27th Mississippi Infantry, 101, 780.

A popular way to gain status was by raising a regiment in one's home region. See McPherson, Ordeal by Fire, 168; Compiled Service Records, Amos McLemore, Co. B, 27th Mississippi Infantry, and John M. Baylis, Co. B, and Joel E. Welborn, Co. E, 7th Battalion, Mississippi Infantry, NA.

35. J. E. Welborn, Major Commander, 7th Mississippi Battalion, to A. A. Gen'l, Nov. 1, 1862, Compiled Service Records, Joel E. Welborn, Co. E, 7th Battalion, Mississippi Infantry, NA.

36. New Orleans Item, Mar. 20, 1921; Compiled Service Records, Newton Knight, Co. F, 7th Battalion, Mississippi Infantry, NA.

37. All correspondence is in Compiled Service Records, Joel E. Welborn, Co. E, 7th Battalion, Mississippi Infantry, NA.

38. J. H. Powell to Governor J. J. Pettus, Feb. 1, 1863, Governors' Papers, RG 27, vol. 50, MDAH.

39. Testimony of John Mathews, H. L. Sumrall, Allen Vallentine (Valentine), James Hinton, and Madison Harrington (Herrington), certified by T. J. Collins, Acting Justice of the Peace, and P. M. Bynum, Clerk of the Circuit Court, Jones County, Oct. 15, 1870, in Newton Knight Folder, HR 1814, RG 233, House of Representatives, Accompanying Papers Files, 42d Congress, box 15, NA.

40. *New Orleans Item*, Mar. 20, 1921; testimony of O. C. Martin, 6 March 1895, Claims of Newton Knight and Others, #8013 and 8464, Committee on War Claims, Records of U.S. Court of Claims, NA.

41. Second Lieutenant H. Mathis, Comdg. Co. K, 8th Mississippi Regiment, to Governor Pettus, June 1, 1863, Governors' Papers, RG 27, vol. 50, MDAH; *Supplement*, 113.

42. Information on John Ellzey is from Winnie Knight Thomas, Earle W. Knight, Lavada Knight Dykes, and Martha Kaye Dykes Lowery, *The Family of John "Jackie" Knight and Keziah Davis Knight, 1773–1985* (Magee, Miss.: Robert and Delores Knight Vinson, 1985), 296–97, and Earle Knight, conversations with author. Ellzey was reported AWOL after his parole from Vicksburg until November 1863, when he returned to his unit. See Compiled Service Records, Co. B, 7th Battalion, Mississippi Infantry, NA. The letter from "many soldiers" to General Pemberton is printed in *Official Records*, 24 (3):982–83. See Address of M. P. Bush, Feb. 17, 1912, Rogers Museum. The 7th Battalion's movements at Vicksburg are reported in *Supplement*, 104–5.

43. Wyatt T. Baylis died on June 28, 1863 (see Compiled Service Records, Wyatt T. Baylis and John M. Baylis, Company B, 7th Battalion, Mississippi Infantry, NA); Earle Knight, conversations with author. For contemporary reports on the siege of Vicksburg, see *Official Records*, 24 (2):146–423, passim. Earle Knight, descendant of William Martin "Dickie" Knight, a member of the Knight Company, recalled hearing that the siege of Vicksburg precipitated the desertions of many Jones County soldiers from the Confederate Army; see Earle Knight, conversation with author, June 30, 1994. After the Vicksburg surrender, soldiers were forced to sign oaths of allegiance to the Union before being paroled. They were then marched to Enterprise, Mississippi, from where many returned home as quickly as they could.

44. Compiled Service Records, Amos McLemore, Co. B, 27th Mississippi Infantry, NA; Rudy Leverett, "Ole Rosinheels: A Genealogical Sketch of the Family of Major Amos McLemore, 27th Mississippi Infantry Regiment, C.S.A." (unpublished manuscript, 1988, in author's possession), 27–36. Joel E. Welborn was granted a medical retirement in January 1863; see Joel E. Welborn to Governor Pettus, Jan. 21, 1963, Governors' Papers, RG 27, vol. 50, MDAH, and Compiled Service Records, Joel E. Welborn, Co. E, 7th Battalion, Mississippi Infantry, NA. Leverett described McLemore's force as consisting mostly of old men, boys, and superannuated veterans. In 1860 William H. Fairchild was fifty years old, married, and had nine children ranging from one to seventeen years old. His real estate was valued at $2,500, his personal worth was $1,800, and he owned no slaves. See U.S. Bureau of the Census, Federal Manuscript Censuses, Population and Slave Schedules, 1860, Jones County, Miss.

45. *New Orleans Item*, Mar. 20, 1921; Earle Knight, conversations with author; Thomas J. Knight, *Life and Activities of Captain Newton Knight*, 74–75. As Rudy Leverett pointed out, Tom Knight's account is riddled with errors, beginning with the statement that McLemore was murdered in his own home. Tom also erroneously placed the murder after the Lowry raids of April 1864, when in fact McLemore was murdered on October 5, 1863; see Leverett, *Legend of the Free State of Jones*, 62–67. In the month following McLemore's death, John M. Baylis returned to his unit, where he remained until his retirement on June 4, 1864; see Compiled Service Records, John M. Baylis, Co. B, 7th Battalion, Mississippi Infantry, NA.

46. Earle Knight, conversations with author; Thomas J. Knight, *Life and Activities of Captain Newton Knight*, 74–75; Ethel Knight, *Echo of the Black Horn*, 165–66. Ethel tells the legend of three men drawing straws in regard to the murder of both McLemore and two Jones County tax agents, Nat Gilgore and William Fairchild; see Ethel Knight, *Echo*

of the Black Horn, 76–77. Gerald Johnson speculates that Joe Gunter was the third man who accompanied Newt and Alpheus Knight the night McLemore was murdered. Gunter had served in the Confederate unit commanded by McLemore and thus could have identified him for his companions on the night of the murder; see Gerald W. Johnson, conversation with author, June 18, 1999, ML-USM.

47. Ethel Knight offered no date for the murder of Amos McLemore but, like Tom Knight, erroneously places it *after* the formation of the Knight Company. See Ethel Knight, Echo of the Black Horn, 166–69.

48. Newton Knight list of battles, undated, Anna Knight Collection, Oakwood Archives and Museum, Oakwood College, Huntsville, Ala.; New Orleans Item, Mar. 20, 1921; Thomas J. Knight, Life and Activities of Captain Newton Knight, 19–20; Ethel Knight, Echo of the Black Horn, 113–224. Leverett, Legend of the Free State of Jones, 68–72, offers a useful corrective to the muddled chronologies of battles presented in the works of both Tom Knight and Ethel Knight.

49. New Orleans Item, Mar. 20, 1921; Thomas J. Knight, Life and Activities of Captain Newton Knight, 30–31, 70; Ethel Knight, Echo of the Black Horn, 187. On the important role of women on the Southern home front during the Civil War, see Whites, Civil War As a Crisis in Gender; Faust, Mothers of Invention; Catherine Clinton and Nina Silber, eds., Divided Houses: Gender and the Civil War (New York: Oxford University Press, 1992); Bynum, Unruly Women; Michael Fellman, Inside War: The Guerrilla Conflict in Missouri during the American Civil War (New York: Oxford University Press, 1989); Rable, Civil Wars; and Paul D. Escott, Many Excellent People: Power and Privilege in North Carolina, 1850–1900 (Chapel Hill: University of North Carolina Press, 1985).

50. The ages of Sally Delancy and Sally Parker were taken from U.S. Bureau of the Census, Federal Manuscript Census, 1860, Jones County, Miss. On the two women's support for the Knight Company, see Thomas J. Knight, Life and Activities of Captain Newton Knight, 30–31, 41–49, and Ethel Knight, Echo of the Black Horn, 114–15, 187–91. Quote from Newt Knight in New Orleans Item, Mar. 20, 1921.

51. Probably the most reliable account of the battle is provided by Company F, 26th Mississippi Infantry, in Supplement, 761–64. Newt Knight recorded the date of the battle as December 24, 1863 (Newton Knight list of battles, Anna Knight Collection) and identified Joseph Richard "Dick" Yawn as having been wounded during the battle (Newton Knight Folder, NA). According to Tom Knight (who mistakenly identified Col. Robert Lowry as the Confederate leader of the December 1863 skirmish), John Valentine, "Mr. Whitehead," and Moses Richardson were wounded; see Thomas J. Knight, Life and Activities of Captain Newton Knight, 41–42.

52. Ethel Knight excused Sally Parker's support for the Knight Company as repayment to Newt for work he had performed for her in the past. See Ethel Knight, Echo of the Black Horn, 82, 115.

53. Thomas J. Knight, Life and Activities of Captain Newton Knight, 55–56; U.S. Bureau of the Census, Federal Manuscript Census, 1870, 1880, Jones County, Miss.

54. Thomas J. Knight, Life and Activities of Captain Newton Knight, 55–56.

55. Minnie S. Davis, Confederate Patriots of Jones County (Ellisville, Miss.: printed by the Progress-Item for Minnie Mae Davis, 1977), 8; Ethel Knight, Echo of the Black Horn, 134–35.

56. Ethel Knight, Echo of the Black Horn, 58–60, 79.

57. George P. Rawick, ed., The American Slave: A Composite Autobiography, supplement, ser. 1, vol. 9, Mississippi Narratives, pt. 4 (Westport, Conn.: Greenwood Press, 1972), 9:1801–2.

58. Ibid., 1623–24. For similar examples of collaboration between deserters, slaves, and free blacks in North Carolina during the war, see Bynum, Unruly Women, 122–24.

59. Ethel Knight, *Echo of the Black Horn*, 260, 283–84. On the image of black women as Jezebels, see esp. Deborah Gray White, *Ar'n't I a Woman: Female Slaves in the Plantation South* (1985; rev. ed, New York: Norton, 1999), 27–46. By the 1920s the public's obsession with interracial sexual relations amounted to what Jacquelyn Dowd Hall labeled a "folk pornography" that underwrote violent systems of racial and sexual domination; see Jacquelyn Dowd Hall, " 'The Mind That Burns in Each Body': Women, Rape, and Racial Violence," in *Powers of Desire: The Politics of Sexuality*, ed. Ann Snitow, Christine Stansell, and Sharon Thompson (New York: Monthly Review Press, 1983), 328–49.

60. Ethel Knight, *Echo of the Black Horn*, 73–77, 122; U.S. Bureau of the Census, Federal Manuscript Census, 1900, Jasper County, Miss. On the history of conjuring powers among slaves, see esp. Theophus H. Smith, *Conjuring Culture: Biblical Formations of Black America* (New York: Oxford University Press, 1994).

61. Compiled Service Records, Tapley Bynum and John H. Harper, Co. F, 7th Battalion, Mississippi Infantry, NA; Wayne and JoAnn Wingate, e-mail message to author, Nov. 21, 24, Dec. 6, 1998, ML-USM; Newton Knight folder, NA; Ethel Knight, *Echo of the Black Horn*, 97; Thomas J. Knight, *Life and Activities of Captain Newton Knight*, 18, 52–53. It is curious that neither Tom Knight nor Ethel Knight mentions the death of John H. Harper, although his name appears on their lists of Knight Company members. Despite problems in chronology, I suspect that the John Parker they report as killed in a shoot-out at Levi Valentine's house (see Chap. 6) was actually John Harper, especially since John Parker is not listed on any version of the Knight Company roster. No official report of Tapley Bynum's execution survives. Newton Knight's 1870 roster reported the date of his execution as January 10, 1865, but it appears that he mistakenly wrote 1865 instead of 1864 on the later roster. Descendants claim that Tapley was shot in January 1864, which conforms with Tom Knight's statement that he was shot on January 10, 1864, information he obtained from his father's original roster. The 1864 date is also consistent with Tapley's daughter's birthdate of January 5, 1864.

62. Ethel Knight, *Echo of the Black Horn*, 152; petition, Arick Coleman and citizens of southeastern part of Smith County and southwestern part of Jasper County to Governor Clark, Jan. 28, 1864, Governors' Papers, RG 27, vol. 56, MDAH.

63. Dabney H. Maury, Major-General, Commanding, to Hon. James A. Seddon, Secretary of War, Mar. 3, 1864, *Official Records*, 32 (2):688–89; L. Polk, Lieutenant General and Adjutant Inspector General, to General S[amuel] Cooper, Mar. 3, 1864, *Official Records*, 32 (3):580; Marie Martin Graham, ed., *John H. Powell and Some of His Descendants* (Oxford, Miss.: n.p., 1985), 18. J. C. Andrews is quoted from "Jones County Historical Research Project," Apr. 24, 1936, reprinted in Jean Strickland and Patricia N. Edwards, comps., *Confederate Records: Covington, Wayne, and Jones County* (Moss Point, Miss.: n.p., 1987), 99. Andrews claimed that the deserters committed numerous robberies and administered many beatings. He also stated that deserters murdered "Preacher Carlisle, B. J. Rushton, and many others." No records of these murders, much less who committed them, survive, but neither do any of these men appear in the 1870 federal manuscript census.

64. L. Polk, Lieutenant General and Adjutant Inspector General, to General S[amuel] Cooper, Mar. 3, 1864, *Official Records*, 32 (3):580; *New Orleans Item*, Mar. 20, 1921.

65. Capt. W. J. Bryant, Post Quartermaster of the seventh district, to James Hamilton, Major and Controlling Quartermaster, Tax-in-Kind, Miss. and La., to Colonel T. M. Jack, Asst. Adj. Gen'l., Mar. 31, 1864, *Official Records*, 32 (3):727 (W. J. Bryant may have been the same "Captain Bryan" whose cavalry killed deserter John Harper); E. M. Devall to Governor Clark, Mar. 21, 1864, Governors' Papers, RG 27 vol. 56, MDAH.

66. Address of M. P. Bush, Feb. 17, 1912, Rogers Museum. On the murders of

McGilvery, Kilgore, and Fairchild, see Thomas J. Knight, *Life and Activities of Captain Newton Knight*, 30–31, 84, and Ethel Knight, *Echo of the Black Horn*, 76–77, 188–89. On the murder of McGilvery, see also J. C. Andrews, "Jones County Historical Research Project." On the probability that Kilgore and Fairchild (who was the uncle of Amos McLemore) were the murdered tax agents referred to above, see Leverett, *Legend of the Free State of Jones*, 81.

None of these three murders is recorded, making the identities of the men difficult as well to document. I have concluded that Nat Kilgore was M. T. G., or Matt, Kilgore (see Chap. 4) because I have found no record of a Nat, whereas M. T. G. Kilgore disappears from Jones County records after the war. In 1860 William McGilvery was forty-two years old, owned six slaves, and owned real estate valued at $5,480 and personal wealth valued at $18,910. Tom Knight identified him only as "Mr. McGilbery," but J. C. Andrews and Ethel Knight identified him as "Angus" McGilvery. However, the two Jones County men named Angus McGilvery were still alive in 1870, whereas the 1864 death of William McGilvery, who had a son named Angus, is documented in the 1868 bankruptcy papers of Amos Deason, who was the administrator of both McGilvery's and William Fairchild's estates. See U.S. Bureau of the Census, Federal Manuscript Census, 1870, Jones County, Miss.; petition for bankruptcy, Amos Deason, filed Dec. 21, 1868, in Leesburg (Ellisville), County of Davis (Jones), District Court, United States, Southern District of Mississippi, NA-SE.

Chapter Six

1. The earliest debates over whether unionism or mere banditry gave rise to the Free State of Jones did not include discussions of Ben Knight's execution. Other than those provided by Confederate cavalrymen, no descriptions of his death appeared in print before that given by Ben Graves in 1926. Deserters and their kinfolk rarely discussed it in interviews conducted before Ethel's book appeared, probably because Ben was only one of ten men killed by Colonel Lowry's band in the space of a few days.

2. Lieut. Gen. L[eonidas] Polk to Gen. [Dabney] Maury, Feb. 7, 1864, in U.S. War Department, *War of the Rebellion: A Compilation of the Official Records of the Union and Confederate Armies* (Washington, D.C.: Government Printing Office, 1880–1901), ser. 1 (hereafter referred to as *Official Records*), 32 (2):688–89. On March 2, according to Rudy Leverett, Col. Henry Maury "left Mobile for Jones County with the Fifteenth Confederate Cavalry Regiment, a battalion of infantry, and a section of artillery" (*Legend of the Free State of Jones* [Jackson: University Press of Mississippi, 1984], 90).

Newt Knight erroneously recorded the date of the battle at Big Creek Church as February 1, 1864. His handwritten list of battles is undated, and he may have recorded the battles some years later from memory, as in the case of his 1870 version of the Knight Company roster. He recorded six battles between his men and Confederate forces after Amos McLemore's murder and before February 1, 1864: two on November 1, 1863, at "Liev old feels [Levi Valentine's Old Field]" and at "Crrey Creek Coventeon Co [Curry Creek in Covington County]"; one on "Talahaley Creek Near Ellisville, Jones Co., December 24, 1863"; one at Ellisville on January 6, 1864; another on January 15 at Reddoch's Ferry in Covington County; and one with "Cornel Marre [Maury] of Mobile Ala and his artilery." He identified the "Rebel command" of one or more of these battles as Liev Hinson [Levi Hinson]. See Newton Knight list of battles, undated, Anna Knight Collection, Oakwood Archives and Museum, Oakwood College, Huntsville, Ala.

3. H. Maury, Colonel, to My Dear General [Dabney H. Maury], Mar. 12, 1864,

enclosed in letter from Dabney H. Maury, Major General, to Colonel T. M. Jack, Assistant Adjutant General, Mar. 15, 1864, *Official Records*, 32 (3):632–33.

4. L[eonidas] Polk, Lt. Gen., to General S[amuel] Cooper, Adjutant and Inspector-General, Mar. 17, 1864, *Official Records* 32 (1):499. J. C. Andrews identified the three executed men as "Mitchell, Blackledge, and Smith" ("Jones County Historical Research Project," Apr. 24, 1936, reprinted in Jean Strickland and Patricia N. Edwards, comps., *Confederate Records: Covington, Wayne, and Jones County* [Moss Point, Miss.: n.p., 1987], 100). Tom Knight identified four men: Morge Mitchell, Jack Smith, Jesse Smith, and Jack Arnal (Arnold); Ethel Knight listed the same men. Rudy Leverett is mistaken in his statement that these men's names do not appear on the Knight Company rosters published by Tom and Ethel Knight. Both Knights also stated unequivocally that they were members of the company at the time of their executions. See Leverett, *Legend of the Free State of Jones*, 93; Thomas J. Knight, *The Life and Activities of Captain Newton Knight and His Company and the "Free State of Jones"* (1935; rev. ed, Laurel, Miss.: n.p., 1946), 17, 39; and Ethel Knight, *The Echo of the Black Horn: An Authentic Tale of "The Governor" of "The Free State of Jones"* (n.p., 1951), 90, 195–96.

5. W. Wirt Thomson, Capt., Co. A, 24th Miss. Reg't., to James A. Seddon, Secretary of War, Mar. 29, 1864, *Official Records*, 32 (3):711–12; B. R. Sumrall, unpublished WPA records, Jones County, RG 60, vol. 316, MDAH.

6. Colonel Lowry and the 6th Mississippi Regiment were ordered to the area between the Pearl and Tombigbee Rivers by T. M. Jack, Assistant Adjutant General, under Command of Lieutenant General Polk, Special Orders No. 80, Mar. 20, 1864; L[eonidas] Polk., Lt. Gen., to President [Jefferson] Davis, Mar. 21, 1864 (first quoted passage); W. Wirt Thomson, Captain, to Secretary of War James Seddon, Mar. 29, 1864, all in *Official Records*, 32 (3):662–63, 711–12.

7. W. Wirt Thomson, Capt., Co. A, 24th Miss. Reg't., to James A. Seddon, Secretary of War, Mar. 29, 1864, and Danl. P. Logan to Major J. C. Denis, Provost Marshal General, Apr. 7, 1864, *Official Records*, 32 (3):711–12, 755. On Yankees in Jones County, see also Ethel Knight, *Echo of the Black Horn*, 205.

8. *New Orleans Item*, Mar. 20, 1921; Thomas J. Knight, *Life and Activities of Captain Newton Knight*, 51. Meigs Frost mistakenly concluded that Newt was referring to the federal raid on Brookhaven, Mississippi, which was routed by Confederate lieutenant W. M. Wilson of the 43d Tennessee Infantry at Rocky Creek, near Ellisville, in Jones County. The Brookhaven raid occurred, however, on June 25, 1863, almost four months before the Knight Company was formed. In contrast to Frost, historian Rudy Leverett cited the Rocky Creek battle as evidence against the existence of union sympathies in Jones County, since Lieutenant Wilson reported that Jones County citizens eagerly appropriated "horses, arms, and equipments" from his Union prisoners. In a region beset by mounting food shortages and death tolls, such behavior need not have reflected a pro-Confederate stance. By 1863 Southern farm families were suffering mightily, and one might expect them to seize whatever goods became available. Leverett further cited Wilson's use of civilian forces to defeat federal raiders as additional evidence of Jones County's Confederate sympathies. Wilson, however, identified the civilians who fought on his side as being primarily from Brookhaven, eighty-six miles away. See Leverett, *Legend of the Free State of Jones*, 61; *Official Records*, 24 (2):514–15.

9. Major-General W. T. Sherman to Major-General Halleck, Feb. 29, 1864, *Official Records*, 32 (2):498–99.

10. Goode Montgomery, "Alleged Secession of Jones County," *Publications of the Mississippi Historical Society* 8 (1904), 15; L[eonidas] Polk, Lieutenant General, to President

[Jefferson] Davis, Mar. 21, 1864, *Official Records*, 32 (3):662–63, 711–12. In A. H. Polk, First Lieutenant and Acting Assistant Inspector General, to Lieutenant Colonel T. F. Sevier, Assistant Inspector General, Mar. 3, 1864, *Official Records*, 32 (3):579, Polk referred to Jones County deserters as "Tories."

11. Colonel Robert Lowry to Lieutenant Colonel T. M. Jack, Assistant General, Apr. 13, 1864, *Official Records*, 52 (2):657.

12. *Mobile Evening News*, 3 May 1864, Power Scrapbook, MDAH. Military records show that Benjamin F. Knight served in Company B, 7th Battalion Infantry (Compiled Service Records, Company B, 7th Battalion, NA). An original copy of Newton Knight's muster list is in Newton Knight Folder, HR 1814, RG 233, House of Representatives, Accompanying Papers File, 42d Congress, box 15, NA.

13. *Mobile Evening News*, May 3, 1864, in Power Scrapbook, MDAH; Ethel Knight, *Echo of the Black Horn*, 134–35; Minnie S. Davis, *Confederate Patriots of Jones County* (Ellisville, Miss.: printed by the *Progress-Item* for Minnie Mae Davis, 1977), 8. Daniel Reddoch deserted Co. G, 7th Battalion, Mississippi Infantry, after his parole from Vicksburg in July 1863. No military records exist for either Sil or Nobe Coleman, presumably because both were too young to serve. I have found no proof that the Confederacy executed Nobe Coleman; however, his name disappears from public records after the war. See Compiled Service Records, 7th Battalion, Mississippi Infantry, M269, roll 167, NA (microfilm). In addition to assuming custody of Tom Coleman's children, Mary Coleman seems to have inherited several of her son's slaves; see U.S. Bureau of the Census, Federal Manuscript Censuses, Population and Slave Schedules, 1860, Covington County, Miss.

14. *Jackson Daily News*, Aug. 1, 1974, Clipping File, and B. D. Graves, Hebron Community Meeting, June 17, 1926, both in Lauren Rogers Museum of Art, Laurel, Miss.

15. B. D. Graves, Hebron Community Meeting, June 17, 1926, Rogers Museum. On genealogical connections between the Colemans, Whiteheads, and Knights, see Appendixes 1–2.

16. B. D. Graves, Hebron Community Meeting, June 17, 1926, Rogers Museum.

17. Martha Wheeler, interview by Addie West, unpublished WPA records, RG 60, vol. 315, MDAH. West's interview of Wheeler may also be found in George P. Rawick, ed., *The American Slave: A Composite Autobiography*, supplement, ser. 1, vol. 10, *Mississippi Narratives*, pt. 5 (Westport, Conn.: Greenwood Press, 1972), 2262–71. That version, however, does not contain the story of Ben Knight's murder. As Leah Townsend noted in her history of South Carolina Baptists, baptism symbolizes "an actual burial in a watery grave from which the regenerate subject arises a conscious member of Christ" (*South Carolina Baptists, 1670–1805* [Florence, S.C.: Florence Printing Co., 1935], 291).

18. Ethel Knight, *Echo of the Black Horn*, 138.

19. Ibid., 135–36.

20. Ibid., 136–37. It may well be that Ben was hanged by Lowry's men because they believed that he was Newt. Ethel claimed that the men realized their mistake only after they flung Ben's body at Serena Knight's feet and she identified him. This might explain why, almost in passing, Col. William N. Brown of the Lowry expedition commented in a letter to Governor Clark that the cavalry had mistakenly killed the husband of one woman. As for Ben being on furlough, however, Ethel probably mistook Ben's parole from Vicksburg as Confederate leave. Many of the men who survived Vicksburg later cited the terms of that parole—that they could never again take up arms against the Union—as justification for not rejoining their units. They were, of course, nonetheless deserters in the eyes of the Confederate Army. See Colonel [William N.] Brown to Governor Clark, May 5, 1864, Governors' Papers, RG 27, vol. 56, MDAH; Paula

Broussard, e-mail message to author, May 8, 2000, and Earle Knight, conversations with author, June 28–30, 1994, ML-USM.

21. Benjamin Knight was reported AWOL from Company B of the 7th Battalion from December 1863 to February 1864, when his record ends. His name also appears on Newton Knight's 1870 handwritten roster. See Compiled Service Records, 7th Battalion, Mississippi Infantry, NA; Newton Knight Folder, NA.

22. Colonel [William N.] Brown to Governor Clark, May 5, 1864, Governors' Papers, MDAH; B. D. Graves, Hebron Community Meeting, June 17, 1926, Rogers Museum. Newton Knight recorded April 15 as the date of the Ates and Whitehead hangings. He also claimed that N. V. Whitehead was "on picket" rather than home sleeping when captured by Lowry's men. See Newton Knight Folder, NA. Ethel Knight's account of the Whitehead hangings differs from that of Graves in that she claims that Noel Whitehead was shot to death while on picket, before his two brothers were hanged; see Echo of the Black Horn, 151. Military records show that James H. Ates and Thomas Ates enlisted together in Company G of the 7th Battalion on May 14, 1862, in Williamsburg, Covington County. Both were reported absent and hospitalized from October 1862 until February 1863. From that point on, both were reported AWOL. Because the "Ates" name is often spelled "Yates," Thomas Ates is easily confused with Thomas Daniel Yates of Smith County, son of Samuel and Rebecca Yates, and a private in Company F of the 7th Battalion. That Thomas Yates was reported AWOL in mid-1863 but survived the war. See Janet Smith, Jean Strickland, and Patricia N. Edwards, Who Married Whom: Covington County, Mississippi (Moss Point, Miss.: n.p., 1991), 3–4, 191–92, and Compiled Service Records, 7th Battalion, Mississippi Infantry, M269, rolls 165, 167, NA.

I have found no record of military service for Thomas and Daniel Whitehead, but Noel Whitehead is the N. V. Whitehead who enrolled in Company G, 7th Battalion, on May 14, 1862, the same day as Tom and Jim Ates, and was reported AWOL by mid-1863. E. D. Whitehead, probably Emerson Whitehead, the oldest son of John and Mary Ann Whitehead, also enrolled on that day. He died in September 1862 at Okalona hospital following the battle of Iuka. See Compiled Service Records, 7th Battalion, Mississippi Infantry, NA.

23. Winnie Knight Thomas, Earle W. Knight, Lavada Knight Dykes, and Martha Kaye Dykes Lowery, The Family of John "Jackie" Knight and Keziah Davis Knight, 1773–1985 (Magee, Miss.: Robert and Delores Knight Vinson, 1985), 141–42. According to Ethel Knight, Lowry's cavalry seized Joe Hatten rather than William H. Knight and threatened to hang the slave if he did not reveal the whereabouts of Newt Knight; see Echo of the Black Horn, 123–25.

24. Ethel Knight, Echo of the Black Horn, 207–10; Thomas J. Knight, Life and Activities of Captain Newton Knight, 38–39. Ethel Knight reported that the dance occurred on December 24, 1864, but there is nothing to corroborate this date. She may be referring to the December 24, 1863, battle recorded by Newt Knight, in Newton Knight list of battles, Anna Knight Collection. Ethel and Tom Knight reported the dead member of the Knight Company as John Parker, but he is not listed on the various Knight Company musters. I suspect that Tom and Ethel Knight were referring to the cavalry's killing of John H. Harper (see Chap. 5).

25. B. R. Sumrall, unpublished WPA records, Jones County, RG 60, vol. 316, MDAH; Colonel Brown to Governor Clark, May 5, 1864, Governors' Papers, MDAH. Most of these women's sons deserted the army following the siege of Vicksburg. Frances Ates's sons, James and Thomas, deserted Co. G, 7th Battalion, in mid-1863. Likewise did George F. Whitehead and Steven R. Whitehead, the sons of John Whitehead's brother

William (who died between 1850 and 1860) and Ali Whitehead. Lucinda Todd's son, Aaron Todd, joined the Knight band after deserting Co. K of the 8th Battalion, Mississippi Infantry. Catherine (Bynum) Welch was the widow of John Ira Welch and the mother of Harrison and Timothy Welch, members of the Knight Company; Harrison Welch deserted Co. F, 7th Battalion, in mid-1863. Susannah Valentine was the widow of Darrel Valentine. Her sons, W. P. (Patrick) and Martin B., had deserted Co. F., 7th Battalion, by early February 1863. Sally Parker's son, George W. Walters, served in Co. K, 8th Mississippi Infantry, Jones Co. (see Strickland and Edwards, *Confederate Records*, 108). Sally Delancy's son Howell was reported AWOL from Co. A, 7th Battalion, on August 23, 1863. He returned to service on September 10, 1863, and received special detail as a nurse from Lt. Gen. Hardee on grounds of a medical disability. See U.S. Bureau of the Census, Federal Manuscript Censuses, 1850, 1860, Covington, Jones, Smith, Jasper Counties, Miss.; Compiled Service Records, 7th Battalion, Mississippi Infantry, NA.

26. Information from Paula Bolan, great-granddaughter of Martha Knight Yawn and Joseph Richard Yawn, e-mail message to author, Apr. 19, 23, 2000, ML-USM.

27. Ethel Knight, *Echo of the Black Horn*, 107–8. Ellafair Chain's daughter Caroline married Henry F. Dykes in 1867.

28. Colonel Brown to Governor Clark, May 5, 1864, Governors' Papers, MDAH.

29. Ibid.; Ethel Knight, *Echo of the Black Horn*, 137.

30. Thomas J. Knight, *Life and Activities of Captain Newton Knight*, 53–55. Full names and ages of Nancy and Calvin Walters are from U.S. Bureau of the Census, Federal Manuscript Census, 1860, Jones County, Miss.

31. Thomas J. Knight, *Life and Activities of Captain Newton Knight*, 53–55. For a more embellished account of this event, see Ethel Knight, *Echo of the Black Horn*, 200–203.

32. *New Orleans Item*, Mar. 20, 1921; Ethel Knight, *Echo of the Black Horn*, 171–74.

33. Compiled Service Records, 1st Regiment, New Orleans Infantry, NA; "Union Army Pension Records," in *Miscellaneous Records of Jones County, MS*, comp. Jean Strickland and Patricia N. Edwards (Moss Point, Miss.: n.p., 1992), 146–49, 155, 157, 177, 186, 189. See Appendixes 3, 4, and 7 for kinship ties among men who joined the Union Army. Most of the men were mustered into Company E of the 1st Regiment of the New Orleans Infantry between April 28 and 30, 1864. Merada Walters enlisted on May 15, 1864; Tolbert Welborn and Prentice Bynum enlisted on May 26, 1864. Richard T. Welch of Company B, 7th Battalion, was wounded and taken prisoner in the battle of Corinth. He deserted on December 11, 1862.

34. Newton Knight Folder, NA; Newton Knight list of battles, Anna Knight Collection. For genealogical links, see Appendixes 1–8. According to Newton Knight's 1870 roster, the men were captured by Lowry's band on April 25, 1864. In addition to the Collinses, Valentines, Welches, and Welborns, Merida M. Coats, Joseph M. Gunter, Richard H. Hinton, and Lazarus Mathews were also captured. James Morgan Valentine eluded capture but may have been wounded; however, there are discrepancies as to when he received his wounds. On his 1870 roster, Newt recorded that James Morgan Valentine was wounded on April 16, 1864, by Lowry's troops. On his undated list of battles, he recorded that Valentine was wounded by Captain Miller's cavalry, which would have been on January 10, 1865. Presumably using his father's earlier roster, Tom Knight wrote that Valentine was wounded on January 10, 1865; see *Life and Activities of Captain Newton Knight*, 20.

Drew (Drury) Gilbert, Merida Coats, Simeon Collins, James Madison (Matt) Collins, and Thomas Jefferson Collins enlisted or reentered Co. F, 7th Battalion of the Mississippi Infantry. Simeon's younger son, Morgan Columbus Collins, claimed to have served in the same company when he applied for a Confederate pension in 1925, but no records of such service exist; see Soldier's Application for Confederate Pension, Aug. 27, 1925, Texas State Archives, Austin. In 1915 Thomas Jefferson Collins's widow applied for a Confederate pension. At that time Morgan C. Collins testified that while he remembered his brother's enlistment in the Confederacy, he himself did not serve because he was too young. See petition of Sarah P. Collins, widow of T. J. Collins, "Form for Use of Widows of Soldiers Who Are in Indigent Circumstances," May 12, 1915, Texas State Archives.

35. Compiled Service Records, 7th Battalion, Mississippi Infantry, NA. Coats, Eulin, and the Collinses were sent to Camp Morton, Indiana; Welch and the Valentines were sent to Camp Douglas, Illinois. On Gen. Joseph E. Johnston's Georgia campaign, see Richard Beringer, Herman Hattaway, Archer Jones, and William N. Still Jr., *Why the South Lost the Civil War* (Athens: University of Georgia Press, 1986), 321–22; James M. McPherson, *Ordeal by Fire: The Civil War and Reconstruction* (New York: Knopf, 1982), 429–36; and J. G. Randall and David Herbert Donald, *The Civil War and Reconstruction*, 2d rev. ed. (Lexington, Mass.: D. C. Heath, 1969), 417–27.

36. Compiled Service Records, 7th Battalion, Mississippi Infantry, NA. For kinship ties, see Appendixes 7–8.

37. Compiled Service Records, 7th Battalion, Mississippi Infantry, NA. F. M. Herrington enlisted in the U.S. military on March 24, 1865; Wilson L. Jones, on April 2, 1865.

38. Steven R. Whitehead was the son of William Whitehead, brother of John Whitehead. William died before 1860. See U.S. Bureau of the Census, Federal Manuscript Censuses, 1850, 1860, Covington County, Miss.

39. "Final Records of the Chancery Court" and "Union Army Pension Records," in Strickland and Edwards, *Miscellaneous Records of Jones County*, 69, 123, 148–49, 177. Riley James Collins died from the effects of chronic rheumatism and diarrhea. Because his wife, Desdemonia, had died two years earlier, older brother Vinson and his wife, Nancy, assumed custody of the couple's four orphans. Sometime after 1870 Simeon Collins's widow, Lydia, and his children moved to Hardin County, Texas, joining those Collinses who moved to Texas during the 1850s. William H. Mauldin died in December 1864 from pneumonia. His widow, Dicey Bynum, relinquished custody of the couple's children to her parents, Peggy and Benjamin Bynum, after her marriage to Benjamin Geiger in 1869. The grandparents presumably raised the Mauldin orphans from that point on.

Archibald Walters died from measles on August 8, 1864; his brother Merada died from the effects of chronic diarrhea on November 27, 1864. Both men died at U.S. General Hospital in New Orleans. Tolbert Welborn, the son of Younger and Betsy Welborn, died of typhoid and pneumonia on February 11, 1865, in the Marine U.S. General Hospital at New Orleans. James W. Lee was probably related to Knight Company member Jeff Lee. His death in August 1864 from typhoid fever left a widow, Delphene, and five children, the youngest of whom was named Abraham Lincoln. Drew Gilbert died on September 13, 1864, at the U.S.A. General Hospital at Chattanooga, Tennessee, two months after his capture on Kennesaw Mountain. James Eulin died February 23, 1865, at Piedmont, West Virginia, en route to be exchanged after imprisonment at Camp Morton. See Compiled Service records, 7th Battalion, Mississippi Infantry, M269, roll 165, 166, NA, and "Union Army Pension Records," 146, 155, 162–63, 192.

40. B. C. Duckworth to Governor Pettus, June 14, 1864, Governors' Papers, RG 27, vol. 56, MDAH.

41. *Natchez Courier*, July 12, 1864, reprinted in *Mississippi in the Confederacy: As They Saw It*, ed. John K. Bettersworth (Jackson: Louisiana State University Press, 1962; reprint, New York: Kraus Reprint Co., 1970), 143.

42. W. L. Brandon, Brigadier General, Commanding, to Maj. General D. H. Maury, Aug. 14, 1864, *Official Records*, 39 (3):777. M. H. Barkley was probably Moses H. Barkley, in 1860 a thirty-five-year-old farmer who claimed $200 in real and $100 in personal property. See Amos Deason et al., petition to Governor Clark, Sept. 1, 1864, Governors' Papers, RG 27, vol. 57, MDAH.

43. Petition of Newton Knight and 63 others to Governor Sharkey, July 15, 1865, and A. P. McGill to Governor Sharkey, July 26, 1865, Governors' Papers, RG 27, vol. 61B, MDAH; U.S. Bureau of the Census, Federal Manuscript Census, Population and Slave Schedules, 1860, Jones County, Miss.; Compiled Service Records, 27th Mississippi Infantry, NA; "Final Records of the Chancery Court," 90–91; Ethel Knight, *Echo of the Black Horn*, 47–48. William Hood served on Jones County's Board of Police during the 1850s. He married Elizabeth S. Windham, daughter of Willis Windham, who owned thirteen slaves in 1860. Ethel Knight described Windham as a pro-secessionist member of the gentry. On intermarriage between the Hood and McLemore families, see Rudy Leverett, "Ole Rosinheels: A Genealogical Sketch of the Family of Major Amos McLemore, 27th Mississippi Infantry Regiment, C.S.A." (unpublished manuscript, 1988, in author's possession), 20.

44. Newt noted on his list of battles that the cavalry were "sed to have belong to Forest Caverle [Forrest's Cavalry]"; however, this is not credible, given Forrest's movements during November. See Newton Knight list of battles, Anna Knight Collection.

45. Ibid. Newt Knight identified the cavalry as Captain Gilles's company. Samuel Gibson Owens was the son of Norris and Celia (Sullivan) Owen. Celia Owen was the daughter of Tom and Maud Elizabeth (Workman) Sullivan. Owens and Joseph Megannon Gunter were both related to the Knights by marriage. Owens married Almeda Knight, daughter of Daniel and Elizabeth (Coleman) Knight; Gunter married Selena Knight, daughter of William H. and Mary (Youngblood) Knight. See Ann R. Hammons, *Wild Bill Sullivan: King of the Hollow* (Jackson: University Press of Mississippi, 1980), 25, 115; Chester Sullivan, *Sullivan's Hollow* (Jackson: University Press of Mississippi, 1978), 10–11; and Thomas et al., *Family of John "Jackie" Knight*, 244.

Newton Knight and Tom Knight both dated the wounding of Owens as December 28, 1864; Ethel Knight dated it January 10, 1865. Gerald W. Johnson, a descendant of the Gunters, believes that Joseph M. Gunter may have been targeted for death by the Confederacy because of his alleged participation in the murder of Amos McLemore; see Gerald W. Johnson, conversation with author, July 18, 1999, ML-USM. Joe Gunter is the only member of the Gunter family listed as a member of the Knight Company by Tom Knight, but Ethel Knight lists Joe, John, and Charley Gunter as members; Lucille Ainsworth adds a fourth Gunter, Americus, who she says was also killed by Confederate cavalry. See Newton Knight Folder, NA; Thomas J. Knight, *Life and Activities of Captain Newton Knight*, 19, 45, 85; Ethel Knight *Echo of the Black Horn*, 89–90, 220; and Lucille Ainsworth quoted in Jan Sumrall and Kenneth Welch, *The Knights and Related Families* (Denham Springs, La.: n.p., 1985), 162.

46. Dickie Knight's full name was William Martin Knight. Mary Knight's sister Martha Ellzey later married Taylor Knight, a brother of Newton Knight and cousin to Dickie Knight (see Appendix 1). Newton Knight's account of the wedding day ambush is from the *New Orleans Item*, Mar. 20, 1921; see also Ethel Knight, *Echo of the Black Horn*, 212–19, and Thomas J. Knight, *Life and Activities of Captain Newton Knight*, 34–36.

47. *New Orleans Item*, Mar. 20, 1921; Ethel Knight, *Echo of the Black Horn*, 212–19.

48. *New Orleans Item*, Mar. 20, 1921. See also Ethel Knight, *Echo of the Black Horn*, 218–19, and Thomas J. Knight, *Life and Activities of Captain Newton Knight*, 34–36.

49. Thomas J. Knight, *Life and Activities of Captain Newton Knight*, 36; Ethel Knight, *Echo of the Black Horn*, 219.

50. Thomas et al., *Family of John "Jackie" Knight*, 252. Like Joe Gunter, Alpheus Knight may have been targeted by the Confederacy because of his alleged participation in the murder of Amos McLemore.

51. R. C. Duckworth to Samuel Duckworth, May 24, 1868, Duckworth-Smith-McPherson Family Papers, Center for the Study of American History, University of Texas, Austin.

52. On the various deserter bands in the Jones County region and their contacts with one another, see Thomas J. Knight, *Life and Activities of Captain Newton Knight*, 69–71, and Ethel Knight, *Echo of the Black Horn*, 121, 200–206. Quote from Prentice Bynum from Wayne and JoAnn Wingate, e-mail message to author, Oct. 18, 2000, ML-USM. Quotes from both Jasper Collins and Newton Knight are from *New Orleans Item*, Mar. 20, 1921. Interestingly, Goode Montgomery did not print Jasper Collins's statement to him about Robert Lowry in his "Alleged Secession of Jones County."

Chapter Seven

1. On similar mythmaking by combatants on both sides of Missouri's inner civil war, see Michael Fellman, *Inside War: The Guerrilla Conflict in Missouri during the American Civil War* (New York: Oxford University Press, 1989), 253–66.

2. On Redeemer Democrats' manipulation of racism in Mississippi, see esp. Bradley G. Bond, *Political Culture in the Nineteenth-Century South: Mississippi, 1830–1900* (Baton Rouge: Louisiana State University Press, 1995), 151–82. For general overviews, see Edward L. Ayers, *The Promise of the New South: Life after Reconstruction* (New York: Oxford University Press, 1992), 8–9, 136–37, and C. Vann Woodward, *Origins of the New South, 1877–1913* (Baton Rouge: Louisiana State University Press, 1951), 51–74. On the connections between national stereotyping of poor rural people as inferior and the eugenics movement of the progressive era, see Nicole Hahn Rafter, ed., *White Trash: The Eugenic Family Studies, 1877–1919* (Boston: Northeastern University Press, 1988).

3. Petition to Governor Sharkey from citizens of Jones County, Miss., July 15, 1865, Governors' Papers, RG 27, vol. 61B, MDAH. On the appointment of William Lewis Sharkey as provisional governor, see William C. Harris, *Presidential Reconstruction in Mississippi* (Baton Rouge: Louisiana State University Press, 1967), 37–60. In addition to Newton Knight, petitioners included William M. Welch, James Morgan Valentine, H. C. and J. A. Delancy (sons of Sarah Delancy), Jeff Collins (son of Simeon Collins), Jasper Collins, and William Wesley Sumrall. Interestingly, the name of Benjamin C. Duckworth, the same conscript officer who complained about deserters to Governor Clark in 1864, appears on this petition and does not appear on the pro-Confederate petitions that followed. Duckworth either switched sides after the war was over or played a double game with pro- and anti-Confederate citizens. Because the men did not sign their own names to the petition (many of them were illiterate), it is also possible that Duckworth's name was forged.

4. Petition to Governor Sharkey from citizens of Jones County, Miss., July 15, 1865, Governors' Papers, RG 27, vol. 61B, MDAH.

5. The appointments of Collins and Huff were made on July 20, 1865; two identically worded petitions to Governor Sharkey from citizens of Ellisville, Jones County, followed on July 29, 1865. See Governors' Papers, RG 27, vol. 61B, MDAH. The first

petition bore forty-one names, including those of three Bynums related by marriage to Hansford D. Dossett; M. H. Barkley, former captain of a local home guard unit; and several relatives of men reportedly slain by deserters during the war, including J. T. Fairchild and Angus and Murdock McGilvery. The second petition contained fifty-eight names, including those of John M. Baylis; Willis Windham (William Hood's father-in-law); Benjamin Hood; several pro-Confederate Welborns, including Joel E. Welborn; former court clerk E. M. Devall; and Daniel McGill, the father of Allan McGill.

6. Dr. J. M. Baylis to Governor Sharkey, July 30, 1865, Governors' Papers, RG 27, vol. 61B, MDAH.

7. Ibid. On postwar harassment of unionists, see Paul D. Escott, *Many Excellent People: Power and Privilege in North Carolina, 1850–1900* (Chapel Hill: University of North Carolina Press, 1985), 152–70; George C. Rable, *But There Was No Peace: The Role of Violence in the Politics of Reconstruction* (Athens: University of Georgia Press, 1984), 13–15; and Eric Foner, *Reconstruction: America's Unfinished Revolution, 1863–1877* (Baton Rouge: Louisiana State University Press, 1988), 17, 427–35. For Mississippi, see William C. Harris, *The Day of the Carpetbagger: Republican Reconstruction in Mississippi* (Baton Rouge: Louisiana State University Press, 1979), 8, and Bond, *Political Culture in the Nineteenth-Century South*, 176–82.

8. Newton Knight is identified as relief commissioner in a letter to N. Knight from J. Fairbanks, Capt., 72d U.S.C. Infantry, Commanding at Raleigh, Miss., July 21, 1865. See also H. T. Elliott, Lieutenant 50th U.S.C. Infantry, Commanding at Raleigh, to Captain Newton Knight, July 31, Aug. 30, 1865, all in Newton Knight Folder, HR 1814, RG 233, House of Representatives, Accompanying Papers Files, 42d Congress, box 15, NA. On Whig unionist William L. Sharkey's Reconstruction career, see William C. Harris, *Presidential Reconstruction*, 43, 116, 239.

9. Duplicate of requisition of O. S. Coffin, Capt. and Assistant Quartermaster, to Mr. Newton Knight, July 16, 1865, and J. Fairbanks, Capt., 72d U.S.C. Infantry, Commanding at Raleigh, Miss., to N. Knight, July 21, 1865, Newton Knight Folder, NA. On Piney Woods destitution, see William C. Harris, *Presidential Reconstruction*, 164.

10. J. A. Hawley, Chaplain and Subcommissioner, to Col. Samuel Thomas, July 4, 1865, in Records of the Assistant Commissioner for the State of Mississippi, Bureau of Refugees, Freedmen, and Abandoned Lands, 1865–69, microfilm, vol. M826, roll 10, Records of the Bureau of Refugees, Freedmen, and Abandoned Lands, RG 105 (microfilm), NA (hereafter cited as Records, BRFAL); J. Fairbanks, Capt., Commanding at Raleigh, to N. Knight, July 24, 1865, Newton Knight Folder, NA. I found no record of an appointment of Newton Knight as provost marshal in the indexes of BRFAL records or in the appointment records of either the Department of Justice or the Department of State (Appointment files for Judicial Districts, 1853–1905, Department of Justice, RG 60, NA; Appointment Records, Letters of Application and Recommendation for Public Office, 1869–1877, Department of State, RG 59, NA; Index to Names of U.S. Marshals, microfilm, T577, NA).

11. Tom Knight claimed that Newt was provost marshal during this event, but no such title appears in his official letters. See Thomas J. Knight, *The Life and Activities of Captain Newton Knight and His Company and the "Free State of Jones"* (1935; rev. ed, Laurel, Miss.: n.p., 1946), 4; see also Ethel Knight, *The Echo of the Black Horn: An Authentic Tale of "The Governor" of "The Free State of Jones"* (n.p., 1951), 231. Kenneth Welch cites evidence that Newt was appointed a deputy U.S. marshal for the Southern District of Mississippi on July 6, 1872; see Jan Sumrall and Kenneth Welch, *The Knights and Related Families* (Denham Springs, La.: n.p., 1985), 160.

12. H. T. Elliott, Lieut., 50th U.S.C. Infantry, to Capt. [Newton Knight], July 31,

1865; R. M. Smith, Capt., Comdg. Det., 70th U.S.C. Infantry, post of Ellisville, to Mr. Newton Knight, Aug. 18, 1865; A. R. M. Smith, Capt. 70th USC Inf., to Mr. Newton Knight, Aug. 19, 1865; H. T. Elliott, Int. 50th U.S.C. Infantry, to Capt. Night, Aug. 30, 1865; S. N. Smith Sr., 70th U.S.C. Infantry, Sept. 2, 1865; and Simon N. Smith, Lieut., 70th U.S.C. Infantry, Sept. 8, 1865, all in Newton Knight Folder, NA.

13. Petition from Jones County citizens to the Senate and House of Representatives, Oct. 16, 1865 (read into record Nov. 29, 1865), RG 47, vol. 88, MDAH.

14. Bond, Political Culture in the Nineteenth-Century South, 156–61; William C. Harris, Presidential Reconstruction, 51–54, 259–60, 371–405; Vernon Wharton, The Negro in Mississippi, 1865–1890 (1947; New York: Harper and Row, 1965), 131–215. Studies of the means by which other Southern states constructed white supremacist governments include Laura Edwards, Gendered Strife and Confusion: The Political Culture of Reconstruction (Urbana: University of Illinois Press, 1997), 184–217; LeeAnn Whites, The Civil War As a Crisis in Gender: Augusta, Georgia, 1860–1890 (Athens: University of Georgia Press, 1995), 132–59; and Escott, Many Excellent People, 126–35.

15. William C. Harris, Presidential Reconstruction, 57; petition from Jones County citizens to the Senate and House of Representatives, Oct. 16 1865, RG 47, vol. 88, MDAH; Laws of the State of Mississippi Passed at a Regular Session of the Mississippi Legislature Held in the City of Jackson, October, November, and December, 1865 (Jackson: J. J. Shannon, 1866), chap. 86, p. 240; address of M. P. Bush, Feb. 17, 1912, Lauren Rogers Museum of Art, Laurel, Miss. (quoted passage). During the same legislative session, Lee County was created in honor of General Robert E. Lee. See David G. Sansing, "The Failure of Johnsonian Reconstruction in Mississippi, 1865–1866," Journal of Mississippi History 34, no. 4 (Nov. 1972): 381).

16. Address of M. P. Bush, Feb. 17, 1912, Rogers Museum; William C. Harris, Day of the Carpetbagger, 1–66; Bond, Political Culture in the Nineteenth-Century South, 156–61. "Black Codes" refers to the collection of laws passed by the Mississippi legislature in 1865 and designed to reinstitute white control over black labor and mobility in the wake of the abolition of slavery.

17. B. D. Graves, Hebron Community Meeting, June 17, 1926, and address of M. P. Bush, Feb. 17, 1912, Rogers Museum; Frances Gandy-Walsh, e-mail message to author, June 28, 2000, ML-USM. For general overviews of the war's stimulation of lawlessness and violence during Reconstruction, see esp. George Rable, But There Was No Peace, and Edward L. Ayers, Vengeance and Justice: Crime and Punishment in the Nineteenth-Century South (New York: Oxford University Press, 1984); also William Lynwood Montell, Killings: Folk Justice in the Upper South (Lexington: University Press of Kentucky, 1986), 9–13; Fellman, Inside War, 231–66; and Altina L. Waller, Feud: Hatfields, McCoys, and Social Change in Appalachia, 1860–1900 (Chapel Hill: University of North Carolina Press, 1988), 32–33. On postwar destitution and violence in Mississippi, see Bond, Political Culture in the Nineteenth-Century South, 135, 155; William C. Harris, Presidential Reconstruction, 34–36, 68–69, 164–65, and Day of the Carpetbagger, 8–9, 62–64; Chester Sullivan, Sullivan's Hollow (Jackson: University Press of Mississippi, 1978), 27–50; and Ann R. Hammons, Wild Bill Sullivan: King of the Hollow (Jackson: University Press of Mississippi, 1980), 64–68.

18. Information on the murder of James Gunter is from Gerald W. Johnson, conversation with author, July 18, 1999, Laurel, Miss., and e-mail message to author, Apr. 27, 1999, ML-USM. Information on Gunter's special assignment at Enterprise is from Compiled Service Records of Confederate Soldiers Who Served in Organizations from the State of Mississippi, 7th Battalion, Mississippi Infantry, NA. In Sumrall and Welch, Knights and Related Families, 162, contributing author Lucille D. Ainsworth claims that Hinton murdered Gunter for "fooling around" with his own wife, rather than a friend's. Before James Gunter died on March 10, 1866, he left a noncupative (oral) will

and testament in which he directed Joel E. Welborn to care for his effects and to erect a marble slab tombstone over his place of burial. See Probate Records, Ellisville Courthouse, Jones County, Miss., courtesy of Gerald W. Johnson.

19. The woman described as the mother of Jim and Tom Ates is quoted in Ruby Huff's account of the Battle of Shiloh, unpublished WPA records, Covington County, Miss., RG 60, vol. 272, MDAH. Huff identified the speaker as "Lou Yates," but Frances Ates was the mother of Tim and Jim Ates and was still alive in 1870. See U.S. Bureau of the Census, Federal Manuscript Census, 1870, Covington County, Miss. For detailed accounts of the Battle of Shiloh, see Chester Sullivan, *Sullivan's Hollow*, 27–50, and Hammons, *Wild Bill Sullivan*, 64–68.

20. U.S. Bureau of the Census, Federal Manuscript Census, 1860, Jones County, Miss.; unpublished WPA records, Jones County, RG 60, vol. 317, MDAH. On the prevalence of horse thieves in postwar Mississippi, see William C. Harris, *Presidential Reconstruction*, 35, and *Day of the Carpetbagger*, 10–11. There are three almost identical accounts of the Dawson Holly Ring in the unpublished WPA records. One interviewee claimed that Mandy White was shot to death; another declared that it was her sister Susie; yet another account stated that both women were killed.

21. U.S. Bureau of the Census, Federal Manuscript Census, Agricultural Schedules, 1860, 1870, Jasper, Jones, Covington Counties, Miss. In 1860 Benjamin Bynum's farm was valued at $4,300; in 1870, $150. Jasper Collins's farm was valued at $2,000 in 1860; in 1870, $1,000. Vinson Collins's farm was valued at $1,500 in 1860; in 1870, $200. Allen Valentine's farm was valued at $1,200 in 1860; in 1870, $150. John M. Baylis's farm was valued at $11,000 in 1860; in 1870, $5,000.

22. Ben Hilbun, "Cracker's Neck," *Mississippi Quarterly* 7 (Jan. 1954): 69.

23. Frances Gandy-Walsh, e-mail message to author, July 5, 2000, ML-USM; Mrs. S. W. Patrick, Rainey Community Meeting, June 10, 1926, and Grandma Smith, "Historical Events in Whitfield Community, Jones County, Mississippi," June 4, 1926, Rogers Museum.

24. Hilbun, "Cracker's Neck," 71.

25. U.S. Bureau of the Census, Federal Manuscript Census, 1880, Jones County, Miss. Federal manuscript censuses and published memoirs provide tantalizing but imprecise images of women's work. In 1880 Jones County's census takers readily identified black women as field laborers but listed white women's occupations as either "keeping house" or "at home," unless they worked outside their own homes. One of Jones County's two enumerators, James L. Welborn, however, deviated from the norm. Welborn identified the occupations of 84 white women from 42 households (in a total of 332 households) as either field hands or day laborers. A sprinkling of other women's occupations noted by Welborn included farmer, nurse, servant, spinner, knitter, weaver, diary hand, milkmaid, and prostitute.

26. Ibid. Although census enumerator James Lawrence Welborn was the son of slaveholder Aaron Welborn and a loyal Confederate soldier during the war, he married Tobitha Welch, who, like him, was kin to many members of the Knight Company (see Appendixes 3 and 7). Perhaps Welborn's kinship ties influenced his decision to label the Dossett sisters as prostitutes.

27. *C. W. Wood v. Mary Coleman*, Jan. 31, 1866, in Special Court of Equity, Jackson, Chancery Court Record Book, 1842–1869, case #129, pp. 158–59, NA-SE; petition of bankruptcy, J. E. Welborn, filed Aug. 23, 1867, in Leesburg, County of Davis, District Court, United States, Southern District of Mississippi, NA-SE. Charges against John M. Baylis and order of his incarceration are mentioned in the case of *John Clark v. Angus McGilvery, Administrator et al.*, and a suit against Amos Deason filed by A. B. Fall et al. A

subpoena was issued to Amos Deason on February 10, 1872; Deason died the following year. Administration papers for the estate of Amos Deason were filed on October 8, 1873. The above cases are abstracted in "Final Records of the Chancery Court," in *Miscellaneous Records of Jones County, MS*, comp. Jean Strickland and Patricia N. Edwards (Moss Point, Miss.: n.p., 1992), 94–97. Unfortunately their details are sketchy and the outcomes inconclusive because of the 1880 burning of the Jones County courthouse in Ellisville.

James Knight, administrator of Benjamin Knight's estate, filed a complaint on November 22, 1869, charging that Joel E. Welborn, administrator of James Gunter's estate, had "converted $500 in gold and silver and U.S. currency to his own use for the purpose of reporting the estate insolvent" (Probate Records, Ellisville Courthouse, Jones County, Miss., courtesy of Gerald W. Johnson).

28. Petition of bankruptcy, Amos Deason, filed Dec. 21, 1868, in Leesburg, County of Davis, District Court, United States, Southern District of Mississippi, NA-SE. Although the Piney Woods was not part of the cotton belt, the Mississippi state legislature's passage of the infamous crop lien laws in 1867 created conflict and confusion between landowners and merchants over claims on crops grown and contributed to conflicts between farmers and merchants. On the legal and economic impact of crop lien laws on the postbellum South, see esp. Harold D. Woodman, *New South—New Law: The Legal Foundations of Credit and Labor Relations in the Postbellum Agricultural South* (Baton Rouge: Louisiana State University Press, 1995), esp. 5–7, 28–66, 108–15. On its effects on farmers and merchants outside the plantation belt, see Steven Hahn, *The Roots of Southern Populism: Yeoman Farmers and the Transformation of the Georgia Upcountry, 1850–1890* (New York: Oxford University Press, 1983), 176–86, and Lawrence Goodwyn, *The Populist Moment: A Short History of the Agrarian Revolt in America* (New York: Oxford University Press, 1978), 20–27, 72–74.

29. U.S. Bureau of the Census, Federal Manuscript Census, 1870, Jones County, Miss.; B. D. Graves, Hebron Community Meeting, June 17, 1926, Rogers Museum. Graves identified Newton Knight as a Republican.

30. William C. Harris, *Day of the Carpetbagger*, 60, 171–80.

31. *Journal of the Proceedings in the Constitutional Convention of the State of Mississippi*, 1868 (Jackson, Miss.: E. Stafford, 1871), 1–20, 145–46, 741. On the tenth day of the convention, fifty-four-year-old Collins requested and received a ten-day leave of absence. He subsequently received at least two more leaves of absence and never appeared for another roll call. He attended long enough to vote against two resolutions, both of which failed. The first would have forbade delegates from assuming "any position of trust or profit in connection with the state government"; the second would have funded the publication of convention proceedings in the *State Journal, Vicksburg Republican*, and *Meridian Chronicle*. Although not reported absent, Collins cast no vote on a resolution to omit the word "white" in regard to qualifications for electors (the measure passed 67 to 15).

Although Newt Knight was identified as a Republican during Reconstruction, the overwhelming majority of voters in Jones and Jasper Counties, even those who deserted the Confederacy, appear to have quickly rejoined the Democratic Party. See Warren A. Ellem, "Who Were the Mississippi Scalawags?," *Journal of Southern History* 38 (May 1972): 217–40. B. D. Graves identified Vinson Collins as a Democrat, indicating that he may have been among the nineteen Democrats who attended the 1869 state convention; see B. D. Graves, Hebron Community Meeting, June 17, 1926, Rogers Museum. In 1904 local lawyer and historian Goode Montgomery remarked that Collins abandoned the "Black and Tan Convention" out of disgust for its "extravagance"

("Alleged Secession of Jones County," *Publications of the Mississippi Historical Society* 8 [1904], 16). For a breakdown of the political affiliations of the delegates to the 1868 constitutional convention and details of its events, see William C. Harris, *Day of the Carpetbagger*, 115, 132–59; Bond, *Political Culture in the Nineteenth-Century South*, 161–65; and Blanche Ames Ames, *Adelbert Ames, 1835–1933* (New York: Argosy-Antiquarian, 1964), 256, 286.

32. William Wesley Sumrall is listed as assistant marshal for Jones County in U.S. Bureau of the Census, Federal Manuscript Census, 1870, Jones County, Miss. The other men's governmental positions are identified in various letters contained in Newton Knight Folder, NA. For genealogical links between the Sumrall and Collins families, see Appendixes 5–6. On the economic recovery of cotton farmers between 1868 and 1870, see William C. Harris, *Day of the Carpetbagger*, 274–80. On James L. Alcorn's political views, see Lillian A. Pereyra, *James Lusk Alcorn: Persistent Whig* (Baton Rouge: Louisiana State University Press, 1966), 90–105. On Adelbert Ames's political appointments, see James W. Garner, *Reconstruction in Mississippi* (1901; Baton Rouge: Louisiana State University Press, 1968), 228–31.

33. Frank Klingberg, *The Southern Claims Commission* (Berkeley: University of California Press, 1955; reprint, New York: Octagon Books, 1978), 17, 25, 38–56; Newton Knight Folder, NA.

34. Newton Knight Folder, NA; Klingberg, *Southern Claims Commission*, 168–73. Klingberg's report of claims from Mississippi lists none from Jones County, presumably because Newt filed his bill before the SCC was established. In regard to Newt's omission in 1870 of many names from his wartime roster, B. A. Mathews stated in a letter contained in Newt's claim file that Newt omitted those who "did not hold out faithful" to the company's cause.

Newt requested the following compensations for individual members of the Knight Company: $2,000 for himself as captain; $1,800 for James Morgan Valentine, whom he moved up in rank from first sergeant to first lieutenant; $1,600 for Simeon Collins, whom he moved up from second sergeant to second lieutenant; $350 for Jasper J. Collins, who was reduced from first lieutenant to first sergeant; $350 for W. P. Turnbow, who was advanced from private to second sergeant; and $325 each for First Corp. Alpheus Knight and Second Corp. Sam G. Owens, who remained at their former ranks. For the remaining thirty-eight privates, who now included William Wesley Sumrall, Newt requested $300 apiece. Personal, political, or economic concerns may account for Newt's changing of men's ranks. Personally, it may reflect simple nepotism. Both James Morgan Valentine and W. P. Turnbow were married to Knight women (as was Samuel G. Owens). Politically, Simeon Collins may have been elevated because his son Thomas Jefferson Collins was the acting justice of the peace who verified Newt's supporting documents. Some changes may also have reflected Newt's economic concerns for certain families. In 1870 William Wesley Sumrall's farm was valued at $500; Jasper Collins's, at $1,000. By contrast, Simeon Collins's widow and grown children all operated farms valued at $400 or less. See U.S. Bureau of the Census, Federal Agricultural Censuses, 1860, 1870, Jasper, Jones, Covington Counties, Miss.

35. William C. Harris, *Day of the Carpetbagger*, 303; William M. Hancock to Honorable L. W. Perce, Dec. 10, 1870; Richard Simmons to Honorable G. C. McKee, Dec. 6, 1870; B. A. Mathews, ex–probate judge of Jones County, Miss., to Honorable L. W. Perce and G. C. McKee, Dec. 8, 1870, all in Newton Knight Folder, NA. For a redeemer overview of Reconstruction that contains lively descriptions of Republican judge William M. Hancock, see W. H. Hardy, "Recollections of Reconstruction in East and Southeast Mississippi," *Publications of the Mississippi Historical Society* 4 (1901): 105–32.

36. Newton Knight's bills before Congress are recorded as follows: HR41-B1, HR 2775, 41st Cong., 3rd sess., Jan. 16, 1871 (referred to Judiciary Committee); HR42A-B1, 42d Cong., 2d sess., HR 1814, Mar 4, 1872 (referred to Military Affairs Committee); HR 43A-B1, 43d Cong., 1st sess., HR 822, Dec. 18, 1873 (referred to Claims Committee), RG 233, NA. Later claims filed in Claims of Newton Knight and Others, #8013 and 8464, U.S. Court of Claims. On Representatives Perce and Howe, see William C. Harris, Day of the Carpetbagger, 123-24, 420. On Sen. Blanche Bruce and Newt's claim, see Daily Clarion, 3 March 1880. My thanks to Grady Howell of the MDAH and Ed Payne for providing me this reference. On the paucity of claims paid by the SCC, see Klingberg, Southern Claims Commission, 55, 70-72.

37. Whitelaw Reid, After the War: A Tour of the Southern States, 1865–1866, ed. with an introduction by C. Vann Woodward (1866; New York: Harper and Row, 1965), 348–49; Sidney Andrews, The South since the War, As Shown by Fourteen Weeks of Travel and Observation in Georgia and the Carolinas (North Stratford, N.H.: Ayer, 1969).

38. William Sparks, The Memories of Fifty Years, 3d ed. (Philadelphia: Claxton, Remsen, and Haffelfinger, 1872), 331–32.

39. Klingberg, Southern Claims Commission, 176–84, 194–209; William C. Harris, Presidential Reconstruction, 34. On the use of racism in Mississippi to unite or coerce white Southern men of diverse political views, see esp. Bond, Political Culture in the Nineteenth-Century South, 151–82; Michael Perman, The Road to Redemption: Southern Politics, 1869–1879 (Chapel Hill: University of North Carolina Press, 1984), 34–37; and William Gillette, Retreat from Reconstruction, 1869–1879 (Baton Rouge: Louisiana State University Press, 1979), 59. On Northern images of the postwar South, see esp. Nina Silber, The Romance of Reunion: Northerners and the South, 1865–1900 (Chapel Hill: University of North Carolina Press, 1993), 48–92.

40. Mary Gladys Watkins, "Reconstruction," unpublished WPA records, June 12, 1937, RG 60, vol. 272, MDAH.

41. William C. Harris, Day of the Carpetbagger, 172; B. D. Graves, Hebron Community Meeting, June 17, 1926, Rogers Museum. On the Ku Klux Klan during Reconstruction, see Allen Trelease, White Terror: The Ku Klux Klan Conspiracy and Southern Reconstruction (New York: Harper and Row, 1971), and Wyn Craig Wade, The Fiery Cross: The Ku Klux Klan in America (New York: Oxford University Press, 1997), 9–111. On the Klan in Reconstruction Mississippi, see esp. Vernon Wharton, Negro in Mississippi, 219–22, and Ames, Adelbert Ames, 331–42, 350–69.

42. Watkins, "Reconstruction." Stories such as this one were often purposely omitted from the WPA publications that followed. Ethel Knight claimed without offering details or proof that "men who had been in the Company of Knight joined the Ku Klux Klan" (Echo of the Black Horn, 250).

43. William C. Harris, Day of the Carpetbagger, 650–90, 663–64; Ames, Adelbert Ames, 385–422; Vernon Wharton, Negro in Mississippi, 181–98. The phrase "political culture of racism" is borrowed from the title of chap. 5 of Bond, Political Culture in the Nineteenth-Century South, 151, 175–81.

Despite the Redeemers' use of democratic rhetoric, they changed crop lien laws to favor planter landlords; see Woodman, New South—New Law, 47, 63–64. On white resistance to Democratic-Conservative appeals, see Michael R. Hyman, The Anti-Redeemers: Hill Country Political Dissenters in the Lower South from Redemption to Populism (Baton Rouge: Louisiana State University Press, 1990). On the era of Redemption, see Perman, Road to Redemption; Gillette, Retreat from Reconstruction; and Terry Seip, The South Returns to Congress: Men, Economic Measures, and Intersectional Relationships, 1868–1879 (Baton Rouge: Louisiana State University Press, 1983).

44. Bond, *Political Culture in the Nineteenth-Century South*, 274; U.S. Bureau of the Census, Federal Manuscript Census, 1870, Jasper County, Miss.

45. Ethel Knight, *Echo of the Black Horn*, 260, 273–300, 310; *State of Mississippi v. Davis Knight*, Dec. 13, 1948, case no. 646, court record and transcript of the Circuit Court, Jones County, Miss. (Clerk's Office, Mississippi Supreme Court, Jackson), transcript, 21, 65, 95–106; Earle Knight, conversations with author, June 28–30, 1994, ML-USM. Molly's full name was Martha Ann Eliza Jane Knight, Mat's was George Madison Knight, Jeff's was Jeffrey Early Knight, and Fannie's was Frances Knight. Rachel may have given birth to as many as ten children; I have verified nine of them through the 1870, 1880, 1900, 1910, and 1920 Federal Manuscript Censuses, Population Schedules, Jasper County, Miss. Censuses indicate that the two couples were married in 1878.

46. Anna Knight, *Mississippi Girl: An Autobiography* (Nashville: Southern Publishing Association, 1952), 11–12. Anna Knight's conversion to Seventh-Day Adventism occurred during the church's intense efforts during the 1880s and 1890s to penetrate the South. The church's evangelistic drive included organizing missions among Mississippi blacks, particularly in the Vicksburg area. Anna, however, discovered Adventism by answering an advertisement in the *Home and Fireside Magazine*. Hungry for personal attention and intellectual stimulation, she wrote away for a listing of various "free samples of books, papers, and catalogues." See Anna Knight, *Mississippi Girl*, 20–29; R. W. Schwartz, *Light Bearers to the Remnant: Denominational History Textbook for Seventh-Day Adventist College Classes* (Mountain View, Calif.: Pacific Press, 1979), 233–49.

47. U.S. Bureau of the Census, Federal Agricultural Censuses, 1870, 1880, Jasper County, Miss. The 1870 agricultural census does not list whether farmers were owners, tenants, or sharecroppers. On Southern blacks and agriculture during Reconstruction, see Jeffrey Kerr-Ritchie, *Freedpeople in the Tobacco South: Virginia, 1860–1900* (Chapel Hill: University of North Carolina Press, 1999); Woodman, *New South—New Law*; Barbara J. Fields, *Slavery and Freedom on the Middle Ground: Maryland during the Nineteenth Century* (New Haven: Yale University Press, 1985), 177–81; and Woodward, *Origins of the New South*, 205–16.

48. Tom Knight, born in 1860, recalled that he was about ten years old when the school was built. See Thomas J. Knight, *Life and Activities of Captain Newton Knight*, 96–97; Ethel Knight, *Echo of the Black Horn*, 266–67; and George P. Rawick, ed., *The American Slave: A Composite Autobiography*, supplement, ser. 1, vol. 10, *Mississippi Narratives*, pt. 5 (Westport, Conn.: Greenwood Press, 1972), 2269. In 1870 the "negro children" alluded to by Wheeler would have been the children of Rachel Knight, who were now part of Newt and Serena's extended family. It is also possible that one or more of these children were fathered by Newt.

49. On black education in the postbellum South, see Leon F. Litwack, *Trouble in Mind: Black Southerners in the Age of Jim Crow* (New York: Knopf, 1998), 52–113. On Mississippi laws regarding education for black children during Reconstruction, see Neil R. McMillen, *Dark Journey: Black Mississippians in the Age of Jim Crow* (Urbana: University of Illinois Press, 1989), 79, and Vernon Wharton, *Negro in Mississippi*, 243–47.

50. On the volatile issue of race and sex in Reconstruction and Redeemer politics and law, see esp. Martha Hodes, *White Women, Black Men: Illicit Sex in the Nineteenth-Century South* (New Haven: Yale University Press, 1997), 147–75; Edwards, *Gendered Strife and Confusion*, 1–23, 186–87, 244–54; Peter Bardaglio, *Reconstructing the Household: Families, Sex, and the Law in the Nineteenth-Century South* (Chapel Hill: University of North Carolina Press, 1995), 176–213; Mary Frances Berry, "Judging Morality: Sexual Behavior and Legal Consequences in the Late-Nineteenth-Century South," *Journal of American History* 78 (Dec. 1991), 835–56; Joel Williamson, *Crucible of Race: Black-White Relations in the American South*

since *Emancipation* (New York: Oxford University Press, 1984), 79–139; McMillen, *Dark Journey*, 14–15; and Vernon Wharton, *Negro in Mississippi*, 227–29. On the construction of a white supremacist government in Mississippi, see Bond, *Political Culture in the Nineteenth Century South*, 156–61; William C. Harris, *Presidential Reconstruction*, 51–54, 259–60, 371–405; and Vernon Wharton, *Negro in Mississippi*, 131–215.

51. William D. McCain, "The Populist Party in Mississippi" (M.A. thesis, University of Mississippi, 1931), 16–17.

52. *Jackson Clarion-Ledger*, June 20, Aug. 8, 1895.

53. Albert D. Kirwan, *Revolt of the Rednecks: Mississippi Politics, 1876–1925* (Lexington: University Press of Kentucky, 1951; reprint, Gloucester, Mass.: Peter Smith, 1964), 93–102; McCain, "Populist Party in Mississippi," 32–35, 43, 73–74; *Jackson Clarion-Ledger*, Aug. 8, 15, 1895.

54. *Jackson Clarion-Ledger*, Sept. 12, 28, Oct. 10, 1895.

55. Ibid., Feb. 27, 1896.

56. On racism among populists, see Stephen Kantrowitz, *Ben Tillman and the Reconstruction of White Supremacy* (Chapel Hill: University of North Carolina Press, 2000); Litwack, *Trouble in Mind*, 221–22; Catherine McNicol Stock, *Rural Radicals: Righteous Rage in the American Grain* (Ithaca, N.Y.: Cornell University Press, 1996), 62; Glenda Elizabeth Gilmore, *Gender and Jim Crow: Women and the Politics of White Supremacy in North Carolina, 1896–1920* (Chapel Hill: University of North Carolina Press, 1996), 76–78, 92; Edwards, *Gendered Strife and Confusion*, 252–53; Hyman, *Anti-Redeemers*, 191, 203; Steven Hahn, *Roots of Southern Populism*, 282–87; Goodwyn, *Populist Moment*, 122–23; Kirwan, *Revolt of the Rednecks*, 101; and C. Vann Woodward, *Tom Watson: Agrarian Rebel* (New York: Oxford University Press, 1963), 216–43.

57. William D. McCain, "Theodore Gilmore Bilbo and the Mississippi Delta," *Journal of Mississippi History* 31, no. 1 (Feb. 1969): 1–27; Kirwan, *Revolt of the Rednecks*, vii, 311–14. Information on Jasper Warren Collins's nomination as a delegate to the Progressive Party is from Daniel C. Vogt, "A Note on Mississippi Republicans in 1912," *Journal of Mississippi History*, 49, no. 1 (Feb. 1987): 54. Personal information on Collins (whose wife was assistant postmaster) is from U.S. Bureau of the Census, Federal Manuscript Censuses, 1870, 1910, Jones County, Miss.

58. Quoted from Ames, *Adelbert Ames*, 506; Addie West, unpublished WPA records, Jones County, RG 60, vol. 317, MDAH. The writing of Southern history from a Confederate perspective had its earliest beginnings with the founding of the Southern Historical Society on May 1, 1869.

Chapter Eight

1. Josie Frazee Cappleman, "Importance of the Local History of the Civil War," *Publications of the Mississippi Historical Society* 3 (1900): 111. For analysis of the means and ends of New South rhetoric, see esp. LeeAnn Whites, *The Civil War As a Crisis in Gender: Augusta, Georgia, 1860–1890* (Athens: University of Georgia Press, 1995), 199–224; Laura Edwards, *Gendered Strife and Confusion: The Political Culture of Reconstruction* (Urbana: University of Illinois Press, 1997), 218–54; Edward L. Ayers, *The Promise of the New South: Life after Reconstruction* (New York: Oxford University Press, 1992), 334–38; and Charles Reagan Wilson, *Baptized in Blood: The Religion of the Lost Cause, 1865–1920* (Athens: University of Georgia Press, 1980), 79–99. On the origins of the Southern Historical Society, founded in 1869, see Richard D. Starnes, "Forever Faithful: The Southern Historical Society and Confederate Historical Memory," *Southern Cultures* 2, no. 2 (winter 1996): 177–94. On the creation of the Myth of the Lost Cause, see also Gaines M. Foster, *Ghosts*

of the Confederacy: Defeat, the Lost Cause, and the Emergence of the New South (New York: Oxford University Press, 1987); Wilson, Baptized in Blood; and Paul M. Gaston, The New South Creed: A Study in Southern Mythmaking (New York: Knopf, 1970).

For Lost Cause versions of the Civil War and Reconstruction in Publications of the Mississippi Historical Society, see esp. J. S. McNeilly, "The Enforcement Act of 1871 and the Ku Klux Klan in Mississippi," vol. 9 (1906): 171; W. H. Hardy, "Recollections of Reconstruction in East and Southeast Mississippi," vol. 4 (1901): 105–32 and vol. 7 (1903): 199–215; and S. S. Calhoon, "The Causes and Events That Led to the Calling of the Constitutional Convention of 1890," vol. 11 (1902): 105–9.

2. Albion Tourgee is quoted from David W. Blight, " 'For Something beyond the Battlefield': Frederick Douglass and the Struggle for the Memory of the Civil War," Journal of American History, Memory and American History: A Special Issue, 75 (Mar. 1989): 1163. On Tourgee's career as a carpetbag judge in North Carolina, see Otto Olsen, Carpetbagger's Crusade: The Life of Albion Winegar Tourgee (Baltimore: Johns Hopkins University Press, 1965).

3. Cappleman, "Importance of the Local History of the Civil War"; Mary V. Duval, "The Making of a State," Publications of the Mississippi Historical Society 3 (1900): 157, 161–65. Cappleman and Duval demonstrated the important role played by women in creating the Myth of the Lost Cause. See Whites, Civil War As a Crisis in Gender, 160–98, and Rebecca Montgomery, "Lost Cause Mythology in New South Reform: Gender, Class, Race, and the Politics of Patriotic Citizenship in Georgia, 1890–1925," in Dealing with the Powers That Be: Negotiating Boundaries of Southern Womanhood, ed. Janet L. Coryell, Thomas H. Appleton, Jr., Anastatia Sims, and Sandra Gioia Treadway (Columbia: University of Missouri Press, 2000). On Mississippi, see Karen L. Cox, "Women, the Lost Cause, and the New South: The United Daughters of the Confederacy and the Transmission of Confederate Culture, 1894–1919" (Ph.D. diss., University of Southern Mississippi, 1997). On the Southern movement to "correct" the historical record in favor of Lost Cause values, see Fred A. Bailey, "The Textbooks of the 'Lost Cause': Censorship and the Creation of Southern State Histories," Georgia Historical Quarterly 75 (fall 1991): 507–33.

4. Neil R. McMillen, Dark Journey: Black Mississippians in the Age of Jim Crow (Urbana: University of Illinois Press, 1989), 245; Jacquelyn Dowd Hall, " 'The Mind That Burns in Each Body': Women, Rape, and Racial Violence," in Powers of Desire: The Politics of Sexuality, ed. Ann Snitow, Christine Stansell, and Sharon Thompson (New York: Monthly Review Press, 1983), 328–49; William Pierce Randel, The Ku Klux Klan: A Century of Infamy (Philadelphia: Chilton, 1965), 82. For an analysis of how dominant beliefs about appropriate race, class, and gender behavior converged to ignite mass hysteria and violence, see Nancy MacLean, "The Leo Frank Case Reconsidered: Gender and Sexual Politics in the Making of Reactionary Populism," Journal of American History 78 (1991): 917–48. For more comprehensive analyses of race relations during this era, see Leon F. Litwack, Trouble in Mind: Black Southerners in the Age of Jim Crow (New York: Knopf, 1998); Grace Elizabeth Hale, Making Whiteness: The Culture of Segregation in the South, 1890–1940 (New York: Pantheon, 1998); Nina Silber, The Romance of Reunion: Northerners and the South, 1865–1900 (Chapel Hill: University of North Carolina Press, 1993), 48–63; and Joel Williamson, Crucible of Race: Black-White Relations in the American South since Emancipation (New York: Oxford University Press, 1984), 111–323.

On other interracial Southern communities of the postbellum South, see esp. Mark R. Schultz, "Interracial Kinship Ties and the Emergence of a Rural Black Middle Class: Hancock County, Georgia, 1865–1920," in Georgia in Black and White: Explorations in the Race Relations of a Southern State, 1865–1950, ed. John C. Inscoe (Athens: University of Georgia

Press, 1994), 141–72; Adele Logan Alexander, *Ambiguous Lives: Free Women of Color in Rural Georgia, 1789–1879* (Fayetteville: University of Arkansas Press, 1991); Kent Anderson Leslie, *Woman of Color; Daughter of Privilege, 1849–1893* (Athens: University of Georgia Press, 1995); Mary R. Bullard, *Robert Stafford of Cumberland Island: Growth of a Planter* (Athens: University of Georgia, 1995).

5. Article from the *Meridian Mercury*, reprinted in the *Ralls County (Mo.) Record*, Apr. 30, 1868 (thanks to Gregg Andrews for bringing this article to my attention).

6. *Jackson Clarion-Ledger*, Oct. 17, 1895.

7. Ibid., Dec. 12, 1895.

8. Dabney Lipscomb, "Mississippi's 'Backwoods Poet,'" *Publications of the Mississippi Historical Society* 1 (June 1898): 11. William C. Harris described Berryhill as a "Bourbon activist in Reconstruction politics"; see his *The Day of the Carpetbagger: Republican Reconstruction in Mississippi* (Baton Rouge: Louisiana State University Press, 1979), 594. On the close connections between racism and Confederate imagery during this era, see Kevin Thornton, "The Confederate Flag and the Meaning of Southern History," *Southern Cultures* 2, no. 2 (winter 1996): 233–45.

9. McMillen, *Dark Journey*, 229, 244–45.

10. James Street, *Look Away! A Dixie Notebook* (New York: Viking, 1936). I have found no evidence to suggest that Street's statement about the sycamore tree was true.

11. Interview with B. A. Boutwell, unpublished WPA records, Jones County, RG 60, vol. 316, MDAH. Boutwell, described as justice of the peace of Jones County at the time, gave the date of the lynching as 1917 but was surely describing the June 26, 1919, lynching of John Hartfield (see African-American Holocaust, http://www .maafa.org).

12. Interview with Hulon Myers by Orley Caudill, Mississippi Oral History Program, vol. 349, 1979, ML-USM, 33–37. On the history of the 1920s Ku Klux Klan, see esp. Nancy MacLean, *Behind the Mask of Chivalry: The Making of the Second Ku Klux Klan* (New York: Oxford University Press, 1994).

13. *New Orleans Item*, Mar. 20, 1921.

14. Thomas J. Knight, *The Life and Activities of Captain Newton Knight and His Company and the "Free State of Jones"* (1935; rev. ed, Laurel, Miss.: n.p., 1946), 96–97. During the trial of Davis Knight, attorney Quitman Ross described Tom Knight as "filled with venom and hatred" (*Knight v. State*, 207 Miss. 564 [1949], at 565). Ethel Knight claimed that Tom "hated any person whom he so much as even suspicioned was not entirely white"; see Ethel Knight, *The Echo of the Black Horn: An Authentic Tale of "The Governor" of "The Free State of Jones"* (n.p., 1951), 312.

15. Ethel Knight, *Echo of the Black Horn*, 293, 300, 315. The phrase "blood and thunder" is from Thomas L. McHaney, "James Street: Making History Live," in *Mississippi's Piney Woods: A Human Perspective*, ed. Noel Polk (Jackson: University Press of Mississippi, 1986), 125. Family genealogist Earle Knight claimed that Ethel Knight used vivid prose in hopes of likewise attracting a movie producer; see Earle Knight, conversations with author, June 28–30, 1994, ML-USM. In 1963 attorney Quitman Ross reportedly labeled *Echo of the Black Horn* "ninety-nine percent fiction." See Johnston to Tubb and Lewis, Dec. 12, 1963, Mississippi State Sovereignty Commission Papers, courtesy of Leesha Faulkner Civil Rights Collection, University of Southern Mississippi, Hattiesburg; thanks to Charles C. Bolton for bringing this collection to my attention.

16. Ethel Knight, *Echo of the Black Horn*, 264–70; U.S. Bureau of the Census, Federal Manuscript Census, 1900, Jasper County, Miss.

17. Ethel Knight, *Echo of the Black Horn*, 315.

18. Ibid., 264–65, 278–79 (quoted passage), 300, 303, 309, 311–12.

19. Paula Giddings, *When and Where I Enter: The Impact of Black Women on Race and Sex in America* (New York: Morrow, 1984), 86–87; Martha Hodes, *White Women, Black Men: Illicit Sex in the Nineteenth-Century South* (New Haven: Yale University Press, 1997), 131–32, 162–63.

20. G. Norton Galloway, "A Confederacy within A Confederacy," *Magazine of American History*, Oct. 1886, 387–90; *Natchez Courier*, July 12, 1864; *New Orleans Times-Picayune*, July 17, 1864.

21. Galloway, "Confederacy within A Confederacy," 387–90. On Northern ridicule of Southern whites as illiterate, feuding, and backward, see Altina L. Waller, *Feud: Hatfields, McCoys, and Social Change in Appalachia, 1860–1900* (Chapel Hill: University of North Carolina Press, 1988), 195, 206–34.

22. Newton Knight to John Knight, Apr. 3, 1887, reprinted in Winnie Knight Thomas, Earle W. Knight, Lavada Knight Dykes, and Martha Kaye Dykes Lowery, *The Family of John "Jackie" Knight and Keziah Davis Knight, 1773–1985* (Magee, Miss.: Robert and Delores Knight Vinson, 1985), 351–53.

23. Albert Bushnell Hart, "Why the South Was Defeated in the Civil War," *New England Magazine*, n.s., 4 (Dec. 1891): 95–120; Dr. Samuel Willard, "A Myth of the Confederacy," *Nation*, Mar. 24, 1892, 227. For a historical overview of the roots of violence in the postwar Southern backcountry, see Samuel C. Hyde Jr., "Backcountry Justice in the Piney-Woods South," in *Plain Folk of the South Revisited*, ed. Samuel C. Hyde Jr. (Baton Rouge: Louisiana State University Press, 1997). On the *Nation's* increasingly pro-Confederate rhetoric during this era, see Silber, *Romance of Reunion*, 171–74.

24. General Dabney Herndon Maury, *Recollections of a Virginian in the Mexican, Indian, and Civil Wars* (New York: Charles Scribner's Sons, 1894), 200–203, 246–47.

25. Alexander L. Bondurant, "Did Jones County Secede?," *Publications of the Mississippi Historical Society* 1 (1898): 103–6; Goode Montgomery, "Alleged Secession of Jones County," *Publications of the Mississippi Historical Society* 8 (1904): 13–22.

26. Bondurant, "Did Jones County Secede?," 106; Goode Montgomery, "Alleged Secession of Jones County," 21.

27. Bondurant interviewed three former Mississippi governors, John M. Stone, Robert Lowry (the Confederate colonel who led a major raid on Knight's band during the war), and Anselm J. McLaurin and a Jones County chancery clerk, E. B. Clark. See Bondurant, "Did Jones County Secede?," 103–6, and Goode Montgomery, "Alleged Secession of Jones County," 13–22. Goode Montgomery was identified as the mayor of Laurel in U.S. Bureau of the Census, Federal Manuscript Census, 1920, Jones County, Miss.

28. Goode Montgomery, "Alleged Secession of Jones County," 18–19; *New Orleans Item*, Mar. 20, 1921.

29. Goode Montgomery, "Alleged Secession of Jones County," 17–19. On increased legal and extralegal persecution of interracial marriages beginning in the 1880s, see Hodes, *White Women, Black Men*, 176–97; Glenda Elizabeth Gilmore, *Gender and Jim Crow: Women and the Politics of White Supremacy in North Carolina, 1896–1920* (Chapel Hill: University of North Carolina Press, 1996), 71; and W. Fitzhugh Brundage, *Lynching in the New South: Georgia and Virginia, 1880–1930* (Urbana: University of Illinois Press, 1993), 58–62.

30. See Appendix 9. Mary E. Welborn and Sarah E. Welborn, daughters of Aaron Terrell Welborn, married Tom Knight and Joseph Sullivan Knight, respectively, in 1878 and 1880. Ulysses Grant Welborn, son of Caroline Welborn, married Susan Knight in 1888.

31. U.S. Bureau of the Census, Federal Manuscript Censuses, 1880, 1900, Jasper

County, Miss. According to the U.S. Dept. of Commerce, *Twenty Censuses: Population and Housing Questions, 1790–1980* (Orting, Wash.: Heritage Quest, 1979), 22, 33, census enumerators for 1880 were instructed to designate people of African ancestry as either "black," or "mulatto," according to their physical appearance. In 1900, just four years after the U.S. Supreme Court sanctioned racial segregation in *Plessy v. Ferguson* (1896), they were instructed to designate people of any degree of African ancestry as simply "black."

32. George P. Rawick, ed., *The American Slave: A Composite Autobiography*, supplement, ser. 1, vol. 10, *Mississippi Narratives*, pt. 5 (Westport, Conn.: Greenwood Press, 1972), 2268. Georgeanne's four children were John Howard, born 1872; Anna (Rachel Ann), born 1874; Grace, born 1891; and Lessie, born 1894. See U.S. Bureau of the Census, Federal Manuscript Census, 1900, Jasper County, Miss. Consistent with census reports, Martha Wheeler claimed that Serena left Newton's household and moved to that of Jeffrey and Molly sometime after 1890. Census reports also confirm that Georgeanne gave birth to daughters in 1891 and 1894 following a seventeen-year period in which she bore no children. The gap in births suggests that Rachel's death may indeed have precipitated a relationship between Georgeanne and Newton. Wheeler claimed that Newton and Georgeanne raised seven children together. Since Georgeanne gave birth to only four children during her lifetime, it is possible that Wheeler included the three children of Rachel—Augusta, Hinchie, and Stewart—that Rachel's descendants most consistently claim were fathered by Newton.

Knight family genealogist Kenneth Welch is convinced from his research into death certificates and obituaries that Newt fathered five of Rachel's children: Martha Ann, Stewart, Floyd, Augusta Ann, and Hinchie. The death certificates of three of Georgeanne's children—Anna, Grace, and Lessie—also list Newt Knight as their father. Although several African American Knights expressed doubt that Georgeanne's children were fathered by Newton, they were certain that several of Rachel's were. Although they disagreed over how many of Rachel's children were fathered by Newton, all agreed that Augusta, Hinchie, and Stewart were his offspring. See Kenneth Welch, telephone interview with author, Nov. 29, 2000; Florence Blaylock, Dorothy Marsh, Annette Knight, Olga Watts, and Lois Knight Wilson, interview with author, Soso, Miss., July 22, 1996; Audrey Knight Crosby, interview with author, Soso, Miss., July 23, 1996; and Annette Knight, taped interview with Florence Blaylock, Soso, Miss., June 29, 1996, ML-USM.

For an even earlier description than Martha Wheeler's of the marriages between Newt's and Rachel's children, and another assertion that Newt had children by Georgeanne Knight, see B. D. Graves, Hebron Community Meeting, June 17, 1926, Lauren Rogers Museum of Art, Laurel, Miss. See also Jan Sumrall and Kenneth Welch, *The Knights and Related Families* (Denham Springs, La.: n.p., 1985), 161.

33. U.S. Bureau of the Census, Federal Manuscript Census, 1880, Jasper County, Miss. Consistent with Anna Knight's memory, the 1880 census enumerator listed Rachel's household separately from Newt and Serena's and reported several adults in the home: Rachel, 40; her daughter Georgeanne, 26; her son Jeffrey, 22; and her daughter Martha, 15. Included also were numerous children: Georgeanne's son John Howard, 9; her daughter Anna, 6; and the youngest children of Rachel—Stewart, 12; Floyd, 10; Augusta, 7; and Hinchie, 5. Two households listed between those headed by Rachel and Newt were comprised of their intermarried adult children and thus were interracial. The census enumerator's listing of the Knight households is a tangle of confusion, however. Several Knights are double-listed: Georgeanne is listed twice in Rachel's household, first as her daughter, age 26, then as her granddaughter, age 25.

Rachel's son Jeffrey is listed as "Geoffrey" in Rachel's household, then again as "Jeff E." as the head of his own household. Similarly, Newt and Serena's son Sullivan is listed both in their household and as head of his own (as "S. Knight"). In Rachel's household, her son Stewart is listed by his given name of Jonathan S.; Augusta is listed as "A. A."; and Anna is listed by her given name of Rachel.

34. U.S. Bureau of the Census, Federal Agricultural Census, 1880, Jasper County, Miss.; Anna Knight, *Mississippi Girl: An Autobiography* (Nashville: Southern Publishing Association, 1952), 12–13, 18, 27. On the lives of black women in the postwar South, see esp. Tera W. Hunter, *To 'Joy my Freedom: Southern Black Women's Lives and Labors After the Civil War* (Cambridge: Harvard University Press, 1997); Leslie Schwalm, *A Hard Fight for We: Women's Transition from Slavery to Freedom in South Carolina* (Urbana: University of Illinois Press, 1997); and Jacqueline Jones, *Labor of Love, Labor of Sorrow: Black Women, Work, and the Family from Slavery to the Present* (New York: Vintage, 1985), 44–151.

35. B. D. Graves, Hebron Community Meeting, June 17, 1926, Rogers Museum.

36. Paula Bolan, e-mail message to author, Apr. 19, 2000, and Lonnie Knight, e-mail messages to author, Jan. 28, 29, 2000, ML-USM.

37. Thomas J. Knight, *Life and Activities of Captain Newton Knight*, 17, 37 (second quoted phrase), and 87 (first quoted phrase), 96–97. Tom Knight provided an obtuse, confused discussion of Rachel and Georgeanne's efforts to send mixed-race Knights to a newly built schoolhouse around 1870, referring to them only as "Negro women." George Valentine was the younger brother of Richard H. Valentine, who appeared on Newton Knight's company "muster list" during the Civil War. Martha Ellzey married Taylor Knight, Newton's brother, in 1871. See Thomas et al., *Family of John "Jackie" Knight*, 31, and U.S. Bureau of the Census, Federal Manuscript Censuses, 1860, 1870, Jones County, Miss.

38. William Pitts, telephone conversation with author, Feb. 16, 2000; DeBoyd Knight, conversation with author, Aug. 9, 1993; Earle Knight, conversations with author, June 28–30, 1994; and Julius Huff, conversation with author, Aug. 8, 1993, ML-USM. When I asked William Pitts what he thought of Ethel Knight's book, he pronounced it unfair to Newt and mostly "fiction." He concluded by remarking, "I don't really have a close feeling for her." DeBoyd Knight and Earle Knight, before his death in 1998, have been the chief collectors of Newt Knight material in Jones County. Together they cared for his gravestone, which has often been defaced, and once even stolen, by vandals.

39. According to Ethel Knight, George "Clean Neck" Knight (who earned his nickname because he wore his collar so high that hair did not grow on his neck) was one of only two whites who attended Newt's funeral; see *Echo of the Black Horn*, 326–27. Also see Sumrall and Welch, *Knights and Allied Families*, 22, and Earle Knight, conversations with author, June 28–30, 1994.

40. On Ellen G. White, see esp. Ronald L. Numbers, *Prophetess of Health: Ellen G. White and the Origins of Seventh-Day Adventist Health Reform*, rev. and enl. ed. (Knoxville: University of Tennessee Press, 1992). Works that illuminate religious movements in which women promoted racial uplift include Nell Irvin Painter, *Sojourner Truth: A Life, a Symbol* (New York: Norton, 1996); Gilmore, *Gender and Jim Crow*; Evelyn Brooks Higginbotham, *Righteous Discontent: The Women's Movement in the Black Baptist Church, 1880–1920* (Cambridge: Harvard University Press, 1993); Mary E. Frederickson, "Each One Is Dependent on the Other: Southern Churchwomen, Racial Reform, and the Process of Transformation, 1880–1940," in *Visible Women: New Essays on American Activism*, ed. Nancy A. Hewitt and Suzanne Lebsock (Urbana: University of Illinois Press, 1993), 296–324; Cynthia Neverdon-Morton, *Afro-American Women of the South and the Advancement of the Race, 1895–*

1925 (Knoxville: University of Tennessee Press, 1989); and Jacqueline Anne Rouse, *Lugenia Burns Hope: Black Southern Reformer* (Athens: University of Georgia Press, 1989).

41. Numbers, *Prophetess of Health*, 93–101. Seventh-Day Adventists strongly supported the Temperance Movement; for this reason, claimed Anna, moonshiners regularly harassed her. See Anna Knight, *Mississippi Girl*, 83–84.

42. The American Medical Missionary College was sponsored by the Seventh-Day Adventist Battle Creek Sanitarium from 1895 until 1910. Its president was the controversial John Harvey Kellogg, medical doctor, health reformer, and developer of many "health" products, including corn flakes. See R. W. Schwartz, *Light Bearers to the Remnant: Denominational History Textbook for Seventh-Day Adventist College Classes* (Mountain View, Calif.: Pacific Press, 1979), 210, 282–97; and Don F. Neufeld, ed., *Seventh-Day Adventist Encyclopedia*, rev. ed. (Washington, D.C.: Review and Herald Publishing Association, 1976), 37, 722–23.

On the origins of Seventh-Day Adventism, see Numbers, *Prophetess of Health*, 48–101, and Ronald L. Numbers and Jonathan M. Butler, eds., *The Disappointed: Millerism and Millenarianism in the Nineteenth Century* (Knoxville: University of Tennessee Press, 1993).

43. Anna Knight, *Mississippi Girl*, 26–27. On the views of the Seventh-Day Adventist Church, especially those of Ellen G. White, on card playing, dancing, and sexual relations, see Numbers, *Prophetess of Health*, 93, 99, 129–59.

44. Annette Knight, interview with author, Soso, Miss., July 22, 1996, ML-USM. As Darlene Clark Hine has written, "The combined influence of rape (or the threat of rape), domestic violence, and a desire to escape economic oppression born of racism and sexism" motivated many young black women during this era to flee the South. See Darlene Clark Hine, "Rape and the Inner Lives of Southern Black Women: Thoughts on the Culture of Dissemblance," in *Southern Women: Histories and Identities*, ed. Virginia Bernhard, Betty Brandon, Elizabeth Fox-Genovese, and Theda Purdue, eds. (Columbia: University of Missouri Press, 1992), 177–89.

45. Ethel Knight, *Echo of the Black Horn*, 265, 309. On efforts by black women to uplift themselves and kin through the founding of churches and schools, see esp. Gilmore, *Gender and Jim Crow*, 12–21, 150–65.

46. Anna Knight, *Mississippi Girl*, 84.

47. Numbers and Butler, *The Disappointed*; Anna Knight *Mississippi Girl*, 20–29, 48–49; Schwartz, *Light Bearers to the Remnant*, 233–49. On Anna Knight's encounter of racial prejudice, see her *Mississippi Girl*, 20–32, 41–47, 71–75. On the role of charismatic evangelical sects in empowering a far more famous black woman, and one with connections to Seventh-Day Adventism in Battle Creek, Michigan, see Painter, *Sojourner Truth*.

48. Anna Knight, *Mississippi Girl*, 14–15, 75–92, 159–70.

49. Quoted from Address of M. P. Bush, Feb. 17, 1912, Rogers Museum.

50. Ethel Knight, *Echo of the Black Horn*, 296–300. On societal condemnation of white women who crossed the color line, see Martha Hodes, "The Sexualization of Reconstruction Politics: White Women and Black Men in the South after the Civil War," *Journal of the History of Sexuality* 3 (Jan. 1993), 402–17, and Laura F. Edwards, "Sexual Violence, Gender, Reconstruction, and the Extension of Patriarchy in Granville County, North Carolina," *North Carolina Historical Review*, 63 (July 1991): 237–60.

51. *Laurel Leader Call*, Dec. 9, 1920; Annette Knight, taped interview with Florence Blaylock, Soso, Miss., June 29, 1996, and Yvonne Bevins and Anita Williams, taped interview with Florence Blaylock, July 4, 1996 (tapes in possession of Florence Blaylock, Soso, Miss.). Evidence that Sharp Welborn was convicted and imprisoned for murdering Stewart Knight is from Kenneth Welch Genealogy Files. An undated, un-

titled newspaper clipping from the 1960s, in possession of DeBoyd Knight of Jones County, Miss., noted that unknown assailants murdered Rachel's fifty-two-year-old son Stewart in 1920. In fact, Sharp Welborn was not only later convicted but also identified as the murder suspect by the *Laurel Leader Call* on December 9, 1920. The newspaper reported that Sharp Welborn, a young white man who lived five miles south of Stringer, was jailed on December 6, 1920, after being accused of the murder of a "Negro," whom it erroneously identified as Dewey Knight, described as "well-to-do" and having lived alone in a house near Welborn. Knight's body was reportedly found by a Mr. Jackson who went several times to visit the victim and finally searched for him and found his body. Knight appeared to have been dead for several days. "His head was partly shot off and had other marks on his body which might have been made by an ax." The newspaper also reported that Knight's gun was found in Welborn's possession. Consistent with this newspaper report, Stewart Knight's gravestone lists his date of death as November 29, 1920. When questioned about the murder, Knight relatives reported hearing that Stewart Knight had intervened on behalf of a white woman rather than having become sexually involved with a white woman.

52. "The Lynching Century: African Americans Who Died in Racial Violence in the United States: Names of the Dead, Dates of Death, Places of Death, 1865–1965" (www.geocities.com/Colosseum/Base/8507/NLPlaces2.htm); *Laurel Daily Leader*, Oct. 23, 1922.

53. *Laurel Daily Leader*, Oct. 20, 21, 1922. In 1979 Hulon Myers recalled how the Klan "would go in and march around and they would hand the preacher a letter, maybe it would have a hundred dollars in it" (interview with Hulon Myers, 33).

54. Florence Blaylock, telephone conversation with author, Mar. 5, 2000, ML-USM.

55. E. Franklin Frazier, *The Negro Family in the United States* (Chicago: University of Chicago Press, 1939), 215–45.

56. Melba Riddle, e-mail message to author, Nov. 3, 1999; Rhonda Benoit, e-mail message to author, Jan. 14, 2000; Frances Jackson, e-mail message to author, Apr. 30, 2000, all at ML-USM.

57. Wade Hall, *Passing for Black: The Life and Careers of Mae Street Kidd* (Lexington: University Press of Kentucky, 1998), 176–77.

58. Anna Knight, *Mississippi Girl*, 14–15; Annette Knight, conversation with author, Soso, Miss., July 22, 1996, and Florence Blaylock, Dorothy Marsh, and Olga Watts, conversation with author, Soso, Miss., July 22, 1996, ML-USM; Deposition of Fannie House (Howze), in *Martha Ann Musgrove et al. v. J. R. McPherson et al.*, Jan. 27, 1914, case no. 675, Chancery Court of Jones County, Laurel, Miss., copy in Kenneth Welch Genealogy Files. Although Georgeanne's youngest daughter, Lessie, moved to Texas at the urging of her cousins to live as a white woman, she continued to visit her Mississippi relatives.

59. *Ellisville Progressive*, Mar. 16, 1922.

60. Memories of the Klan's harassment of whites were described by Frances Gandy-Walsh, e-mail message to author, June 28, 2000, ML-USM. Dates of deaths are from individual tombstones. Newt Knight and Georgeanne Knight are both buried in the Newt Knight Cemetery near Soso, in Jones County. Serena Knight is buried in the cemetery of the Palestine Primitive Baptist Church in Laurel, Jones County.

61. Ardella Knight Barrett Papers, property of Florence Blaylock, Soso, Miss. On July 27, 1980, the Central States Conference of Seventh-Day Adventists held a testimonial banquet in St. Louis, Missouri, in honor of Ardella Knight Barrett's thirty-five years as a Christian educator.

62. Ibid. Ardella Barrett's description of white people setting fire to her mother's home is corroborated by Frances Gandy-Walsh's statement that the Klan was deter-

mined to "burn the Knights out" of their property (e-mail message to author, June 28, 2000, ML-USM).

63. Unpublished poem by Rachel Watts (Green) provided courtesy of Wynona Green Frost and Olga Watts Nelson, e-mail message of Jan. 20, 2000, ML-USM.

64. John Shelton Reed, "Mixing in the Mountains," *Southern Cultures* 3, no. 4 (spring 1998), 29.

65. On developing notions of race and "whiteness," see esp. Litwack, *Trouble in Mind*; Hale, *Making Whiteness*; and David R. Roediger, *The Wages of Whiteness: Race and the Making of the American Working Class* (New York: Verso, 1991).

Epilogue

1. David L. Cohn, *Where I Was Born and Raised*, 3d ed. (Notre Dame, Ind.: University of Notre Dame Press, 1948), xi. For more on Cohn, see James C. Cobb, ed., *The Mississippi Delta and the World: The Memoirs of David L. Cohn* (Baton Rouge: Louisiana State University Press, 1995). On the segregated South's unwritten racial code, see Leon F. Litwack, *Trouble in Mind: Black Southerners in the Age of Jim Crow* (New York: Knopf, 1998), 327–36.

2. State of Mississippi v. Davis Knight, Dec. 13, 1948, case no. 646, court record and transcript of the Circuit Court, Jones County, Miss. (Clerk's Office, Mississippi Supreme Court, Jackson), transcript, 4–6 (hereafter these two separately paged sections of the record of the case are cited as either *State v. Knight*, record, or *State v. Knight*, transcript).

3. Thomas J. Knight, *The Life and Activities of Captain Newton Knight and His Company and the "Free State of Jones"* (1935; rev. ed, Laurel, Miss.: n.p., 1946), 82; Ethel Knight, *The Echo of the Black Horn: An Authentic Tale of "The Governor" of "The Free State of Jones"* (n.p., 1951), 229–30. For a firsthand account of the effects of the Myth of the Lost Cause on Southern white children of the early twentieth century, see esp. Katharine Du Pre Lumpkin, *The Making of a Southerner* (New York: Knopf, 1947; reprint, Athens: University of Georgia Press, 1991), and Jacquelyn Dowd Hall, " 'You Must Remember This': Autobiography as Social Critique," *Journal of American History* 85 (Sept. 1998): 439–65.

4. Patricia Sullivan, *Days of Hope: Race and Democracy in the New Deal Era* (Chapel Hill: University of North Carolina Press, 1996), 97–100; John Egerton, *Speak Now against the Day: The Generation before the Civil Rights Movement in the South* (Chapel Hill: University of North Carolina Press, 1995), 81; 102–4, 288–92; Adam Fairclough, *Race and Democracy: The Civil Rights Struggle in Louisiana, 1915–1972* (Athens: University of Georgia Press, 1995), 46–73.

5. *Laurel Leader Call*, Mar. 8, 1939. The agrarian romanticism of this era is best expressed in a collection by Twelve Southerners, *I'll Take My Stand: The South and the Agrarian Tradition* (1939; reprinted with a new introduction by Louis D. Rubin Jr., Baton Rouge: Louisiana State University Press, 1978). For a history of the Old South written from an agrarian perspective, see Frank L. Owsley, *Plain Folk of the Old South* (Baton Rouge: Louisiana State University Press, 1949). On continuing efforts among Laurel reformers to link Newt Knight and the Free State of Jones to issues of class and racial exploitation, see David Moberg, "Puttin' Down Ol' Massa: Laurel, Mississippi, 1979," in *Working Lives: The Southern Exposure History of Labor in the South*, ed. Marc S. Miller (New York: Pantheon, 1980), 291–301.

6. Patricia Sullivan, *Days of Hope*, 70; Jacquelyn Dowd Hall, *Revolt against Chivalry: Jessie Daniel Ames and the Women's Campaign against Lynching*, 2d ed. (New York: Columbia University Press, 1993). On Operation Dixie, see Michael K. Honey, *Southern Labor and Black Civil Rights: Organizing Memphis Workers* (Urbana: University of Illinois Press, 1993), and Barbara S. Griffith, *The Crisis of American Labor: Operation Dixie and the Defeat of the CIO* (Phila-

delphia: Temple University Press, 1988). On Southern black labor radicalism, see also Robin D. G. Kelley, *Hammer and Hoe: Alabama Communists during the Great Depression* (Chapel Hill: University of North Carolina Press, 1990), and Nell Irvin Painter, *The Narrative of Hosea Hudson: The Life and Times of a Black Radical* (New York: Norton, 1994).

7. On red-baiting of Union and civil rights organizations, see Egerton, *Speak Now against the Day*, 292–301, and Patricia Sullivan, *Days of Hope*, 230–47. On Theodore Bilbo, see Honey, *Southern Labor and Black Civil Rights*, 245 (quoted phrase); John Dittmer, *Local People: The Struggle for Civil Rights in Mississippi* (Urbana: University of Illinois Press, 1995), 2; Steven F. Lawson, *Running for Freedom: Civil Rights and Black Politics in America since 1941* (New York: McGraw Hill, 1991), 17, 23; and William F. Winter, "Piney Woods Politics and Politicians," in *Mississippi's Piney Woods: A Human Perspective*, ed. Noel Polk (Jackson: University Press of Mississippi, 1986), 134–43. For an overview of the origins of Bilbo's ideas in the postbellum South, see Litwack, *Trouble in Mind*, esp. 206–16.

8. Patricia Sullivan, *Days of Hope*, 191, 117–18, 153; Egerton, *Speak Now against the Day*, 340; Fairclough, *Race and Democracy*, 74–105; Lawson, *Running For Freedom*, 32–40; Donald G. Nieman, *Promises to Keep: African-Americans and the Constitutional Order, 1776 to the Present* (New York: Oxford University Press, 1991), 141.

9. *State v. Knight*, transcript, 3–8. As Joel Williamson argues, the economic, physical, and social sanctions against race-mixing were often more effective than legal barriers; see Joel Williamson, *Crucible of Race: Black-White Relations in the American South since Emancipation* (New York: Oxford University Press, 1984), 247.

10. *State v. Knight*, transcript, 3–8. On the racial etiquette that made the sight of white women publicly consorting with black men unthinkable to the court clerk, see Litwack, *Trouble in Mind*, 36, and Neil R. McMillen, *Dark Journey: Black Mississippians in the Age of Jim Crow* (Urbana: University of Illinois Press, 1989), 23–28.

11. Williamson, *Crucible of Race*, 467. Attorney Quitman's Mississippi roots provide an ironic contrast to the Pennsylvania roots of prosecutor Paul Swartzfager, who was the son of Yankee entrepreneurs James H., a bookkeeper, and Helen C. Swartzfager, a retail merchant of ladies' clothing, who moved to Laurel, Mississippi, sometime before 1920. See U.S. Bureau of the Census, Federal Manuscript Census, 1920, Jones County, Miss.

12. *State v. Knight*, transcript, 4, 55–56, 67, 92.

13. Ibid., 55.

14. Ibid., 32–40.

15. Ibid., 39.

16. Ibid., 108. D. H. Valentine was probably Darrell Valentine. In 1920 he was twenty-eight, married, and living with his parents, William P. (grandson of Susannah Valentine, a widow by the time of the Civil War) and Nancy Valentine, and six siblings in Laurel, Mississippi. See U.S. Bureau of the Census, Federal Manuscript Census, 1920, Jones County, Miss.

17. See Appendix 8. D. H. Valentine's father, William P. Valentine, was the grandson of Susannah and Darrel Valentine and probably the son of their son, William P. The full name of the elder William P. was William Patrick Valentine—Patrick Valentine, a member of the Knight Company.

18. *State v. Knight*, transcript, 1, 33, 70–71, and 78–79. Complete lists of all witnesses summoned for the defendant, June 25, 1948, and for the state, December 16, 1948, are in the *State v. Davis Knight* folder, case #646, Ellisville Circuit Court, Ellisville, Miss.

On the use of the epithet "white nigger," see Williamson, *Crucible of Race*, 465–68. Witness "Mrs. Bertis Ellzey" is referred to as such because I have not identified her beyond her married name. She, court clerk Nell Graves, and court reporter Hettie Bell

Stevens were all identified respectfully as "Mrs." In contrast, none of the black female witnesses were identified as either "Miss" or "Mrs." Kate Spradley Till, the mother of Junie Lee Knight, was identified only by her full name in the original trial witness list; in the final trial record, however, she was identified as "Mrs. Kate S. Till." The custom of degrading black women (and white women who associated too closely with blacks) by refusing to address them as "Miss" or "Mrs." was routine during the era of segregation. See Glenda Elizabeth Gilmore, *Gender and Jim Crow: Women and the Politics of White Supremacy in North Carolina, 1896–1920* (Chapel Hill: University of North Carolina Press, 1996), 180, and McMillen, *Dark Journey*, 23–24.

19. *State v. Knight*, transcript, 61.

20. Ibid., 83–89; Anna Knight, *Mississippi Girl: An Autobiography* (Nashville: Southern Publishing Association, 1952), 19.

21. Annette Knight, conversation with author, July 22, 1996, ML-USM.

22. *State v. Knight* transcript, 84–85, 88–90.

23. Ibid., 84, 109–10.

24. See Appendix 9. Davis Knight was the great-great-grandson of Rachel Knight through his mother Addie's line; he was her great-grandson through his father Otho's line.

25. *State v. Knight*, transcript, 96–100.

26. Ibid. 101–6.

27. Ibid., 97–100.

28. *State v. Knight*, record, 32. I am surmising that Grace Knight attended Davis's trial because she was listed among his sureties when he appealed his case. Anna Knight was not.

29. *State v. Knight*, transcript, 88. Dr. John M. Stringer, who among white witnesses was most likely to have known Anna Knight, merged her identity with that of Grace Knight by referring to Grace as Gracie *Ann* Knight and describing her as a "missionary."

30. Ibid., 6, 10, 19.

31. Ibid., 11–12. Description of Tom as a disheveled old man by Flo Wyatt and Florence Blaylock, interview by author, Soso, Miss., July 24, 1996; as a peddler, by the *Laurel Leader Call*, Dec. 19, 1951; as a storekeeper, by the 1920 federal manuscript census for Jones County, Miss.; as a former storekeeper who operated a street stand in later years, by Earle Knight, conversations with author, June 28–30, 1994, ML-USM.

32. *State v. Knight*, record, 25–29, 33.

33. Ibid., 27–30; *Knight v. State*, 207 Miss. 564 (1949). The *New York Times*, Dec. 19, 1948 published a story about Knight titled "Wed to White Girl, Gets 5-Year Term." The *Ellisville Progress-Item*, Dec. 23, 1948, underplayed the verdict with a short, purely factual article titled "Davis Knight Found Guilty."

Evidently civil rights groups were watching the case closely. Quitman Ross reportedly received "telephone calls, letters, and other communications from nearly every state in the Union and three European countries" (memo from Erle Johnston Jr., Director of the Mississippi Sovereignty Commission, to Jack Tubb, Superintendent of Education, and F. Gordon Lewis, Jasper County Superintendent of Education, Dec. 12, 1963, in Leesha Faulkner Civil Rights Collection, University of Southern Mississippi, Hattiesburg). According to Ethel Knight, Ross told her that "various institutions having to do with the Negro race sought to inject themselves into the matter but their offers of assistance were courteously and firmly declined" (Ethel Knight, *Echo of the Black Horn*, 9).

34. Bureau of Vital Statistics, *An Index to Death Records: Texas, 1959*, 2:735, State Department of Health, Austin, Tex. Information on Anna Knight was taken from programs prepared for her 90th Birthday Testimonial, March 12, 1964, by the National Oak-

wood College Alumni Association, and from announcements of her Memorial Service, held June 8, 1972, at Oakwood College (Oakwood Archives and Museum, Oakwood College, Huntsville, Ala.). On the founding of Oakwood College, see R. W. Schwartz, *Light Bearers to the Remnant: Denominational History Textbook for Seventh-Day Adventist College Classes* (Mountain View, Calif.: Pacific Press, 1979), 242–44, and Don F. Neufeld, ed., *Seventh-Day Adventist Encyclopedia*, rev. ed. (Washington, D.C.: Review and Herald Publishing Association, 1976), 1017–19.

35. Report of a meeting with the West Jasper County School Board at Bay Springs, Miss., from A. L. "Andy" Hopkins and Tom Scarbrough, Aug. 22, 1960, Mississippi State Sovereignty Commission Papers, Faulkner Civil Rights Collection.

36. Report, Further Investigation of Louvenia Knight Case, from A. L. Hopkins and Erle Johnston Jr., Dec. 19, 1963, and Johnston Jr. to Tubb and Lewis, Dec. 12, 1963, ibid. For Johnston's remarks on the need to avoid media coverage, see Memorandum to All Members of the Sovereignty Commission from Director, Jan. 24, 1964, ibid., and Memorandum to Governor Paul B. Johnson from Director, Sovereignty Commission, Feb. 14, 1964, box 135, Paul B. Johnson Jr. Papers, ML-USM.

37. Johnston to Tubb and Lewis, Dec. 12, 1963; Memorandum to All Members of the Sovereignty Commission from Director, Jan. 24, 1964; Memorandum from Director, Sovereignty Commission, to File, Nov. 9, 1965, all in Sovereignty Commission File, Faulkner Civil Rights Collection.

38. Johnston to Tubb and Lewis, Dec. 12, 1963, ibid.

39. In 1930, for example, the U.S. Federal Census Bureau instructed its enumerators to designate anyone with any degree of African blood as "Negro." The same instructions applied to people of mixed Indian and European ancestry, *except* where the amount of Indian blood was minute or the person was accepted in their community as white. The race of an individual born to one white and one nonwhite parent (defined as Negro, Indian, Chinese, Japanese, or Mexican) was to be reported according to the race of the *nonwhite* parent. See U.S. Dept. of Commerce, *Twenty Censuses: Population and Housing Questions, 1790–1980* (Orting, Wash.: Heritage Quest, 1979), 52.

40. C. Vann Woodward, *Origins of the New South, 1877–1913* (Baton Rouge: Louisiana State University Press, 1951).

41. Quoted passage from the dust jacket of Ethel Knight, *Echo of the Black Horn*. According to Ethel, Tom Knight sold her his manuscript materials and copyright shortly after the Davis Knight trial. Though Tom presumably agreed that Ethel should tell the story of Rachel, his cousin Earle Knight stated that Tom was unaware that his father's political principles and goals would be recast as well. See Earle Knight, conversations with author, June 28–30, 1994, ML-USM.

42. On Newt's Knight Company roster, he inverted John Thomas Whitehead's first two initials as "T. J." The citizens who ordered the tombstone misread the initials as "T. H." They recorded Thomas Ates as Thomas Yates because that is what Newt recorded on his roster. Newton Knight is buried in the Newton Knight cemetery, Soso, Mississippi. The John "Jackie" Knight cemetery is in Covington County, Mississippi.

43. Earle Knight, conversations with author, June 28–30, 1994, ML-USM.

Bibliography

Primary Sources

Manuscript Collections
Atlanta, Georgia
   Georgia Department of Archives and History
      Name Index
      Stone Creek Baptist Church Minutes, 1808–1954
      Superior Court Records (microfilm)
         Deeds and Mortgages, Book C, 1811–1812
Austin, Texas
   Center for the Study of American History, University of Texas
      Duckworth-Smith-McPherson Family Papers
      Natchez Trace Collection
Columbia, South Carolina
   South Carolina Department of Archives and History
      County Records
         Wills
      General Assembly Records
         Petitions to the Legislature
East Point, Georgia
   National Archives, Southeast Region
      Records of the U.S. Courts, Southern District, Mississippi, Jackson
         Chancery Court Record Book, 1842–1869, #259
         General Index, 1848–1879
         Petitions of Bankruptcy

Hattiesburg, Mississippi
   University of Southern Mississippi, McCain Library and Archives
      Conversations with Author (deposited transcripts)
         Florence Blaylock, July 22, 1996
         Gerald W. Johnson, July 18, 1999
         Annette Knight, July 22, 1996
         Earle Knight, June 28–30, 1994
         Ethel Knight, August 10, 1993
         Dorothy Knight Marsh, July 22, 1996
         Olga Watts Nelson, July 22, 1996
         William Pitts, February 16, 2000
         Kenneth Welch, November 29, 2000
      Electronic Messages to Author (deposited transcripts)
         Rhonda Benoit
         Florence Blaylock
         Paula Bolan
         Paula Broussard
         Patricia Bryan
         Eleanore Crespo
         Ann Beason Gahan
         Mary Gamero-Adams
         Frances Gandy-Walsh
         Frances Jackson
         Gerald W. Johnson
         Eddie Josey-Wilson
         Lonnie Knight
         Olga Watts Nelson
         Frances Nosser
         Jean Duckworth Paleschic
         Melba Riddle
         Regina Roper
         Kenneth Slade
         Judy Smith
         Wayne and JoAnn Wingate
      Genealogy File Cabinet
         Collins Folder
         Knight Folder
         Welborn Folder
      Mississippi Oral History Program
         Interview with Hulon Myers
         Interview with Elly Dahmer
Huntsville, Alabama
   Oakwood Archives and Museum, Oakwood College
      Anna Knight Collection
Jackson, Mississippi
   Mississippi Department of Archives and History
      Confederate Records, RG 9
      County Records (microfilm)
         Jones County Chancery Court, Final Records, First District, 1857–1890

Genealogical Vertical Files
   Collins Folder
   Knight Folder
   Sumrall Folder
   Welborn Folder
Governors' Papers, RG 27
   James L. Alcorn
   Adelbert Ames
   Charles Clark
   Robert Lowry
   J. J. Pettus
   William L. Sharkey
Legislative Records, RG 47
   Petitions and Memorials, 1817–1839
   Senate Journal, vol. 88
Private Manuscripts
   Thomas J. Knight, "Intimate Sketch of Activities of Newton Knight and 'Free State of Jones County'" (1935)
   James L. Power Scrapbook
   Records of the Acts and Doings of the Baptist Church of Christ at Leaf River, Covington County, Mississippi (microfilm)
   U.S. Work Projects Administration, RG 60
      Unpublished WPA Files, Jones, Covington, and Jasper Counties
   Mississippi Supreme Court, Clerk's Office
      State of Mississippi v. Davis Knight, December 13, 1948, Case No. 646, court record and transcript of the Circuit Court, Jones County
Laurel, Mississippi
   Lauren Rogers Museum of Art
      Address of Mr. M. P. Bush before the Meeting of the DAR, February 17, 1912
      Hebron Community Meeting, June 17, 1926
      History of Union Line Community, compiled by Mrs. J. W. Moss, 1926
      Historical Events in Whitfield Community, Meeting June 4, 1926
      Johnson School Community Meeting, July 1, 1926
      Jones County's Agricultural and Industrial Development, B. L. Moss; read at Centennial Celebration, December 16, 1926
      Newspaper Clipping File
      Rainey Community Meeting, June 10, 1926
Raleigh, North Carolina
   North Carolina Department of Archives and History
      County Court Records
      Wills
      General Assembly Session Records
      Petitions to Assembly
Richmond, Virginia
   Virginia Historical Society
      Elder Norvell Robertson Sr., "An Autobiography, 1765–1846" (typed copy)
Tuscaloosa, Alabama
   William Stanley Hoole Special Collections Library, University of Alabama
      Mississippi Territorial Records
         "Causes Ended in the Superior Court, 1812," box 73

Civil trial docket, October 1810–November 1814, box 72
Trial and appearance dockets, July 1810–January 1812, box 72
U.S. General Land Office (microfilm)
    Ledger 3, 1805–1840
    Ledger 13, 1738–1813

Private Collections

Ardella Knight Barrett Papers, in possession of Florence Blaylock, Soso, Mississippi
Genealogy Files, Rhonda Benoit, DeQuincy, Louisiana
Genealogy Files, Florence Knight Blaylock, Soso, Mississippi
Genealogy Files, Versie McKnight Frederick, Vidor, Texas
Genealogy Files, Mary Bess Gamero-Adams, Mesquite, Texas
Genealogy Files, Frances Jackson, Broken Arrow, Oklahoma
Genealogy Files, Gerald W. Johnson, Laurel, Mississippi
Genealogy Files, Olga Watts Nelson, Sumrall, Mississippi
Genealogy Files, Regina Roper, Gainesville, Florida
Genealogy Files, Judy Smith, Dallas, Texas
Genealogy Files, Wayne and JoAnn Wingate, Baker, Louisiana
Genealogy Files, Kenneth Welch, Soso, Mississippi

Local Court Records

Collins, Mississippi
  Office of the Chancery Clerk, Covington County
    Chancery Court, Book 1
    Chancery Court Docket, 1857–1904
    Circuit Court, Book 2
    Circuit Court Minutes, Book 2, 1858–1866
    Probate Court, Book 3A
    Probate Minutes, Book 1, 1854–1861
Ellisville, Mississippi
  Office of the Circuit Clerk, Jones County
    Circuit Court Minutes, First District, Books 3, 5, 7, 1902–1937
    Folder, Trial Papers of Davis Knight, 1948, case #646
    Justice's Docket, 1887–1895

Official Records

Washington, D.C.
  National Archives
    Records of the Adjutant General's Office, 1780s–1917, RG 94
      Compiled Service Records of Volunteer Union Soldiers Who Served in
        Organizations from the State of Louisiana, M396, 50 rolls
    Records of the Bureau of Refugees, Freedmen, and Abandoned Lands, RG 105
      (microfilm)
    Records of the Assistant Commissioner for the State of Mississippi, Bureau of
      Refugees, Freedmen, and Abandoned Lands, 1865–1869, M826, 50 rolls
    Records of the Department of Justice, RG 60
      Appointment files for Judicial Districts, 1853–1905
      Index to names of U.S. Marshals, 1789–1960 (microfilm) T577, 1 roll
      Letters Received by the Department of Justice from Mississippi, 1871–1884
        (microfilm) M970

Records of the Department of State, RG 59
Appointment Records, Letters of Application and Recommendation for Public
Office, 1869–1877
Records of the Department of the Treasury, RG 56
Registers of Letters Received, 1834–1872, 1873–1902
Records of the U.S. House of Representatives, RG 233
Barred and Disallowed Case Files of the Southern Claims Commission, 1871–
1880, M1407, 4,829 cards (microfiche)
Newton Knight Folder, box 15
Records of the Veterans Administration, RG 15
Revolutionary War Pension and Bounty-Land Application Files (microfilm),
M804, 2,670 rolls
Records of U.S. Court of Claims, RG 123
Committee on War Claims, Claims of Newton Knight and Others, #8013
and 8464
War Department Collection of Confederate Records, RG 109
Records of the Adjutant and Inspector General's Department relating to
Conscripts, Exemptions, and Details, Mississippi, 1864–65, 1 vol.
Compiled Service Records of Confederate Soldiers Who Served in
Organizations from the State of Mississippi, M269, 427 rolls (microfilm)

Published and Unpublished U.S. Censuses and Census Reports
U.S. Bureau of the Census. Federal Manuscript Agricultural and Manufacturing
Schedule, 1850, 1860, 1870, 1880, Covington, Jones, and Jasper Counties, Miss.
(microfilm).
U.S. Bureau of the Census, Federal Manuscript Census, Population Schedule, 1790,
North Carolina and South Carolina (published).
U.S. Bureau of the Census, Federal Manuscript Census, Population Schedule, 1820,
1830, 1840, 1850, 1860, 1870, 1880, 1900, 1910, 1920, Covington, Jasper,
Jones, Smith, and Perry Counties, Miss. (microfilm).
U.S. Bureau of the Census, Federal Manuscript Census, Slave Schedule, 1850, 1860,
Covington, Jasper, Jones, Smith, and Perry Counties, Miss. (microfilm).
U.S. Department of Commerce. *Twenty Censuses: Population and Housing Questions, 1790–
1980*. Orting, Wash.: Heritage Quest, 1979.

Published Proceedings of the U.S. Congress
Journal of the House of Representatives of the United States, 3d Session of 41st Congress. December 5,
1870. Washington, D.C.: Government Printing Office, 1871.
Journal of the House of Representatives of the United States, 2d Session of 42d Congress. December 4,
1871. Washington, D.C.: Government Printing Office, 1872.
Journal of the House of Representatives of the United States, 1st Session of 43d Congress. December 1,
1873. Washington, D.C.: Government Printing Office, 1873.

**Published Proceedings of the Mississippi Supreme Court
and Mississippi Legislature**
Journal of the Proceedings in the Constitutional Convention of the State of Mississippi, 1868. Jackson,
Miss.: E. Stafford, 1871.
*Laws of the State of Mississippi Passed at a Called Session of the Mississippi Legislature held in Columbus,
February and March 1865*. Jackson, Miss.: J. J. Shannon, 1865.
*Laws of the State of Mississippi Passed at a Called Session of the Mississippi Legislature held in the City of
Jackson, October 1866 and January and February, 1867*. Jackson, Miss.: J. J. Shannon, 1867.

Laws of the State of Mississippi Passed at a Regular Session of the Mississippi Legislature held in the City of Jackson, October, November, and December, 1865. Jackson: J. J. Shannon, 1866.

Mississippi Reports: Cases Argued and Decided in the Supreme Court of Mississippi. Vols. 15, 32, 37, 207.

Published Documents and Compilations of Records

Barefield, Marilyn Davis. *Clarke County, Alabama, Records, 1814–1885.* Easley, S.C.: Southern Historical Press, 1983.

Bell, Mary Best, comp. *Colonial Bertie County, North Carolina.* Vol. 2, *Abstracts of Deed Books, 1725–1730 and 1739.* Windsor, N.C.: Colonial Bertie, 1963.

Bettersworth, John K., ed. *Mississippi in the Confederacy: As They Saw It.* Baton Rouge: Louisiana State University Press, 1962. Reprint, New York: Kraus Reprint Co., 1970.

Blair, Ruth, ed. *Some Early Tax Digests of Georgia.* Vidalia, Ga.: Georgia Genealogical Reprints, 1971. Reprint, Georgia Department of Archives and History, 1926.

Candler, Allen D. *The Colonial Records of Georgia.* Atlanta: Franklin-Turner, 1907.

———, comp. *The Revolutionary Records of the State of Georgia.* Atlanta: Franklin-Turner, 1908.

Carter, Clarence Edwin, ed. *The Territory of Mississippi, 1807–1817.* Vols. 5 and 6 of *The Territorial Papers of the United States.* Washington, D.C.: Government Printing Office, 1938.

Clark, Murtie June. *Loyalists in the Southern Campaign of the Revolutionary War: Official Rolls of Loyalists Recruited from North and South Carolina, Georgia, Florida, Mississippi, and Louisiana.* Baltimore: Genealogical Pub. Co., 1981.

Clark, Walter, ed. *The State Records of North Carolina.* Goldsboro, N.C.: Nash Brothers, 1906.

Davis, Robert Scott, Jr. *Georgia Citizens and Soldiers of the American Revolution.* Easley, S.C.: Southern Historical Press, 1983.

———. *Georgians in the Revolution: At Kettle Creek (Wilkes Co.) and Burke County.* Easley, S.C.: Southern Historical Press, 1986.

Davis, Robert Scott, Jr., and Rev. Silas Emmett Lucas Jr., comps. *The Families of Burke County, 1755–1855: A Census.* Easley, S.C.: Southern Historical Press, 1981.

De Lemar, Marie, and Elisabeth Rothstein, eds. *The Reconstructed 1790 Census of Georgia: Substitutes for Georgia's Lost 1790 Census.* Baltimore: Genealogical Pub. Co., 1989.

Dunstan, Edythe Smith, comp. *The Bertie Index for Courthouse Records of Bertie Co., N.C., 1720–1875: Deeds, Land Divisions, Grants, Abstracts of Wills and Marriage Bonds, Maps, Illustrations.* N.p., 1966.

Ervin, Sara Sullivan. *South Carolinians in the Revolution.* 1949. Reprint, Baltimore: Genealogical Pub. Co., 1981.

Fleet, Beverly. *Virginia Colonial Abstracts: The Original Thirty-four Volumes Reprinted in Three.* Baltimore: Genealogical Pub. Co., 1988.

Green, Fletcher M., ed. *Lides Go South . . . and West: The Record of a Planter Migration in 1835.* Columbia: University of South Carolina Press, 1952.

Hahn, Marilyn Davis. *Old St. Stephens Land Office Records and American State Papers, Public Lands.* Easley, S.C.: Southern Historical Press, 1983.

Hendrix, Mary Louise Flowers, comp. *Mississippi Court Records from the Files of the High Court of Errors and Appeals, 1799–1859.* N.p., 1950.

Hofman, Margaret M., comp. *Abstracts of Deeds, Edgecombe Precinct, Edgecombe County, North Carolina, 1732–1758.* Weldon, N.C.: Roanoke News Co., 1969.

———. *Abstracts of Land Patents, Province of North Carolina, 1663–1729.* Weldon, N.C.: Roanoke News Co., 1979.

———. *The Granville District of North Carolina, 1748–1763: Abstracts of Land Grants.* N.p., 1986.

Holcomb, Brent, comp. *Anson County, N.C., Deed Abstracts.* Vol. 2, *1757–1766 and 1763 Tax List.* N.p., 1975.

———. *Spartanburg County: South Carolina Will Abstracts, 1787–1840.* Columbia, S.C.: n.p., 1983.

Hornaday, Mr. and Mrs. L. S., comps. *Piedmont North Carolina Cemeteries: Spring, Eno, South Fork, Chatham, and Plainfield Friends Meeting Cemetery Records with Additional Records from Spring Friends Meeting.* Burlington, N.C.: n.p., 1991.

Lackey, Richard S., comp. *Frontier Claims in the Lower South: Records of Claims Filed by Citizens of the Alabama and Tombigbee River Settlements in Mississippi Territory for Depredations by the Creek Indians during the War of 1812.* New Orleans: Polyanthos, 1977.

———, ed. *East Mississippi Source Material.* Vol. 1, Newspaper Abstracts. Forest, Miss.: n.p., 1968.

———. "Minutes of Zion Baptist Church of Buckatunna, Wayne County, Mississippi." *Mississippi Genealogical Exchange* 19, nos. 1–4 (spring 1973): 13–21, 59–65, 85–93, 123–25. Original manuscript is at Mississippi Baptist Historical Commission Library, Mississippi College, Clinton.

———. "Petition to the Legislative Council by Inhabitants Living on the Chickasawhay River, 1808." *Journal of Mississippi History* 37, no. 3 (Aug. 1975): 279–82.

Linn, Jo White, comp. *Abstracts of the Deeds of Rowan County, N.C., 1753–1785.* N.p., n.d.

———. *Abstracts of the Minutes of the Court of Pleas and Quarter Sessions, Rowan County, N.C., 1775–1789.* N.p., 1982.

———. *Rowan County Deed Abstracts.* Vol. 1, 1753–1762: Abstracts of Books 1–4. N.p., n.d.

Lowrie, Walter, ed. *Early Settlers of Mississippi As Taken from Land Claims in Mississippi Territory.* Easley, S.C.: Southern Historical Press, 1986.

McBee, May Wilson, comp. *Anson County, North Carolina: Abstracts of Early Records.* Baltimore: Genealogical Pub. Co., 1978.

Moss, Bobby Gilmer. *Roster of South Carolina Patriots in the American Revolution.* Baltimore: Genealogical Pub. Co., 1983.

Powell, William S., James K. Huhta, and Thomas J. Farnham, eds. *The Regulators of North Carolina: A Documentary History, 1759–1776.* Raleigh: State Department of Archives and History, 1971.

Price, William S., Jr., ed. *The Colonial Records of North Carolina.* 2d series. Vol. 5, North Carolina Higher-Court Minutes, 1709–1723. Raleigh: Department of Cultural Resources, Division of Archives and History, 1977.

Rawick, George P., ed. *The American Slave: A Composite Autobiography.* Supplement, ser. 1, vols. 7–10, Mississippi Narratives, pts. 2–5. Westport, Conn.: Greenwood Press, 1972.

Reamy, Bill, and Martha Reamy. *St. George's Parish Registers, 1689–1793.* Silver Spring, Md.: Family Line Publications, 1988.

Reeves, Henry, and Mrs. G. D. Koch. *Cemetery Inscriptions, Davidson (Old Rowan) Co., North Carolina.* N.p., 1970.

Saunders, William L. *The Colonial Records of North Carolina.* Raleigh: Josephus Daniels, 1890.

Strickland, Ben, and Jean Strickland. *Records of Jones County, Mississippi: Deed Book A and B, 1827–1856.* Moss Point, Miss.: n.p., 1981.

Strickland, Jean, and Patricia N. Edwards, comps. *Confederate Records: Covington, Wayne, and Jones County.* Moss Point, Miss.: n.p., 1987.

———. *Miscellaneous Records of Jones County MS.* Moss Point, Miss.: n.p., 1992.

———. *Records of Jones County, Mississippi: Deed Book A & B, 1827–1856.* Moss Point, Miss.: n.p., 1981.

U.S. War Department. *Supplement to the Official Records of the Union and Confederate Armies.* Edited by Janet B. Hewett. Wilmington, N.C.: Broadfoot Pub. Co., 1996.

———. *War of the Rebellion: A Compilation of the Official Records of the Union and Confederate Armies.* Washington, D.C.: Government Printing Office, 1880–1901.

Walker, Alexander McDonald, comp. *New Hanover Co. Court Minutes, 1794–1800.* N.p., 1962.

Warren, Mary Bondurant, ed. "Colonial Records, Attainders, and Confiscations."
   Carolina Genealogist (1970), no. 2, 1–4; no. 3, 5–6; no. 4, 7–10.
Wheeler, John Hill. *Historical Sketches of North Carolina from 1584 to 1851: Compiled from
   Original Records, Official Documents, and Traditional Statements, with Biographical Sketches of Her
   Distinguished Statesmen, Jurists, Lawyers, Soldiers, Divines, etc.* 2 vols. in 1. Philadelphia, 1851.
   Reprint, Baltimore: Regional Pub. Co., 1964.
White, Virgil D., abstractor. *Genealogical Abstracts of Revolutionary War Pension Files.* 3 vols.
   Waynesboro, Tenn.: National Historical Pub. Co., 1991.
Williams, Carolyn White. *History of Jones County, Georgia: One Hundred Years, Specifically, 1807–
   1907.* Macon, Ga: J. W. Burke, 1957.
Williams, Ruth Smith, and Margaret Glenn Griffin, comps. *Abstracts of the Wills of Edge-
   combe County, North Carolina, 1733–1856.* Rocky Mount, N.C.: Joseph W. Watson, 1980.
Winslow, Ellen Goode. *History of Perquimans County: As Compiled from Records Found There and
   Elsewhere, by "Mrs. Watson Winslow."* Raleigh: Edwards and Broughton, 1931.
Wood, Virginia S., and Ralph V. Wood. *1805 Georgia Land Lottery.* Cambridge, Mass.:
   Greenwood Press, 1964.

Newspapers
Ellisville (Miss.) Progress-Item
Ellisville (Miss.) Progressive
Jackson (Miss.) Clarion-Ledger
Laurel (Miss.) Leader Call
Laurel (Miss.) Daily Leader
Meridian (Miss.) Daily Clarion
Natchez (Miss.) Courier
New Orleans Item
Ralls County (Mo.) Record

Books
Andrews, Sidney. *The South since the War, As Shown by Fourteen Weeks of Travel and Observation in
   Georgia and the Carolinas.* North Stratford, N.H.: Ayer, 1969.
Benedict, David. *General History of the Baptist Denomination in America and Other Parts of the
   World.* 2 vols. Boston: Manning and Loring, 1813.
Christian Index. *History of the Baptist Denomination in Georgia.* Atlanta: James P. Harrison,
   1881.
Hooker, Richard J., ed. *The Carolina Backcountry on the Eve of the Revolution: The Journal and Other
   Writings of Charles Woodmason, Anglican Itinerant.* Chapel Hill: University of North
   Carolina Press, 1953.
Maury, General Dabney Herndon. *Recollections of a Virginian in the Mexican, Indian, and Civil
   Wars.* New York: Charles Scribner's Sons, 1894.
Pitts, Dr. J. R. S. *Life and Confession of the Noted Outlaw James Copeland.* Introduction by John D.
   W. Guice. Jackson: University Press of Mississippi, 1992. Facsimile of 1909 edition.
Reid, Whitelaw. *After the War: A Tour of the Southern States, 1865–1866.* Edited with an
   Introduction by C. Vann Woodward. 1866. Reprint, New York: Harper and Row,
   1965.
Sparks, William. *The Memories of Fifty Years.* 3d ed. Philadelphia: Claxton, Remsen, and
   Haffelfinger, 1872.

Articles
Claiborne, J. F. H. "A Trip through the Piney Woods." 1841–42. Reprinted in
   Publications of the Mississippi Historical Society 9 (1906): 487–538.

Secondary Sources

Family Genealogies and Biographical Dictionaries

Baird, Robert W. *Bynum and Baynham Families of America, 1616–1850.* Baltimore: Gateway Press, 1983.

Boyd, Sandra E., comp. and ed. *Benjamin Duckworth: His Descendants and Related Families.* Hattiesburg, Miss.: n.p. 1989.

Collins, A. O. *"Ole Man Moses and His Chillun": The Story of Moses Collins of South Carolina, Georgia, Alabama, and Mississippi, and His Descendants.* Aransas Pass, Tex.: Biography Press, 1974.

Collins, Carr P., Jr. *Royal Ancestors of Magna Charta Barons.* Dallas, Tex.: n.p., 1959.

Collins, Vinson Allen. *A Story of My Parents: Warren Jacob Collins and Tolitha Eboline Valentine Collins.* Livingston, Tex.: n.p., 1962.

Davis, Minnie S. *Confederate Patriots of Jones County.* Ellisville, Miss.: Printed by the Progress-Item for Minnie Mae Davis, 1977.

Edwards, Patricia N., and Jean Strickland. *Who Married Whom: Jones County, Mississippi.* Moss Point, Miss.: n.p., 1986.

Graham, Marie Martin. *John H. Powell and Some of His Descendants.* Oxford, Miss.: n.p., 1985.

Hammons, Ann R. *Wild Bill Sullivan: King of the Hollow.* Jackson: University Press of Mississippi, 1980.

Hines, James H. *The Families Somerville, Somervaill, Summerall, Summerell, Summerill, Summerlin, Sumlin, Sumrall, and Sumril.* N.p., 1981.

Leverett, Rudy. "Ole Rosinheels: A Genealogical Sketch of the Family of Major Amos McLemore, 27th Mississippi Infantry Regiment, C.S.A." Unpublished manuscript, 1988.

Maddox, Joseph T., and Mary Carter, comps. *North Carolina Soldiers, Sailors, Patriots, and Descendants.* Albany: Georgia Pioneers Publications, n.d.

Sanders, Ruby Bynum, comp. *The Bynum and Herrington Connections.* Ellisville, Miss.: n.p., 1994.

Smith, Janet, Jean Strickland, and Patricia N. Edwards. *Who Married Whom: Covington County, Mississippi.* Moss Point, Miss.: n.p., 1991.

Sumrall, Jan, and Kenneth Welch. *The Knights and Related Families.* Denham Springs, La.: n.p., 1985.

Thomas, Winnie Knight, Earle W. Knight, Lavada Knight Dykes, and Martha Kaye Dykes Lowery. *The Family of John "Jackie" Knight and Keziah Davis Knight, 1773–1985.* Magee, Miss.: Robert and Delores Knight Vinson, 1985.

Tyler, Ron, ed. in chief. *New Handbook of Texas.* 6 vols. Vol. 2. Austin: Texas State Historical Association, 1996.

Welborn, Gene. *Welborn and Related Families with Roots in North and South Carolina.* N.p., 1994.

Wharton, Clarence Ray. *Texas under Many Flags.* Chicago: American Historical Society, 1930.

Wooley, James E., ed. *A Collection of Upper South Carolina Genealogical and Family Records.* 3 vols. Easley, S.C.: Southern Historical Press, 1979.

Youngblood, Frances, and Floelle Youngblood Bonner. *Youngblood-Armstrong and Allied Families.* N.p., 1962.

Books

Abernethy, Thomas Perkins. *The Formative Period in Alabama, 1815–1828.* 1965. Tuscaloosa: University of Alabama Press, 1990.

Alexander, Adele Logan. *Ambiguous Lives: Free Women of Color in Rural Georgia, 1789–1879.* Fayetteville: University of Arkansas Press, 1991.

Ames, Blanche Ames. *Adelbert Ames, 1835–1933.* New York: Argosy-Antiquarian, 1964.

Ayers, Edward L. *The Promise of the New South: Life after Reconstruction.* New York: Oxford University Press, 1992.

———. *Vengeance and Justice: Crime and Punishment in the Nineteenth-Century South.* New York: Oxford University Press, 1984.

Bardaglio, Peter W. *Reconstructing the Household: Families, Sex, and the Law in the Nineteenth-Century South.* Chapel Hill: University of North Carolina Press, 1995.

Bass, Robert D. *Ninety Six: The Struggle for the South Carolina Backcountry.* Lexington, S.C.: Sandlapper Store, 1978.

Bearss, Edwin C. *Decision in Mississippi: Mississippi's Important Role in the War between the States.* Jackson: Mississippi Commission on the War between the States, 1962.

Beringer, Richard, Herman Hattaway, Archer Jones, and William N. Still Jr. *Why the South Lost the Civil War.* Athens: University of Georgia Press, 1986.

Bettersworth, John K. *Confederate Mississippi: The People and Policies of a Cotton State in Wartime.* Baton Rouge: Louisiana State University Press, 1963.

Blassingame, John. *The Slave Community: Plantation Life in the Antebellum South.* New York: Oxford University Press, 1972.

Boles, John. *The Great Revival, 1787–1805.* Lexington: University Press of Kentucky, 1972.

Bolton, Charles C. *Poor Whites of the Antebellum South: Tenants and Laborers in Central North Carolina and Northeast Mississippi.* Durham, N.C.: Duke University Press, 1994.

Bolton, Charles C., and Scott Culclasure, eds. *The Confessions of Edward Isham: A Poor White Life of the Old South.* Athens: University of Georgia Press, 1998.

Bond, Bradley G. "Herders, Farmers, and Markets on the Inner Frontier: The Mississippi Piney Woods, 1850–1860." In *Plain Folk of the South Revisited,* edited by Samuel C. Hyde Jr., 73–99. Baton Rouge: Louisiana State University Press, 1997.

———. *Political Culture in the Nineteenth-Century South: Mississippi, 1830–1900.* Baton Rouge: Louisiana State University Press, 1995.

Boyd, Jesse Laney. *A Popular History of Baptists in Mississippi.* Jackson, Miss.: Baptist Press, 1930.

Brasseaux, Carl A., Keith P. Fontenot, and Claude F. Oubre. *Creoles of Color in the Bayou Country.* Jackson: University Press of Mississippi, 1994.

Brekus, Catherine A. *Strangers and Pilgrims: Female Preaching in America, 1740–1845.* Chapel Hill: University of North Carolina Press, 1998.

Brown, Kathleen M. *Good Wives, Nasty Wenches, and Anxious Patriarchs: Gender, Race, and Power in Colonial Virginia.* Chapel Hill: University of North Carolina Press, 1996.

Brown, Richard Maxwell. *The South Carolina Regulators.* Cambridge, Mass.: Belknap Press of Harvard University Press, 1963.

Brundage, W. Fitzhugh. *Lynching in the New South: Georgia and Virginia, 1880–1930.* Urbana: University of Illinois Press, 1993.

Bullard, Mary R. *Robert Stafford of Cumberland Island: Growth of a Planter.* Athens: University of Georgia Press, 1995.

Bynum, Victoria E. "Mothers, Lovers, and Wives: Images of Poor White Women in Edward Isham's Autobiography." In *The Confessions of Edward Isham: A Poor White Life of the Old South,* edited by Charles C. Bolton and Scott Culclasure. Athens: University of Georgia Press, 1998.

———. *Unruly Women: The Politics of Social and Sexual Control in the Old South.* Chapel Hill: University of North Carolina Press, 1992.

Carr, Lois Green, and David William Jordan. *Maryland's Revolution of Government, 1689–1692.* Ithaca, N.Y.: Cornell University Press, 1974.

Carr, Lois Green, and Russell R. Menard. "Immigration and Opportunity: The Freedman in Early Colonial Maryland." In *The Chesapeake in the Seventeenth Century: Essays on Anglo-American Society*, edited by Thad W. Tate and David L. Ammerman, 206–42. New York: Norton, 1979.

———. "Political Stability and the Emergence of a Native Elite in Maryland." In *The Chesapeake in the Seventeenth Century: Essays on Anglo-American Society*, edited by Thad W. Tate and David L. Ammerman, 243–73. New York: Norton, 1979.

Cashin, Edward. "From Creeks to Crackers." In *The Southern Colonial Backcountry: Interdisciplinary Perspectives on Frontier Communities*, edited by David Colin Crass, Steven D. Smith, Martha A. Zierden, and Richard D. Brooks, 69–75. Knoxville: University of Tennessee Press, 1998.

Cashin, Joan E. *A Family Venture: Men and Women on the Southern Frontier*. Baltimore: Johns Hopkins University Press, 1991.

Cathey, Cornelius O. *Agriculture in North Carolina before the Civil War*. Raleigh: North Carolina Department of Archives and History, 1974.

Cecil-Fronsman, Bill. *Common Whites: Class and Culture in Antebellum North Carolina*. Lexington: University Press of Kentucky, 1994.

Chaplin, Joyce E. *An Anxious Pursuit: Agricultural Innovation and Modernity in the Lower South, 1730–1815*. Chapel Hill: University of North Carolina Press, 1993.

Clinton, Catherine. *The Plantation Mistress: Woman's World in the Old South*. New York: Pantheon, 1982.

Clinton, Catherine, and Michele Gillespie, eds. *The Devil's Lane: Sex and Race in the Early South*. New York: Oxford University Press, 1997.

Clinton, Catherine, and Nina Silber, eds. *Divided Houses: Gender and the Civil War*. New York: Oxford University Press, 1992.

Coates, Robert M. *The Outlaw Years: The History of the Land Pirates of the Natchez Trace*. New York: Macauley Co., 1930. Reprint, Lincoln: University of Nebraska Press, 1986.

Cobb, James C., ed. *The Mississippi Delta and the World: The Memoirs of David L. Cohn*. Baton Rouge: Louisiana State University Press, 1995.

Cohen, William. *At Freedom's Edge: Black Mobility and the Southern White Quest for Racial Control, 1861–1915*. Baton Rouge: Louisiana State University Press, 1991.

Cohn, David L. *Where I Was Born and Raised*. 3d ed. Notre Dame, Ind.: University of Notre Dame Press, 1948.

Cozzens, Peter. *The Darkest Days of the War: The Battles of Iuka and Corinth*. Chapel Hill: University of North Carolina Press, 1997.

Dailey, Jane. *Before Jim Crow: The Politics of Race in Postemancipation Virginia*. Chapel Hill: University of North Carolina Press, 2000.

De Vorsey, Louis, Jr. *The Indian Boundary in the Southern Colonies, 1863–1775*. Chapel Hill: University of North Carolina Press, 1966.

Dittmer, John. *Local People: The Struggle for Civil Rights in Mississippi*. Urbana: University of Illinois Press, 1995.

Dominquez, Virginia R. *White by Definition: Social Classification in Creole Louisiana*. New Brunswick, N.J.: Rutgers University Press, 1968.

Dorman, James H. "Ethnicity and Identity: Creoles of Color in the Twentieth-Century South." In *Creoles of Color in the Gulf South*, edited by James H. Dorman, 166–79. Knoxville: University of Tennessee Press, 1996.

Durrill, Wayne K. *War of Another Kind: A Southern Community in the Great Rebellion*. New York: Oxford University Press, 1990.

Dyer, Thomas G. *Secret Yankees: The Union Circle in Confederate Atlanta*. Baltimore: Johns Hopkins University Press, 1999.

Edwards, Laura. *Gendered Strife and Confusion: The Political Culture of Reconstruction*. Urbana: University of Illinois Press, 1997.

Egerton, John. *Speak Now against the Day: The Generation before the Civil Rights Movement in the South*. Chapel Hill: University of North Carolina Press, 1995.

Escott, Paul D. *Many Excellent People: Power and Privilege in North Carolina, 1850–1900*. Chapel Hill: University of North Carolina Press, 1985.

——. *Slavery Remembered: A Record of Twentieth-Century Slave Narratives*. Chapel Hill: University of North Carolina Press, 1979.

——, ed. *North Carolina Yeoman: The Diary of Basil Armstrong Thomasson, 1853–1862*. Athens: University of Georgia Press, 1996.

Fairclough, Adam. *Race and Democracy: The Civil Rights Struggle in Louisiana, 1915–1972*. Athens: University of Georgia Press, 1995.

Faust, Drew Gilpin. *Mothers of Invention: Women of the Slaveholding South in the American Civil War*. Chapel Hill: University of North Carolina Press, 1996.

Fellman, Michael. *Inside War: The Guerrilla Conflict in Missouri during the American Civil War*. New York: Oxford University Press, 1989.

Fields, Barbara J. "Ideology and Race in American History." In *Region, Race, and Reconstruction: Essays in Honor of C. Vann Woodward*, edited by J. Morgan Kousser and James M. McPherson, 143–78. New York: Oxford University Press, 1982.

——. *Slavery and Freedom on the Middle Ground: Maryland during the Nineteenth Century*. New Haven: Yale University Press, 1985.

Foner, Eric. *Reconstruction: America's Unfinished Revolution, 1863–1877*. Baton Rouge: Louisiana State University Press, 1988.

Foster, Gaines M. *Ghosts of the Confederacy: Defeat, the Lost Cause, and the Emergence of the New South*. New York: Oxford University Press, 1987.

Fox-Genovese, Elizabeth. *Within the Plantation Household: Black and White Women of the Old South*. Chapel Hill: University of North Carolina Press, 1988.

Frazier, E. Franklin. *The Negro Family in the United States*. Chicago: University of Chicago Press, 1939.

Frederickson, Mary E. "Each One Is Dependent on the Other: Southern Churchwomen, Racial Reform, and the Process of Transformation, 1880–1940." In *Visible Women: New Essays on American Activism*, edited by Nancy A. Hewitt and Suzanne Lebsock, 296–324. Urbana: University of Illinois Press, 1993.

Freehling, William W. *The Road to Disunion: Secessionists at Bay, 1776–1854*. New York: Oxford University Press, 1990.

Gallay, Alan. *The Formation of a Planter Elite: Jonathan Bryan and the Southern Colonial Frontier*. Athens: University of Georgia Press, 1989.

Gardner, Robert G. *A Decade of Debate and Division: Georgia Baptists and the Formation of the Southern Baptist Convention*. Macon, Ga.: Mercer University Press, 1995.

Garner, James W. *Reconstruction in Mississippi*. 1901. Baton Rouge: Louisiana State University Press, 1968.

Gaston, Paul M. *The New South Creed: A Study in Southern Mythmaking*. New York: Knopf, 1970.

Genovese, Eugene D. *The Political Economy of Slavery: Studies in the Economy and Society of the Slave South*. New York: Random House, 1965.

——. *Roll, Jordan, Roll: The World the Slaves Made*. New York: Pantheon, 1974.

Giddings, Paula. *When and Where I Enter: The Impact of Black Women on Race and Sex in America*. New York: Morrow, 1984.

Gillette, William. *Retreat from Reconstruction, 1869–1879*. Baton Rouge: Louisiana State University Press, 1979.

Gilmore, Glenda Elizabeth. *Gender and Jim Crow: Women and the Politics of White Supremacy in North Carolina, 1896–1920.* Chapel Hill: University of North Carolina Press, 1996.

Goen, C. C. *Broken Churches, Broken Nation: Denominational Schisms and the Coming of the American Civil War.* Macon, Ga.: Mercer University Press, 1985.

Goodwyn, Lawrence. *The Populist Moment: A Short History of the Agrarian Revolt in America.* New York: Oxford University Press, 1978.

Greenberg, Kenneth S. *Honor and Slavery: Lies, Duels, Noses, Masks, Dressing As a Woman, Gifts, Strangers, Humanitarianism, Death, Slave Rebellions, the Proslavery Argument, Baseball, Hunting, and Gambling in the Old South.* Princeton: Princeton University Press, 1996.

Griffith, Barbara S. *The Crisis of American Labor: Operation Dixie and the Defeat of the CIO.* Philadelphia: Temple University Press, 1988.

Groce, W. Todd. "Social Origins of East Tennessee's Confederates." In *The Civil War in Appalachia: Collected Essays,* edited by Kenneth W. Noe and Shannon H. Wilson, 30–54. Knoxville: University of Tennessee Press, 1997.

Guice, John D. W. Introduction to *Frontier Claims in the Lower South: Records of Claims Filed by Citizens of the Alabama and Tombigbee River Settlements in the Mississippi Territory for Depredations by the Creek Indians during the War of 1812,* compiled by Richard S. Lackey, xi–xiii. New Orleans: Polyanthos, 1977.

Hackett-Fischer, David. *Albion's Seed: Four British Folkways in America.* New York: Oxford University Press, 1989.

Hahn, Steven. *The Roots of Southern Populism: Yeoman Farmers and the Transformation of the Georgia Upcountry, 1850–1890.* New York: Oxford University Press, 1983.

Hale, Grace Elizabeth. *Making Whiteness: The Culture of Segregation in the South, 1890–1940.* New York: Pantheon, 1998.

Hall, Jacquelyn Dowd. " 'The Mind That Burns in Each Body': Women, Rape, and Racial Violence." In *Powers of Desire: The Politics of Sexuality,* edited by Ann Snitow, Christine Stansell, and Sharon Thompson, 328–49. New York: Monthly Review Press, 1983.

———. *Revolt against Chivalry: Jessie Daniel Ames and the Women's Campaign against Lynching.* 2d ed. New York: Columbia University Press, 1993.

Hall, Wade. *Passing for Black: The Life and Careers of Mae Street Kidd.* Lexington: University Press of Kentucky, 1998.

Harris, J. William. *Plain Folk and Gentry in a Slave Society: White Liberty and Black Slavery in Augusta's Hinterlands.* Middletown, Conn.: Wesleyan University Press, 1985.

Harris, William C. *The Day of the Carpetbagger: Republican Reconstruction in Mississippi.* Baton Rouge: Louisiana State University Press, 1979.

———. *Presidential Reconstruction in Mississippi.* Baton Rouge: Louisiana State University Press, 1967.

Hatley, Tom. *The Dividing Paths: Cherokees and South Carolinians through the Revolutionary Era.* New York: Oxford University Press, 1995.

Heinegg, Paul. *Free African Americans of North Carolina and Virginia.* Baltimore: Genealogical Pub. Co., 1994.

Heyrman, Christine Leigh. *Southern Cross: The Beginnings of the Bible Belt.* Chapel Hill: University of North Carolina Press, 1997.

Higginbotham, A. Leon. *In the Matter of Color: Race and the American Legal Process: The Colonial Period.* New York: Oxford University Press, 1978.

Higginbotham, Evelyn Brooks. *Righteous Discontent: The Women's Movement in the Black Baptist Church, 1880–1920.* Cambridge, Mass.: Harvard University Press, 1993.

Hilliard, Sam Bowers. *Hog Meat and Hoe Cake: Food Supply in the Old South, 1840–1860.* Carbondale: Southern Illinois University Press, 1972.

Hine, Darlene Clark. "Rape and the Inner Lives of Southern Black Women: Thoughts on the Culture of Dissemblance." In *Southern Women: Histories and Identities*, edited by Virginia Bernhard, Betty Brandon, Elizabeth Fox-Genovese, and Theda Purdue, 177–89. Columbia: University of Missouri Press, 1992.

Hine, Darlene Clark, and Barry David Gaspar, eds. *More Than Chattel: Black Women and Slavery in the Americas*. Bloomington: University of Indiana Press, 1996.

Hodes, Martha, ed. *Sex, Love, Race: Crossing Boundaries in North American History*. New York: New York University Press, 1999.

——. *White Women, Black Men: Illicit Sex in the Nineteenth-Century South*. New Haven: Yale University Press, 1997.

Hoffman, Ronald. "The 'Disaffected' in the Revolutionary South." In *The American Revolution: Explorations in the History of American Radicalism*, edited by Alfred F. Young, 273–316. DeKalb: Northern Illinois University Press, 1976.

Hoff-Wilson, Joan. "The Illusion of Change: Women and the American Revolution." In *The American Revolution: Explorations in the History of American Radicalism*, edited by Alfred F. Young, 383–445. DeKalb: Northern Illinois University Press, 1976.

Honey, Michael K. *Southern Labor and Black Civil Rights: Organizing Memphis Workers*. Urbana: University of Illinois Press, 1993.

Hunter, Tera W. *To 'Joy My Freedom: Southern Black Women's Lives and Labors after the Civil War*. Cambridge, Mass.: Harvard University Press, 1997.

Hyde, Samuel C., Jr. "Backcountry Justice in the Piney-Woods South." In *Plain Folk of the South Revisited*, edited by Samuel C. Hyde Jr. Baton Rouge: Louisiana State University Press, 1997.

——, ed. *Plain Folk of the South Revisited*. Baton Rouge: Louisiana State University Press, 1997.

Hyman, Michael R. *The Anti-Redeemers: Hill Country Political Dissenters in the Lower South from Redemption to Populism*. Baton Rouge: Louisiana State University Press, 1990.

Inscoe, John. *Mountain Masters: Slavery and the Sectional Crisis in Western North Carolina*. Knoxville: University of Tennessee Press, 1989.

——, ed. *Georgia in Black and White: Explorations in Race Relations of a Southern State, 1865–1950*. Athens: University of Georgia Press, 1994.

Isaac, Rhys. *The Transformation of Virginia, 1740–1790*. Chapel Hill: University of North Carolina Press, 1982.

Jeffrey, Julie Roy. *Frontier Women: The Trans-Mississippi West, 1840–1880*. New York: Hill and Wang, 1979.

Jennings, Francis. "The Indians' Revolution." In *The American Revolution: Explorations in the History of American Radicalism*, edited by Alfred F. Young, 319–48. DeKalb: Northern Illinois University Press, 1976.

Johnston, Erle, Jr. *Mississippi's Defiant Years, 1953–1973: An Interpretative Documentary with Personal Experiences*. Forest, Miss.: Lake Harbor, 1990.

Jones, Jacqueline. *Labor of Love, Labor of Sorrow: Black Women, Work, and the Family from Slavery to the Present*. New York: Vintage, 1985.

Jordan, Terry G., and Matti Kaups. *The American Backwoods Frontier: An Ethnic and Ecological Interpretation*. Baltimore: Johns Hopkins University Press, 1989.

Jordan, Winthrop D. *White over Black: American Attitudes toward the Negro, 1550–1812*. Chapel Hill: University of North Carolina Press, 1968.

Kantrowitz, Stephen. *Ben Tillman and the Reconstruction of White Supremacy*. Chapel Hill: University of North Carolina Press, 2000.

Kars, Marjoleine. *"Breaking Loose Together": How North Carolina's Colonial Farmers Came to Fight the War of the Regulation*. Chapel Hill: University of North Carolina Press, forthcoming.

Kay, Marvin L. Michael. "The North Carolina Regulation, 1766–1776: A Class
 Conflict." In *The American Revolution: Explorations in the History of American Radicalism*, edited
 by Alfred F. Young, 73–123. DeKalb: Northern Illinois University Press, 1976.
Kelley, Robin D. G. *Hammer and Hoe: Alabama Communists during the Great Depression*. Chapel
 Hill: University of North Carolina Press, 1990.
Kennedy, N. Brent, with Robyn Vaughan Kennedy. *The Melungeons: The Resurrection of a
 Proud People, an Untold Story of Ethnic Cleansing in America*. Macon, Ga.: Mercer University
 Press, 1994.
Kerr-Ritchie, Jeffrey. *Freedpeople in the Tobacco South: Virginia, 1860–1900*. Chapel Hill:
 University of North Carolina Press, 1999.
Kirwan, Albert D. *Revolt of the Rednecks: Mississippi Politics, 1876–1925*. Lexington:
 University Press of Kentucky, 1951. Reprint, Gloucester, Mass.: Peter Smith, 1964.
Klein, Rachel N. *Unification of a Slave State: The Rise of the Planter Class in the South Carolina
 Backcountry, 1760–1808*. Chapel Hill: University of North Carolina Press, 1990.
Klingberg, Frank. *The Southern Claims Commission*. Berkeley: University of California Press,
 1955. Reprint, New York: Octagon Books, 1978.
Knight, Anna. *Mississippi Girl: An Autobiography*. Nashville: Southern Publishing
 Association, 1952.
Knight, Ethel. *The Echo of the Black Horn: An Authentic Tale of "The Governor" of "The Free State of
 Jones."* N.p., 1951.
Knight, Thomas J. *The Life and Activities of Captain Newton Knight and His Company and the "Free
 State of Jones County."* 1935. Rev. ed., Laurel, Miss.: n.p., 1946.
Kousser, J. Morgan, and James M. McPherson, eds. *Region, Race, and Reconstruction: Essays in
 Honor of C. Vann Woodward*. New York: Oxford University Press, 1982.
Kulikoff, Allan. "The Revolution, Capitalism, and the Formation of the Yeoman
 Classes." In *Beyond the American Revolution: Explorations in the History of American Radicalism*,
 edited by Alfred F. Young. DeKalb: Northern Illinois University Press, 1993.
———. *Tobacco and Slaves: The Development of Southern Cultures in the Chesapeake, 1680–1800*.
 Chapel Hill: University of North Carolina Press, 1986.
Lamplugh, George R. *Politics on the Periphery: Factions and Parties in Georgia, 1783–1806*.
 Newark: University of Delaware Press, 1986.
Landrum, J. B. O. *History of Spartanburg County*. Atlanta: Franklin Printing and Publishing,
 1900.
Lawson, Steven F. *Running for Freedom: Civil Rights and Black Politics in America since 1941*. New
 York: McGraw Hill, 1991.
Leavell, Z. T., and T. J. Bailey. *A Complete History of Mississippi Baptists from the Earliest Times*.
 2 vols. Jackson: Mississippi Baptist Pub. Co., 1904.
Lefler, Hugh T., and William S. Powell. *Colonial North Carolina: A History*. New York:
 Charles Scribner's Sons, 1973.
Leslie, Kent Anderson. *Woman of Color: Daughter of Privilege, 1849–1893*. Athens:
 University of Georgia Press, 1995.
Leverett, Rudy. *Legend of the Free State of Jones*. Jackson: University Press of Mississippi, 1984.
Litwack, Leon F. *Been in the Storm So Long: The Aftermath of Slavery*. New York: Knopf, 1979.
———. *Trouble in Mind: Black Southerners in the Age of Jim Crow*. New York: Knopf, 1998.
Lonn, Ella. *Desertion during the Civil War*. New York: Century, 1928. Reprint, Lincoln:
 University of Nebraska Press, 1998.
Loughmiller, Campbell, and Lynn Loughmiller. *Big Thicket Legacy*. Austin: University of
 Texas Press, 1977.
Loveland, Anne C. *Southern Evangelicals and the Social Order, 1800–1860*. Baton Rouge:
 Louisiana State University Press, 1980.

Lumpkin, Katharine Du Pre. *The Making of a Southerner*. New York: Knopf, 1947. Reprint, Athens: University of Georgia Press, 1991.

Lumpkin, William L. *Baptist Foundations in the South: Tracing through Separates the Influence of the Great Awakening, 1754–1787*. Nashville: Broadman Press, 1961.

Lyerly, Cynthia Lynn. "Enthusiasm, Possession, and Madness: Gender and the Opposition to Methodism in the South, 1770–1810." In *Beyond Image and Convention: Explorations in Southern Women's History*, edited by Janet L. Coryell, Martha H. Swain, Sandra Gioia Treadway, and Elizabeth Hayes Turner, 53–73. Columbia: University of Missouri Press, 1998.

Lynch, John R. *The Facts of Reconstruction*. Edited by William C. Harris. 1913. Indianapolis: Bobbs-Merrill, 1970.

McCoy, Drew R. *The Elusive Republic: Political Economy in Jeffersonian America*. Chapel Hill: University of North Carolina Press, 1980.

McCurry, Stephanie. *Masters of Small Worlds: Yeoman Households, Gender Relations, and the Antebellum South Carolina Low Country*. New York: Oxford University Press, 1995.

McHaney, Thomas L. "James Street: Making History Live." In *Mississippi's Piney Woods: A Human Perspective*, edited by Noel Polk, 121–33. Jackson: University Press of Mississippi, 1986.

McLaurin, Melton A. *Celia, a Slave*. Athens: University of Georgia Press, 1991.

MacLean, Nancy. *Behind the Mask of Chivalry: The Making of the Second Ku Klux Klan*. New York: Oxford University Press, 1994.

McMillen, Neil R. *Dark Journey: Black Mississippians in the Age of Jim Crow*. Urbana: University of Illinois Press, 1989.

McPherson, James M. *Ordeal by Fire: The Civil War and Reconstruction*. New York: Knopf, 1982.

McWhiney, Grady. "Antebellum Piney Woods Culture: Continuity over Time and Place." In *Mississippi's Piney Woods: A Human Perspective*, edited by Noel Polk, 40–58. Jackson: University Press of Mississippi, 1986.

Main, Jackson Turner. *The Social Structure of Revolutionary America*. Princeton: Princeton University Press, 1965.

Marten, James. *Texas Divided: Loyalty and Dissent in the Lone Star State, 1856–1874*. Lexington: University Press of Kentucky, 1990.

Medley, Mary. *History of Anson County, North Carolina, 1750–1976*. Wadesboro, N.C.: Anson County Historical Society, 1976.

Merrens, H. Roy. *Colonial North Carolina in the Eighteenth Century: A Study in Historical Geography*. Chapel Hill: University of North Carolina Press, 1964.

Miles, Edwin Arthur. *Jacksonian Democracy in Mississippi*. Chapel Hill: University of North Carolina Press, 1960.

Mills, Gary B. *The Forgotten People: Cane River's Creoles of Color*. Baton Rouge: Louisiana State University Press, 1977.

Moberg, David. "Puttin' Down Ol' Massa: Laurel, Mississippi, 1979." In *Working Lives: The Southern Exposure History of Labor in the South*, edited by Marc S. Miller, 291–301. New York: Pantheon, 1980.

Montell, William Lynwood. *Killings: Folk Justice in the Upper South*. Lexington: University Press of Kentucky, 1986.

Montgomery, Rebecca. "Lost Cause Mythology in New South Reform: Gender, Class, Race, and the Politics of Patriotic Citizenship in Georgia, 1890–1925." In *Dealing with the Powers That Be: Negotiating Boundaries of Southern Womanhood*, edited by Janet L. Coryell, Thomas H. Appleton Jr., Anastatia Sims, and Sandra Gioia Treadway. Columbia: University of Missouri Press, 2000.

Moore, Albert Burton. *Conscription and Conflict in the Confederacy*. New York: Macmillan, 1924.

Morgan, Edmund. *American Slavery, American Freedom: The Ordeal of Colonial Virginia*. New York: Norton, 1975.

Morris, Christopher. *Becoming Southern: The Evolution of a Way of Life: Warren County and Vicksburg, Mississippi, 1770–1860*. New York: Oxford University Press, 1995.

Morton, Patricia, ed. *Discovering the Women in Slavery: Emancipating Perspectives on the American Past*. Athens: University of Georgia Press, 1996.

Myrdal, Gunnar. *An American Dilemma: The Negro Problem and American Democracy*. New York: Harper and Brothers, 1944.

Myres, Sandra. *Westering Women and the Frontier Experience, 1800–1915*. Albuquerque: University of New Mexico Press, 1982.

Neufeld, Don F., ed. *Seventh-Day Adventist Encyclopedia*. Rev. ed. Washington, D.C.: Review and Herald Publishing Association, 1976.

Neverdon-Morton, Cynthia. *Afro-American Women of the South and the Advancement of the Race, 1895–1925*. Knoxville: University of Tennessee Press, 1989.

Nieman, Donald G. *Promises to Keep: African-Americans and the Constitutional Order, 1776 to the Present*. New York: Oxford University Press, 1991.

Noe, Kenneth W., and Shannon H. Wilson. *The Civil War in Appalachia: Collected Essays*. Knoxville: University of Tennessee Press, 1997.

North, Douglass C. *The Economic Growth of the United States, 1790–1860*. New York: Norton, 1966.

Numbers, Ronald L. *Prophetess of Health: Ellen G. White and the Origins of Seventh-Day Adventist Health Reform*. Rev. and enl. ed. Knoxville: University of Tennessee Press, 1992.

Numbers, Ronald L., and Jonathan M. Butler, eds. *The Disappointed: Millerism and Millenarianism in the Nineteenth Century*. Knoxville: University of Tennessee Press, 1993.

Olsen, Otto. *Carpetbagger's Crusade: The Life of Albion Winegar Tourgee*. Baltimore: Johns Hopkins University Press, 1965.

Ownby, Ted. *Subduing Satan: Religion, Recreation, and Manhood in the Rural South, 1865–1920*. Chapel Hill: University of North Carolina Press, 1990.

Painter, Nell Irvin. *The Narrative of Hosea Hudson: The Life and Times of a Black Radical*. New York: Norton, 1994.

——. *Sojourner Truth: A Life, a Symbol*. New York: Norton, 1996.

——. *Standing at Armageddon: The United States, 1877–1919*. New York: Norton, 1987.

Paludan, Phillip Shaw. *Victims: A True Story of the Civil War*. Knoxville: University of Tennessee Press, 1981.

Paschal, George Washington. *History of North Carolina Baptists*. 2 vols. Raleigh: General Board of the Baptist State Convention, 1930, 1955.

Perdue, Theda. *Slavery and Evolution of Cherokee Society, 1540–1866*. Knoxville: University of Tennessee Press, 1979.

Pereyra, Lillian A. *James Lusk Alcorn: Persistent Whig*. Baton Rouge: Louisiana State University Press, 1966.

Perman, Michael. *The Road to Redemption: Southern Politics, 1869–1879*. Chapel Hill: University of North Carolina Press, 1984.

Polk, Noel, ed. *Mississippi's Piney Woods: A Human Perspective*. Jackson: University Press of Mississippi, 1986.

Rable, George C. *But There Was No Peace: The Role of Violence in the Politics of Reconstruction*. Athens: University of Georgia Press, 1984.

——. *Civil Wars: Women and the Crisis of Southern Nationalism*. Urbana: University of Illinois Press, 1989.

Rafter, Nicole Hahn, ed. *White Trash: The Eugenic Family Studies, 1877–1919*. Boston: Northeastern University Press, 1988.

Rainwater, Percy. *Mississippi: Storm Center of Secession, 1856–1861*. Baton Rouge: Otto Claitor, 1938.

Randall, J. G., and David Herbert Donald. *The Civil War and Reconstruction*. 2d rev. ed. Lexington, Mass.: D. C. Heath, 1969.

Randel, William Pierce. *The Ku Klux Klan: A Century of Infamy*. Philadelphia: Chilton, 1965.

Remini, Robert V. *Henry Clay, Statesman for the Union*. New York: Norton, 1991.

Robinson, W. Stitt. *The Southern Colonial Frontier, 1607–1763*. Albuquerque: University of New Mexico Press, 1979.

Roediger, David R. *The Wages of Whiteness: Race and the Making of the American Working Class*. London: Verso, 1991.

Rosengarten, Theodore. *Tombee: Portrait of a Cotton Planter*. New York: McGraw-Hill, 1987.

Rouse, Jacqueline Anne. *Lugenia Burns Hope: Black Southern Reformer*. Athens: University of Georgia Press, 1989.

Rowland, Dunbar. *History of Mississippi, the Heart of the South*. 2 vols. Chicago-Jackson: S. J. Clarke, 1925.

Schultz, Mark R. "Interracial Kinship Ties and the Emergence of a Rural Black Middle Class: Hancock County, Georgia, 1865–1920." In *Georgia in Black and White: Explorations in the Race Relations of a Southern State, 1865–1950*, edited by John C. Inscoe. Athens: University of Georgia Press, 1994.

Schwalm, Leslie. *A Hard Fight for We: Women's Transition from Slavery to Freedom in South Carolina*. Urbana: University of Illinois Press, 1997.

Schwartz, R. W. *Light Bearers to the Remnant: Denominational History Textbook for Seventh-Day Adventist College Classes*. Mountain View, Calif.: Pacific Press, 1979.

Scott, Anne Firor. *The Southern Lady: From Pedestal to Politics, 1830–1930*. Chicago: University of Chicago Press, 1970.

Seip, Terry. *The South Returns to Congress: Men, Economic Measures, and Intersectional Relationships, 1868–1879*. Baton Rouge: Louisiana State University Press, 1983.

Silber, Nina. *The Romance of Reunion: Northerners and the South, 1865–1900*. Chapel Hill: University of North Carolina Press, 1993.

Smith, Alfred Glaze, Jr. *Economic Readjustment of an Old Cotton State: South Carolina, 1820–1860*. Columbia: University of South Carolina Press, 1958.

Smith, Mark M. *Mastered by the Clock: Time, Slavery, and Freedom in the American South*. Chapel Hill: University of North Carolina Press, 1997.

Smith, Theophus H. *Conjuring Culture: Biblical Formations of Black America*. New York: Oxford University Press, 1994.

Southerland, Henry deLeon Jr., and Jerry Elijah Brown. *The Federal Road through Georgia, the Creek Nation, and Alabama, 1806–1836*. Tuscaloosa: University of Alabama Press, 1989.

Sparks, Randy J. *On Jordan's Stormy Banks: Evangelicalism in Mississippi, 1773–1876*. Athens: University of Georgia Press, 1994.

Stampp, Kenneth M. *The Peculiar Institution: Slavery in the Antebellum South*. New York: Random House, 1956.

Stevenson, Brenda E. *Life in Black and White: Family and Community in the Slave South*. New York: Oxford University Press, 1996.

Stock, Catherine McNicol. *Rural Radicals: Righteous Rage in the American Grain*. Ithaca, N.Y.: Cornell University Press, 1996.

Stokes, Melvyn, and Stephen Conway. *The Market Revolution in America: Social, Political, and Religious Expressions, 1800–1900*. Charlottesville: University Press of Virginia, 1996.

Street, James. *Look Away! A Dixie Notebook*. New York: Viking, 1936.
——. *Oh, Promised Land*. New York: Dial Press, 1940.
——. *Tap Roots*. Garden City, N.Y.: Sun Dial Press, 1943.
Sullivan, Chester. *Sullivan's Hollow*. Jackson: University Press of Mississippi, 1978.
Sullivan, Patricia. *Days of Hope: Race and Democracy in the New Deal Era*. Chapel Hill: University of North Carolina Press, 1996.
Sutherland, Daniel. *Seasons of War: The Ordeal of a Confederate Community, 1861–1865*. New York: Free Press, 1995.
——, ed. *Guerrillas, Unionists, and Violence on the Confederate Home Front*. Fayetteville: University of Arkansas Press, 1999.
Sydnor, Charles E. *Slavery in Mississippi*. 1933. Baton Rouge: Louisiana State University Press, 1966.
Tatum, Georgia Lee. *Disloyalty in the Confederacy*. Chapel Hill: University of North Carolina Press, 1934. New ed. with an introduction by David Williams, Lincoln: University of Nebraska Press, 2000.
Thornton, J. Mills, III. *Politics and Power in a Slave Society: Alabama, 1800–1860*. Baton Rouge: Louisiana State University Press, 1978.
Thorp, Daniel B. "Taverns and Communities: The Case of Rowan County, North Carolina." In *The Southern Colonial Backcountry: Interdisciplinary Perspectives on Frontier Communities*, edited by David Colin Crass, Steven D. Smith, Martha A. Zierden, and Richard D. Brooks, 76–86. Knoxville: University of Tennessee Press, 1998.
Tillson, Albert H., Jr. *Gentry and Common Folk: Political Culture on a Virginia Frontier, 1740–1789*. Lexington: University Press of Kentucky, 1991.
Townsend, Leah. *South Carolina Baptists, 1670–1805*. Florence, S.C.: Florence Printing Co., 1935.
Trelease, Allen. *White Terror: The Ku Klux Klan Conspiracy and Southern Reconstruction*. New York: Harper and Row, 1971.
Twelve Southerners. *I'll Take My Stand: The South and the Agrarian Tradition*. 1939. Reprinted with a new introduction by Louis D. Rubin Jr. Baton Rouge: Louisiana State University Press, 1978.
Usner, Daniel H., Jr. *Indians, Settlers, and Slaves in a Frontier Exchange Economy: The Lower Mississippi Valley before 1783*. Chapel Hill: University of North Carolina Press, 1992.
Wade, Wyn Craig. *The Fiery Cross: The Ku Klux Klan in America*. New York: Oxford University Press, 1997.
Waller, Altina L. *Feud: Hatfields, McCoys, and Social Change in Appalachia, 1860–1900*. Chapel Hill: University of North Carolina Press, 1988.
Watson, Harry L. *Jacksonian Politics and Community Conflict: The Emergence of the Second American Party System in Cumberland County, North Carolina*. Baton Rouge: Louisiana State University Press, 1981.
——. "Slavery and Development in a Dual Economy: The South and the Market Revolution." In *The Market Revolution in America: Social, Political, and Religious Expressions, 1800–1800*, edited by Melvyn Stokes and Stephen Conway. Charlottesville: University Press of Virginia, 1996.
Weaver, Herbert. *Mississippi Farmers, 1850–1860*. Nashville: Vanderbilt University Press, 1945. Reprint, Gloucester, Mass.: Peter Smith, 1968.
Wessinger, Catherine, ed. *Women's Leadership in Marginal Religions: Explorations outside the Mainstream*. Urbana: University of Illinois Press, 1993.
Wharton, Vernon. *The Negro in Mississippi, 1865–1890*. 1947. New York: Harper and Row, 1965.

White, Deborah Gray. *Ar'n't I a Woman: Female Slaves in the Plantation South.* 1985. Rev. ed. New York: Norton, 1999.

Whites, LeeAnn. *The Civil War As a Crisis in Gender: Augusta, Georgia, 1860–1890.* Athens: University of Georgia Press, 1995.

Williams, David. *Rich Man's War: Class, Caste, and Confederate Defeat in the Lower Chattahoochee Valley.* Athens: University of Georgia Press, 1998.

Williamson, Joel. *Crucible of Race: Black-White Relations in the American South since Emancipation.* New York: Oxford University Press, 1984.

——. *New People: Miscegenation and Mulattoes in the United States.* New York: Free Press, 1980.

Wilson, Charles Reagan. *Baptized in Blood: The Religion of the Lost Cause, 1865–1920.* Athens: University of Georgia Press, 1980.

Winter, William F. "Piney Woods Politics and Politicians." In *Mississippi's Piney Woods: A Human Perspective,* edited by Noel Polk, 134–43. Jackson: University Press of Mississippi, 1986.

Woodman, Harold D. *New South—New Law: The Legal Foundations of Credit and Labor Relations in the Postbellum Agricultural South.* Baton Rouge: Louisiana State University Press, 1995.

Woodward, C. Vann. *Origins of the New South, 1877–1913.* Baton Rouge: Louisiana State University Press, 1951.

Wright, Gavin. *The Political Economy of the Cotton South: Households, Markets, and Wealth in the Nineteenth Century.* New York: Norton, 1978.

Wyatt-Brown, Bertram. *Southern Honor: Ethics and Behavior in the Old South.* New York: Oxford University Press, 1982.

Young, Alfred F. "English Plebeian Culture and Eighteenth-Century American Radicalism." In *The Origins of Anglo-American Radicalism,* edited by Margaret Jacob and James Jacob, 185–212. Boston: Allen and Unwin, 1983.

——, ed. *The American Revolution: Explorations in the History of American Radicalism.* DeKalb: Northern Illinois University Press, 1976.

——, ed. *Beyond the American Revolution: Explorations in the History of American Radicalism.* DeKalb: Northern Illinois University Press, 1993.

Journal Articles, Essays, Papers, Dissertations, and Theses

Auman, William T. "Neighbor against Neighbor: The Inner Civil War in the Randolph County Area of Confederate North Carolina." *North Carolina Historical Review* 61 (Jan. 1984): 60–90.

Ayers, Edward L. "Memory and the South." *Southern Cultures* 2, no. 1 (fall 1995): 5–8.

Bailey, Fred A. "The Textbooks of the 'Lost Cause': Censorship and the Creation of Southern State Histories." *Georgia Historical Quarterly* 75 (fall 1991): 507–33.

Berry, Mary Frances. "Judging Morality: Sexual Behavior and Legal Consequences in the Late-Nineteenth-Century South." *Journal of American History* 78 (Dec. 1991): 835–56.

Blight, David. " 'For Something beyond the Battlefield': Frederick Douglass and the Struggle for the Memory of the Civil War." *Journal of American History.* Memory and American History: A Special Issue, 75 (Mar. 1989): 1156–78.

Bode, Frederick A. "The Formation of Evangelical Communities in Middle Georgia: Twiggs County, 1820–1861." *Journal of Southern History* 60 (Nov. 1994): 711–48.

Bondurant, Alexander L. "Did Jones County Secede?" *Publications of the Mississippi Historical Society* 1 (1898): 103–6.

Briceland, Alan V. "Land, Law, and Politics on the Tombigbee Frontier, 1804." *Alabama Review* 33 (Apr. 1980): 67–92.

——. "The Mississippi Territorial Land Board East of the Pearl River, 1804." *Alabama Review* 32 (Jan. 1979): 38–68.

Calhoon, S. S. "The Causes and Events That Led to the Calling of the Constitutional Convention of 1890." *Publications of the Mississippi Historical Society* 11 (1902): 105–9.

Cappleman, Josie Frazee. "Importance of the Local History of the Civil War." *Publications of the Mississippi Historical Society* 3 (1900): 107–12.

Countryman, Edward. "The Price of Cotton: The Human Cost of Slavery in Mid-Nineteenth-Century Mississippi." Paper prepared for the Milan Biennial Conference on Early American History, June 19–23, 1992.

Cox, Karen L. "Women, the Lost Cause, and the New South: The United Daughters of the Confederacy and the Transmission of Confederate Culture, 1894–1919." Ph.D. diss., University of Southern Mississippi, 1997.

Donald, David. "The Scalawag in Mississippi Reconstruction." *Journal of Southern History* 10 (Nov. 1944): 447–60.

Downey, Tom. "Riparian Rights and Manufacturing in Antebellum South Carolina: William Gregg and the Origins of the 'Industrial Mind.' " *Journal of Southern History* 65 (Feb. 1999): 77–108.

Duckworth, W. A. "A Republic within the Confederacy and Other Recollections of 1864." *Annals of Iowa* 4 (1914): 342–51.

Dupre, Daniel. "Ambivalent Capitalists on the Cotton Frontier: Settlement and Development in the Tennessee Valley of Alabama." *Journal of Southern History* 56 (May 1990): 215–40.

Duval, Mary V. "The Making of a State." *Publications of the Mississippi Historical Society* 3 (1900): 155–65.

Edwards, Laura F. "Sexual Violence, Gender, Reconstruction, and the Extension of Patriarchy in Granville County, North Carolina." *North Carolina Historical Review* 63 (July 1991): 237–60.

Ellem, Warren A. "Who Were the Mississippi Scalawags?" *Journal of Southern History* 38 (May 1972): 217–40.

Ford, Lacy K., Jr. "Making the 'White Man's Country' White: Race, Slavery, and State Building in the Jacksonian South." *Journal of the Early Republic* 19, no. 4 (winter 1999): 713–38.

French, Scot A. "What Is Social Memory?" *Southern Cultures* 2, no. 1 (fall 1995): 9–18.

Galloway, G. Norton. "A Confederacy within a Confederacy." *Magazine of American History*, Oct. 1886, 387–90.

Gildemeister, Enrique Eugene. "Local Complexities of Race in the Rural South: Racially Mixed People in South Carolina." Unpublished paper in author's possession, June 1977.

Gjerde, Jon. " 'Here in America there is neither king nor tyrant': European Encounters with Race, 'Freedom,' and Their European Pasts." *Journal of the Early Republic* 19, no. 4 (winter 1999) 673–90.

Goins, Craddock. "The Secession of Jones County." *American Mercury*, Jan. 1941, 33–35.

Gorn, Elliot J. "Gouge and Bite, Pull Hair and Scratch: The Social Significance of Fighting in the Southern Backcountry." *American Historical Review* 90 (Feb. 1985): 18–43.

Hall, Jacquelyn Dowd. " 'You Must Remember This': Autobiography As Social Critique." *Journal of American History* 85 (Sept. 1998): 439–65.

Hardy, W. H. "Recollections of Reconstruction in East and Southeast Mississippi." *Publications of the Mississippi Historical Society* 4 (1901): 105–32; 7 (1903): 199–215.

Harris, William C. "A Reconsideration of the Mississippi Scalawag." *Journal of Mississippi History* 32, no. 1 (Feb. 1970): 3–42.

Hart, Albert Bushnell. "Why the South Was Defeated in the Civil War." *New England Magazine*, n.s., 4 (Dec. 1891): 95–120.

Hilbun, Ben. "Cracker's Neck." *Mississippi Quarterly* 7 (Jan. 1954): 67–71.

Hodes, Martha. "The Sexualization of Reconstruction Politics: White Women and Black Men in the South after the Civil War." *Journal of the History of Sexuality* 3 (Jan. 1993): 402–17.

Hodge, Jo Dent. "The Lumber Industry in Laurel, Mississippi, at the Turn of the Nineteenth Century." *Journal of Mississippi History* 34, no. 4 (Nov. 1972): 361–79.

Holmes, Jack D. L. "The Mississippi County That 'Seceded' from the Confederate States of America." *Civil War Times Illustrated* 3 (Feb. 1965): 85–94.

Horton, Lois E. "From Class to Race in Early America: Northern Post-Emancipation Racial Reconstruction." *Journal of the Early Republic* 19, no. 4 (winter 1999): 629–50.

Kars, Marjoleine. " 'Breaking Loose Together': Religion and Rebellion in the North Carolina Piedmont, 1730–1790." Ph.D. diss., Duke University, 1994.

Liddle, William D. " 'Virtue and Liberty': An Inquiry into the Role of the Agrarian Myth in the Rhetoric of the American Revolutionary Era." *South Atlantic Quarterly* 77, no. 1 (winter 1978): 15–38.

Lipscomb, Dabney. "Mississippi's 'Backwoods Poet.' " *Publications of the Mississippi Historical Society* 1 (June 1898): 1–15.

Looram, Mary. "A Little-Known Republic." *Outlook*, Mar. 17, 1920, 484–85.

McCain, William D. "The Populist Party in Mississippi." M.A. thesis, University of Mississippi, 1931.

———. "Theodore Gilmore Bilbo and the Mississippi Delta." *Journal of Mississippi History* 31, no. 1 (Feb. 1969): 1–27.

McCurry, Stephanie. "The Two Faces of Republicanism: Gender and Proslavery Politics in Antebellum South Carolina." *Journal of American History* 78 (Mar. 1992): 1245–63.

McGlone, Robert E. "Rescripting a Troubled Past: John Brown's Family and the Harpers Ferry Conspiracy." *Journal of American History*. Memory and American History: A Special Issue, 75 (Mar. 1989): 1179–1200.

McNeilly, J. S. "The Enforcement Act of 1871 and the Ku Klux Klan in Mississippi." *Publications of the Mississippi Historical Society* 9 (1906): 109–71.

Mandell, Daniel R. "Shifting Boundaries of Race and Ethnicity: Indian-Black Intermarriage in Southern New England, 1760–1880." *Journal of American History* 85 (Sept. 1998): 466–510.

Manring, Maurice M. "Aunt Jemima Explained: The Old South, the Absent Mistress, and the Slave in a Box." *Southern Cultures* 2, no. 1 (fall 1995): 19–44.

Mathews, Donald G. "The Second Great Awakening As an Organizing Process." *American Quarterly* 21 (1969): 23–43.

Melish, Joan Pope. "The 'Condition' Debate and Racial Discourse in the Antebellum North." *Journal of the Early Republic* 19, no. 4 (winter 1999): 651–72.

Montgomery, Goode. "Alleged Secession of Jones County." *Publications of the Mississippi Historical Society* 8 (1904): 13–22.

Nash, Gary. "The Image of the Indian in the Southern Colonial Mind." *William and Mary Quarterly* 29 (Apr. 1972): 197–230.

Payne, Roger M. "New Light in Hanover County: Evangelical Dissent in Piedmont Virginia, 1740–1755." *Journal of Southern History* 61 (Nov. 1995): 665–94.

Reed, John Shelton. "Mixing in the Mountains." *Southern Cultures* 3, no. 4 (winter 1998): 25–36.

Richter, Daniel. " 'Believing That Many of the Red People Suffer Much for the Want of Food': Hunting, Agriculture, and a Quaker Construction of Indianness in the Early Republic." *Journal of the Early Republic* 19, no. 4 (winter 1999): 601–28.

Riley, Franklin L. "Life of Col. J. F. H. Claiborne." *Publications of the Mississippi Historical Society* 7 (1903): 217–43.

Robertson, Heard. "A Revised, or Loyalist Perspective of Augusta during the American Revolution." *Richmond County History* 1 (summer 1969): 5–24.

Roediger, David R. "The Pursuit of Whiteness: Property, Terror, and Expansion, 1790–1860." *Journal of the Early Republic* 19, no. 4 (winter 1999): 579–600.

Ronda, James P. " 'We Have a Country': Race, Geography, and the Invention of Indian Territory." *Journal of the Early Republic* 19, no. 4 (winter 1999): 739–56.

Sansing, David G. "The Failure of Johnsonian Reconstruction in Mississippi, 1865–1866." *Journal of Mississippi History* 34, no. 4 (Nov. 1972): 373–90.

Sedevie, Donna Elizabeth. "The Prospect of Happiness: Women, Divorce, and Property." *Journal of Mississippi History* 57, no. 1 (Feb. 1995): 189–206.

Starnes, Richard D. "Forever Faithful: The Southern Historical Society and Confederate Historical Memory." *Southern Cultures* 2, no. 2 (winter 1996): 177–94.

Stewart, James Brewer. "Modernizing 'Difference': The Political Meanings of Color in the Free States, 1776–1840." *Journal of the Early Republic* 19, no. 4 (winter 1999): 691–712.

Storey, Margaret M. "Southern Ishmaelites: Wartime Unionism and Its Consequences in Alabama, 1860–1874." Ph.D. diss., Emory University, 1999.

Thelen, David. "Memory and American History." *Journal of American History* 75, no. 4 (Mar. 1989): 1120.

Trelease, Allen W. "Who Were the Scalawags?" *Journal of Southern History* 29 (Nov. 1963): 445–68.

Vogt, Daniel C. "A Note on Mississippi Republicans in 1912." *Journal of Mississippi History* 49, no. 1 (Feb. 1987): 49–55.

Watson, Harry L. " 'The Common Rights of Mankind': Subsistence, Shad, and Commerce in the Early Republican South." *Journal of American History* 83 (June 1996): 13–43.

Whittenburg, James P. "Planters, Merchants, and Lawyers: Social Change and the Origins of the North Carolina Regulation." *William and Mary Quarterly* 34 (Apr. 1977): 215–38.

Willard, Dr. Samuel. "A Myth of the Confederacy." *Nation*, Mar. 24, 1892, 227.

Woods, Thomas H. "A Sketch of the Mississippi Secession Convention of 1861: Its Membership and Work." *Publications of the Mississippi Historical Society* 11 (1902): 91–104.

Wyatt-Brown, Bertram. "The Antimission Movement in the Jacksonian South: A Study in Regional Folk Culture." *Journal of Southern History* 36 (Nov. 1970): 501–29.

———. "The Mask of Obedience: Male Slave Psychology in the Old South." *American Historical Review* 93 (Dec. 1988): 1228–52.

Internet Sources

Carlson, Christopher Lee. "The South's Strangest Army: Newt Knight and the Deserters of Jones County, Mississippi." www2.ebicom.net/~mallett/freejone.htm.

Heinegg, Paul. "Free African Americans of Virginia, North Carolina, South Carolina, Maryland, and Delaware." Mar. 4, 1999. http://www.freeafricanamericans.com/introduction.htm, 8–9.

Inter-University Consortium for Political and Social Research Archive. Study 3, Historical, Demographic, Economic, and Social Data, the United States, 1790–1970. University of Virginia Geospatial & Statistical Data Center. http://fisher.lib.Virginia.edu/.

"The Lynching Century: African Americans Who Died in Racial Violence in the United States: Names of the Dead, Dates of Death, Places of Death, 1865–1965." www.geocities.com/Colosseum/Base/8507/NLPlaces2.htm.

WGBH/Frontline, Mario de Valdes y Cocom. "The Blurred Racial Lines of Famous Families." Memo of April 25, 1996. http://www.pbs.org/wgbh/pages/frontline/shows/secret/famous/april25.html.

Index

Grant, Gen. Ulysses S., 104–5; as U.S. president, 140, 142
Graves, Benjamin D., 56, 64, 72–73, 85, 98, 100, 119, 121, 140, 143, 160
Graves, Nell, 180–81
Graves, Robert, Jr., 56
Graysville Academy, 163
Great Awakening, 21, 24
Great Britain, 34
Gregg, Tucker, 118
Griffin, Martha, 39
Griffith, Rebecca. See Knight, Mason Rainey
Guerrilla warfare, 94. See also Deserters; Free State of Jones; Jones County, Miss.; Knight Company
Gunter, Albert, 183
Gunter, Allen, 126
Gunter, James, 135–37, 139
Gunter, Joseph Megannon, 126
Gunter, Selena Knight, 126

Halleck, Maj. Gen. Henry, 118
Hamilton, Maj. James, 112
Hancock, Judge William M., 142
Harper, John H., 101, 111
Harper, Mary "Polly," 39–40, 79
Harris, William C., 142
Hart, Albert Bushnell, 157
Hartfield, John: lynching of, 151–52, 165
Harvey, E. B., 84
Hatten, Joe, 121
Hattiesburg, Miss.: Ku Klux Klan in, 166
Hawley, J. A., 134
Hayes, Rutherford B., 144
Hebert's Brigade: at Vicksburg, 104
Hebron community, 46, 119
Hendricks, John Williams, 45
Hendricks, Lucy, 45
Hendricks, Rachel, 45. See also Collins, Rachel
Hendricks family, 45
Henry (slave), 76
Herders: of livestock in Piney Woods, 50, 52, 56, 60
Herrington, Francis M., 124
Herrington, Jesse, 124
Herrington, Nora, 157
Hilbun, Bill, 138

Hill, Sarah, 80–81
Hinton, Richard, 136–37
Holifield, Joshua, 84
Holifield, William, 124
Holland, Moses, 24
Holliman, Thomas, 36–37
Holly, Dawson: alleged leader of outlaw band, 137
Holly Springs, Miss., 101
Honey Island, Miss., 117
Honor: among white men, 15–16, 19, 37, 76, 95–96, 128, 131, 137; among slaves, 19; among white women, 19, 138, 152
Hood, William, 126, 132
Howe, Rep. Albert R., 142
Howze, Dock, 168, 171
Hudson, Judge Robert S., 94
Huff, Julius, 161
Huff, Ruby, 96–97
Huff, Thomas Jefferson, 124–25, 132–33, 161
Huldy (slave), 62
Hunting: importance to Piney Woods economy, 58

Interracial relations, 2, 14–16, 40–41, 82, 86–87, 110, 144–45; in Knight community, 153–88 passim
Isaac, Rhys, 15
Iuka, battle of, 100–101, 103

Jack, Lt. Col. T. M., 118
Jackson, Gen. Andrew, 38
Jackson, Wiley, 183–84, 186
Jasper County, Miss.: West Jasper County School Board, 187
Jefferson, Thomas, 30, 33–34
Jessie (slave), 77
Johnson, Andrew, 128, 135
Johnson, Gerald W., 64, 78, 99, 101, 136
Johnston, Erle, Jr., 187
Johnston, Gen. Joseph E., 124–28
Jones, Mandy, 41
Jones, Capt. S. E., 125
Jones, Willis B., 124
Jones County, Miss.: Ellisville circuit court located in, 1, 177, 186; formation of, 30, 50; inner civil war in,

Lumber industry: in Jones County, 156
Lynching: of Jasper County slave, 86; in Jones County, 150–52; in Mississippi, 151

McGee, Alzade Courtney. See Courtney, Alzade
McGee, James, 83, 108
McGee, John D., 83
McGill, Allan P., 126, 132
McGill, Sandy, 143–44
McGilvery, Angus, 353 (n. 66)
McGilvery, William, 112
McHenry, Wiley, 181
McLemore, Abraham, 67–68, 105
McLemore, Maj. Amos, 97, 102–3; background of, 67, 68; murder of, 105–6, 135
McLemore, Amos (grandfather of Maj. Amos McLemore), 67
McLemore, Amos (uncle of Maj. Amos McLemore), 78
McLemore, John, 67
McLemore family, 32, 49
McLeod, Roy E., 67
Madison, James, 30, 33
Madison County, Miss., 94
Manhood: symbols of, 32, 37, 71–75, 96. See also Honor
Marietta, Ga., 124
Marshall, Daniel, 21–23, 27, 42
Marshall, Eunice, 22
Marshall, Martha Stearns, 22–23, 79
Mathews, B. A., 140, 142
Mathis, 2d Lt. Harmon, 104
Mauldin, William H., 125
Mauldin family, 41
Maury, Maj. Gen. Dabney H., 103, 111–12, 116, 126, 157
Maury, Col. Henry, 112, 116, 157
Mayfield, John, 76
Mayfield, Tom, 134
Melungeons, 15
Memphis, Tenn., 117–18
Mercer, Jesse, 42
Mercer, Thomas, 43
Meridian, Miss., 117, 133
Methodists: in Jones County, 119
Michaux, Joseph, 38

Michaux, Judith, 38
Millerites, 163
Mills, John, 35
Mills, Mary, 39. See also Coleman, Mary
Milsaps, Uriah, 66
Miscegenation, 1, 3, 153, 175, 177, 180, 183, 186–87. See also Interracial relations
Mississippi Constitutional Convention: of 1865, 135; of 1868, 140; of 1890, 158
Mississippi Historical Society, 149, 157
Mississippi legislature, 135–36, 139
Mississippi River, 34, 124
Mississippi State Convention of 1861, 98
Mississippi State Sovereignty Commission, 187–88
Mississippi Supreme Court: Davis Knight trial, 3
Mississippi Territory, 29, 39–40; achievement of statehood, 32; Tensaw settlement of, 34, 36
Mississippi troops, Confederate Army: 7th Battalion, Mississippi Infantry, 94, 99, 100–101, 103–4, 120, 124–25, 136; 8th Mississippi Infantry, 101, 104; 27th Mississippi Infantry, 102–3, 126; 26th Mississippi Infantry, 107; 6th Mississippi Infantry, 117
Mississippi Valley: commercial development of, 34
Mitchell, Margaret: and Gone with the Wind, 2
Mobile, Ala., 33, 50, 128; as center of trade, 40, 53, 59, 67
Mobile River, 34
Montgomery, Goode, 118, 129, 157–58, 168, 171
Morgan, Bill: murder of, 100, 122
Moselle, Miss., 61
Moselle Baptist Church: visited by Ku Klux Klan, 166
Mulattoes, 15, 40, 86, 88, 144, 159
Mulkey, Nancy, 22
Mulkey, Philip, 21–24, 42
Murrell, John A.: frontier bandit, 88
Mustees, 15
Myers, Hulon, 152
Myrick, Miss., 137

differences between in North Carolina and South Carolina, 24; in Wrightsboro, Georgia, 46
Reid, Whitelaw, 142
Republican ideology, 32, 35–37, 40, 53, 96, 146
Republican Party, 180; in Mississippi, 131–32, 140, 142–43, 147
Republic of Jones: historical views on, 5. See also Free State of Jones; Knight Company
Rhoda (slave), 84
Richmond, Va., 100
Roberts, Jesse N., 81
Robertson, Jeffery, 43
Robertson, Norvell, Jr., 51
Robertson, Norvell, Sr., 30–32, 41, 46, 51, 77, 161; pro-missionary Baptist views of, 43, 73–75; as slaveholder, 45, 52–53; images of women in autobiography of, 79–81
Robertson family, 49
Rocky Creek, Miss., 117
Roosevelt, Eleanor, 179
Roosevelt, Franklin D., 179
Ross, Quitman, 180–82, 184, 186
Rush, Synthia, 81–82

Salsbattery: Jones County battlefield, 106
Saluda River, 24
Scalawags: in Mississippi, 132, 140, 142, 148, 178
Second Great Awakening, 30, 41, 75
Seddon, James (secretary of war), 111, 116
Segregation, 4, 144–45, 153–54, 158–59, 175, 178, 180, 184, 187
Seventh-Day Adventists, 145, 161–63, 172
Seven Years' War, 16
Sherman, Gen. William T., 117–18, 124, 128
Shows, A. G., 56
Shows, Adam, 51
Shows, Daniel M., 62
Shows, James K. Polk, 62
Shows, John, Sr., 51–52
Shows family, 32, 49
Shubuta, Miss., 133
Simmons, Richard, 142

Sims, Berry, 99
Slaveholders, 19–20, 30, 77, 86, 109; in Jones County, 48, 52–53, 56, 62–64, 68; support for Confederacy, 101–2
Slavery, 15, 28, 31; on frontier, 15, 21, 30, 40–42; in Jones County, 47–48, 96; in Mississippi, 48, 59, 71; among Baptists, 84
Slaves: during Creek War, 36; in Piney Woods, 76–77, 86–89; support for deserters, 106, 109–10, 121. See also Interracial relations; Knight, Rachel; Lynching
Slave traders, 86
Smith, Capt. A. R. M., 135
Smith, Frances, 66
Smith, Grandma, 138
Smith, Rebecca, 83
Smith, Tobias, 83
Smith County, Miss., 46, 66, 75, 111
Soso, Miss., 106, 163
South Carolina, 11, 24, 29, 67
Southern Claims Commission (SCC), 141–43
Southern Conference for Human Welfare (SCHW), 179
Spain: control over West Florida, 34
Sparks, William, 142
Spartanburg, S.C., 30
Spears, Amos J., 65
Spradley, Junie Lee, 1, 180–81
Stearns, Shubal, 21, 42
Street, James, 12, 13, 93, 152
Stringer, Dr. John W., 183, 186
Stuart, Col. John, 24
Sullivan, Neace, 137
Sullivan, Patricia, 179
Sullivan, Tom, 76, 126
Sullivan family, 35
Sullivan's Hollow, 75–76, 126
Summerall, Jacob, 52
Summerall, Jesse, 52
Summerlin, Peggy, 40, 79
Sumrall, Benjamin R., 96, 98–99, 116, 121
Sumrall, Calvin, 35, 51
Sumrall, Giles, 35, 46, 74, 77
Sumrall, Harmon Levi, 62, 96
Sumrall, Mollie Olivia Knight, 161
Sumrall, Tom, Jr., 37, 69